Understanding

Phonology

Third edition

Understanding

Phonology

Third edition

Carlos Gussenhoven
and
Haike Jacobs

**Understanding
Language Series**

Series Editors:
Bernard Comrie
and
Greville Corbett

HODDER
EDUCATION
PART OF HACHETTE LIVRE UK

British Library Cataloguing in Publication Data
A catalogue record for this title is available from the British Library

ISBN: 978 1 444 11204 7

First Published 2011
Impression number   10 9 8 7 6 5 4 3
Year   2017 2016 2015 2014 2013 2012

First edition published in Great Britain in 1998 by Hodder Arnold.
Second edition published in Great Britain in 2005 by Hodder Arnold.
Third edition published in Great Britain in 2011 by Hodder Education.

Cover photo © Zoran Ivanovich Photo/iStockphoto.com
Typeset by MPS Limited, a Macmillan Company
Printed in Great Britain for Hodder Education, part of Hachette UK, 338 Euston Road, London
NW1 3BH by CPI Group (UK) Ltd, Croydon, CRO 4YY

Contents

Preface

There are about 6000 languages in the world today. Almost certainly, no two of them have the same sound structure: they vary widely in the number of consonants and vowels they have, in their use of tonal contrasts, in their stress patterns, in the shape of their syllables, and so on. At the same time, all these languages show striking similarities in the way they structure their sound systems. Phonology is a thriving field of linguistic research that strives to understand the structure behind these systems. How do these similarities arise? Or again, why is there so much variation? How is our knowledge of the pronunciation of our language represented in our brain? How can we describe the pronunciation of a language? What do people do when they play language games? Why do loanwords often sound so totally different from the way they are pronounced in the donor languages? These and many other questions are dealt with in this book. In our discussion, we have tried to sketch the development of scientific thinking about the sound structure of languages and to take an unbiased view of the cognitive or physiological nature of the explanations. We hope we have succeeded in this task in at least some places in the book, and have got close enough to this ideal for it to serve as a reliable and relevant introduction to an important and exciting field.

This book reflects the thoughts and discoveries of many phonologists. We have learnt to appreciate the value and implications of these theoretical positions not only by reading their publications, but also by attending their classes and discussing the issues with them. Needless to say, our debt to then is inestimable.

A number of people deserve thanks for providing us with data. These are Wilber van der Beek, Barbara van den Brekel, Aoju Chen, Frederic Gaggeri, Kees Groenewoud, Jandranka Gvozdanhović, Özden Heebink-Mandaci, Joost Kremers, Eric Kellerman, Aditi Lahiri, Will Leben, Manjari Ohala, Michael Redford, Leo Wetzels and Young-mee Yu Cho.

The second edition of this book benefited from the comments made by Elan Dresher, San Duanmu, Ed Flemming, Ingmar Steiner, Bo Hagström, Victoria Rosén, Rik van Gijn, Jeroen van der Weijer, Leo Wetzels, Maria Wolters and those who responded to the publisher's questionnaire.

In this third edition, we have made a number of additions and in part rearranged the old text. The new Chapter 1 places our subject in a more general scientific context. It includes the first half of the old Chapter 2 on the difference between morphosyntactic structure and phonological structure. Chapter 2 is essentially the old Chapter 1, while Chapter 3 is a revised version of old Chapter 2. Chapter 8 is again largely new and deals with responses to phonological opacity in Optimality Theory.

Carlos Gussenhoven and Haike Jacobs
Radboud University Nijmegen, The Netherlands 2011

Acknowledgments

The International Phonetics Alphabet (2005) is reproduced by kind permission of the International Phonetic Association (Department of Theoretical and Applied Linguistics, School of English, Aristotle University of Thessaloniki, Thessaloniki 54124, Greece).

The authors would like to thank Janine Berns, Hyong-Sil Cho, Bert Cranen, Anne Cutler, Marinda Hagen, Robert Kennedy, Hikaru Osawa and Henning Reetz for their help with this third edition.

THE INTERNATIONAL PHONETIC ALPHABET (revised to 2005)

CONSONANTS (PULMONIC)

	Bilabial	Labiodental	Dental	Alveolar	Postalveolar	Retroflex	Palatal	Velar	Uvular	Pharyngeal	Glottal
Plosive	p b			t d		ʈ ɖ	c ɟ	k ɡ	q ɢ		ʔ
Nasal	m	ɱ		n		ɳ	ɲ	ŋ	N		
Trill	B			r					R		
Tap or Flap		ⱱ		ɾ		ɽ					
Fricative	ɸ β	f v	θ ð	s z	ʃ ʒ	ʂ ʐ	ç ʝ	x ɣ	χ ʁ	ħ ʕ	h ɦ
Lateral fricative				ɬ ɮ							
Approximant		ʋ		ɹ		ɻ	j	ɰ			
Lateral approximant				l		ɭ	ʎ	L			

Where symbols appear in pairs, the one to the right represents a voiced consonant. Shaded areas denote articulations judged impossible.

CONSONANTS (NON-PULMONIC)

Clicks		Voiced implosives		Ejectives	
ʘ	Bilabial	ɓ	Bilabial	ʼ	Examples:
ǀ	Dental	ɗ	Dental/alveolar	pʼ	Bilabial
ǃ	(Post)alveolar	ʄ	Palatal	tʼ	Dental/alveolar
ǂ	Palatoalveolar	ɠ	Velar	kʼ	Velar
ǁ	Alveolar lateral	ʛ	Uvular	sʼ	Alveolar fricative

OTHER SYMBOLS

ʍ	Voiceless labial-velar fricative	ɕ ʑ	Alveolo-palatal fricatives
w	Voiced labial-velar approximant	ɺ	Voiced alveolar lateral flap
ɥ	Voiced labial-palatal approximant	ɧ	Simultaneous ʃ and X
ʜ	Voiceless epiglottal fricative		
ʢ	Voiced epiglottal fricative	Affricates and double articulations can be represented by two symbols joined by a tie bar if necessary.	k͡p t͡s
ʡ	Epiglottal plosive		

VOWELS

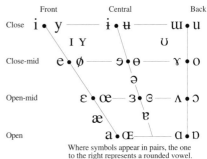

Where symbols appear in pairs, the one to the right represents a rounded vowel.

SUPRASEGMENTALS

ˈ	Primary stress	ˌfoʊnəˈtɪʃən
ˌ	Secondary stress	
ː	Long	eː
ˑ	Half-long	eˑ
˘	Extra-short	ĕ
ǀ	Minor (foot) group	
‖	Major (intonation) group	
.	Syllable break	ɹi.ækt
‿	Linking (absence of a break)	

DIACRITICS

Diacritics may be placed above a symbol with a descender, e.g. ŋ̊

̥	Voiceless	n̥ d̥	̤	Breathy voiced	b̤ a̤	̪	Dental	t̪ d̪
̬	Voiced	s̬ t̬	̰	Creaky voiced	b̰ a̰	̺	Apical	t̺ d̺
ʰ	Aspirated	tʰ dʰ	̼	Linguolabial	t̼ d̼	̻	Laminal	t̻ d̻
̹	More rounded	ɔ̹	ʷ	Labialized	tʷ dʷ	̃	Nasalized	ẽ
̜	Less rounded	ɔ̜	ʲ	Palatalized	tʲ dʲ	ⁿ	Nasal release	dⁿ
̟	Advanced	u̟	ˠ	Velarized	tˠ dˠ	ˡ	Lateral release	dˡ
̠	Retracted	e̠	ˤ	Pharyngealized	tˤ dˤ	̚	No audible release	d̚
̈	Centralized	ë	̴	Velarized or pharyngealized	ɫ		
̽	Mid-centralized	e̽	̝	Raised	e̝	(ɹ̝ = voiced alveolar fricative)	
̩	Syllabic	n̩	̞	Lowered	e̞	(β̞ = voiced bilabial approximant)	
̯	Non-syllabic	e̯	̘	Advanced Tongue Root	e̘		
˞	Rhoticity	ɚ a˞	̙	Retracted Tongue Root	e̙		

TONES AND WORD ACCENTS

LEVEL			CONTOUR		
e̋ or ˥	Extra high		ě or ˩˥	Rising	
é or ˦	High		ê or ˥˩	Falling	
ē or ˧	Mid		e᷄ or ˧˥	High rising	
è or ˨	Low		e᷅ or ˩˧	Low rising	
ȅ or ˩	Extra low		e᷈ or ˧˩˧	Rising-falling	
↓	Downstep		↗	Global rise	
↑	Upstep		↘	Global fall	

Structures in languages

1.1 INTRODUCTION

All human languages have two kinds of structure: a **phonological** structure and a **morphosyntactic** structure. Before this point can be made, we need to make it clear what it means for languages to have 'structure'. We will do this in section 1.2, where we also point out that languages vary in the extent to which they allow particular kinds of structure to be 'seen', or observed. Phonological structure is not the same as the orthography in alphabetic writing systems, and we urge you to keep the notions of 'letter' and 'sound' distinct in your thinking about pronunciation. In section 1.3, we explain briefly what is meant by morphosyntactic structure, and then move on to a thought experiment in which you are invited to imagine a world without phonological structure, a mental exercise that is intended to make you see more clearly what phonological structure really is. Its independence from the morphosyntactic structure is brought out by another thought experiment, where we imagine a world in which all languages have the same phonological structure. Finally, we will make the point that all languages have phonological structures, but that sign languages express their phonological elements visually, as manual and facial gestures, rather than acoustically.

1.2 OBSERVING LINGUISTIC STRUCTURE

By the time he or she is five years old, every child in this world has learnt to speak a human language. Today, this event happens about 16,000 times every hour.[1] It is hard to say how many of the 6,000 or so languages spoken in the world today are still being used by care-givers to communicate with their children, but one thing is certain—those languages vary greatly in their structure. Some of them will have a passive verb form and others will not; some will have five vowels, some thirteen and yet others 25, and likewise the number of consonants will vary greatly; some will use pitch to distinguish words (see section 2.2.4) and some will not, and so on. Children of that age are usually capable of saying that they have five fingers on each of their two hands, but if you were to ask them how many vowels their language has, your

---

[1] Estimate based on Median Crude Birth Rate for 2010–2015 (http://data.un.org), minus Under-5 Child Mortality (http://www.who.int/features/qa/13/en/index.html).

question would be royally ignored. This is not because the child does not necessarily know the meaning of the word 'vowel', but because the question goes well beyond what humans can naturally know. The structure of our language is not accessible to us in the way the outward shape of our bodies is; in fact, people are normally not even aware that their language has any structure at all.

How then can we ever develop an awareness of that structure? In countries in which children are taught to write in an alphabetic orthography, awareness of segments typically arises because to a large extent the letters used to write words stand in some regular relationship to the sounds—we will often call them 'segments'—in those words. It is in fact quite a mental step to realize that an English word like *tea* consists of two segments, a [t] and an [iː], rather than being a single unit of sound. In general, awareness of structural elements will depend on two factors. First, there are the demands that are made on you—as well as the natural inclination you have—to look into such issues. Illiterates are typically unaware of the existence of segments, and it will take more than a little work to reach that understanding (Morais *et al.* 1979). Second, the language itself will reveal some elements of structure more readily than others. That is, the structural elements of any one language vary in 'salience', and it is understandably easier to become aware of more striking elements than of less striking elements. For instance, the notion 'lexical word' naturally develops fairly easily for speakers of most languages. Pre-school speakers of English usually know that *Johnny shouted!* consists of two words, and *No!* of one, even though they will be less sure in cases like *Don't!* or *Shaggy dog story*.

But again, we must remember that languages vary, and thus also vary in the salience of comparable notions. Inuit, spoken in northern Alaska, northern Canada and western Greenland, has a complex system of suffixes and incorporates nouns with verbs: all its words or sentences are much like *Don't!* and *Shaggy dog story*. Inuit children may therefore not be equally comfortable with the notion 'word' as are English children, because there is no evident one-to-one correspondence between some meaning and a word, or between a word and some syntactic position. Or again, if you ask a speaker of German how many syllables there are in a particular German word, you will typically get a quick and correct answer, but if you pose the same question to a speaker of Japanese about a Japanese word, you may well draw a blank, or get the wrong answer. This is because syllables are not particularly salient; or rather, another structural element, smaller than the syllable, is more salient in Japanese, the 'mora' (Hyman 1992). This phonological element will be discussed in Chapter 11. So if you want a quick answer, you should ask how many moras there are in some Japanese words. A 'mora' is a short vowel as well as each half of a long vowel, so that *hi* 'day' is one mora and *boo* 'stick' is two. In addition, *a consonant in the coda of the syllable* is a mora: this goes for the first half of a long consonant, as occurring in *nattoo* 'fermented soy beans', and for a nasal consonant like [n] as in *kéndoo* 'swordsmanship'. So in *kéndoo* there are four moras: [e], [n], [o] and another [o], just as in *nattoo*, where [a], the first [t], [o] and another [o] are the moras.

In general, there tend to be various regularities in the language that make reference to salient structural elements, which may in part explain *why* these elements are salient and thus open to the intuition of speakers (Kubozono 1999). In Japanese, for instance, there are many ways in which the moraic structure of words is relevant to the way you pronounce words and the way words are structured. However, the syllable, too, is a structural element in Japanese. For instance, it determines the possible locations of the word accent. Japanese words are idiosyncratically either accented or unaccented, and if a word is accented, an accent occurs on one of its syllables. In other words, the number of syllables determines the potential locations of the Japanese accent. Although both *kéndoo* and *bokokugo* each have four moras, there are in principle four locations in which the word accent could have occurred in *bokokugo* (which word happens to be unaccented), but only two in *kéndoo* (which word happens to have an accent on the first syllable). Given the relatively low salience of Japanese syllables, it will take a speaker of Japanese more effort to be able to say how many syllables there are in *kéndoo* than it would take a speaker of German to do the same for the comparable German word *Handy* [hɛndi] 'mobile phone; cell phone'. Conversely, even though the phonology of German contains an element 'mora', the German speaker would probably give you a blank stare if you asked him or her how many moras there are in that word.

Q1	The lines of the lyric *Do-re-me* from the 1956 musical *The Sound of Music* (Richard Rogers and Oscar Hammerstein) have the same number of syllables as the notes in the song. They are given in (1). In (2), a popular Japanese version of this song is given, again with the numbers of syllables in each line.

(1)	Doe, a deer, a female deer	7	
	Ray, a drop of golden sun	7	
	Me, a name I call myself	7	
	Far, a long, long way to run	7	
	Sew, a needle pulling thread	7	
	La, a note to follow sew	7	
	Tea, I drink with jam and bread	7	
(2)	Do wa donatu no do	7	'*Do* is *do* of *donatu* (donuts)'
	Re wa remon no re	6	'*Re* is *re* of *remon* (lemon)'
	Mi wa minna no mi	6	'*Mi* is *mi* of *minna* (everyone)'
	Fa wa faito no fa	6	'*Fa* is *fa* of *faito* (fight)'
	So wa aoi sora	6	'*So* is of the blue *sora* (sky)'
	Ra wa rappa no ra	6	'*Ra* is *ra* of *rappa* (trumpet)'
	Si wa siawase yo	7	'*Si* is of *siawase* (happy)'

Why do only the first and last lines of the Japanese version have seven syllables?

Above, we saw that awareness of segmental structure can be induced by cultural factors like learning an alphabetic writing system. At the same time, however, a language's orthography can be a hindrance to understanding the structure of language, because of the irregularities in the relations between letters and segments. The English word *laugh* has five letters, but three segments, [l], [ɑː] or [æ], depending on the dialect, and [f], while the French word *taxi* has four letters and five segments [t], [a], [k], [s] and [i]. Speakers of such languages will tend to mix up letters and segments in their attempts to become aware of the pronunciation of words. This is the reason why segments have been assigned unique symbols by the International Phonetic Association (IPA), which are generally used by linguists. They are written in square brackets, as has been done here. The IPA has a website featuring all these symbols, many of which were taken from the Roman alphabet, and their meanings, with sound files giving examples.[2]

Q2 In one of his sketches, the American comedian and singer Tom Lehrer referred to an eccentric friend of his called ['hɛnri], who spelled his name 'h', 'e', 'n', '3', 'r', 'y'. After allowing his audience to ponder the merits of the spelling *Hen3ry* for a couple of seconds, he added: 'The '3' is silent, you know'.

(a) What is meant by a 'silent letter'?
(b) Argue on the basis of the English word *light* that 'silent letter' is not a particularly helpful notion.

1.2.1   What linguists do

As a group, linguists try to become aware of the entire structure of the languages they study, even if each individual linguist is usually concerned with a specific aspect of those structures. The difference between the incipient awareness that lay language users have—which apart from being hopelessly incomplete is often grossly mistaken—and the work of linguists is that their efforts take place in a scientific context. Thus, they will typically give evidence why they assume some structure to exist and will hold themselves accountable for mistakes by publishing their hypotheses in peer-reviewed journals.

In principle, linguists aim to discover the entire structural system of every language, motivating hypothesized structures as they go along. Of course, this goal is unrealistic, because languages are dying out at a rapid rate and the number of linguists falls far short of what would be needed for that task. It is hard to say how many languages would be sufficient to be able to answer the question that defines a further goal of linguistics: what factors allow linguistic structures to exist, or rather, what factors account for the distribution of those structures across the languages of the world? Why are some elements common and others rare, and yet other imaginable ones apparently non-existent? Those factors will come from many different domains, like our brains (**cognitive** factors), our perceptual system and our speech production system (together, these are **phonetic** factors), as well as **social** factors. To go further still, how do these factors explain the way that languages are acquired by infants? And what is the explanation for the finding that from one generation to the next the linguistic structures that are acquired are slightly different, such that over time languages change in a way that makes it hard to see that stages of a language that are a thousand years apart actually are 'the same language'?

The evidence they present is of two kinds, one of which is language-internal. In this case, the assumption is backed up by regularities in the language that refer to the hypothesized element. We have seen an example of this above: the syllable determines

---

[2] http://web.uvic.ca/ling/resources/ipa/charts/IPAlab/IPAlab.htm

where the accent can come in Japanese. To repeat this point, a disyllabic structure like [hasi] could be *hási, hasí* or *hasi* (recall that a Japanese word may be unaccented), and these actually happen to be words: 'chopsticks', 'bridge' and 'edge', respectively. By contrast, there are only two theoretically possible words that consist of the syllable [ree]: *rée* and *ree*, which again are real words, 'a bow in greeting' and 'gratitude', respectively. It doesn't make sense to ask what *reé* might mean in Japanese: it couldn't *be* a word, because the accent never occurs on half of a syllable. Now, for it to be the case that the number of accentable positions is equal to the number of syllables it must of course be the case that the syllable exists.

Q3

(a) How many Japanese words could be formed from [hi]? And how many words could be formed from [kentoo]?

(b) There are, in fact, two Japanese words that are pronounced [rée]: 'example' and 'bow, greeting'. What do you call words that have the same pronunciation?

In addition to the language-internal evidence illustrated with the example of the Japanese syllable, there are many other sources of evidence. Most importantly, linguists can make phonetic measurements. They can measure the acoustic properties of speech, track the articulatory gestures by speakers and register listeners' responses to speech stimuli in perception experiments. These measurements enable them to understand better just what is going on when people communicate through spoken language. Such phonetic research not only reveals in detail the physiological, physical and psychological events that together make up the 'speech chain', but can also be used to provide evidence for or against a particular structural hypothesis. For instance, to show that the mora is an important element in the structure of Japanese, we could collect Japanese words varying in the number of syllables and the number of moras. One category would have words of one mora, like *go* 'word, language', another words with two moras and one syllable, like *kúu* 'bite, eat (by insects)', a third have words with two moras and two syllables, like *motí*, and so on. If we then measured the durations of the words, we could see whether word duration is better explained by how many moras a word has or by how many syllables a word has. If it turned out that the mora explains better than the syllable how long a word is, we would have phonetic evidence for the greater relevance of the mora in Japanese.

Behavioural experiments try to find evidence for linguistic structure by registering subjects' responses to specifically designed tasks. Such tasks should, of course, never directly ask subjects to give answers to questions about linguistic structures, or at least never take such data at face value, because this carries the obvious risk of including all sorts of misconceptions in the evidence. To return to language art forms, we could use the rhythm of poetry to investigate the syllabic structure of words. If we wanted to know how many syllables there are in an English word like *hire*, we could ask whether names like *Hire Fire* and *Mo Toe* could take the place of *Humpty-Dumpty* in the nursery rhyme *Humpty-Dumpty sat on a wall*. If all is well, there would be significantly more votes for *Hire Fire* than for *Mo Toe*, which difference could then be argued to be due to the fact that *hire* and *fire* are disyllabic words, like *Humpty* and *Dumpty*, while *Mo* and *Toe* are not. As you may have guessed, real-life experimental questions and tasks are more complex than these examples suggest.

The research agenda of psychologists, who started to take a serious interest in language in the 1960s, was to unravel the mental processes that allow listeners to understand speech and the processes that allow speakers to produce it. You will be familiar with the sensation you have that when listening to a foreign language you cannot tell where the words are. The reason for this is of course that, within a coherent phrase, there are no pauses between the words, any more than there are pauses between the syllables or moras of words (Cutler 2011). In fact, if by 'pauses' we were to think of brief periods of silence, then we will find quite a number of 'pauses' in coherent phrases, but these will occur within words as well as at the edges of words with reckless abandon. In an English phrase like *paper napkins*, there are two such silent intervals, one corresponding to the second *p* in *paper* and one to the *pk* combination in *napkins*. The boundary between the two words does not correspond to any silent interval at all. If there are no audible word beginnings, the question arises how native speakers of English avoid hearing words made up of sound sequences inside words, like *pay* in *paper* or *nap* in *napkin*, or even across word boundaries. Figure 1.1 shows a speech waveform of this phrase, with lines indicating the beginning and ending of sounds, as well as the word boundary. In this case, we cannot even say where the word begins. This could be defined as the moment that the lips close for the formation of [p], but since this action produces no acoustic energy, it cannot be distinguished from the silence that occurred before this event.

In fact, psycholinguists have shown that during speech perception, listeners do hear strings of sounds inside words as possible words, but this happens very briefly and below our awareness. Word strings across word boundaries may also 'activate' words that were never said, such as *income* in *mustering compassion* (..*muster income passion*..), but because of the particular ways in which sounds combine into words, cross-word strings of sounds are less likely to form words.

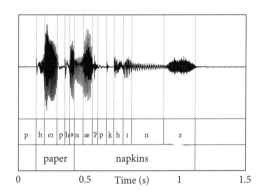

Figure 1.1

Speech waveform of a British English utterance of *paper napkins*. Segment boundaries within words have interrupted lines, the one separating the words is uninterrupted.

> **Q4** Why would the English phrase *Call the police!* never cause a word to be heard made up of a cross-word string of segments, while this may well happen in *Wildest endings*?

Other research has shown that it is easier to think of a word, as measured by the time it takes to say the word for an object in a picture, when the speaker has just been alerted to some other word that begins in the same way. That is, after just hearing *checkers*, people are quicker to say 'Cherry!' when presented with a picture of a cherry than after just hearing *backgammon*. Priming research of this sort can go some way towards understanding how speakers retrieve the pronunciation of a word before they actually pronounce it (Meyer & Belke 2007).

Psycholinguistic research into the processing of language in the brains of speakers and hearers and, more recently, neurological research into brain activity during language processing should of course be informed by the results of linguistic research into the structures of languages. Equally, structural linguistic research should take place in the wider context of psychological, neurological and sociological research, something that has not always been the case. In fact, some people would say that linguists are notorious for working out their problems in isolation from other fields.

1.3 MORPHOSYNTACTIC STRUCTURE

Phonology is concerned with a particular aspect of linguistic structure. In order to see what part of linguistic structure is phonological, we will first briefly consider that part of the linguistic structure which is *not* phonological, the **morphosyntactic structure**. The morphosyntactic structure of a language can be seen in the arrangement of the meaningful units of any linguistic expression. A distinction is made between **morphology**, which deals with the structure up to the level of the word, and **syntax**, which deals with the structure above the word.

1.3.1 Morphological structure

The smallest morphosyntactic unit is known as the **morpheme**. The word *scratch* is a single morpheme, but the word *pens* contains two morphemes. A morpheme that can be a word by itself is a **free morpheme**. The morpheme *pen* could form a word by itself, and is for that reason an example of a free morpheme, while the morpheme *s* is a **bound morpheme**, because it must combine with some other morpheme in order to be part of a word. A word consisting of a single (necessarily free) morpheme is a **simplex** word, other words being **complex**. An important group of bound morphemes are **affixes**, which can be divided into **prefixes** and **suffixes**, depending on whether they are placed before or after what is known as the **base**. Thus, the *s* in our example is a suffix because it is placed after the base *pen*, and so is *able* in the complex word *scratchable*.

Most words have a **category membership**, which allows them to be used in certain positions in sentence structure. If we assume that a sentence consists of a Noun and a Verb, in that order, then the sentence *Pens scratch* is well-formed, while **Scratch* *pens* is an ill-formed sentence (as indicated by the *). Affixes are **subcategorized** for a category membership, meaning that they only attach to bases that are members of a particular category. Thus, the plural suffix *s* attaches to nouns, while the suffix *able* attaches to transitive verbs, i.e. verbs that take a Direct Object, such as *scratch*, *read* and *drink* (but not *sleep*: **sleepable*). Affixes are also distinguished on the basis of whether they create new words, in which case they are known as **derivational** affixes, or merely create new forms of the same word, like the plural suffix *s* or the past-tense suffix in *scratched*, in which case they are **inflectional**. Derivational suffixes come with their own category membership, which is frequently different from the category of their base. Thus, *able* has the category Adjective, and every complex word ending in *able* is therefore an Adjective. In (1), the structural information for these two affixes is given in a notation known as **labelled bracketing**.

(1)   a.   [[   ]$_N$ s]   PLURAL
        b.   [[   ]$_{Vtrans}$ able]$_{Adj}$ 'is able to *Verb*'

Observe that a base can be simplex or complex. In *scratchers*, the plural suffix was attached to *scratcher*, itself composed of *scratch* and *er*. A simplex base which is a free morpheme is also known as a **stem**, while a simplex base that is not, like the English verbal base *mit* in *transmit*, is also known as a **root**.

Q5   Explain why there are no words *dieable and *seemable in English, and why *imaginable* is a word.

1.3.2   Syntactic structure

Words do not directly enter into sentence structure. If the structure of our simple sentence S were simply [N V], it would only be possible to form sentences of the type *Kittens scratch*, *Pens leak* and *Time flies*. In fact, we can also form *A good pen mustn't scratch* or *The pen I bought in Italy leaks*. Here, the structural position of *Pens* in our original example sentence *Pens scratch* is occupied by the word groups *A good pen* and *The pen I bought in Italy*. This is the reason why, in between the structural level of the word, illustrated in (1), and the structural level of the **sentence** (or **clause**), we need to recognize the structural level of the **(syntactic) phrase**. That is, instead of [N V], our simple sentence has the structure [Noun Phrase – Verb Phrase], or [NP VP]. In addition to the NP and the VP, another frequent type of phrase is the Prepositional Phrase, or PP, which consists of a preposition plus an NP, such as *with the leaky pen*, *on the surface* or *in Italy*.

The introduction of a level of phrasal structure allows us to point to two properties of morphosyntactic structure. One is that this structure is **hierarchical**. This means that we can distinguish higher and lower levels of structure: a word level, a phrase level and a sentence level. The second property is **recursiveness**. This means that a unit of a given structural level can be incorporated into a unit of the same structural level, or that a unit of a higher level of structure can be incorporated into a unit of a lower level. For example, the sentence *The pen I bought in Italy leaks* consists of two phrases, the NP *The pen I bought in Italy* and the VP *leaks*. The first of these is made up of an NP *The pen* and an S *(which) I bought in Italy*, which sentence in turn consists of the NP *I* and a VP *bought which* (i.e. *the pen*) *in Italy*. The structure in (2) expresses this. In (3), we give the mini-grammar that will produce this sentence. Recursiveness is shown in (3b), first, by the fact that we can feed a higher-level S into a lower-level NP and, second, by the fact that we can feed an NP into an NP. As you will have guessed, we can – at least in theory – apply the same rules again and again. It may be fun to do this, as illustrated by the children's verse *This is the farmer that kissed the girl that chased the cat that killed the mouse*, etc.

(2) $_S[_{NP}[_{NP}[$The pen$]_{NP}$ $_S[_{NP}[$I$]_{NP}$ $_{VP}[$bought (*sc*. the pen) in Italy$]_{VP}]_S]_{NP}$ $_{VP}[$leaks$]_{VP}]_S$

(3)   a.   S: NP VP
       b.   NP: NP S

There is much that is universal about the syntax of the languages of the world, but, of course, there is also a good deal of variation. Some languages have a VP in which the Verb precedes the rest (i.e. [V NP] or [V PP]), while other languages maintain the opposite order (i.e. [NP V] and [PP V]). Moreover, some languages have a syntactic rule that moves the Verb to initial position in the sentence. This type of variation is often referred to as that between S(ubject)V(erb)O(bject), SOV and VSO.

Q6   Identify the nouns and verbs in the following words:

1.   *unscratchable*
2.   *road tax increase*

Q7   Identify all the NPs in the following sentence:

He wrote the letter with a pen he bought in Italy

1.4   A WORLD WITHOUT PHONOLOGICAL STRUCTURE

Spoken languages use human vocal sound to give shape to their morphemes. Phonology is the branch of linguistics that aims to describe the way in which this medium of human vocal sound is structured, in languages generally as well as in individual languages. To see what is meant by the sound structure of languages, it may be instructive to pretend for a while that languages do not have it. Imagine that every morpheme of a language were assigned some vocalization. Conceivably, these vocalizations could be quite lengthy in view of the large number that would be needed to distinguish all the morphemes of the language. But, importantly, there would be no implication that they should have structure in the sense that they are composed of subparts, any more than abstract paintings are. To give a hypothetical example, vocalization (4) might be the morpheme meaning 'oak tree' in some language.

(4)   'oak tree': high-pitched wheeze, trailing off into a voiced cough with central, nasal vowel quality

The wide variation in morphosyntactic structure that is found in the languages of the world could exist without there being any structure to the human vocal sounds that languages use as a medium. Clearly, in the hypothetical situation described above, languages could still have SVO or VSO as their basic word order. They could either have an extensive Case system (i.e. be strongly inflectional) or have many prepositions; they may or may not have articles, they may or may not mark plural in both Subjects and Verbs ('Concord') and so on. Where our hypothetical situation is different from the situation in the real world is that nothing would have to be said about the sound structure, because there would not be any. All that anyone could do is make a list of descriptions like the one in (4).

Q8   Why, in the hypothetical situation above, would it be impossible for speech errors like [klɪs kɛə] for *kiss Claire* to occur?

Now let us turn to real life. The first observation to be made about the pronunciation of morphemes is that there are **recurring** elements. For instance, the sound patterns used for morphemes can be analysed as strings of **segments**. This is the basis on which we can say that English *cat* has the same segments as *tack* or *act*, although the segments occur in different orders. Minimally, then, the task of phonology is to state what these recurring elements are.

The second observation to be made is that the recurring elements do not occur in all possible orders. For example, while *cat, act, tack* are possible combinations in English of the segments [k], [æ] and [t], the same does not go for [ætk]. Notice that it is not the case that the sequence [ætk] never occurs in English. This sequence is part of the word *Atkins*, for instance, and occurs in the sentence *The cat killed the mouse*. What this shows is that there is some constituent higher than the segment which imposes constraints on what sequences of segments it may contain. In the example, that constituent is the **syllable**. That is, *[ætk] cannot occur as a sequence of segments inside the syllable. In general, elements at one level of structure combine in restricted ways to form elements of a higher level of structure. We will see in Chapter 6 that the segment is to be looked upon as an element that itself combines elements of a lower structural level, called **distinctive features**. So a second task for phonological theory is to state what the permitted patterns of arrangement of the phonological elements are.

A third important observation is that segments may be pronounced differently depending on their environment. This is because languages usually have processes that affect ('change') segments in particular contexts. In English, for example, [p,t,k] are aspirated when they are the first consonant of a syllable. Hence, *tack* is pronounced [tʰæk], but *stack* is [stæk]. Similarly, the Dutch [z] in [zeː] 'sea' is pronounced [s] when it is preceded by an obstruent, as in [ɔp seː] 'at sea'. Or again, in French the final consonant of an adjective like [pətit] 'small' is pronounced in *le petit autobus* 'the little bus', but not in *le petit camion* 'the little lorry', as a result of the difference in the first segment in the following noun. As these examples make clear, one and the same morpheme may have different pronunciations in different contexts as a result of the existence of these processes.

Phonological theory, then, will have to account for these three aspects of phonological structure.

Q9 Do you think that sign languages for the deaf have phonologies?

1.4.1 One phonology for all languages?

Now, it might have been the case that all human languages had the **same** sound structure. In order to see what this would mean, let's once more enter into an imaginary world. We will make up a 'universal phonology', and then give partial descriptions of two – very different – languages. The universal sound structure is given in (5), and (6) gives partial descriptions of the two languages.

(5) a.   Segment inventory:

C	V
p t k	i u
b d g	a
m n	
l	

   b.   Arrangement:
         A word consists of one, two or three syllables.
         A syllable consists of CV.

   c.   Process:
         FRICATION Initial obstruents in non-initial words are fricatives.

Because of FRICATION, [p,t,k] will be [f,θ,x] and [b,d,g] will be [v,ð,ɣ] in the context specified. Because the fricatives are variants of the plosives, they are not listed separately in (5a).

(6)		Language I	Language II
	Syntax	SVO	VSO
	Subject–Verb Concord	*yes*	*no*
	'cow'	pi	kapu
	'graze'	namu	ni
	'field'	diku	pu
	Plural	[[ ]ₙ/ᵥ lu]PLUR	[[ ]ₙ ti]PLUR
	'in' (Preposition)	ma	–
	Locative Case	–	[[ ]ₙ la]LOC

Using the data in the first column of (6), we find that in Language I the sentence meaning 'Cows are grazing in the field' would be [pilu namulu ma ðiku]. Here, Subject – Verb Concord is expressed by the double occurrence of [lu], while the position of the PP 'in the field' is that of the O in SVO.

Q10

1. Why does the word for 'field' in the sentence of Language I begin with [ð], and not with [d]?
2. What is the translation of this sentence into Language II?
3. Why would the process we assumed in (5c) be a convenient feature of human language, as seen from the point of view of the listener?

The reason why a single phonology for all languages is so improbable is that the phonologies of languages change over time, just as does the morphosyntax. One general factor inducing change affects both aspects of structure. When learning their language, infants may make different generalizations over the data from what their parents did when they learnt the language. Changes induced by such generalizations will affect word order as well as the forms of specific words. To begin with a syntactic example, the position of the verb changed from an earlier SOV in proto-Germanic to SVO in English. Other Germanic languages remained SOV, except in that they moved the finite verb form to the second position in main clauses. As a result, English now has SVO in both dependent clauses (7a) and main clauses (7b), but Dutch has SOV in dependent clauses and a partial SVO, known as 'Verb-Second', in main clauses: S-Vfinite-O-Vnonfinite (Koster 1975). Here, English acquired a more general rule than did Dutch and other Germanic languages.

(7)	*English*	*Dutch*
a.	I think she *would like to buy* fish	Ik denk dat ze vis *wil kopen*
b.	She *would like to buy* fish	Ze *wil* vis *kopen*

A morphological example concerns the Dutch 3rd SG verbal suffix [t]. It appears after stems like *ken* 'know' and *raak* 'hit', which thus change to *kent* and *raakt* when used with a singular 3rd subject NP. However, auxiliary verbs like *wil* 'would like' and *kan* 'can' don't take this [t]: *De jongen kent het* 'The boy knows it', but *De jongen kan het* 'The boy can (do) it'. Children often generalize t-suffixation to the auxiliary verb *wil* and say *De jongen wilt het* for the parental *De jongen wil het* 'The boy wants it'. In this case, the treatment of *wil* is probably inspired by the meaning 'want-to', which is expressed by a non-auxiliary verb in many languages, even though Dutch *wil* behaves just like the other auxiliaries in other respects. Such novel generalizations are usually modified in later stages of the acquisition process, as when children acquiring English will start using *mice* instead of the *mouses* which they may have produced before, but some stay and lead to language change.

A second factor relies on changes in the pronunciation of specific sounds, or of specific sounds in specific contexts. Such changes are very common, although we may not always realize that the variation we observe between speakers may be an indication of change. Such changes are sociologically determined in the sense that they arise within a smaller group of speakers. Again, some of these changes will become more general, as happened in the case of the disappearance of [r] from the ends of syllables in a number of varieties of English. In the English spoken in England, this disappearance caused *court* to have the same pronunciation as *caught* and *garter* to rhyme with *sonata*. As a result, the phonology of the innovating 'r-less' speakers represents a fairly drastic change relative to that of the older system, for instance in having additional, new vowels, like the vowel in a word like *beer*. In the English spoken in England, *beer* rhymes with *idea*, but in the English spoken in the USA and Canada, which preserves an 'r-full' version of the language, they do not.

1.5   TWO KINDS OF STRUCTURE

The fact that the vocalizations that are used to represent the meaningful units of language themselves have structure has an important consequence. This is that terms like 'constituent' or 'unit' are ambiguous. The speaker or writer might be referring to a morphosyntactic unit, such as 'the morpheme *hill*' or 'the sentence *I like it*', or to a phonological unit like 'the segment [ɛ]' or 'the syllable [kɛt]'.

Q11   Divide the following English words up into (a) morphemes and (b) syllables:

elephants
palm oil
unsettling

Q12

1. In the case of English [æ], [k] and [t] all permitted arrangements are in fact words: *cat, tack, act*. But if we replace [æ] with [ɪ], combining the three segments yields only two words: *kit* and *tick*. Would it be correct to say that [ɪkt] is an ill-formed combination in English?
2. Can you explain why [mrʌt] would never be introduced as a brand-name in English, while [trʌm] might well be?

Thus, a linguistic expression always has two structures, a morphosyntactic one, which reflects the meaningful elements in the expression, and a phonological one, which is the structure most immediately relevant to the pronunciation of the expression. The distinction is a very real one, because the morphosyntactic constituents do not map one to one onto the phonological constituents; to use a technical term, they are not **isomorphic**. That is, morphemes do not exclusively correspond to segments, or exclusively to syllables, etc. While the Dutch polite second person pronoun consists of the one segment [y], the morpheme [ɪk] 'I' consists of two. And while these two pronouns each consist of one syllable, the informal second person plural pronoun consists of two: [jy.li]. (The period '.' is often used to indicate syllable boundaries.) In English, the single syllable [suːz] can represent two morphemes, *Sue* and *is*, as pronounced in the sentence *Sue is ticklish*. In (7), the morphosyntactic structure of that sentence is given. The way the sentence is analysed in morphosyntactic constituents should be compared with the (partial) phonological constituent analysis of that same sentence, given in (8). Notice that just like the morphosyntactic structure, the phonological structure is hierarchical. There is a layer of **segments**, which build a layer of **syllables** (symbolized σ) which build a layer of **feet** (symbolized F), which build a layer of **phonological words** (symbolized ω), and so on. In addition to the different constituent structures for *Sue is*, for example, notice that *ticklish* consists of two syllables as well as of two morphemes, but that the syllables and the morphemes do not divide the word up in the same way. The dual structure outlined in this section exists in all languages. It is dealt with in more detail in Chapter 16.

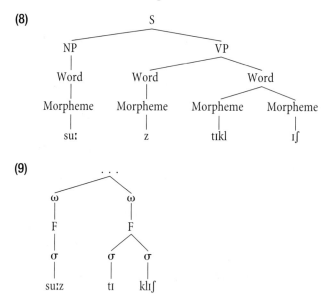

1.6   CONCLUSION

This chapter has made the point that linguistic expressions have two parallel hierarchical structures. One of these, the morphosyntactic structure, reflects the meaning of the linguistic expression, while the other—the phonological structure— reflects its pronunciation. A given constituent in either structure will typically not map onto any single constituent in the other structure, a point that will be worked out more in Chapter 16. Before we move on to a further discussion of the phonological structure, we first deal with the way we produce and articulate speech in Chapter 2.

2

The production of speech

2.1   INTRODUCTION

To describe how we produce speech and what speech looks like acoustically in the space of a single chapter is a tall order, and you would do well to consult other textbooks that deal more specifically with the phonetics of speech, like Ladefoged (2006), Catford (1988), Laver (1994), Ladefoged & Maddieson (1996) or Reetz & Jongman (2009). We describe the speech production process in two stages. First, we consider the role of the lungs and the larynx. This part of the speech organs is responsible for the actions of the vocal folds, which are located inside the larynx. A common and spectacular action of the vocal folds occurs when they vibrate against each other so as to produce a buzzing sound, which can be varied in pitch and loudness. Second, we deal with the role of the channel extending from the larynx onwards, called the **vocal tract**. It is formed by the pharynx, the mouth and, for nasal and nasalized sounds, the nasal cavity. The vocal tract modifies the buzzing larynx sound—which we cannot reproduce here in its pristine form, unless the vocal folds are made to vibrate artificially in a headless cadaver. Because the vocal tract can assume many different shapes, these modifications are highly varied. The most striking effect here is the production of different vowel sounds. The term **organs of speech** is used to refer to parts of the body in the larynx and the vocal tract that are involved in the production of speech. It is a misleading term in that it suggests that we have special physical organs for speaking. This is not so: all our so-called 'organs of speech' have primary biological functions relating to our respiratory system and the processing of food.

The pronunciation of words is conventionally represented with the help of **phonetic symbols**, any such representation being a phonetic transcription. The symbols used in this book are those proposed by the International Phonetic Association (IPA), which can be found on page x. A phonetic symbol stands for a particular speech sound, or **segment**, which is defined independently of any language. Phonetic symbols may be accompanied by **diacritics**, signs which are printed above or below a phonetic symbol or with which the symbol is superscripted, and which specify particular features of pronunciation. For example, in the transcription [kʰæt], which indicates the pronunciation of the English word *cat*, [kʰ] represents a [k] which is accompanied by aspiration, a brief [h]-like sound occurring between the [k] proper and the following [æ]. It is not always necessary, or even desirable, to indicate all the features of the pronunciation of a word in a transcription: the transcription [kæt] is often sufficiently informative if the reader knows the language concerned. A transcription that includes a great deal of detail is called **narrow**.

2.2   THE LUNGS AND THE LARYNX

A crucial requirement for the production of acoustic energy is a mechanism to create an air pressure difference in the appropriate locations in the larynx and the vocal tract. There are a number of ways in which air pressure differences for speech production are created, called **air stream mechanisms** (Abercrombie 1967). The most commonly used by far is the **pulmonic** air stream mechanism, and the great majority of speech sounds are produced with the help of increased air pressure created by our lungs. Before we begin to speak, we breathe in, taking in sufficient air to produce an utterance of reasonable length. Instead of simply letting go of the muscular tension and allowing our lungs to collapse, pushing the air from them (which is what we would do if we were breathing normally), we slowly ease up on the tension, thereby slowing down the exhalation phase. This artificially extended period of pressure from our lungs is used to produce speech. Because it is the exhalation phase rather than the inhalation phase that is used, these speech sounds are called **egressive**. Most languages, only have pulmonic egressive sounds. In section 2.8, we will briefly describe the production mechanisms of three types of nonpulmonic sounds (clicks, implosives and ejectives).

After passing through the bronchi and the trachea, the first organ the airstream will meet on its path from the lungs is the **larynx**. The outward part of this organ can be felt – and, especially in men, be seen – at the front of the neck (the Adam's apple). The larynx is a valve, which can be opened and closed by two thickish flaps that run from back to front inside the larynx (see Figure 2.1). These flaps are primarily there to prevent food or saliva from entering the lungs, but because they also have a function in speech they are known as the **vocal folds** or the **vocal cords**.[1] The aperture between them is called the **glottis**. No air can pass through the glottis when it is closed, while the air can flow quite freely through an open glottis.

Q13   When you pretend to lift a heavy object, like a table or large stone, you naturally close your vocal folds. You do this in order to prevent your contracting muscles from losing their leverage due to a yielding of the surface over which they are stretched. While holding your breath in this way, try to make noises in your mouth. You will find you can make various sounds, by clicking with your tongue or making a popping sound by suddenly opening your lips. Why can't these sounds be classed as 'pulmonic'?

---

[1] There is an additional valve, called the epiglottis, positioned above the larynx where the root of the tongue begins. It normally points upwards, but it flaps down to channel food and saliva into the oesophagus – the tube behind the larynx leading to the stomach – when we swallow.

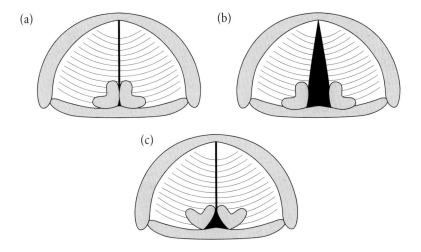

Figure 2.1
Schematic drawings of (a) a closed glottis, as during the closure stage of a glotttal stop or during the closed phase of the vibrating glottis; (b) an open glottis; (c) a narrowed glottis.

The pulmonically produced pressure difference is used for three purposes. First, it can be used to drive the vibratory opening and closing actions of organs like the vocal folds, as explained in section 2.2.1. During the articulation of [m], for instance, vocal-fold vibration can easily be felt by placing one's fingertips on one's 'Adam's apple'. Second, it can be used to generate a flow of air that can be channelled through a narrow opening to create audible air turbulence, or friction. This happens during the articulation of [s], for instance. Third, it can be used to build up pressure behind a complete blockage of the vocal tract in order to create an explosive sound when the blockage is suddenly removed. This occurs in the articulation of plosive consonants like [p], such as when we say [pa].

2.2.1　The vocal folds: the open and vibrating glottis

There are many consonants that are produced with the glottis held **open**, as in ordinary breathing. Such sounds are called **voiceless**, and we hear them because other speech organs, the tongue or the lips, are used to generate fricative or explosive sounds further up in the vocal tract. Examples of voiceless sounds are [f] and [ʃ] in *fish* and [st] in *stay*.

The vocal folds are exploited in various ways to create sound which can be used as a basis for speech. This is known as **phonation**. The most important type of phonation is **voice**, which is produced when the vocal folds vibrate. Vocal-fold vibration occurs when the closed glottis is subjected to increased subglottal air pressure which is sufficient to blow the vocal folds apart, but not enough to prevent them from falling together again when the air pressure between them drops as a result of the Bernoulli effect, a physical effect which causes pressure mimima at points where the flow of gases or liquids is high. As soon as they have been sucked together, the vocal folds are once more blown apart as a result of the subglottal air pressure. This process typically repeats itself more than 100 times per second for the larger and laxer vocal folds of men, and over 200 times per second for the smaller vocal folds of women. Consonants like [m], [l] and [j] (which we will see are sonorant consonants) and vowels are normally **voiced**. Voiced obstruent consonants also exist, such as [b] in English *abbey* and [z] in *lazy*, and usually contrast with their voiceless counterparts (in these cases with [p] and [s], as in *happy, lacy*).

2.2.2   Devoicing and aspiration

When a consonant that is normally voiced is pronounced without vocal-fold vibration in some context, it is said to be **devoiced**. Devoiced segments are symbolized with a circle below the symbol (which may also appear above it, if there is no space below it). For example, devoicing may follow voiceless obstruents, in particular plosives. In many languages, the vocal folds may begin to vibrate immediately after the release of the closure made for the plosive for a following voiced segment, as in [pa], but in other languages the vocal folds may remain open for a while. In the latter case, the plosives are said to be **aspirated**. As shown above, aspirated plosives are symbolized with a superscript [h], as in [pʰa]. English has voiceless aspirated plosives at the beginning of the syllable, as in *tea, pea, key*. If a sonorant consonant rather than a vowel follows the aspirated plosive, the aspiration is indicated by means of the devoicing diacritic, as in English [pl̥eɪ] *play*.

The timing relation between plosive releases and the onset of vocal-fold vibration is expressed as Voice Onset Time, or VOT. The VOT is zero when the plosive release and the onset of vocal-fold vibration are simultaneous; when the onset of vocal-fold vibration is earlier than the release of the plosive, VOT is negative, and when it is later, it is positive. Typical values for aspirated plosives are between VOT +50 ms and VOT +80 ms.

Figure 2.2 shows a **speech wave form** of the word *pass*, spoken by a speaker of British English as [pɑːs]. The first acoustic event is the burst of [p]. (Recall from Chapter 1 that we cannot tell from the acoustics when a [p] begins if it occurs after silence.) Then there is some weak turbulence, which is the aspiration as indicated by [h]. The VOT is measured from the beginning of the burst to the beginning of the vowel, and is 61 ms in this example. The waveform during the vowel shows the vibrating vocal folds. Finally, the voiceless [s] consists of loud turbulence. Voiced sounds like [m] and [ɑː] are 'periodic sounds', because the waveform shows a repeating pattern. Each of the repeated portions of the waveform corresponds to an opening-and-closing action of the vocal folds and is known as a **period**. Figure 2.3 reproduces a section from the waveform in Figure 2.2, with one period marked out. Notice that the shape of the waveform during this period is more or less the same as those of the periods before and after. The duration of the period, usually measured in milliseconds (ms), depends on the frequency with which the vocal folds carry out their opening-and-closing actions. If these occur 200 times per 1,000 ms (expressed as 200 Hz), the period will be exactly 5 ms. The frequency of vibration of the vocal folds is the **fundamental frequency** of the speech signal, also referred to as the F0 ('F-zero'). The shape of the waveform during a period determines the quality of the sound, in this case that of the British English vowel [ɑː]. Panel (b) shows a period of

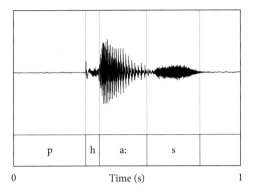

Figure 2.2
Speech waveform of the British English word *pass*. The vertical lines demarcate the release of the bilabial [p], the beginning of the vocal fold vibration for [ɑː], the beginning of [s] and the end of [s]. The Voice Onset Time (VOT) is given by the duration between the first two demarcation lines.

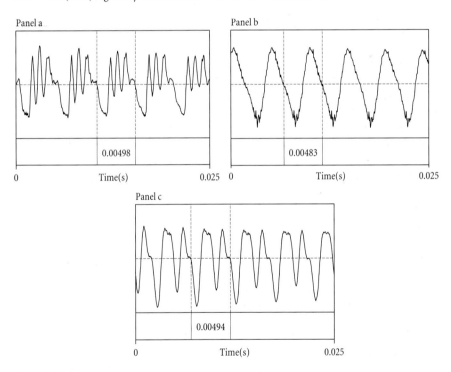

Figure 2.3
Waveforms for [ɑː] (panel a), [iː] (panel b) and [ʊ] (panel c) with approximately equally long periods.

about the same duration for the vowel [iː] in *peace*, and panel (c) does the same for [ʊ] in *foot*. The different shapes are due to the different shapes the vocal tract assumes during the production of these vowels: the resonances that are set up in the air in the vocal tract depend on its length and shape. The relation between these resonance frequencies, known as **formants**, and vowel qualities is briefly indicated in section 2.4.

The turbulent signal for [s] has no fundamental frequency. It consist of 'noise', a largely random pattern of vibrations in which broad frequency zones are more emphasized than others. These different emphases in the frequency spectrum determine whether the turbulence sounds more like a high-friction [s], or a low-friction [f], etc. When turbulence and vocal-fold vibration are produced simultaneously, we produce sounds like [z] and [v].

Q14   What would the speech waveform of the word *ceased* look like?

Q15   What is the approximate fundamental frequency of the vowel shown in panel (c) of Figure 2.3?

2.2.3   Special types of phonation

Three special types of phonation are mentioned here, whisper, breathy voice and creaky voice.

1. The vocal folds can be brought together to form a **narrowing** which produces **friction** when air passes through it. This is how people whisper: instead of voice, glottal friction may be used as the acoustic source to be modified. A whispered speech sound occurring in otherwise voice-phonated speech is [h], as in English [hæt] *hat*. Whisper can be indicated by the devoicing symbol, as has been done in [æ̥t].

2. **Breathy voice** occurs when the closing phase of the vibration is not complete, so that air is allowed to flow through with friction during phonation. Breathy voice is used in European languages to signal confidentiality (Laver 1994: 200), and is sometimes jocularly used to create the effect of a sexy voice. Voiced aspirated plosives, which occur in many languages spoken on the Indian subcontinent, are produced by allowing breathy voice to be used throughout the plosive and the following vowel, as in Hindi [bʱal] 'forehead'. Breathy voice can be indicated by [̤].

3. **Creaky voice** or **laryngealized voice** is produced with tight vocal folds, and often allows the listener to hear the opening actions of the vocal folds as separate events. (The effect may remind you of the sound produced when running a fingernail across the teeth of a comb.) British English speakers may break into creak at the ends of their utterances, when the pitch is low. Many Nilotic languages use laryngeal voice contrastively (Ladefoged 1971). Dinka has a set of vowels with creaky voice, symbolized by means of [̰], which contrast with a set with breathy voice, as in [rò̰ːr] 'forest' – [rò̤ːr] 'men' (Andersen 1987; symbols for long segments are followed by [ː]).

2.2.4 Pitch

Variations in the frequency of vibration are heard by the listener as variations of **pitch**: the more frequently the vocal folds open and close, the higher the pitch. In languages like English, French, German and Spanish, variations in pitch are used to signal different discoursal meanings. For instance, in the utterance *But I don't want it!*, the syllable *want* will be higher than the syllable *it*, but in *Want it?*, *it* will be the higher syllable. These two intonation patterns are known as the 'fall' and the 'rise', and add a 'declarative' and 'interrogative' meaning to the utterance, respectively. In other languages, called **tone languages**, different pitch patterns are used in the same way vowels and consonants are used in all languages, i.e. to distinguish words from one another. Dinka has low tone ['], high tone ['] and falling tone [^], as illustrated by [rɒ̀w] 'two' *vs* [rɒ́w] 'thirst' and [yọ́ːw] 'bones' *vs* [yộːm] 'wind' (Andersen 1987). Karen has three level tones, high, mid [ˉ] and low, as illustrated by [tá] 'one', [tā] 'spoon' and [tə̀] 'ant' (Jones 1961).

2.2.5 The glottal stop

It is possible during phonation to suddenly **close** the glottis, hold that closure briefly and then, equally suddenly, allow the vocal folds to vibrate again. The resulting speech sound is known as the **glottal stop**, symbolized by [ʔ]. A glottal stop requires voicing on one side only; hence it can be initial, as in Hawaiian [ʔu] 'to moan' and final, as in Tsou [suʔ] 'to fall'. English has the paralinguistic item [ʔm̩ʔm̩], with the first [m] higher in pitch than the second, meaning 'no', used in informal settings. In German, [ʔ] occurs before the second syllable of *Beamter* ([bəˈʔamtəʁ]).

Summarizing section 2.2, the larynx produces either no sound (open glottis) or a phonated sound. In the former case, the segment is said to be **voiceless**, and the acoustic energy created for the speech sound lies at a location above the larynx. In the other case, the phonation could be normal voice, breathy voice or creaky voice, in which cases the speech sound is **voiced**, or whisper. Finally, a brief closure before or after voicing represents a glottal stop. In the next section, we consider the ways in which an acoustic source can be created at a location above the larynx, as well as the ways in which the phonated laryngeal sound source can be modified by differences in the shape of the supralaryngeal cavities, which together form the vocal tract.

2.3 THE VOCAL TRACT

The vocal tract extends all the way to the lips (see Figure 2.4). It consists of the **pharynx** and the **mouth**, to which an extra tube extending to the nostrils may be coupled, the **nasal cavity**. This (potentially bifurcating) tube acts as a resonator, modifying the sound produced at the glottis. The sound produced by a vibrating glottis can be modified by changing the position of the tongue or jaw so as to produce

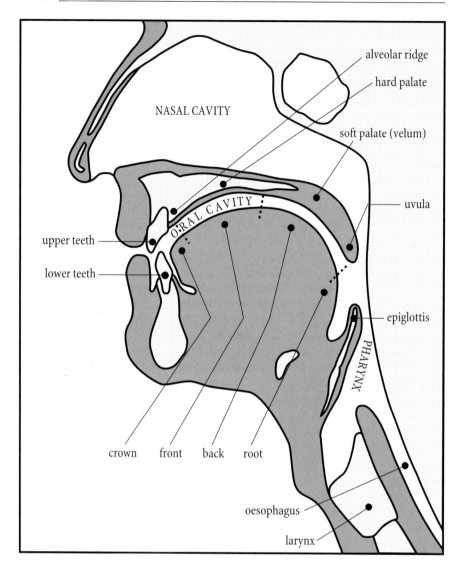

Figure 2.4
Cross-section of the vocal tract.

a range of different vowel qualities. Second, inside the vocal tract there are further opportunities for generating sound, which – in their turn – will be modified by the shape of the vocal tract in front of the sound source. For instance, the tongue can be brought up against the roof of the mouth to form a constriction that generates friction when air is passed through it. In this section, we describe the three parts of the vocal tract mentioned above, and in section 2.4 we deal with the positions that the tongue, jaw and lips may assume to produce different vowels. In section 2.5 we identify the various places at which languages make articulatory constrictions. In the same section, we will classify the types of constriction that are used.

2.3.1 The pharynx

The pharynx is the vertical part of the tube extending up from the larynx to the velum. The forward wall is formed by the **root** of the tongue, which faces the back wall of the pharynx.

2.3.2 The nasal cavity

The **soft palate**, or **velum**, is a valve which closes off the entrance to the nasal cavity when it is pressed up, but opens the cavity when it is allowed to hang down, as in ordinary breathing (When we have a cold, the entrance to the nasal cavity may be blocked by mucus, which forces us to breathe through the mouth, and hence to produce only oral sounds). The velum ends in a pear-shaped little blob of flesh, which can be seen during the speaker's articulation of [aː]. It is called the **uvula**.

2.3.3 The mouth

The **mouth** is the most important part of the vocal tract because it is here that the most drastic modifications of its shape are achieved and the majority of the articulatory contacts are made. The roof of the mouth is formed by the soft palate, with the **uvula** at the extreme end, and the **hard palate**, which lies to the front of the soft palate (also known simply as the **palate**). With a curled-back tongue, it is possible to feel the hard palate arching back to where the soft palate begins. Immediately behind the front teeth is the **alveolar ridge**, which is touched by the tongue during the pronunciation of *dada*; then there are the **front teeth** themselves and the **upper lip**. Below these parts there are the more active speech organs: the **lower lip** and the **tongue**. The zone immediately behind the **tip** of the tongue is called the **blade**. You use it when imitating the sharp, hissing sound of a snake. Together, tip and blade are called the **crown**, which term is from Clements (1989). The part of the tongue opposite the hard palate is called the **front**, the part opposite the soft palate is called the **back**. The section comprising both front and back is known as the **dorsum**.

2.4 VOWELS

For vowels, the vocal folds vibrate. The crown is held behind the lower teeth, while the dorsum is bunched, forming a constriction that allows a frictionless escape of the air. The lips may be rounded, causing the vocal tract to be lengthened. The location of the bunch can be varied in a vertical dimension, as well as in a horizontal dimension. In the British English phonetic tradition, four steps are recognized in the vertical dimension: **close**, **close-mid**, **open-mid** and **open**. In the American English tradition, the three terms **high**, **mid** and **low** are used to distinguish three vowel heights. Horizontally, the bunch can go from **front** to **back**, with **central** being used as an in-between value. If we disregard the open vowel [a], most languages just have front unrounded and back rounded vowels. Italian, for instance, has the vowels shown in (1). The position of the lips is rounded for [u], [o] and [ɔ], and unrounded for [i], [e], [ɛ] and [a]. (Deviating from IPA conventions, authors normally use the symbol [a] to represent a central or central to back open unrounded vowel like [ɑ].)

(1)

	Front unrounded	Back unrounded	Back rounded
High	i		u
Mid	e		o
Low	ɛ	a	ɔ

If the tongue positions used for [i], [e] and [ɛ] are combined with rounded lips, the vowels [y], as in French [lyn] 'moon', [ø], as in [pø] '(a) little' and [œ], as in [sœl] 'alone' are produced. A rounded [ɑ] is [ɒ], and may occur in *dog* as pronounced in varieties of English spoken in England and on the east coast of the USA. Unrounded vowels with the bunch in the back or centre exist also. The unrounded counterpart of [ɔ] is [ʌ], that of [o] is [ɤ], and that of [u] is [ɯ].

Rounded front vowels are somewhat more central than unrounded ones, while unrounded back vowels are somewhat more central than rounded back vowels. Frequently, of the low vowels only the back member is ever rounded, and many languages avoid low round vowels altogether. The vowels of conservative Korean, given in (2), illustrate the avoidance of low round vowels. (The vowel [æ] has merged with [e] for many speakers, while [y] and [ø] have become [wi] and [we] in the speech of younger speakers.) Example words are given in (3).

(2)

	Front unrounded	Centralized front rounded	Centralized back unrounded	Back rounded
High	i	y	ɯ	u
Mid	e	ø	ɤ	o
Low	(æ)		a	

(3)

mi	'beauty'	ky	'ear'	kɯ	'he'	ku	'sphere'
pe	'hemp'	mø	'mountain'	nɤ	'you'	co	'millet'
pæ	'pear'			na	'I'		

While a central position of the tongue bunch is thus quite common, central vowels pattern like back vowels if they are unrounded, and like front vowels if they are rounded.

Diphthongs. A vowel whose quality remains stable during its production, like [æ] in English *hat* or [uː] in German [guːt] 'good', is known as a **monophthong**. When two different vowels appear in the same syllable, the combination is known as a **diphthong**. English has diphthongs in [laɪ] *lie*, [naʊ] *now* and [dʒɔɪ] *joy*, while German has the diphthongs [ai], [ɑu] and [ɔi] in [tsait] 'time', [hɑus] 'house' and [ɔiç] 'you (OBJ PL)', respectively.

Nasalization. Vowels can be **nasalized**: if during their production the soft palate is lowered (so that the nasal cavity is opened up), a nasal quality is added to them. Nasalized vowels occur in Portuguese and French, and are symbolized by placing a tilde over the symbol. Thus, French has three nasalized vowels, occurring in [ṽɛ̃] 'wine', [tɑ̃t] 'aunt' and [ʃɔ̃t] 'shame'.

Q16 Are there any close, close-mid or open-mid front vowels in the English phrase *I'm not here to make friends*? Any velar sounds? Any fricatives whose friction is produced upstream from the larynx?

The acoustic structure of vowels is determined by the resonances of the air in the vocal tract which modify the glottal waveform. These resonance frequencies or formants are counted from lowest to highest (formant 1, or F1, is thus the lowest). F1 corresponds to the degree of opening of the oral cavity. It is low for close vowels like [i, y, u] and high for an open vowel like [a]. F2 approximately depends on the distance between the lips and the main constriction in oral cavity: a forward constriction as for [i] results in a high F2, while a velar or uvular constriction results in a low F2. The effect of F2 is similar to the resonance heard in a bottle under a tap: as it fills up towards the beginning of the neck and the column of air gets shorter, the resonance caused by the splashing water is higher. F1 is rather related to the size of the opening of the bottle: a thin neck creates a duller effect (low F1, as for close vowels) than a wide neck (high F1, as for open vowels). In the next chapter we will see how the distance between the lips and the constriction is a determining factor in explaining the frequencies of occurrence of vowel sounds in the languages of the world.

You can hear the effect of your second formant independently of the laryngeal source sound when you whistle. High notes are produced with the tongue in the position for [i] (or better, [y], because of the lip rounding), low notes with the tongue in the position for [u] and intermediate notes with intermediate tongue positions for high vowels, like [ʉ]. You can hear your first formant if you close your glottis (see Q13) and flick a finger against the side of your throat going from [i] via [e], [a], [o] to [u], once per vowel position. Figure 2.5 plots the first two formant frequencies of a male speaker of the seven Italian vowels in (1). The horizontal axis represents F2, with its origin on the right, while the vertical axis represents F1,

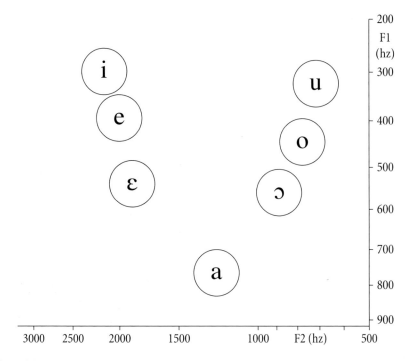

Figure 2.5
Plots of F1 and F2 of seven Italian vowels as spoken by a male speaker in a space with inverted, logarithmic axes. By courtesy of Antti Iivonen http://www.helsinki.fi/speechsciences/projects/vowelcharts/.

with its origin at the top. Both axes are nonlinear, with higher values being more compressed than lower values. By arranging the axes in this way, the vowels get to be spatially arranged as in a conventional impressionistic vowel diagram or vowel trapezoid (see the vowel trapezoid IPA chart on page x) or as in diagrams like those in (1). Incidentally, you may now see why people started calling the fundamental frequency the 'F0'.

Because of the shorter length and smaller width of a child's vocal tract, the formant frequencies of vowels produced by children are higher than those of adults, particularly those of F2. Likewise, women, whose vocal tracts are approximately 15 cm long as compared to 17.5 cm in men, have higher formant frequencies than men for the 'same' vowels. Listeners normalize for those differences after extracting the information about the sex and maturation of the speaker from the speech waveform.

2.5 CONSTRICTIONS

In the vocal tract various types of **constriction** can be made in different places. We will first go through the different places, and then discuss the different kinds of constriction that exist for consonants. The expression 'to articulate with X' is used to mean 'to form a constriction at X'.

2.5.1   Places of articulation

Pharyngeal

The **root** of the tongue articulates with the back wall of the pharynx. Gulf Arabic has a voiceless pharyngeal fricative, as in [laħam] 'meat'.

Dorsal

The **dorsum** articulates with the roof of the mouth. If it is the back that articulates with the soft palate, the term **velar** is used. This place is used for [k] in French *quand* 'when', for [ŋ] in English *hang*, for [g] in English *good* and for [x] in Scottish English *loch*. If it is the front which articulates with the hard palate, the term **palatal** is used. It is found in German *nicht*, where [ç] occurs, and in French *qui*, where a voiceless plosive [k̟] occurs. Such consonants are really 'fronted velars', and should be distinguished from palatals or palatoalveolars that are produced somewhat further forward, like the [c] in Dutch ['kacjə] 'cat+DIM', or English [ʃ] in *ship*. These type of segment also involve a raising of the crown, and are therefore treated under 'Coronal' below. Retraction of the dorsum allows the back of the tongue to articulate with the uvula. A voiceless uvular fricative [χ] occurs in Western Dutch, as in [χeːl] 'yellow'. The uvular stops [q,ɢ] occur in Tlingit, for instance.

Coronal

The **crown** may articulate with the teeth, the alveolar ridge or the forward part of the hard palate immediately behind the alveolar ridge. When the crown articulates with the upper teeth, **dental** segments are produced, like [θ] in English *thing* and [ð] in *this* and *that*; the dental plosives [t̪,d̪] occur for instance in Sinhalese [t̪ad̪ə] 'hard'. The label **alveolar** is used if the crown articulates with the alveolar ridge. Examples are [t] and [d] in German [tʰuːn] 'do', [duː] 'you', [n] in [naxt] 'night' or [l] as in ['aləs] 'everything'. If the crown articulates with the rear edge of the alveolar ridge, a **postalveolar** consonant is produced. English [ʃ] in *shore*, [ʒ] in *measure*, [tʃ] in *chip* and [dʒ] in *jet* are articulated with the crown of the tongue, while the front of the tongue is raised towards the hard palate. Often, as in Dutch, the tip is held behind the lower teeth for this type of consonant, in which case the contact is alternatively labelled **prepalatal**. A postalveolar articulation with just the tip of the tongue occurs in English [tɹ] as in *try*. If this type of contact is made with the lower surface of the tongue blade, keeping the tongue tip curled back, the term **retroflex** is used. Like many languages spoken in India, Hindi has retroflex consonants such as [ʈ,ɖ,ɳ] as in [tʰəɳɖi] 'cold' and [gʱəɳʈa] 'hour'.

Labial

If the *lips* articulate with each other, as in English [p, b, m] in *spot, bell, mad*, the place is **bilabial**. If the lower lip articulates with the upper teeth, the place is **labiodental**. It is used for [f] in German [fiː] 'cattle' or French [fɛʀ] 'do'.

2.5.2   Types of constriction

A first subdivision distinguishes between two kinds of constriction.

1. A constriction that is tight enough to lead to friction when a (voiced or voiceless) airstream is passed through it, as used with **obstruents**.
2. A type of constriction that it allows a voiced airstream to pass through without friction, which is used for **sonorants**.

In the case of obstruents, an acoustic source is actually created at the point of articulation: either a popping sound is produced (for plosives) or friction is produced at that spot (for fricatives and affricated plosives). The auditory quality of sonorants relies exclusively on the different shapes the vocal tract is given, i.e. on the resulting modifications of the acoustic characteristics of the sound produced by phonation in the larynx.

Obstruents are subdivided into **plosives** (also called **stops**), **fricatives** and **affricates**.

Plosives

These are formed by creating a **complete closure** at some point in the speech tract, behind which the air from the lungs is compressed until the closure is abruptly released so that the air explodes outwards. Since the soft palate is raised, the air cannot escape through the nasal cavity. Examples are French voiceless [p,t,k], as in [pip] 'pipe', [tip] 'type', [e'kip] 'crew'. Voiced plosives occur in French [bi'de] 'bidet' and [gã] 'glove'. Plosives have a very brief friction burst when they are released, which is not usually heard as friction, but is responsible for the popping quality of plosive releases.

Fricatives

These are formed by **narrowing** the speech tract to such a degree that audible **friction** is produced when air passes through. English has the voiceless labiodental fricative [f] in *fee*, the voiceless dental fricative [θ] in *thigh*, the voiceless alveolar [s] in *sigh* and the voiceless palatoalveolar [ʃ] in *shy*. The voiced counterparts [v,ð,z,ʒ] occur in *vie, that, zoo* and *measure*, respectively. (At the beginning of the syllable, English [v,ð] frequently are pronounced without friction.)

Affricates

Affricates are plosives whose release is slow instead of sudden, causing a longer phase of turbulence. The affricates [pf] and [ts] occur in German [pfaifə] 'pipe' and [tsait] 'time', and the palate-alveolar affricate [tʃ, dʒ] occur in English *cheer* and *jeer*, respectively.

Sonorants

These divide into **nasals** and **approximants**.

Nasals

For nasals the soft palate is lowered, and the oral cavity is blocked completely at some point. A slow, deliberate pronunciation of *morning* will allow us to observe how each of the three nasal consonants in the word has a different place of articulation: a bilabial [m], an alveolar [n] and a dorsal [ŋ]. (Pre-)palatal [ɲ] occurs in Dutch, as in ['spɑɲjə] 'Spain', and in French, as in [a'ɲo] 'lamb'.

Approximants

Approximants derive their name from the approximation of the articulators which gives rise to a **light** or **near-contact**, the airstream being so weak that no friction is produced. The (pre-)palatal approximant [j] occurs in English *yes*, while a bilabial one ([β̞]) occurs in Southern Dutch [β̞at] 'what'. (When combined with a symbol for a voiced fricative, the subscript [̞] indicates an approximant, i.e. frictionless pronunciation.) Frequently, languages have rhotics, or [r]-type segments, that are approximant, such as the postalveolar approximant [ɹ] in English *ray*. Also **trills** occur, during which the uvula is allowed to vibrate against the back of the tongue [ʀ], as in European Portuguese [kaʀu] 'car', or the tongue tip against the alveolar ridge [r], as in Spanish [pɛro] 'dog'. When, instead of a series of vibratory taps, a single such brief contact is made, a flap is produced ([ɾ]). In Spanish and Catalan the alveolar flap contrasts with a trill, a minimal pair in Catalan being ['parə] 'father' – ['para] 'grapevine'. In Arawak, the alveolar flap contrasts with a retroflex flap, which involves flicking the curled back tongue forward, causing the tip to hit the rear edge of the alveolar ridge, as illustrated in [hoɾoro] 'swampy' – [hòɽoɽo] 'cloud' (Pet 1979), while Toda contrasts three places of articulation for trills (or flaps), postdental, alveolar and retroflex, as in [kar̪] 'border of cloth', [kar] 'juice' and [kaɽ] 'pen for calves' (Spajić et al. 1996).

For [l], as in German [aləs] 'everything', the airstream is partly blocked by the tongue tip contact with the alveolar ridge, but allowed to escape freely on one or both sides. Sounds which have this type of partial occlusion are called **lateral**. Because the air escapes without friction through the lateral opening, the German lateral is an approximant. The voiceless lateral fricative ([ɬ]) has a turbulent escape of air along the lateral opening(s); it occurs in Welsh, as in the place-name [ɬan'dɪdno] (*Llandudno*). Laterals are usually alveolar: the crown articulates with the alveolar ridge. A palatal (approximant) lateral [ʎ] occurs in Italian ['zbaʎːo] 'mistake' or Catalan [ʎop] 'wolf'.

2.6 SEGMENTAL DURATION

In many languages, duration contrasts exist in the group of vowels, as in Hawaiian, or in the group of consonants, as in Italian, or both, as in Finnish and Japanese. Long consonants are also called *geminates*. Italian and Japanese have long consonants in intervocalic position. An illustration of such a quantity contrast is Italian [fato] 'fate' versus [fatːo] 'fact'. Imonda has this type of contrast in initial position, as illustrated by [nːõl] 'uncle' versus [nõl] 'seed' (Seiler 1985). Frequently, only a subset of the consonants occurs both long and short. Thus, only [p,t,k,s] occur as long consonants in the native vocabulary of Japanese. Vocalic quantity contrasts, such as exist in Hawaiian, are more common. As in the case of consonantal duration contrasts, sometimes only a subset of the vowels occurs both long and short. Thus, Chipewyan has five short vowels ([i,e,a,o,u]), but only three of them have long variants ([iː,aː,uː]). Moreover, the quality of the long vowels may differ somewhat from that of the short vowels. Finnish, for instance, has eight monophthongal vowels appearing both short and long, but long [eː] has a closer quality than short [ɛ].

In German, the durational contrast coincides with a difference in the position of the root of the tongue, which is advanced somewhat during the pronunciation of the long vowels. Such vowels are known as **tense**, while their unmodified counterparts are **lax**. As a result of the widening of the pharynx, the tongue body will tend to be higher for tense vowels than for lax vowels, at least for vowels that are not fully open. In (4), which gives the vowel system of Standard German, the symbol on the left in each box is a lax, short vowel, while the symbol on the right represents a long, tense vowel. Examples of words with these vowels can be found on p. 85.

(4)

	Front unrounded	Centralized front rounded	Centralized back unrounded	Back rounded
High	ɪ, iː	ʏ, yː		ʊ, uː
Mid	ɛ, eː	œ, øː		ɔ, oː
Low	(æː)		a, aː	

In more conservative German, there is also a long lax vowel [æː] (bracketed in (4)), which has merged with [eː] in the speech of many speakers.

2.7   COMPLEX CONSONANTS

Complex consonants are single segments which in some way have two distinguishable articulations. We distinguish consonants with a secondary articulation, consonants with a double articulation, and manner-contour consonants.

2.7.1   Secondary articulations

The articulation of a consonant does not require the services of the entire tongue as well as the lips. For [t,d], for instance, only the crown is used, and for [f,p,m] only the lips. In fact, the lips and tongue can be used to form a vocalic articulation simultaneously with the production of the consonant. The result is what is known as a consonant with **secondary articulation**. The following types of secondary articulation can be distinguished:

1. Labialization. During the articulation of the consonant, the lips are rounded. A labialized velar plosive, for instance, is symbolized [kʷ].
2. Palatalization. The front of the tongue is raised (as for [i] or [j]) during the pronunciation of a consonant. A palatalized bilabial plosive, for instance, is symbolized [pʲ].
3. Velarization. The back of the tongue is raised (as for [u] or [ɯ]), during the pronunciation of a consonant. A velarized alveolar lateral approximant ('dark l'), symbolized [ɫ], is used postvocalically in most varieties of English, as in *all*.
4. Pharyngealization. The root of the tongue is retracted towards the back wall of the pharynx. Arabic 'emphatic' consonants are pharyngealized. This is indicated by placing a dot below the phonetic symbol concerned (e.g. [ṣ]).

2.7.2 Double articulations

Some consonants have two consonant-type constrictions at the same time, such that it is not possible to say which is 'primary' (i.e. consonant-like) and which 'secondary' (vowel-like). Well-known examples are [kp] and [ɡb], labial-velar plosives, which occur in many Niger-Congo languages. The English consonant [w] is a labial-velar approximant: it is pronounced with a raising of the back, as well as with rounding of the lips. Such consonants are said to involve a **double articulation**.

2.7.3 Manner-contour consonants

Some consonants change their constriction-type half-way through. An example is provided by **prenasalized stops**, which occur for instance in Bantu languages. Such consonants begin like nasals and end like plosives at the same place of articulation ([mb], [nd], [ŋg]).

2.8 NONPULMONIC CONSONANTS

We briefly describe the three classes of nonpulmonic segment here.

1. **Clicks.** Clicks are produced with the help of a velar closure (as for [k]) plus a closure somewhere further forward. This forward closure may be located at the lips (rare) or at, or immediately behind, the alveolar ridge. The trapped air in the pocket in front of the velar closure is rarefied by lowering the body of the tongue, or – in the case of a bilabial click – of the jaw. When the forward closure is released to allow outside air to rush into the pocket of rarefied air, a clacking noise-burst results. This way of creating an air pressure difference is known as the VELARIC AIR STREAM MECHANISM (Abercrombie 1967).

Clicks may be contrastively accompanied by a glottal stop at the beginning of the postclick vowel, by nasalization on the following vowel, by aspiration preceding the following vowel, or by a slow (affricated) release of the velar closure. Five articulation places for the forward contact occur. Their symbols are included under 'Other symbols' in the IPA chart on page x. The alveolar click is used paralinguistically in English as a sign of disapproval (rendered *tut, tut* in British English and *tsk, tsk* in American English), while repeated lateral alveolar clicks are sometimes used to imitate the noise a horse's hooves make on the pavement. Clicks only occur in languages spoken in southern Africa, !Xũ, Nama and Xhosa being well-known examples of such languages.

2. **Implosives.** Implosives have a closure as for plosives, as well as a closed glottis. By lowering the larynx, the air in the mouth and pharyx is rarefied, so that a noise-burst will result when the oral closure is released. Because on its way down, the speaker relaxes his glottal closure, phonation will occur as the glottis meets the air in the trachea. Such speech segments occur in Vietnamese, as well as in some Niger-Congo languages. Their symbols are [ɓ,ɗ,ɠ].

3. **Ejectives.** The initial articulatory configuration of ejectives is like that used for implosives, but instead of being pulled down, the larynx is pushed up. The air inside the pharynx and mouth is compressed, so that upon the release of the oral closure, an egressive noise-burst occurs. Ejectives are reasonably common, and are symbolized [p',t',k']. Implosives and ejectives are produced with the GLOTTALIC AIR STREAM MECHANISM.

2.9   STRESS

Words consist of rhythmic units called **feet**, the most common foot type being disyllabic. One of the syllables of the foot is more prominent or stronger than the other syllable(s) in it, which for this reason is called the **stressed** syllable. In *city*, this is the first syllable. There are two types of foot, and languages have either the one or the other. In **left-dominant** feet, the first syllable is the stressed syllable and the others are **unstressed**. In **right-dominant** feet, the rightmost syllable is the stressed syllable. English has left-dominant feet. A word like *celebration* contains the two feet [sɛlə] and [breɪʃn]. One of the feet in a word has the **primary stress** or **word stress**. In *cele-bration*, this is the last foot. The other feet have **secondary stress**. The IPA notation for primary stress is [ˈ], and for secondary stress is [ˌ], to be placed before the syllables concerned. In many publications on this topic, [ˊ] is used over the vowel for primary stress, and [ˋ] for secondary stress. The English word ˌceleˈbration (or cèlebrátion) contrasts with ˈalliˌgator (or álligàtor) in the location of the primary stress: while both *alligator* and *celebration* consist of two feet, the first foot has primary stress in *alligator*, but the second in *celebration*. In addition to disyllabic feet, there may also be monosyllabic feet, as in *cat*, and ternary feet, as in *origin* [ˈɔrədʒən]. Examples of English disyllabic words that consist of two monosyllabic feet are ['sɪn,tæks] *sýntàx* and [ˌkæn'tiːn] *cànteén*. Thus, within the foot, a distinction between stressed and unstressed syllables is made; among the different feet in a word, a distinction between primary stress and secondary stress is made. Notice that ['] and [ˋ] are also used to indicate tone (cf. section 2.2.4).

2.10 CONCLUSION

This chapter has outlined the workings of the speech production mechanism in a way that will enable you to follow the discussion in the rest of this book. For many users of the book, it will have served as a brief refresher course while for others, who may be new to the topic, it will have served as an introduction.

Some typology: sameness and difference

3.1   INTRODUCTION

The phonologies of different languages are in many respects very similar, to the extent that some features appear to be part of every language. These cross-linguistic similarities are in large measure due to the ergonomics of the speech process. Speakers, and languages, prefer distinctions that are easy to perceive and easy to produce. The difference between [t] and [n] is very clear to the perceiver and not too difficult to make for the producer. The contact made by the tongue tip and rims with the upper gums is the same, while the velum is lowered for [n], opening up the nose at the back, and raised for [t], trapping the air behind the oral closure. In the open-velum position, very little effort is needed to bring the vocal folds somewhat closer together than during breathing in order for them to start vibrating. This is so easy that voicing during sonorant consonants and vowels has been called 'spontaneous vibration'. By contrast, if we block the egressive flow by closing off both the mouth and the nose, it will take some effort to create a sufficiently powerful air stream through the glottis to make them vibrate at all: we are pumping more air into a small, closed pocket of air. Speakers would be well advised therefore not to be too eager to vibrate their vocal folds while their vocal tract is significantly obstructed, as maintaining an air pressure difference across the glottis takes some effort. (You can increase the pressure from the lungs, or make more room by pulling up the velum for [d, g] or blowing out your cheeks for [b].) That is why almost all languages have a dental/alveolar [t] and [n], but only 64% have the voiced counterpart of [t] ([d]), and less than 0.5% the voiceless counterpart of [n] ([n̥]).[1] It would be extremely improbable to find a language that had no [t, n], but did have [d, n̥]. Another speaker interest is to duplicate contrasts. If a language has the vowels [i, e, a, o, u] and you find it has a nasalized [õ], you can bet it also has [ã], and probably there will also be [ẽ]. The speaker's phonetic routine of nasalization is exploited so as to maximize contrasts with the same velum lowering gesture. But here too the hearer is not forgotten. For high vowels like [i, u], nasalization does not have a whole lot of acoustic effect, and many languages, like French, therefore leave them out of their subsystem of nasal vowels (system 'gaps').

---

[1] Based on the UCLA Phonological Segment Inventory Database (UPSID), which can be conveniently approached with the help of Henning Reetz' search program at http://web.phonetik.uni-frankfurt.de/ upsid_info.html.

Low-cost contrasts are thus frequent. Some sound contrasts are so easy to make and so clear to the ear that they are found in every language that has been described. For instance, no language has been found without vowels and no language has been found without consonants. There are two responses to this state of affairs. One is to assume that whatever languages have in common is **universal** and that the explanation for the universality is that this is hard-wired in our brains, **innate**. The other is to assume that the neurological, physiological, physical and social conditions under which languages arose and developed are the same across our species and the forces that determine their structure are the same. Those forces must allow for a fair number of degrees of freedom in order to explain the variation that is seen. Apparently, after going for the obvious sound contrasts, which occur in the great majority of languages, weighing up the cost to the speaker and the benefit for the hearer may lead to a large number of options. Also, there are apparently other factors that explain why some languages have many sound contrasts and others few. The only factor that we can at this point be certain of is the historical dimension: the complexity of languages changes very little in its transfer from one generation to the next. Old English, for example, had broadly the same level of complexity as most contemporary varieties of English, even though it has changed virtually beyond recognition after some 1,500 years of development.

Q17 Why is [i, e, a, a̧, o, õ ,u] an implausible vowel system?

Q18 Assume that all the languages that were ever spoken in the world have at least three vowels. What explanation would be given of this fact by someone who rejects the theory that human brains are genetically programmed to have at least three vowels?

3.2 VARYING COMPLEXITY

Languages differ in their morphosyntax just as they differ in their phonologies. To begin with, they differ greatly in the number of segments they have. In UPSID (see footnote 1, page 34) a corpus of segment inventories of 451 languages (approximately 7% of all the languages of the world), the smallest number appears to be 11 (e.g. Rotokas, spoken in Papua New Guinea) and the largest a staggering 141 (!Xũ, spoken in Namibia and Angola) (Maddieson 1984: 9). And when two languages have the same number of segments, they are unlikely to have identical sets. Another language that, like Rotokas, has 11 segments is Mura, also known as Pirahã, which is spoken in Colombia. It shares [p,t,k,g,i,o,a] with Rotokas, but while Rotokas has [e,u] and the consonants [β] and a flap, Mura has [ʔ,b,s,h].

Second, different languages will have different constraints on the way segments are combined to form syllables. The initial consonant(s) of the syllable are known as the **onset**, the vowel is in the **peak** and the closing consonant(s) form the **coda**.

Coda and peak form a constituent called the **rhyme** (also spelled *rime*). In (1), we show these constituents in a tree diagram.

(1)

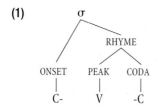

According to Blevins (1995), the lowest degree of complexity in syllable structure is represented by languages that have a single (short) vowel in the peak and optionally allow maximally one consonant in the onset. The syllable structure of such languages is (C)V. Further complexity can be achieved in a number of ways:

1. The Onset may be obligatory: CV. In such languages, of which Maba, Klamath and Arabela are examples, syllables cannot begin with a vowel.

2. There may be a coda. Languages that don't allow a coda include Hawaiian, Arabela and Fijian. If the language allows a coda, a further option is that the coda may be complex, i.e. may be a **cluster** containing more than one C. Spanish, Japanese and Italian allow only one C, but Klamath and French allow two.

3. The onset may be complex. Some languages allow only one C in the onset, like Finnish, Hawaiian and Klamath; others allow two or more, such as Arabela, Dutch and Spanish.

4. The peak may be complex, i.e. be VV. This is the case if, by the side of short vowels, the language has long vowels (in which case the peak is filled by a double occurrence of the same vowel, V_iV_i) and/or has diphthongs (in which case the peak is filled by two different vowels, V_1V_2). Spanish has the diphthong [ue], but no long vowels, while Wolof has long and short vowels but no diphthongs. Dutch and Finnish have both long vowels and diphthongs. Dinka and Estonian are rare examples of languages with overlong vowels, i.e. they have the peaks V, VV and VVV. Phonological vowel-length contrasts are known as **quantity** distinctions.

Some languages allow the syllable peak, i.e. the structural position indicated by 'V', to be filled with a consonant. Thus, in Czech, the liquids [r,l] appear in the peak, as in the geographical names ['br̩.no], ['vl̩.tava], *Brno*, *Vltava* and American English has words like *girl* [gr̩l] and *mountain* ['mauntn̩]. Where languages agree in the number of consonants they allow in the coda or onset, they will still differ in how these consonant positions can be filled. In German, [kn-, ʃn-] are possible onsets, as in ['knaː.bə] 'boy', ['ʃnɛ.kə] 'snail', and so are [ps-, ks-], as in [psy.ço.'loː.gɪʃ] 'psychological', [ksan.tn̩] 'Xanten', all of which are lacking in English. ([ts-] as in [tsaːr] 'Czar' is usually interpreted as a single segment, an affricate.) Conversely,

English has [lj-] in *lure*, which is absent in German. An unexceptional implicational relationship is that the presence of a complex constituent implies the permissability of less complex constituents. Thus, a language that allows two consonants in the onset will also allow one consonant in the onset.

Third, different languages will have different phonological processes. A process that occurs in British English but not in German is PREGLOTTALIZATION, by which [p,t,k] are [ʔp, ʔt, ʔk] when they occur at the end of a syllable before another consonant, as in *ripped, mats, thickness*. And an example of a process in German that does not exist in English is FINAL DEVOICING, by which all obstruents (i.e. plosives and fricatives) are voiceless when they occur at the end of a syllable. This rule is responsible for the fact that in German no voiced fricative or plosive appears at the end of a word, even though voiced obstruents occur in the inflected forms of such words. For instance, the nominative form for 'dog' is [hʊnt], while the genitive form is [hʊndəs]. Many languages have a rule of FINAL DEVOICING, including Polish, Dutch and Catalan.

Q19   The following words, taken from Huisman et al. (1981), illustrate the syllable structure of Angaatiha (the period separates the syllables):

kə.mo.ai	'him'
a.ti.ʔə.rə	'thunder'
ai.n.tə.ʔo	'bird type'
ma.nji.njai	'children (Objective)'
ta.m.pwai.ʔo	'lizard type'

1.   Give the Angaatiha syllable structure as a CV-formula, placing optional elements in brackets.
2.   Does the language have syllabic consonants?

Q20

1.   Can you think of (a) a segment which exists in English but not in your own language, and (b) a segment that exists in your own language, but not in English? If your native language is English, answer the question for any foreign language you are familiar with.
2.   What would the final consonant of the German word for *Kiev* be? Why?

3.3   UNIVERSALS AND IMPLICATIONAL RELATIONS

While it is clear that different languages may have very different phonologies, at the same time it is clear they have many things in common. For a start, all languages have syllables, and all segment inventories can be split into consonants and vowels. All consonant inventories include voiceless plosives, i.e. all languages have at least two of the three consonants [p,t,k]. Then, there are near-universals. For instance, only two languages in UPSID, Rotokas and Mura, have no sonorant consonants. Or again, all languages in UPSID except Hawaiian (i.e. 99%) have some kind of [t], and 90% have [i]. It is also striking that the coronal place of articulation is much commoner generally, and also shows more subdivisions, than either the labial or the dorsal places of articulation.

When the group of more common segments is compared with the group of unusual segments, there are two observations to be made:

1. Unusual segments tend to occur in larger segment inventories. For instance, an unusual segment like [k^{wh}], a [k] with rounding and aspiration, typically occurs in languages with large consonant inventories, like that of Igbo, which has 20 pulmonic egressive plosives in addition to three implosives, or Haida, which has 46 consonants in all.

2. Unusual segments tend to be phonologically more complex than common segments. For example, a common segment like [k] (99.4%) just involves a complete closure between the back of the tongue and the soft palate. The articulation of [k] allows organs of speech other than the back of the tongue to take the line of least resistance, requiring no accompanying actions of the vocal folds (like aspiration, or voicing during the closure, or a glottal closure), of the lips (lip rounding) or of the front of the tongue (palatalization). On the other hand, an unusual segment like [k^{wh}] requires the same oral closure as [k], but in addition has aspiration as well as lip rounding. The relationship is not absolute, however. Although [θ], for instance, is phonologically simple, it is nevertheless a rare segment.

What do these facts suggest about the phonological structure of language? The first fact suggests that languages 'build up' their phonologies in an ordered fashion. It suggests that a language will only have segment X if it already has segment Y. There are in fact many such implicational relationships, as Roman Jakobson had already taught the world in 1928 (Jakobson 1990, Chs 9, 10, 18). Thus, no language has a voiceless nasal without also having its voiced counterpart, and no language has [z] without also having [s]. With very few exceptions, languages do not have front rounded vowels ([y,ø]) if they do not also have front unrounded ([i,e]) and back rounded ([u,o]) vowels. As will be clear, most of these implications are tendential, and true only in a statistical sense. For instance, the presence of [f] generally implies the presence of [p], but Chuave is an example of a language for which this is not true. Apparently, there is no such thing as an absolute order in which languages avail themselves of the universal phonological resources.

The second fact suggests that one way in which languages construct their segment inventories is by adding elements to already existing segments. If we continue to use the metaphor of 'building up' the segment inventory, it is as if you begin by making some choices from a collection of fairly run-of-the-mill segments, and then, as you require more of them, select further elements which you can use to create more segments. For example, many languages have [p,t,k], while a smaller number have [p,t,k] and [b,d,g]. These languages can be seen to have increased their inventory by adding the element 'vibrating vocal cords' to the plosive segments they already had. Then, a smaller number still has these, plus [pʰ, tʰ, kʰ], for instance. Here, the language can be seen to have added 'aspiration' to the [p,t,k] it already had. (But, again, instead of 'aspiration', languages may employ other elements that serve to expand the segment inventory [p,t,k; b,d,g].)

Q21	The mean number of consonants in UPSID is 22.8, with a range of 6–95. The mean number of vowels is 8.7, with a range of 3–46. In what respects are the following languages atypical?

1. !Xũ has 95 consonants and 46 vowels.
2. Pawaia has 10 consonants and 12 vowels.
3. Haida has 46 consonants and 3 vowels.
4. Norwegian has 22 consonants and 19 vowels.

As Jakobson (1968) emphasized in a famous monograph, children learn the sounds of their language in a particular order, regardless of the language, which reflects the scale of complexity implied in this paragraph: the unusual tends to be rare and tends to be acquired late. Thus, the metaphor of 'building up' the phonology in a sense comes true every time a child learns a language.

3.3.1 Plain or special?

A third observation is made by Maddieson (1984): the number of vowels and the number of consonants are positively correlated. That is, when one language has more consonants than another, it is likely that it also has more vowels. This suggests that languages that are more complex in one area of the phonology (in this case, the consonant inventory) also tend to be complex in other areas (in this case, the vowel inventory). It is apparently not the case that complexity in one area is somehow compensated for by simplicity in other areas: phonologies differ in complexity. For instance, languages with larger inventories tend to have more complex syllable structures. That is, languages that allow only simple syllable structures like CV tend to have smaller inventories than languages that, like English and German, allow up to three consonants at the beginning of the syllable (cf. Eng [strɔː] *straw*, German [ʃtroː] 'straw'), as well as more than one at the end (cf. English [læmp] *lamp*). In tone languages, the number of different pitch patterns typically lies between two and six, but the number of such patterns does not appear to be greater in languages with smaller inventories or in languages with simpler syllable structures. UPSID does not list permitted syllable structures, or prosodic distinctions, so the facts here are not easy to give. Maddieson (1984: 22), however, does present the total number of possible syllables in a small corpus of languages. The total number is determined by (a) the number of different vowels and consonants, (b) the permitted syllable structures and (c) the number of tonal (prosodic) distinctions. If complexity in one area of the phonology goes hand in hand with complexity in another, then the greater the number of possible syllables in a language, the larger should be the number of segments, and the larger should be the number of permitted syllable structures, as well as the number of prosodic distinctions. In the representative list of languages Maddieson gives, this is indeed the case. To give some idea of the multiplicative effect of these three factors: the language with the largest number of different syllables in Maddieson's minicorpus (Thai) has 146 times as many possible syllables as the language with the smallest number (Hawaiian).

Q22

In a corpus of 10 languages, the number of segmental contrasts was found to be related to the mean word length expressed as the number of segments in the word, in the sense that the smaller the segment inventory was the greater was the mean word length (Nettle 1995). Speculate on the cause of this negative correlation.

3.3.2   Avoiding complexity

There is another, somewhat more tenuous, relation worth drawing attention to. Unusual segments are not just unusual because they occur in relatively few languages, they also tend to be less frequent in the languages that have them. That is, as languages increase their phonological resources, they tend to do less with them. For instance, Dutch has front unrounded, back rounded and front rounded vowels. First, the set of front unrounded vowels contains one segment more than either the front rounded or the back rounded sets. Then, in almost every case, the frequency of occurrence of the front rounded vowels is lower than those of the corresponding front unrounded or back rounded vowels. The figures in Table 3.1 are based on the frequencies of the vowels in the 1000 most common Dutch words, expressed as percentages of the total number of segments. What can also be seen by comparing the figures in the second row with those of the first and fourth rows is that lax (short) vowels are more common than tense vowels.

3.3.3   A word of caution

You may by now have gained the erroneous impression that it is in fact easy to count the segments, or syllables, or prosodic distinctions, in a language. We hasten

Table 3.1
Frequency of occurrence (%) of Dutch front unrounded, front rounded and back rounded vowels (van den Broecke 1976)

	Front unrounded		Front rounded		Back rounded	
Tense, short	i	2.00	y	0.39	u	0.56
Lax, short	ɪ	2.79	ʏ	0.48	ɔ	2.50
Lax, short	ɛ	4.54				
Tense, long	eː	2.54	øː	0.06	oː	2.11
Diphthong	ɛi	1.93	œy	0.37	ʌu	0.35

to dispel this notion: it is not easy to count these things at all. There are two reasons for this. One is that languages frequently have what are sometimes called **marginal segments** or patterns of arrangements (Moulton 1962). These are restricted to onomatopoeic words, in which the phonology echoes the meaning of the word, and (recent) loanwords. For instance, Dutch has a number of such vowels, among which [ɛː], which occurs in loans (e.g. [krɛːm] 'cream') and in the onomatopoeic ['blɛːrə] 'cry, bawl'. Should it be counted as a Dutch vowel? Or again, no Dutch words begin with [fj-], except [fjɔrt] 'fjord'. Is [fj-] a Dutch onset, or is it a Norwegian onset which speakers of Dutch have taken in their stride? Depending on the answers to such questions, the number of Dutch vowels will vary between 16 and 25. The second reason why it is difficult to count these things is that the count will depend on the **analysis**. Suppose a language has the five vowel qualities [i,e,a,o,u]. Suppose further that they can be either long or short and, moreover, that every combination occurs as a diphthong. The number of different vowels in a sense is five, but in another sense it is 30. UPSID would in a case like this give the number as five, but if, say, the combinations [ae], [uu], [eo] had been missing from the language, then, paradoxically, the number of vowels would have been given as 27. Because of the large number of languages involved, the trends noted in UPSID are unlikely to depend very much on how these decisions are arrived at. What is important is that you should not get the idea that it is easy to say what a segment is, and that counting things is no problem.

3.3.4 Speech ergonomics

Clearly, languages somehow monitor the development of their phonologies, and check segments and inventories off against two very general guidelines: 'Don't make things difficult for the speaker' and 'Don't make things difficult for the listener'. That is, the best systems are those in which contrasts are maximally distinct with the least amount of articulatory effort (Flemming 1995; Boersma 1998). The reasons for specific statistical tendencies may therefore be either articulatory or perceptual. In some cases, the speaker's and the listener's interests may go hand in hand, but often the explanation of the statistical fact lies either in the speaker's interest or the listener's:

1. Plosives are more common than fricatives. Plosives require a brief closure of the oral tract in order for air pressure to build up behind it. This is all it takes to create a brief friction-burst at the release. By contrast, fricatives require considerable airflow for the full duration of the consonant to keep the air turbulence going and produce audible friction. The speaker's interest here favours plosives over fricatives.

2. Voiceless plosives are more common than voiced ones. With every opening action of the vibrating vocal folds, the speaker releases some air from the trachea into the vocal tract. Because the vocal tract is closed off during the closure phase of the plosive, the air pressure in it will rise until it equals the air pressure below the vocal folds that drives their vibration. Just as we stop

pushing the lever of a bicycle pump when the tube is full, so we will avoid continuing the vocal-fold vibration much during the closure stage of the plosive. No such ergonomic conflict arises during voiceless plosives, there being no requirement for any airflow during an open glottis. Again, the speaker's interest is at stake here.

3. Voiceless fricatives are more common than voiced fricatives. The relatively low airflow that results from the release of a rapid series of small air puffs into the vocal tract during vocal-fold vibration conflicts with the requirement of a generous airflow through the narrowed passage where the fricative is articulated. As a result, voiced friction is weaker than voiceless friction.

4. Front rounded and back unrounded vowels are less common than either front unrounded or back rounded vowels. When you place an empty bottle under a running tap, the resonance in the bottle set up by the jet of air hitting the bottom of the bottle or the surface of the water already in it, increases from low pitched to high pitched. Starting from [u], you can reproduce this effect by moving into the articulatory position for [i]. At [u], the lips are rounded, pouted even, so as to increase the distance between the raised back of the tongue and the aperture at the lips, creating the longest distance between them. But when saying [i], we spread the lips, so as to shorten the distance between the raised front of the tongue and the lip aperture. While the articulation of [i] corresponds to the fullest state of the bottle and that of [u] to the most empty one, front rounded [y] and back unrounded [ɯ] represent intermediate positions, which are less likely to be used than the perceptually more extreme vowels. Here, the hearer's interest appears to be the decisive factor.

Ease of production is most clearly seen in the tendency for particular articulations to persist. Prenasalized stops, for instance, always have the same place of articulation for the nasal and the oral stop, as in labial, coronal and dorsal [mb,nd,ŋg]: segments like *[mk] or *[nb] have not been attested. Similarly, nasal consonants in the coda tend to share the place of articulation of the following plosive, as in Japanese [rampɯ] 'lamp', [jonda] 'read' and [maŋgan] 'manganese'. And most languages have rules of **assimilation**, which cause some articulatory feature of one segment to be transferred to an adjacent one, such as when English *in* is pronounced [ɪm] in *in Paris* or [ɪŋ] in *in Copenhagen*. While for the speaker there are obvious advantages in extending the scope of an articulatory gesture, for the listener it is better to be able to hear differences. Paradoxically, therefore, there is also the tendency for languages to avoid repetition of the same thing. For instance, many languages that have labialized consonants lack labialized labials. Thus, Bakairí has [tʷ, kʷ, dʷ, gʷ], but lacks [pʷ, bʷ], even though the nonlabialized plosive series shows no gaps (Wetzels 1997a). Likewise, there are many languages that allow complex onsets like [pn,kn] or [pl,kl] but disallow [tn] and [tl] and these last combinations have a single place of articulation. In Chapter 10, we will introduce and exemplify the OBLIGATORY CONTOUR PRINCIPLE, which is held to be responsible for this avoidance of repetition.

3.3.5   System gaps

We have seen that the segment inventories of languages tend to be constructed as if languages drew on the stock of phonological resources by adding elements to sets of segments. By adding to [p,t,k] the element 'vocal-fold vibration', you will produce the series [b,d,g]; further adding 'aspiration' will produce [pʰ,tʰ,kʰ], as in Burmese, for instance, and so on. Or if you have five vowels, you may allow them to be long as well as short, you may nasalize them, or provide them with pharyngealization. (This is part of the answer to the secret of the 46 vowels of !Xũ.) If phonological resources are typically made available per set of segments rather than per individual segment, as indeed shown by Clements (2004), you may well wonder why languages so often have **system gaps**. For instance, Dutch has the voiceless unaspirated series [p,t,k], but only the voiced [b,d]. So where is [g]? Dutch is not alone in having this gap. It is in fact the most commonly occurring gap among the voiced stops (e.g. Czech, Hixkaryana, Thai), just as [p] is the most common among the voiceless stops, the latter being absent from languages as diverse as Arabic, Chuave, Dizi, Hausa, Vietnamese and Yoruba. In the examples given here, there appears to be a relation between the gaps and efficiency. The voiceless plosive [p] is relatively inefficient from the point of view of the listener, because the stop burst, which is one of the major cues to the presence of a plosive, is of much lower intensity in the case of [p] than in the case of other plosives, due to the lack of a resonating cavity in front of the point of release, where the burst is created (Stevens 1997: 494). The voiced [g] is relatively inefficient from the point of view of the speaker, because the relatively small air cavity behind the velar closure causes the air to accumulate below it, thus increasing the supraglottal air pressure and diminishing the glottal airflow, and thereby causing voicing to stop (Ohala 1989). That is, [p] is relatively hard to hear, and [g] is relatively hard to say. Again, while these statistical tendencies are very clear, languages may deviate from them. Thus Hawaiian, quite exceptionally, has [p, k], but not [t]. In this case, an earlier stage of the language did have [p, t, k], but somehow [t] was replaced with [k], after [k] had become [ʔ].

Q23

In the above discussion on system gaps, the assumption was that [g] was the voiced stop whose place of articulation is closest to the larynx. Which voiced stop would you expect to be least frequent among languages that have plosive systems that include uvular stops as well as velar ones? Motivate your answer.

Q24

1. On average, voiceless plosives are more frequent than voiced plosives, and coronal segments are more frequent than noncoronal segments. This holds true both for the occurrence of these segments in the inventories in the languages of the world, and for their occurrence in the words (or texts) of any individual language. To represent this situation graphically, draw a set of two coordinates, with frequency of occurrence of the y-axis and the three places of articulation LABIAL, CORONAL and DORSAL on the x-axis. Draw two theoretical graphs, one for the voiceless plosives and one for the voiced plosives.
2. English [p,t,k] have frequencies of 1.78, 6.42 and 3.09, while [b,d,g] have frequencies of 1.97, 5.14 and 1.05 (Gimson 1989: 219). In a set of two coordinates, with frequency of occurrence along the y-axis and the three places of articulation on the x-axis, draw two graphs, one for the voiceless plosives and one for the voiced plosives. Explain why the positions of [p] and [g] differ from those in the 'theoretical' graphs of the previous question.

3.6   CONCLUSION

Obviously, the fact that languages show so many similarities in their sound structures cannot be accidental. This fact has been taken to mean that this structure is in part an inherent, 'innate' property of human beings. And, as we have seen, the universally observed frequency distributions appear to be reflected in the frequency of occurrence of segments in individual languages. That is, phonologies of different languages are variations on the same theme. Ideally, phonological theory provides a model that explains this situation. The most general statement of the aims of phonology is that it seeks to establish the 'possible space' of phonological structure, and show that the actual phonological systems we find in languages fit into that space, while showing that nonexistent structures do not. There are, for instance, many processes, but the number of possible processes that are never attested is very much larger. By postulating an innate, universal element, we may explain why children learn phonological structures so quickly. Conceivably, humans may start out with a certain amount of 'skeletal' information, which they fill in with language-specific information on the basis of the language they are exposed to. With regard to syllable structure, for instance, the innate information might be that there are syllables, and that syllables have peaks and onsets. What the child would want to know next is (1) whether the onset may remain empty, and/or (2) whether there may be a coda (Clements and Keyser 1983: 29; Kaye 1989: 56; Blevins 1995).

A crucial assumption that underlies the notion of a phonological system is that the pronunciation of a language can be described with the help of a finite set of discrete constituents, i.e. segments, syllables, feet, etc. The pronunciation of every morpheme consists of a particular configuration of those constituents. These phonological constituents are meaningless, and distinct from the meaningful, morphosyntactic constituents of the language, such as morphemes, morphological words, syntactic phrases and sentences. In Chapter 16, we will see how phonological structure continues above the level of the word.

4

Making the form fit

4.1 INTRODUCTION

In Chapter 1 we saw that different languages have different phonologies. One of the clearest illustrations of this fact is provided by the adaptation of loanwords to the phonology of the borrowing language. In this process, speakers will interpret the pronunciation of the words of the foreign language in terms of the phonological elements of their own. The way in which they do this can tell us a great deal about the phonology of the speaker's native language. For example, the French pronunciation [fi'liŋ] for English ['fiːlɪŋ] reveals that French does not distinguish tense and lax vowels, and uses [i] for both [iː] and [ɪ]. Second, it places the stress on the last syllable, regardless of where the stress was in the original word. In this chapter we will discuss the process of nativization, and illustrate it mainly on the basis of English loans in Hawaiian and one Indonesian loanword in Konjo. These languages have very different phonologies, the phonology of English being much more complex than that of Hawaiian, in particular. After showing how the pronunciation of foreign words is constrained – or shaped – by the phonological structure of the native language, it is pointed out that the phonological representation of native morphemes, too, may need to be adjusted. This need may arise when morphemes are combined. If a language with the syllable structure (C)V(C) only allows a coda consonant in word-final position, something will have to be done whenever a consonant-initial suffix like [ka] is attached to a consonant-final base like [taf], since *[tafka] would be ill-formed. In order to describe phonological adjustments, two approaches have been adopted: rules and constraints. The difference between these two approaches is briefly explained and illustrated.

4.2 HAWAIIAN

First, we give a brief outline of Hawaiian phonology, based on Elbert and Pukui (1979). The syllable structure is characterized by the formula in (1).

(1) (C)V(V)

That is, syllables do not have codas, vowels can be long or short, and the onset contains maximally one consonant. The Hawaiian phoneme inventory is extremely small. It is given in tabular form in (2). The rows in the C-system stand for manners of articulation, usually in the order 'plosive (and affricate)', 'fricative', 'nasal', 'approximant', while the columns stand for places of articulation, ordered from labial to glottal. Voiceless and voiced obstruents are usually presented in separate rows. For vowels, the rows stand for degrees of tongue height, while the columns have the order 'front unrounded', 'front rounded', 'back unrounded' and 'back rounded'.

(2)   V   C
    i   u   p   k   ʔ
    e   o   h
         a   m   n
                       w   l

Consecutive vowels sound like diphthongs if the second is higher than the first (e.g. [au] or [oi]), and like long vowels if they are identical (i.e. [aa] sounds like [aː].) In terms of (1), these vowel sequences are VV, and are monosyllabic. Other sequences of vowels are divided over two syllables. A [j] is inserted between [i,e] and a lower vowel, and [w] is inserted between [u,o] and a lower vowel. The latter consonant is indistinguishable from the unpredictable occurrence of the [w] listed in (2). A sequence like [ua] is therefore equivalent to [uwa], and [ia] is pronounced [ija]. Possible Hawaiian words are [iwa] 'nine', [niʔihao] (geographical name), [honolulu] (geographical name), [aa] 'jaw', [ʔaa] 'fiery', [puaʔohi] 'chatter', [kaukau] 'admonish' and [hoʔolauleʔa] 'celebration'. Impossible words are *[tuʔa], *[plai] and *[kehunanal].

Q25 Explain why the last three items cannot be Hawaiian words.

4.3 ADJUSTMENT PROCESSES

4.3.1 The process of nativization

A speaker of Hawaiian speaking English might well wish you [mele kelikimaka] on 25 December. This utterance is the result of the interpretation of [mɛri krɪsməs]. The situation exemplified here is representative of the sort of thing that happens when speakers of one language decide to speak another language without adopting any of the phonology of that other language. When faced with the task of pronouncing an expression in a foreign language while using only the phonology of their native language, speakers need to (a) interpret each of the segments in the foreign word in terms of the native segment system; and (b) make sure that no strings arise that break the syllable structure constraints or any other phonotactic constraints of their language. These two types of processes should be seen as different parses, according to Silverman (1992). The first parse takes place at the **Perceptual Level**: the acoustic input, or the acoustic image that the speaker has of the foreign word, is interpreted as a string of native segments. In the case of *Merry Christmas*, this process must have resulted in the segments in the second column of (3). The segments in the first column represent the English interpretation of this expression.

(3)	*Input*	*Perceptual Level*	*Operative Level*
	m	m	m
	ɛ	e	e
	ɹ	l	l
	i	e	e
	k	k	k
			e (cf. (1))
	ɹ	l	l
	ɪ	i	i
	s	k	k
			i (cf. (1))
	m	m	m
	ə	a	a
	s	k	k
			a (cf. (1))

Compared to the English segments, Hawaiian has phonetically quite similar segments available in most cases. The fact that there is no [r] type consonant accounts for the interpretation of [ɹ] as [l], while [k], being the only lingual nonsonorant consonant, is the best interpretation of [s]. Now notice that this string of segments (those in the second column) is not well-formed. In particular, it cannot be analysed as sequences of (1), with or without the optional elements in that formula. The aim of the second parse, referred to as the **Operative Level**, is to make the string of segments perceived at the Perceptual Level conform to the phonotactic constraints of the language. Most importantly, the segments will have to be accommodated by giving them legitimate positions in syllable structure. Rather than throwing [l] in *Christmas* out, therefore, a vowel is inserted between [k] and [l]. As a result, both [k] and [l] are now single consonants in their onsets, as required by (1). Similarly, vowels are inserted after the second and third [k]. (The new vowel would appear to be a copy of a nearby vowel, but we will ignore this aspect.)

Silverman's division of the process of nativization into a Perceptual Level and an Operative Level is convenient, and allows us to see the distinction between the phonological elements (vowels, consonants) and the phonological structure containing the segments. Respectively, they may be thought of as the things that need to be packaged and the legitimate ways of packaging them. However, we cannot really separate the two processes in the sense that the segments produced by the perceptual parse must be accommodated by the phonological structure at all costs: it is not always the most likely segmental interpretations that survive. Instead of supplying a vowel in order to make the segment string conform to the native syllable structure, the language might adjust the string of segments by replacing a consonant with one that is not too different from it, but which *can* be accommodated without the addition of a syllable. For instance, German does not allow voiced obstruents in the coda, which do occur in English. In (4), a [b] in the English input for a German loanword is ultimately replaced with a [p], because the presence of [b] is ill-formed in that position. A solution that the German speaker does not resort to is to supply a vowel after the [b] so that it can be preserved as an onset consonant.

(4)	*Input*	*Perceptual Level*	*Operative Level*
	p	p	p
	ʌ	a	a
	b	b	p (to preserve final position of plosive)

Another case of an alternative choice of consonant comes from Konjo. In this language a word must minimally consist of a foot, which in Konjo is disyllabic and has the stress on the first syllable. It has the vowels [i,e,a,o,u], and its syllable structure is (C)V(C). Word-finally, the coda can only be [ʔ] or [ŋ]. It has a full set of nasals ([m,n,ɲ,ŋ]) as well as a lateral (Friberg and Friberg 1991).

Q26   Why are the phonological representations [meŋ] and [leʔem] not possible Konjo words?

Konjo has adopted the Indonesian word [lɛm] 'glue' (itself a loan from Dutch [lɛim]) as ['leʔeŋ]. At first sight, this may be a little surprising. Note that ['leme] would be a possible word; in fact, the form ['lame] is an actual word: 'tuber'. The form ['leʔeŋ] conforms to Konjo phonology in that it is disyllabic and does not have [m] word-finally. Here, the Perceptual Level analysis must be [lem], but as in the case of the German loan from English, the first decision at the Operative Level was to replace an impossible coda consonant with a possible one that is similar: [m] is replaced with [ŋ] (see (5)).

(5) | *Input* | *Perceptual Level* | *Operative Level* |
|---|---|---|
| l | l | l |
| ɛ | e | e |
| | | ʔ (to serve as C in inserted CV syllable) |
| | | e (to serve as V in inserted CV syllable) |
| m | m | ŋ (to preserve final position of the nasal) |

Incidentally, sometimes a segment that is present in the original form is not translated in the loanword, something that is likely to happen if the segment is not particularly salient. An example is the Cantonese word [lip] 'lift', an adaptation of English [lɪft]. Here, while the first three segments in the English original have been translated, the final [t] was simply left uninterpreted.

In this section it has been shown that the pronunciation of foreign words is adjusted to the phonological structure of the native language. In the next section we will see that in the native phonology similar adjustment processes may occur.

Q27   Japanese has the following processes, which apply additively.

1.   The coronal plosive [t] is affricated to [ts] before [i, ʉ].
2.   The coronal obstruent [s] is prepalatal [ʃ] before [i].
3.   In casual speech, close vowels [i, ʉ] are devoiced to [i̥, ʉ̥] between voiceless obstruents or after a voiceless obstruent at the word end.

Give the narrow transcriptions of /tʉkemono/ 'pickled vegetables', /sitá/ 'tongue', /ótiba/ 'fallen leaves'.

Q28   To salvage consonants that would otherwise be illegitimate codas, Japanese provides the vowel [ʉ] to allow them to be onsets, as in [tʃiːzʉ] 'cheese' and [masʉkʉ] 'mask'. However, after [t] the vowel [o] is used, as in [toːsʉto] 'toast'. Referring back to Q27, can you explain this fact?

A quick way of learning something about the phonology of a language is to look at loanwords borrowed from languages that you do know the phonology of. The adjustments that are made will indicate what structures are ungrammatical in the borrowing language.

| Q29 | Here are some Japanese loans from Dutch (Vos 1963; de Graaf 1990). | |

Loanword	Dutch origin	Gloss
soːda	soːdaː	'soda'
koːhiː	kɔfi	'coffee'
korera	xoːləraː	'cholera'
meraŋkoriː	meːlaŋxoːli	'melancholy'
hipokonderiː	hipoːxɔndri	'hypochondria'
maŋgan	maŋyaːn	'manganese'
bombon	bɔmbɔn	'kind of sweet'
gomɨ	ɣʏm	'rubber'
kari	kaːli	'potash'
kiniːne	kininə	'quinine'
mesɨ	mɛs	'knife'
karɨkɨ	kalək	'chalk'
masɨto	mɑst	'mast'
bɨriki	blɪk	'tin'
orɨgoːrɨ	ɔryəl	'pipe organ'
sɨkopːɨ	sxɔp	'spade'
pompɨ	pɔmp	'pump'
pisɨtorɨ	pistoːl	'pistol'
gipɨsɨ	ɣɪps	'plaster cast'
kan	kɑn	'kettle'
rampɨ	lɑmp	'lamp'

1. List the consonants that appear word-finally in the Japanese words.
2. List the consonants that can appear in the coda of nonfinal syllables.
3. Why is a vowel added after the word for 'rubber', but not after the word for 'manganese'?
4. On the basis of these data, what would you say are the voiceless fricatives of Japanese?
5. What evidence is there that Japanese does not allow CC-onsets? (In fact, Japanese allows CC-onsets, provided the second C is [j], as in the geographical name [kjoːto].)

Q30 Study the following Hawaiian loanwords from English carefully.

English	Hawaiian		English	Hawaiian	
'ælbət	ʔalapaki	'Albert'	waɪn	waina	'wine'
'tɪkɪt	kikiki	'ticket'	raɪs	laiki	'rice'
səʊp	kopa	'soap'	bɛl	pele	'bell'
bɪə	pia	'beer'	'flaʊə	palaoa	'flour'
kɪlt	kiliki	'kilt'	'zəʊdiæk	kokiaka	'zodiac'
brʌʃ	palaki	'brush'	θaʊzənd	kaukani	'thousand'
stɔːri	kole	'story'	pɑːm	paama	'palm'
skuːl	kola	'school'	'ɛləfənt	ʔelepani	'elephant'

1. List the onset and coda clusters in the input forms that are broken up into different syllables in the Hawaiian output forms.
2. List the consonant clusters that are not so broken up, i.e. that are not fully interpreted.
3. List the English consonants for which Hawaiian [p] is used. What articulatory aspect do these consonants have in common?
4. List the English consonants for which Hawaiian [k] is used. What articulatory aspect do these consonants have in common?
5. Can you make a guess as to what the nativized Hawaiian form for English *false* might be?
6. If someone asked you why the Hawaiian speaker shouldn't simply say [s] instead of [k] in words like *soap* and *Christmas*, what would your answer be? Would it be correct to answer that the fully native speaker of Hawaiian cannot hear the difference between [s] and [k]?

4.3.2 Adjustments in the native vocabulary

It may seem self-evident that the phonological shape of the morphemes of a language will conform to the structural constraints holding in that language. By and large, this is true: a language that disallows complex onsets will typically not have words with complex onsets. Yet it frequently happens that ill-formed structures arise in native forms. For one thing, the phonological shape of morphemes that cannot by themselves be words, like affixes, need not conform to the constraints on syllable structure. An affix may consist of a single consonant, for instance, and as such cannot be a good syllable. Usually, well-formed syllables are only required at the level of the word. More generally, when suffixes are attached to bases to form complex words, or when words come together to form phrases, there is no guarantee that the phonological shape of the combination is well-formed, and adjustments are therefore frequently called for. For example, as will be seen in Chapter 6, the form of the English nominal plural suffix is [z]. This particular phonological representation is fine when the morpheme attaches to *eye* to form [aɪz], but it cannot be used in that same form in combination with either *nose* or *back*. In the first case, a vowel is inserted between the stem and the suffix, to form [nəʊzɪz], as the form *[nəʊzz] is ill-formed; in the second case, [bæks] is formed, it being impossible to have two adjacent obstruents in the same syllable that differ in voicing (*[bækz]). As a result, the suffix [z] has three different pronunciations, or **morpheme alternants**, [z], [s] and [ɪz].

4.4   TWO APPROACHES

There have been two approaches to the question of how phonological adjustments of (native) morphemes should be described, one based on rules that change representations and one based on constraints that require representations to have certain forms.

4.4.1   Rules

The traditional approach, associated with the monumental work by Noam Chomsky and Morris Halle, *The Sound Pattern of English* (*SPE*) (1968), uses rules that change the phonological representation of the morpheme in particular phonological contexts. These rules are ordered: each rule except the first applies to the output of the preceding rule. After all the appropriate changes have been made, the correct form surfaces. This is a **derivational** approach, in the sense that the surface form of the expression is derived in a series of structure-changing operations from the underlying form.

In the case of the English plural suffix, the derivational approach postulates two rules. One, I-INSERTION (6), inserts a vowel between two sibilants ([s,z,ʃ,ʒ]). The other, DEVOICING (7), devoices an obstruent after a voiceless obstruent in the same syllable.

> **(6)**   I-INSERTION: Insert [ɪ] between two adjacent sibilants in the same word.

> **(7)**   DEVOICING: A voiced obstruent becomes voiceless after a voiceless obstruent.

The adjustments are given in the derivation (8). The first line represents the underlying forms and the last line the surface forms. Intervening lines show the work of the phonological rules, in the order in which they apply. Thus rule (6), I-INSERTION, does not apply to [bæk-z] and [aɪ-z] because these forms have no instances of adjacent sibilants, but it does apply to [kɪs-z], which contains a sequence of [z] and [s] in a single word. Non-application is sometimes explicitly indicated by *(n.a.)*, as has been done here.

(8)	Input representations	bæk-z	kɪs-z	aɪ-z
	Rule (6)	*(n.a.)*	ɪ	*(n.a.)*
	Rule (7)	s	*(n.a.)*	*(n.a.)*
	Output representations	bæks	kɪsɪz	aɪz

An important advantage of applying rules in sequence is that they can express generalizations in simple ways. Notice, for example, that DEVOICING can be formulated in the simple way that is has been in (7), thanks to the work of I-INSERTION. If we were to apply DEVOICING *before* I-INSERTION, it would change the [z] after [kɪs] into [s], because it appears after a voiceless obstruent in the input. By first inserting the [ɪ], the [z] is no longer adjacent to [s], and is skipped by DEVOICING. We will discuss this point further in Chapter 5.

4.4.2 Constraints

Over the last few years, a different approach has been taken to the adjustments. In this **constraint-based** approach, demands are put on the surface form, and any form that does not comply with these constraints is rejected in favour of a form that does. The most successful constraint-based theory is Optimality Theory (Prince and Smolensky 1993, McCarthy and Prince 1993a, Kager 1999). This theory holds that constraints are universal. There are two important features of the theory that explain why languages nevertheless have different phonologies. First, languages differ in the importance they attach to the various constraints. That is, the phonology of a language is given by the **ranking** of the set of universal constraints, known as that language's **constraint hierarchy**. Second, constraints may be contradictory, and thus be violated: if two constraints are contradictory, the one that is ranked higher will have priority.

A constraint-based approach to the English nominal plurals might postulate constraints (9) and (10). According to (9), sequences of sibilants are excluded within the same word. And according to the constraint in (10), we cannot have a sequence of obstruents that differ in that one is voiced and the other is voiceless. Thus, a form like *[nəʊzz] violates the first constraint, and a form like *[bækz] the second.

(9) *SɪʙSɪʙ: Sequences of sibilants are prohibited within the word.

(10) *αVOICE–αVOICE: Sequences of obstruents within the syllable must agree for voicing.

So how does Optimality Theory determine what the output form must be? For any given input form, there will initially be an unlimited set of output forms. This free generation of potential output forms is taken care of by a function called GEN (for 'Generator'), which is subject only to very general constraints of well-formedness. Let us illustrate this with the plural for [kɪs]. For an input form [kɪs-z], some of the generated outputs will be: [kɪsɪz], [kɪsz], [kɪs], [kɪzz], but also forms like [pets] or [tæpt]. There are two general forces at work that determine which of these numerous potential output forms is chosen by the language. One of these forces is called **faithfulness**: it is the force that tries to make the output form identical to the input form. Thus, if English were completely faithful, the plural of *kiss* would be [kɪsz]. The other force might be said to be the **unmarked** way of pronouncing things. If this force were allowed to have its way, unchecked by any other force, all words in the language, or indeed in all languages, would end up as something like [ba], or perhaps [tə]: anything more than this would be more 'marked' in the sense of less common, more complex and more difficult to pronounce. In reality, the outcome is determined by how these two forces interact. Each of the forces is represented by a set of universal constraints, and every language ranks these constraints in its own way. Again, if all the Faithfulness constraints are ranked above all the phonological constraints, no phonological adjustments will be made to the input form. However, typically one or more phonological constraints are ranked above one or more Faithfulness constraints, which means that in the case of a conflict, the phonological constraint wins. Every constraint that is inspected will thus throw out a number of candidate forms, and this process goes on until there is only one form left. Optimality Theory thus holds that the output form is the **optimal form**, the form that is left as the only survivor of all candidate forms after an inspection of the constraint hierarchy.

McCarthy and Prince (1995) propose three important constraints to express Faithfulness. MAX-IO requires that each segment in the input form ('I') has a corresponding segment in the output form ('O'). That is, the input is 'maximally' represented in the output, and the constraint is therefore violated if a segment is deleted. DEP-IO requires that each segment in the output form has a corresponding segment in the input form. That is, the output must be entirely 'dependent' on the input, and the constraint is violated by any inserted segment. Third, IDENT(F) requires that every feature ('F') of the input segment is 'identical' to every feature in the output segment. That is, this constraint is violated if a segment changes from voiceless [t] to voiced [d], say, or from bilabial [m] to dorsal [ŋ]. (The theory allows these constraints to be split up into detailed subconstraints, and they are therefore better seen as constraint families.) There are many phonological constraints, some of which we will present informally below. It will be clear that the output form will be as close as possible to the input form, and that every deviation must be forced by some higher-ranking phonological constraint. It will thus be clear that an output [tæpt] for an input [kɪsz] is unlikely to survive an evaluation by the Faithfulness constraints, which will quickly see to it that [tæpt] is discarded in favour of forms that make a better job of preserving the input.

(11)   MAX-IO: Deletion of segments is prohibited.

(12)   DEP-IO: Insertion of segments is prohibited.

(13)   IDENT(F): A segment in the input is identical to the corresponding segment in the output.

The operation of evaluating the collection of possible output forms is called EVAL (for 'Evaluation'). This evaluation is shown in **tableaux**. The tableau in (14) will serve as an illustration. The constraints are arranged in the columns, and the forms to be evaluated are arranged in the rows. The input form to be evaluated is given in the top left corner. A * in a cell indicates that the form of that row breaks the constraint in that column, and *! indicates that such a violation eliminates that form from further consideration: the violation is fatal. The optimal form, the winner, is marked ☞. Shaded cells indicate that the constraint in that column has become irrelevant to the fate of the form in the row concerned. As is shown in (14), it is more important in English to obey *SIBSIB than to obey DEP-IO: in order to prevent the adjacency of [s] and [z], a segment [ɪ] is inserted between them. However, as shown in tableau (15), the language is less concerned about *αvoice–αvoice: although it could have saved the voiced [z] from 'becoming' [s] in [bækz] by inserting a vowel to form [bækɪz], it chooses not to break Dep-IO for this purpose. To satisfy *αvoice–αvoice, it is however prepared to violate Ident(F) in the matter of the voicing of [z]: the input [z] corresponds to a non-identical output [s].

(14)

kɪsz	*SibSib	Dep-IO	*αvoice–αvoice
kɪsz	*!		*
☞ kɪsɪz		*	
kɪzz	*!		
kɪss	*!		

(15)

bækz	*SibSib	Dep-IO	*αvoice–αvoice	Ident (F)
bækɪz		*!		
bækz			*!	
☞ bæks				*

Incidentally, in addition to (9) and (10), there would have to be a constraint requiring that the phonological content of the stem must be retained. Otherwise, *[bægz], which satisfies *αvoice–αvoice, would also be described as a correct form, by the side of [bæks].

Q31 The form *[kɪs] is an incorrect output form for the plural *kisses*.

1. Which constraint (not listed in tableaux (14) and (15)) is responsible for ruling this form out?
2. Draw a tableau for the input form [kɪsz] (i.e. the plural of *kiss*), with the two potential output forms [kɪs] and [kɪsɪz]. There should only be two constraints in your tableau: Dep-IO and the constraint you gave as the answer to the previous question. Would you rank the latter constraint above or below Dep-IO? Motivate your answer.

Q32 The consonant inventory of Mauritian Creole contains the coronal fricatives [s,z]. Palatoalveolar fricatives are absent. French words containing such fricatives, like [ʃəˈvø] 'hair' and [ʒeneˈral] 'general', are adapted as [seˈve] and [zeneˈral], respectively. Assume the two constraints Ident(F) and *ʃ/ʒ. Draw a constraint tableau with the correct ranking of these two constraints which shows the fate of the possible output form [seˈve] and [ʃeˈve] in Mauritian Creole.

4.5   CHOOSING BETWEEN RULES AND CONSTRAINTS

You may now think that there is not much difference between the two approaches. There are, however, two important differences. First, in a derivational approach, constraints and rules will sometimes both be needed and, moreover, appear to do the same work. Crucially, a rule-based grammar will also need constraints to characterize the phonological well-formedness of morphemes that have only a single form. For instance, the constraint *αVOICE–αVOICE (10) is generally needed to characterize the well-formed syllables of English: *[æbs], [*æpz], *[ztiː], *[sbiː] are ungrammatical, while [ɔks] and [ædz] are fine, and are indeed used for the words *ox* and *adze*. However, because the form [bæks] needs to be derived from [bæk-z], a rule of DEVOICING (7) is required to effect the change from [z] to [s]. That is, the rule-based approach needs both (7) and (10), even though they would appear to be describing the same regularity of English. This inherent drawback of the rule-based approach is known as the **duplication problem** (Kenstowicz and Kisseberth 1977: 136). A constraint-based approach does not run into this problem: the constraint on English syllable structure will act as a condition on all forms, regardless of whether they are morphologically derived or not.

A second difference concerns the phonological adjustments that only appear in loanwords. For the purposes of the native phonology, Hawaiian does not require a rule that breaks up consonant clusters, since all the morphemes of the language conform to the requirement of the structure (C)V(V): there simply are no morphemes that begin with consonant clusters. In order to account for the adjustment made when a word containing a complex onset like [kr] is adapted to the native phonology, the derivational approach will have to add such a rule to the phonology (in this case, one to change [r] into [l], and one to insert a vowel between the [k] and the [l]). In a constraint-based description, no such 'extra' grammar would need to be supplied. To characterize the native Hawaiian forms, a constraint forbidding complex onsets would need to be **undominated** anyway, as the language allows no exceptions. That is, in general, in an OT description, the constraints would be ranked so as to bring any new input forms in line with the structural demands of the language.

To illustrate this last point, consider again the Konjo word for 'glue', ['leʔeŋ]. The input form is the Indonesian word [lem]. Among the generated output forms there will be forms like [lem], ['lemem], [leʔ], etc. Why isn't the output [lem]? This is because the language has phonological constraints that are ranked higher than the Faithfulness constraints. One such constraint is that the output should minimally be a disyllabic foot, a constraint that is undominated in the language, so that there are no exceptions.

(16)   MɪɴWᴏʀᴅ: A word is minimally a (binary) foot.

Since MɪɴWord outranks Dᴇᴘ-IO, a disyllabic form will be preferred to the monosyllabic [lem]. Let us suppose that we have evaluated the potential outputs up to a point where all monosyllabic candidates (e.g. [leŋ], [lem], [leʔ]) have been discarded by MinWord. There are two further constraints that are relevant at this point. One, CodaCondition (17), forbids the presence of consonants other than [ŋ,ʔ] in the coda.

(17)   CodaCondition: A coda consonant is [ʔ] or [ŋ].

After inspection of CodaCondition, there are two reasonably faithful candidates left: ['le.ʔeŋ] and ['le.me]. (We will ignore the question why [ʔ] and [e] are the best choices here for the inserted segments.) The second constraint that is relevant at this point is Align-Stem-Right (18), which requires that no segments should be added to, or removed from, the end of the input. Formally, the requirement is that the end of [lem] should coincide with the end of a syllable in the output, but we give a simplified formulation here.

(18)   Align-Stem-Right: The last segment of the input corresponds with the last segment of the output.

In Konjo, Align-Stem-Right outranks Dep-IO. The form ['leʔeŋ] passes the higher-ranked constraint, because the end of the last syllable, [ʔeŋ], coincides with the end of the input form [lem], and ['leme] fails it, because the end of the syllable [me] does not. These correspondences are shown in (19). (We could of course, perversely, assume different correspondences. For instance, the output [m] in (19a) might be taken to correspond to the second [e] in the input, but that output form would be thrown out on the grounds of multiple violations of specific versions of Ident(F). Not even the consonantal nature of [m] would have been preserved, and an assumption of a high-ranking Ident([consonantal]) would be enough to discard that output form.)

(19)   a. l e ʔ e ŋ   b. l e m e
             | | | | | |
           l e   m   l e m

The fact that ['leʔeŋ] fails the lower ranking Dep-IO is of no importance: since there are no other candidates left, it is irrelevant whether the successful candidate breaks any constraints ranked below the constraint that eliminated the last rival form(s). Neither is it of any relevance that forms that failed to pass a constraint satisfy any lower-ranked constraints. The tableau in (20) schematizes the situation.

(20)

lem	Align-stem-right	Dep-IO
leme	*!	*
☞ leʔeŋ		**

In other words, the adjustment of Indonesian [lem] to Konjo ['leʔeŋ] is accounted for with the help of the same constraint hierarchy as is used for characterizing the native forms of the language (Yip 1993; Jacobs and Gussenhoven 2000). It would therefore appear that, at least in principle, OT scores over a description that uses structure-changing rules in two ways. First, OT can characterize the phonological grammar of a language in a way that avoids having to state the same information twice, once as a constraint on monomorphemic forms and once in terms of a rule that changes polymorphemic forms so as to conform to that constraint. Second, to account for phonological adjustments that are only observed in the adaptation of loanwords (i.e. never in the native forms), a rule-based analysis must add rules to the native grammar that bring those adaptations about. By contrast, the constraints that in an OT analysis characterize the native forms should equally characterize the optimal form of any incoming loanword.

Q33 In Japanese words, only a single voiced obstruent may occur. This constraint is known as Lyman's Law. As a result, [pato], [bato] and [pado] are possible words, but *[bado] is not.

1. Explain why *[gazi] isn't, but [gami] is a possible word.

Compounds are formed from two words, like English *armchair* from *arm* and *chair*. Each of the words making up a compound forms a separate domain for Lyman's Law. In Japanese compounds, the initial consonant of the second word is voiced, as shown in (1). This is known as Rendaku.

(1) ori   'coloured'   kami 'paper'   ori-gami   'coloured paper'
    take   'bamboo'   sao   'pole'   take-zao   'bamboo pole'
    garasɨ   'glass'   tama 'beads'   garasɨ-dama   'glass beads'

Rendaku fails systematically in the compounds illustrated in (2).

(2) kita   'north'   kaze   'wind'   kita-kaze   'north wind'
    tsɨno   'horn'   tokage   'lizard'   tsɨno-tokage   'horned lizard'
    siro   'white'   tabi   'tabi'   siro-tabi   'white tabi'

2. What might be the reason that Rendaku fails in (2)?

3. If you were to give an OT analysis of compounds, and RENDAKU and LYMAN'S LAW are two constraints, how would you rank them? Put the the two constraints in a tableau with /kita-kaze/ as input, and *[kita-gaze] and [kita-kaze] as outputs.

4.5.1 Gradient violation and unranked constraints

Sometimes, two forms break the same constraint, but one of them can be said to violate the constraint *more* than the other form. Also, it will frequently happen that two constraints are never contradictory and therefore that their ranking makes no difference. We illustrate the first point with the help of a hypothetical language, Un-Konjo, in which the ranking of Align-Stem-Right and Dep-IO is the reverse of that in Konjo. This has been done in tableau (21). Notice that inspection of the form ['leʔeŋ] leads to two violations of Dep-IO, compared with only one in the case of ['leme]. Multiple (or 'gradient') violation is shown by the number of stars in the relevant cells. Since the form ['leʔeŋ], with two inserted segments, is a worse candidate for the purposes of this constraint than ['leme], which has only one inserted segment, it is eliminated. Thus ['leme] is the winner in Un-Konjo, and Align-Stem-Right, along with all other lower-ranked constraints, is left uninspected.

(21)

lem	Dep-IO	Align-stem-right
☞ le.me	*	*
le.ʔeŋ	**!	

Let us go back to Konjo. Observe, again, that the potential output form *[leʔem] is non-optimal because it breaks CodaCond. Like Align-Stem-Right, this constraint must therefore be ranked above Ident(F), which requires that [m] remains [m]. However, the ranking of CodaCond with respect to the two constraints in tableau (20) is indifferent. We could either insert it before or after them. In tableau (22) we have placed it in first position; to indicate that its ranking is indifferent, it is separated from Align-Stem-Right by a dotted line. Likewise, while Ident(F) is ranked below CodaCond and Align-Stem-Right, it does not interact with Dep-IO.

(22)

lem	CodaCond	Align-stem-right	Dep-IO	Ident(F)
leme		*!	*	
leʔem	*!		**	
☞ leʔeŋ			**	*

Q34 Draw two tableaux that are identical to tableau (22), except that CodaCond is, respectively, in third and in fourth position. Please motivate your answers to the questions below.

1. Is Dep-IO crucially ranked above CodaCond?
2. Is CodaCond crucially ranked above Ident(F)?

These brief illustrations of the rule-based approach (section 4.4) and of a constraint-based approach (this section) give only the main ideas behind the derivational theory of *SPE* and of Optimality Theory. In later chapters we will illustrate both approaches more extensively. In Chapter 7 we present a description of the diminutive forms in two dialects of Dutch in the derivational framework of *SPE*, and in Chapter 15 we give an account of the word-stress locations in a number of languages in the framework of Optimality Theory.

4.6   CONCLUSION

In this chapter we have seen that the phonologies of languages actively impose phonological adjustments on input forms. Such adjustments are most readily observable in loanwords. However, the need to make adjustments also arises in the native vocabulary of the language when morphemes are combined in words and phrases, since such combination may lead to the creation of phonological representations that are ill-formed. There are two ways in which phonological adjustments have been described. They can be described with the help of a series of rules, which successively change the representation so as to make it conform to the requirements of the language. Second, they can be described by means of output constraints that state what forms must look like. Optimality Theory is a constraint-based theory that postulates that a language can be characterized by a ranking of a set of violable, universal output constraints, and that the correct form is the form that violates the constraints least.

Underlying and surface representations

5.1 INTRODUCTION

The variation in the pronunciation of words is truly mind-boggling. Biological differences between speakers lead to different acoustic outputs, and independently of whether they are adult or child and male or female, people speaking the same language will have different accents, depending on their social class and the region they grew up in. Within the speech of any one speaker, the pronunciation of words will vary with the degree of formality. And even if we tried to remove all variation from our speech, we could not produce acoustically identical pronunciations of the same word, due to the inevitable variation in the physiological mechanics and physical conditions of our environment. One specific type of within-speaker variation is central to our concern. The same speaker speaking in the same style will systematically vary the pronunciation of the same word *as a function of the phonological context*. In the English spoken in North America, the final consonant in an expression like *Right!* will be an unreleased [t˺], but in *Right on!*, this same /t/ will be an alveolar flap [ɾ]. The pronunciation of the English past tense suffix is either [t] or [d], depending on the voicing of the preceding segment, giving [lʊkt] as the past tense of *look* [lʊk], but [bɛgd] as the past tense of *beg* [bɛg]. And if the verb stem ends in [t] or [d], we find it is pronounced [ɪd], as in ['bʌfətɪd] and ['niːdɪd], the past tense forms of *buffet* ['bʌfət] and *need* [niːd].

Phonologists have responded to this situation by assuming multiple levels of representation. As a result, it will be possible to say that a morpheme has a single pronunciation at some cognitive level of representation, and that the variation between its various pronunciations, the morpheme alternants of Chapter 4, can be explained by phonological processes that operate in certain linguistic contexts. This is further discussed in section 5.3, where three arguments are evaluated that have been advanced for the assumption of underlying representations.

Then, zooming in on the segments involved in the variation, it also enables us to say that different sounds at one level of representation may correspond to the same sound at another level of representation. This merging of 'different' sounds to the 'same' sound can occur when going from the surface level to the underlying level. In this case, we speak of 'allophony', or allophonic variation. This is discussed in section 5.2, where a distinction is made between allophonic variation, which is explained by the linguistic context, and stylistic variation, which is explained by the degree of formality of the speech. When different underlying sounds correspond to the same sound on the surface, we have 'neutralization' of a contrast. This is discussed in section 5.4. Finally, in 5.5, we consider the question of how the phonological representation of the underlying form is determined.

5.2   ALLOPHONIC VARIATION

The 'segments' referred to so far in this book typically display a good deal of variation, even in the speech of a single speaker. Some of this variation is apparently random, but much of it is systematic. Two factors are responsible for this intraspeaker variation. One is **style**, or the degree of formality of the speech situation. For instance, in American English, an utterance like *Right!* will frequently have an unreleased final plosive (symbolized by means of the symbol for the plosive and a superscript [˺], as in [raɪt˺]), but in formal speech styles the [t] may well be released (so that you can hear a weakish [s]-like sound after it). In sociolinguistic studies, the **stylistic variants** [t˺] and [tˢ] are accordingly seen as the possible values of a phonological variable (t), whose frequencies of occurrence are compared across different speech styles for different groups of speakers. The second type of variation is due to variation in the **phonological context**. Such context-dependent variants are called **allophones**. The term **phoneme** is used to refer to the segment category that the various allophones are variants of. To distinguish the phoneme as a segment category from the individual allophones, it is often placed between slashes: / /. For example, in British English, there exist two rather different pronunciations of the phoneme /l/. When it occurs in the onset, it is pronounced as an alveolar lateral approximant, perhaps with some slight palatalization, as in *leek, follow*, a segment which is known as 'clear l'. In the coda, as in *ill, cold*, its alveolar contact is accompanied by retraction of the tongue body towards the uvula, a sound symbolized by [ɫ] and commonly known as 'dark l'. Again, in many languages, coronal consonants alternate with palatoalveolar or alveolo-palatal consonants, whereby the palatoalveolar one appears before [i], or sometimes before other front vowels as well. Thus, in Korean, underlying [sipsam] is pronounced [çipsam] 'thirteen', while Igbo has [ʃ] before [i,e] and [s] elsewhere, as shown by [oʃiri] 'he cooked', [ɔʃere] 'he said' vs [osɛrɛ] 'he wrote' and [ɔsara] 'he washed' (Jones 1967: 21). These examples illustrate the two kinds of phonological contexts that determine allophony. One is a particular segment or segment group, and the other is a structural position like the coda or the onset of the syllable.

Although allophonic variation in different languages may show some similarity, as suggested by the example of [s] before front vowels, it is important to see that languages will differ in the way they use segmental differences to differentiate between morphemes. That is, a given segmental difference may be phonemic in one language and allophonic in another. While the difference between [s] and [ʃ] is allophonic in Igbo, i.e. fully conditioned by whether [i,e] or one of the other vowels of the language follows in the word, in English the difference is **contrastive**: it is used to differentiate between morphemes. When a segmental difference is contrastive, there will typically be pairs of words that are distinguished only in that one has one segment where the other has the other segment. Examples of such **minimal pairs** in English are [sɪp – ʃɪp] (*sip – ship*) and [liːs – liːʃ] (*lease – leash*).

<table>
<tr><td>

Q35 For each of the three following languages, say whether the difference between [r] and [ʀ] is (a) allophonic, (b) phonemic or (c) stylistic. Motivate your answers.

1. In some types of Southern Swedish, [ʀ] always appears at the beginning of a syllable and [r] always at the end.
2. In some types of Dutch, [r] is the usual realization in words like [proˈχramaː] 'programme'. Some speakers of those varieties use this pronunciation in everyday life, but use [ʀ], as in [pʀoˈχramaː], when announcing programmes on national television.
3. In Provençal, the word for 'evening' is [sɛʀo] and the word for 'saw (noun)' is [sɛro] (Jones 1967).
</td></tr>
</table>

Allophonic variation is entirely predictable. As such, there is no reason to supply allophonic variation in the lexicon. The only lateral segment to appear in the lexicon of British English is just plain [l]. In a rule-based description, a rule of l-VELARIZATION would be postulated that adds the velarization to the specification of this consonant in the context 'end of syllable'. This is shown in (1) for the words *leak* and *ill*.

(1) Underlying   liːk   ɪl
     l-VELARIZATION (*n.a.*)   ɫ
     Output   liːk   ɪɫ

Allophonic differences typically arise because particular contexts invite particular adaptations in the production of the segment. As a result, allophones are in **complementary distribution**. The phonological context in which [ʃ] occurs in Igbo, i.e. before [i,e], is the complement of the phonological context in which [s] occurs, viz. before the remaining vowels of the language: together they make up the phonological context in which the underlying segment [s] occurs.

<table>
<tr><td colspan="4">

Q36 In Tolitoli, an alveolar lateral approximant [l] is in complementary distribution with a retroflex lateral flap, given as [ɭ]. What determines their distribution (Himmelman 1991)?
</td></tr>
<tr><td>moɭogo</td><td>'wash hands'</td><td>toɭitoɭi</td><td>'Tolitoli'</td></tr>
<tr><td>uɭag</td><td>'snake'</td><td>kikilo</td><td>'firefly'</td></tr>
<tr><td>membembelan</td><td>'to tremble'</td><td>moŋgiuɭan</td><td>'to choke'</td></tr>
<tr><td>labia</td><td>'sago'</td><td>lelembaɭan</td><td>'to carry on the shoulder with a stick'</td></tr>
</table>

Q37 In Plautdiitsch, the distribution of [x] and [ç] is illustrated by [axt] 'eight', [açt] 'real', [laxt] 'laughs' and [laçt] 'lays'. Are [x] and [ç] different phonemes, different allophones, or different stylistic variants in Plautdiitsch? (Nieuweboer 1998)

Q38 In Old English, [ç] and [x] are in complementary distribution. State the contexts in which each of these allophones occur.

kniçt	'boy'	feːçθ	'takes'
meəx	'manure'	broːxtə	'brought'
faːx	'hostile'	nɛəlæːçtə	'approached'
liːçtɑn	'alleviate'	bɔxtə	'bought'
uːxt	'daybreak'	hiːç	'high'

Q39 Korean has adopted a number of loan words from English, like those in (1).

(1) *English*   *Korean*
    [hoʊtɛl]   [ho.tʰɛl]   'hotel'
    [mɛlən]   [mɛ.ron]   'melon'
    [leɪzə]   [rɛ.i.sa]   'laser'
    [skændəl]   [sɯ.kʰɛn.dal]   'scandle'
    [mɪstəri]   [mi.sɯ.tʰɛ.ri]   'mystery'

Are [r] and [l] allophones in Korean?

A complementary distribution of segments can also arise in a different way, such as when one segment happens to be restricted to the onset position and another to the coda position. In such cases, the segments are not historically related in the way that contextual allophones like [s] and [ʃ] are. It will then depend on the similarity of the two segments whether the phonology – and the speaker's intuition – treats them as contextual variants of the same underlying segment. A well-known case is presented by [ŋ] and [h] in English. Because [h] may not occur at the end of a syllable and [ŋ] may not occur at the beginning of a syllable, the two segments are in complementary distribution. (That is, [hæŋ] 'hang' is a word, but neither *[tæh] nor *[ŋæt] could be a word.) There is general agreement that [h] and [ŋ] are underlying segments, since there is no plausible way in which one can be derived from the other.

5.3 TWO LEVELS OF REPRESENTATION

Why do phonologists assume that there are two levels of representation, an underlying one and a surface one? Three arguments have been advanced.

1. One argument is economy. Why supply allophonic information in the lexical entries if it can be stated in a set of allophonic rules that are valid for all morphemes of the lexicon? The strength of this argument has been called into question by Kenstowicz (1994a: 69), who points out that it is not self-evident that the descriptive economy achieved by having allophonic information supplied by rules should be reflected in the actual phonological representations in the mental lexicon. There is apparently no reason to assume that the brain could not store all that redundant information for each word in which it occurs. However, the issue here is not just storage

capacity, but also, or even mainly, search time in speech perception (Lahiri and Marslen-Wilson 1991). It may be expected to be more difficult to retrieve the correct phonological form from a set of fully specified, hence complex, representations than from a set of more economical representations.

2. A second argument for the assumption of two levels of representation is that with a single level it would not be possible to express the phonological relatedness of morpheme alternants. We take the English plural suffix as an example. Suppose that instead of saying that there is a morpheme [z] which in different phonological contexts is adjusted in order to obey the phonological constraints of English, we were to say that three **allomorphs** are listed in the lexicon, [z], [s] and [ɪz], each of which is used in a specific phonological environment: [ɪz] after sibilants, [s] after (other) voiceless segments and [z] in other cases. This description of the regular plural formation would be correct, in that for every noun we can predict the plural form. What the description fails to express, however, is that, somehow, the three alternants [z], [s] and [ɪz] are the same morpheme. It is not adequate to say that this identity is expressed in the semantics. Morphemes that mean the same thing can have different phonological forms. An example is provided by the English comparative, which is expressed by the suffix *-er* in some adjectives, like *nice*, but by means of the 'periphrastic' *more* in the case of others, like *esthetic*. In the case of the plural suffix, the availability of two levels of representation makes it possible to state that underlyingly the phonological form is [z], even though in surface representations it shows up as [z], [s] and [ɪz] (Anderson 1974). Phonologically motivated morpheme alternation can thus be characterized as variation in the shape of the same underlying form in a way that differentiates such variation from cases in which the different phonological forms are unrelated, like *more* and *-er*, as well as from irregular forms, like *went*, the past-tense form of *go*, for example, or *feet*, the plural form of *foot*. In such cases, the allomorphs must be listed in the lexicon, since there is no plausible phonological generalization which could account for them.

While the case for a single underlying form for the English plural is intuitively very clear, there has been no answer to the general question when different forms should be related to a single underlying form and when they must be listed as separate word forms. Chomsky and Halle (1968) derived words like *sane* and *sanity* from the same underlying form [sǣn], just as *profound* and *profundity* are derived from a common [profūnd] (where the overbar indicates tenseness). Others have questioned whether this is realistic, and have attempted to develop experimental procedures to answer such questions empirically (McCawley 1986; Ohala 1986; Wang and Derwing 1986).

Q40	Which of the following pairs of English words would you say contain a common underlying form?
sew – sewage	*cork – corkage*
blow – blew	*conceive – conception*
talk – talked	*fraternal – brother*

3. The third reason for the postulation of an underlying representation is that many generalizations are only valid at a level other than the surface level. Kenstowicz (1994a: 72), citing Mohanan (1992), gives as an example the generalization that sequences of sibilants are broken up by a vowel in English, which is responsible for the fact that the plural of English *bus* is ['bʌsɪz], rather than *[bʌsz] (or *[bʌss]). The generalization also holds in Singapore English: the plural of *kiss* is *kiss*[əz] and that of *nose* is *nos*[əz]. In this variety of English, there is the further fact that plosives are deleted in the coda after fricatives, so that *lift, list, task* are [lɪf, lɪs, tɑːs]. When these words are pluralized, they come out as [lɪfs, lɪss, tɑːss], respectively. Apparently, the generalization that adjacent sibilants must be separated by a vowel does not hold at the surface level in Singapore English, but *is* true at a level of representation at which the final plosive must still be present. Clearly, if we took it to be true at the surface level, the generalization would predict that the plural of *list*, with its surface pronunciation [lɪss], was *['lɪsəz]. If instead we assume that, underlyingly, the form [lɪst] exists, it quite happily allows [z] to be added, without the need for an inserted [ə]. There is in fact independent evidence that the plosives exist at a deeper level of representation, because they show up in verbal forms before vowel-initial suffixes, as in *lif*[t]*ing, lis*[t]*ing, tas*[k]*ing*. (The assumption here is that the noun *list* and the verb *list* have the same phonological form.) In (2), the situation is schematized. The plural morpheme [z] is attached to the underlying forms of *kiss* and *list*. The [ə] is inserted between the adjacent sibilants in the form for *kisses*, but not in that for *lists*, since in the latter form the sibilants are separated by [t]. Only after the vowel has been supplied can [t] be deleted. From (2), it is clear that the generalization ə-INSERTION is only true for the underlying representation, not for the surface representation.

(2)

UNDERLYING	kɪs-z	lɪst-z	lɪst-ɪŋ
ə-INSERTION	kɪsəz	(*n.a.*)	(*n.a.*)
t-DELETION	(*n.a.*)	Ø	(*n.a.*)
OTHER RULES	(*n.a.*)	Ø s	(*n.a.*)
SURFACE	kɪsəz	lɪss	lɪstɪŋ

Q41

1. If it were assumed that the underlying form of the verb *list* was [lɪs], what incorrect pre-diction would be made about the pronunciation of the present participle form of this verb?
2. The past participle of regular Singapore English verbs is formed by suffixing [d] to the stem, as in [saɪd] *sighed*, [faɪld] *filed*. Like the plural suffix [z], it is devoiced after voiceless obstruents, as in [wɔːkt] *walked*, while [ə] is inserted if the stem ends in [t,d]. If the verb *list*, whose past participle form is [lɪstəd], were underlyingly [lɪs], what incorrect prediction would be made about its past participle form? Why does the assumption of underlying [lɪst] make the correct prediction?

Surface forms that contradict a phonological generalization, like [lɪss] in the last line of (2), are **opaque**, that is, nontransparent. Taking a rule-based perspective, opacity can arise because some rule has failed to apply and the rule's structural description is met in the surface form. This occurs in the case of [lɪss], in which I-INSERTION appears ineffective. Equally, a rule may apply even though the context of the rule is not – any longer! – present in the surface form. An example of this type of opacity may occur in Japanese, when a vowel is deleted after causing a preceding [t] to be [ts](cf. Q27). When the underlying form [tɯkemono] is pronounced [tskemono], the [ɯ] that triggered the affrication of [t] has disappeared between voiceless consonants. Opacity is typically dealt with quite adequately in a rule-based description, because rules can be ordered so that segments can be allowed to have active or passive effects before they are deleted. In OT, however, opacity is not easily dealt with, not that is, if all constraints are by definition valid for output forms. We return to this point in Chapter 8.

5.4   NEUTRALIZATION

In the case of British English 'dark l', the rule we postulated produces a novel segment: before the application of the rule, no morpheme contained that segment. However, it is frequently the case that the output of a rule is an already existing segment. This is true, for instance, for the rule of DEVOICING that devoices the [z] of the English plural suffix to [s] after voiceless obstruents, as when [kæt-z] is changed to [kæts]. It also holds good for FINAL DEVOICING, which exists in German and Dutch, among many other languages. These rules produce segments (voiceless obstruents) in positions where such segments already appear. In a Dutch word like [pɑd] 'toad', the final [d] will be devoiced to [t], because the consonant occurs in the coda of the syllable. As a result, the singular form is pronounced [pɑt], but when the plural suffix [ən] is attached, the form is ['pɑdən]. Since [t] appears in that position in words like [kɑt] 'cat' (whose plural is ['kɑtən]), the opposition between [d] and [t] is neutralized in syllable-final position. A rule like English DEVOICING or Dutch FINAL DEVOICING, therefore, is a **neutralization rule**, while British English l-VELARIZATION is an **allophonic rule**.

5.5   CHOOSING THE UNDERLYING FORM

When a morpheme has a number of alternants, one of these will have to be chosen as the underlying form by the phonologist, and—if the phonological model reflects our mental world—by the infant acquiring his language. A good underlying form satisfies two requirements. First, it should allow you to write rules that do not destroy a segmental contrast of the language. Second, the rule or rules that are needed to produce the allophony or allomorphy will be easy to state. As for the first requirement, remember that a neutralization occurs whenever a rule produces an output that already existed in the context concerned. A particularly bad choice therefore would be to choose a neutralized segment. 'Don't lose contrasts!' is the important advice here. Take

FINAL DEVOICING, discussed in section 5.4. Recall that the Dutch morpheme for 'toad' has two alternants, [pɑd] and [pɑt], occurring in the plural [pɑdən] and the singular [pɑt], respectively. If we assume that the underlying form is indeed [pɑd], we can derive the two alternants with the help of (3).

(3) FINAL DEVOICING: Obstruents are voiceless in coda position.

Notice that this rule also applies in the case of [kɑt] 'cat', which has a plural form ['kɑtən]. It just so happens that the form already incorporates the voiceless segment the rule is designed to produce. Such application-without-effect is known as **vacuous** rule application. The derivation is given in (4).

(4)	UNDERLYING REPRESENTATION	pɑd	pɑ.d-ən	kɑt	kɑ.t-ən
	FINAL DEVOICING	t	*n.a.*	*vac.*	*n.a.*
	OUTPUT	pɑt	pɑ.dən	kɑt	kɑ.tən

But why do it this way round? Why don't we assume that there is a voicing rule that voices obstruents in the plural? Let's assume – for the sake of argument – that the underlying form of 'toad' is [pɑt]. Instead of a rule devoicing obstruents in the coda, we would need a rule that voices obstruents in the onset, i.e. (5). A situation would arise which is shown in (6). Clearly, this description produces the wrong results in the case of the plural of 'cat'. Rule (5) is not a correct generalization about Dutch, and the description in (4) must be considered superior.

(5) ONSET VOICING: Obstruents in the onset are voiced.

(6)	UNDERLYING REPRESENTATION	pɑt	pɑ.t-ən	kɑt	kɑ.t-ən
	ONSET VOICING	*n.a.*	d	*n.a.*	d
	OUTPUT	pɑt	pɑ.dən	kɑt	*kɑ.dən

The same reasoning applies to the choice between the [s] and [z] allomorphs of the English plural suffix, discussed in section 4.4.1. With /z/ as the underlying form, we need a devoicing rule to take /bæk-z/ to [bæks]. But if we were to assume /s/ as the underlying form, a voicing rule would apply to so as to change [s] to [z] after voiced segments. At first sight, this may seem fine: a form like /bʊk-s/ can now surface unchanged as [bʊks], while forms like /pɛn-s/ *pens* and /kaʊ-s/ *cows* are changed to [pɛnz] and [kaʊz] by the voicing rule. However, [s] and [z] contrast after voiced sounds, as shown by *dose* [dəʊs] versus *doze* [dəʊz] and by *pence* [pɛns] versus *lens* [lɛnz], or indeed *pens* [pɛnz]. Taking the neutralized [s] as underlying would therefore lead to the incorrect voicing of [s] in *pence* /pɛns/ to *[pɛnz], along with the correct creation of [pɛnz] out of /pɛn-s/. By contrast, if we take the underlying form to be /z/, we can safely devoice it to [s], since there is no contrast with [z] that we need to worry about.

The second requirement is simplicity of the rules or constraints that are needed. A correct choice of the underlying form leads to correct linguistic generalizations. Thus, it is correct to say that all obstruents are voiceless in the coda in Dutch and, conversely, it is incorrect to say that all obstruents are voiced in the onset in Dutch. Similarly, it is correct to say that all word-final coronal fricatives in English are voiceless after voiceless sounds, but it is incorrect to say that all word-final coronal fricatives are voiced after voiced sounds[1]. In order to illustrate that correct generalizations are simple to state, often more simple than if we took another morpheme alternant as the underlying form, let us consider the choice between /ɪz/ and /z/. Notice that the context for the insertion rule is simpler than that of the deletion rule. Insertion occurs 'between sibilants', deletion between 'plosives, nasals, approximants, vowels and non-sibilant fricatives on the one hand and sibilants on the other'. In Chapter 6, we will see that incongruous groupings are difficult to state in formal notation. The fact that contexts in rules and constraints are simple to state must reflect the fact that infants acquiring the language make generalizing hypotheses about the grammar.

The choice between /ɪz/ and /z/ could equally be motivated on the basis of the first requirement, that of no loss of contrasts, but the effect is a little more difficult to see. If we choose /z/ and an insertion rule, we correctly predict that there are no sequences of sibilants at the end of the word. That is, English has no words like *[kɪss], *[sɪʃs] or *[stɪzz]. However, if we choose /ɪz/ and a deletion rule, we predict that there are no words ending in non-sibilants and [z], like [-lɪz]. Such (non-plural) words are actually rare, but do exist. One variant pronunciation of *Los Angeles* is [lɒs 'ændʒəlɪz], by the side of [lɒs 'ændʒəliːz] and [lɒs 'ændʒəlɪs] (Wells 2008). With a deletion rule, we would end up with non-existent *[lɒs 'ændʒəlz]! Clearly, we would want to preserve the contrast between [ɪz] and [z] that exists after nonsibilants.

Q42

['hwan ðat 'aːpril 'wiθ hiz 'ʃuːrəz 'soːtə]
when that April with his showers sweet
[ðə 'druxt ɔv 'martʃ haθ 'pɛrsəd 'toː ðə 'roːtə]
the drought of March has pressed to the root

are the first two lines of Geoffrey Chaucer's *The Canterbury Tales*, with word-by-word glosses. The pronunciation of his words has been changed drastically by the many generations of speakers that have acquired the language since he wrote them some 620 years ago. For instance, the consonant [x] disappeared after making the vowel before it long, and Chaucer's [uː] corresponds to [au] today (i.e. [druxt] went from [druːt] to [draut]), and diphthongs before [r] acquired an extra syllable from the schwa-like transition between [au] and [r] (i.e. [ʃuːr] went from [ʃaur] to [ʃau.ər]).

a. There are two words that suggest that the present-day morpheme alternation for the plural suffix and for the past/participle suffix did not exist in Chaucer's time. What are they?
b. What does this suggest about the relation between the generalizations in grammars and the historical processes of language change?

In practice, it is usually easier to see whether our choice of underlying form leads to a good generalization than whether it preserves the language's contrasts. The place

---

[1] In fact, the English generalization is much more general than this. It holds that no voicing differences exist within sequences of obstruents inside the footed word, for which concept see Chapter 15. But this observation is somewhat beside the point here.

of articulation of nasal consonants in the syllable coda alternates in many languages as dictated by the place of articulation of the following consonant. In English, for instance, the preposition *in* is [ɪn] before the [t] of *Tallinn*, [ɪm] before the [p] of *Paris*, and [ɪŋ] before the [k] of *Copenhagen*. The rule is neutralizing in the case of [m] and [ŋ]: original [m] exists in *di*[m] *Paris*, which is *di*[m] in isolation, and original [ŋ] exists in *lo*[ŋ] *Copenhagen*, which is *lo*[ŋ] in isolation. Nothing merges with [n], as there is no assimilation in *di*[m] *Turin* and *lo*[ŋ] *Turin*. On the basis of these facts, we must avoid including a neutralizing [m] or [ŋ] in the underlying form, and instead take [n], to give the UR /ɪn/. But if we *had* incorrectly taken /ɪŋ/, say, as underlying, we would probably have been alerted that something was wrong once we got to writing the assimilation to coronal [n]. This would occur before coronal [t, d, s, z, n, l, r], as in *in Tallinn, in Dublin, in Stockholm, in Zagreb, in Nicosia, in London, in Rome*, but oddly also before vowels, as in *in Athens*. In Chapter 6, we will see that odd groupings like 'coronal consonants and vowels' cannot be properly described with the help of distinctive features. Clearly, a rule taking either /m/ or /ŋ/ to [n] will be more complex that one taking /n/ to either [m] or [ŋ].

Allophonic variation, too, should be described with 'correct linguistic generalizations'. In Q36, we saw that in Tolitoli [l] appears after front vowels and at the word beginning, while [ʟ] occurs after back vowels. It is thus simpler to state when /l/ is realized as [ʟ] than it is to state when /ʟ/ is realized as [l]. For this reason, /l/ is the better choice for the underlying segment. The more complex context can then be given, or implicitly understood, as 'elsewhere'. This is shown in (7).

(7)   Tolitoli l-FLAPPING: /l/ → [ʟ] after back vowels
                                        [l] elsewhere

> **Q43**   Both [tɔn] and [tɔm] are common Dutch first names, derived from *Anthonius* and *Thomas*, respectively. If the child's surname was ['bleːkfɛlt] *Bleekveld* and the choice was between those two names, which would you advise the parents to choose for their new son?

5.6   CONCLUSION

The recognition of two levels of representation, a surface representation (SR) and a more abstract underlying representation (UR), is the cornerstone of phonological theory. It makes it possible to describe morpheme alternants as variants of the same morpheme, and opens the way to a description in which the differences in phonological form between the alternants are expressed in terms of general statements about contextually defined phonological adjustments. URs and SRs usually differ from each other in that URs are more detailed than SRs, but SRs may also obliterate distinctions that exist in URs, and thus neutralize contrasts. There is no easy algorithm which, given a range of surface morpheme alternants, will lead to the 'correct' UR. URs are chosen so that the resultant grammar is the simplest that can be constructed and no incorrect predictions are made. Another question that is hard to answer is whether forms are to be regarded as morpheme alternants that have a common UR or as forms that are listed separately in the lexicon. In practice, these questions will not often vex the phonologist, since they do not seem too difficult to answer in the majority of cases. It may be expected that psycholinguistic research will provide new insights here, in particular where the second question is concerned. The next chapter turns to another aspect of phonological structure. It will identify and motivate the the smallest unit of analysis, the phonological feature.

Q44 The Balantak nouns in the first column of the first data set have the derived forms in the second column when prefixed with an affix meaning 'one'. The second data set shows verbs stems and their derivations with a prefix meaning 'unintentionally' (Busenitz and Busenitz 1991; some of the data are inferred).

Noun stem	Prefixed form	Gloss for stem
wuras	sawuras	'seed'
bitu?on	sambitu?on	'month'
loloon	saloloon	'thousand'
ta:?	santa:?	'word'
koeŋ	saŋkoeŋ	'head of grain'
utok	saŋutok	'brain'
sumpir	sansumpir	'beard'
apu	saŋapu	'fire'
noa	sanoa	'breath'
gampal	saŋgampal	'underlayer'
ŋo:r	saŋo:r	'nose'
malom	samalom	'night'
roon	saroon	'banana leaf'

Verb stem	Prefixed form	Gloss for stem
giok	toŋgiok	'move'
pi:le?	tompi:le?	'see'
jo:ŋ	tojo:ŋ	'shake'
kana	toŋkana	'hit'
wawau	towawau	'do'
tobok	tontobok	'stab'
lua?	tolua?	'vomit'
sosop	tonsosop	'suck'
ŋoap	toŋoap	'yawn'
dawo?	tondawo?	'fall'
balo	tombalo	'throw'
tunu	tontunu	'burn'
roŋor	toroŋor	'hear'
u:s	toŋu:s	'chew'

1. List the alternants of each prefix.
2. For each alternant, list the initial segment of each base before which the alternant occurs.
3. For each prefix, decide which alternant is the UR. Assume two rules, a place assimilation rule for nasals and either a nasal insertion rule or a nasal deletion rule.
4. Motivate your choice of the URs.

Distinctive features

6.1   INTRODUCTION

In Chapters 2 and 3 we saw that the segment inventories of languages can be divided into subgroups. Thus, we have separated the group of vowels from the group of consonants, and when we discussed the way languages 'build up' their inventories, we distinguished groups of voiceless obstruents (e.g. [p,t,k]) from voiced groups that are otherwise the same (i.e. [b,d,g] in our example). This would appear to suggest that the segment is not the smallest constituent of phonological structure. In this chapter, we will motivate this assumption. We will introduce the **distinctive features** that will in principle enable us to describe the segments in the world's languages, and to refer to those groups of segments that play a role in their characteristic phonological processes and constraints. The latter consideration will be shown to provide an important motivation for the assumption of distinctive features. In this perspective, these features are the elements by which we can refer to **natural segment classes**, groups of segments that are treated as groups by languages.

   We will see that some features are either present or absent in the representation of segments, like LABIAL (**univalent** features), while others may be present with a minus value or a plus value, like [±voice] (**binary** features). Also, we will argue that not even all binary features need to be present in the representation of all segments. Segments may either be unspecifiable for some feature, in which case the feature is **irrelevant** for the segment concerned, or be **underspecified** for some feature(s), in which case the segment will only be provided with those feature(s) in the surface representation.

6.2   MOTIVATING DISTINCTIVE FEATURES

As we have seen in the previous chapter, it is possible to see inventories of segments as composed of intersecting sets of segments, like 'all the voiceless segments' or 'all the segments articulated with lip rounding' or 'all the segments with a coronal place of articulation'. This fact does not in itself imply that a segment is represented in the synchronic structure in terms of a number of separate features, rather than as an unanalysable constituent. It could be the case that we are simply dealing with a reflex of the way segment inventories developed historically. Many cathedrals in Europe contain elements of earlier buildings, but this does not mean that these elements are in any sense functional today.

The chief motivation for the introduction, and hence definition, of a feature is that it enables us to characterize a **natural segment class**. It appears to be the case that languages frequently refer to particular groups of segments, while other conceivable groupings are never referred to. Thus, languages frequently ban voiced obstruents from the final position in the word or from the syllable coda, but no language would ban [m,d,ʒ] from the coda, while allowing [b,n,ɣ]. This forces us to recognize that the segments in the 'real' groups have something in common. If particular groups of segments figure again and again in phonological generalizations about syllable structure constraints or contextual variation, then evidently those groups must share some feature by which phonological grammars can recognize them.

Q45

1. Which consonants are aspirated syllable-initially in English?
2. If we ignore the ordinal suffix [θ], as occurring in *sixth*, which consonants can appear word-finally after [s] in English?
3. Which consonants can occur between [s] and [r] in English words?
4. What is the significance of the fact that the preceding three questions have the same answer?

In addition to the requirement that distinctive features should enable us to refer to natural segment classes, we should require of a feature analysis that the distinctive features can characterize the segment inventories of the languages of the world. That is, all segments must be characterizable in terms of some unique combination of features. This requirement is quite self-evident: we don't want to end up with a list of features that cannot characterize the difference between [m] and [n], say.

There is a third requirement placed on distinctive features. Consider first that there is no a priori reason to suppose that natural segment classes should consist of phonetically similar segments. Instead of [p,t,k], it might have been the case that it was [p,tʃ] which were aspirated in English. If more and more natural segment classes were found to be phonetically arbitrary, we might be led to believe that a distinctive feature was an abstraction, i.e. that it could be given no definition other than in terms of the collection of segments that had it. To continue the hypothetical example, we would say that [p,tʃ] are [+delta], and that [+delta] consonants are aspirated in some context. In reality, we see time and again that the segments in natural segment classes are **phonetically similar**. This has led to the requirement of the Naturalness Condition (Postal 1968: 73), according to which distinctive features must have a phonetic (articulatory or acoustic) definition. Notice that the relationship is not the other way around. We need not – should not – postulate a distinctive feature purely because there is some phonetic property that a group of segments has in common. As Kaye (1989: 27n.) puts it: 'One could group sounds according to the total energy involved in their production, the number of different muscles involved in their articulation, their length in milliseconds, the distance an articulator moves from some predefined neutral position, and so on.' Obviously, none of those definitions corresponds to a natural segment class.

The three requirements we must impose on a **distinctive feature system**, therefore, are that:

1. They should be capable of characterizing natural segment classes.

2. They should be capable of describing all segmental contrasts in the world's languages.

3. They should be definable in phonetic terms.

6.3   FEATURE VALUES

Features may or may not have **values**. A **binary** feature either has the value '+' or the value '−'. The claim here is that both the group of segments that has the minus value and the group that has the plus value form natural classes. For instance, the assumption of the binary feature [±voice] implies that languages refer to groups of voiceless segments as well as to groups of voiced segments. Ever since they were first proposed in Jakobson et al. (1952), distinctive features have standardly been assumed to be binary. In recent years, phonologists have proposed **univalent features** (e.g. Ewen 1995). In this case, reference can only be made to the class of segments that has the feature, not to the collection of segments that does not possess it. Other terms for univalent are **unary**, **single-valued** or **privative**. For instance, the feature [LABIAL] allows reference to the group of labial segments, but we cannot express any generalization involving all non-labial segments. When assuming a univalent feature like [LABIAL], therefore, a phonologist makes the claim that no language ever refers to the class of non-labial segments. (Multivalued features are no longer used. One that was common in the heyday of *SPE* was the feature [*n* stress], where *n* was a number to indicate the degree of stress of the vowel that was specified with the feature.) There is no reason why all features should be of the same type. In the next section we will introduce a set of distinctive features, some of which are binary and some univalent.

6.4   A SET OF DISTINCTIVE FEATURES

The following set of features represents a modified version of the set introduced by *SPE*. It largely follows Halle and Clements (1983), but has also been informed by Sagey (1986). The features come in the following groups: **major-class features**, which classify segments into segment types like 'vowel' and 'obstruent'; **laryngeal features**, which specify the glottal properties of the segment, **manner features**, which specify the type of constriction, or more generally the manner of articulation; and **place features**, which encode the place of articulation.

6.4.1 Major-class features

There are three major-class features, [±consonantal], [±sonorant] and [±approximant].

1. [±consonantal]. [+cons] segments have a constriction somewhere along the centre line in the vocal tract which is at least as narrow as that required for a fricative; [−cons] segments lack such a constriction. Thus, [+cons] are plosives, affricates, fricatives, nasals, laterals and [r], while [−cons] are vowels, glides like [ʋ,w,j], and – because their stricture is in the larynx rather than the vocal tract – [h,ɦ,ʔ].

2. [±sonorant]. This feature distinguishes obstruents ([−son]) from sonorant consonants and vowels ([+son]). [+son] segments are produced with a constriction in the vocal tract which allows the air pressure behind it and in front of it to be relatively equal, while this is not the case for [−son] segments. That is, either [−son] segments have an oral constriction which causes a significant increase in the air pressure behind it (e.g. [s], [d]), or there is no constriction in the vocal tract. Since the vocal tract does not include the larynx, [h] and [ʔ] are [−son]. So [+son] are all vowels, glides like [ʋ,w,j], liquids and nasals, while [−son] are plosives, fricatives, affricates and laryngeal segments.[1]

Q46

1. How many (possibly overlapping) natural segment classes can be referred to with two binary features at one's disposal? Hint: A natural class can be captured by one feature or by a combination of features.
2. Use [±cons] and [±son] to characterize four classes, giving examples of segments for each class.

Q47 In Dutch, there is a rule that places a [ə] between the noun stem and the diminutive ending [tjə], as when [bɑl] 'ball' is affixed with [tjə] and becomes ['bɑlətjə]. On the basis of the following data, characterize the group of segments after which this [ə] is inserted.

bɑl	bɑlətjə	'ball'	dɪŋki tɔj	dɪŋki tɔjtjə	'Dinky Toy'
kɔm	kɔmətjə	'bowl'	kap	kapjə	'hood'
lax	laxjə	'laugh'	bɛs	bɛʃə	'berry'
kan	kanətjə	'jug'	rɔk	rɔkjə	'skirt'
kar	karətjə	'cart'	dɪŋ	dɪŋətjə	'thing'
pɛt	pɛtjə	'cap'	sɔk	sɔkjə	'sock'

---

[1] The characterization of [h, ʔ] as [−son] is controversial. It is sometimes assumed that they are [+son], as in *SPE*, Trommelen and Zonneveld (1983) and Halle and Clements (1983).

Q48   In the variety of Spanish as spoken in the state of Cordoba in Colombia, there has been a process which assimilates the first of two adjacent consonants to the second, creating a geminate consonant (Charette 1989). For example, the word for 'door', which is [pwerta] in Peninsular Spanish, is [pwetta] in the Cordoba variety. The process did not always apply. Study the following data and characterize the class of consonants that underwent the process.

Earlier form	Later form	Gloss
serdo	seddo	'pork'
awto	awto	'car'
talko	takko	'talc'
doktor	dottor	'doctor'
algo	aggo	'something'
neptuno	nettuno	'Neptune'
fohforo	fohforo	'match'
magdalena	maddalena	'Madeleine'
ojgo	ojgo	'onion'
arma	amma	'weapon'
ahno	ahno	'donkey'

Q49   In Dutch, sequences of identical consonants are degeminated. These sequences will arise when the last consonant of one morpheme is the same as the first consonant of the next. However, not all such sequences are degeminated. Characterize the class of sounds that is subject to the rule in terms of distinctive features.

Input	Output	Gloss	
χeːl lampjə	χeː lampjə	'yellow lamp'	
fis sapjə	fi sapjə	'nasty drink'	
leːχ χaːtjə	leː χaːtjə	'empty hole'	
fraːj jɑχt	fraːj jɑχt	'beautiful yacht'	*fraː jɑχt
løːk kɪnt	løː kɪnt	'nice child'	
dɔm mɛns	dɔ mɛns	'unwise woman'	
ryʊ ʋeːr	ryʊ ʋeːr	'stormy weather'	*ry ʋeːr
doːf fɛntjə	doː fɛntjə	'deaf fellow'	
χutkoːp pak	χutkoː pak	'cheap suit'	
fɛin naːχəltjə	fɛi naːχəltjə	'fine nail'	
niʋ ʋɔntjə	niʋ ʋɔntjə	'new wound'	*ni ʋɔntjə
kar radɛiʃəs	kɑ radɛiʃəs	'cartload of radishes'	

Q50	In Dutch, certain consonants must be voiceless at the end of a syllable. Characterize that class of consonants with the help of distinctive features.

SG	PL	*Gloss*	SG	PL	*Gloss*
lir	lirən	'pulley'	kaːrt	kaːrtən	'card'
mɛp	mɛpən	'slap'	rant	randən	'edge'
spɛlt	spɛldən	'pin'	bɑl	bɑlən	'ball'
kɑnt	kɑntən	'side'	ʒiˈrɑf	ʒiˈrɑfən	'giraffe'
rɛis	rɛizən	'journey'	ʋɛp	ʋɛbən	'web'
dœyf	dœyvən	'pigeon'	paːrt	paːrdən	'horse'
ʋɑŋ	ʋɑŋən	'cheek'	sxun	sxunən	'shoe'
kʌus	kʌusən	'sock'	leːʋ	leːʋən	'lion'

3. [±approximant]. [+approx] are those segments which have a constriction in the vocal tract which allows a free (frictionless) oral escape of air, while for [−approx] segments this is not the case (Ladefoged 1971: 46, Clements 1989). Vowels and non-nasal sonorants, like [l, ɹ, ʌ], are [+approx] segments. (The term 'lateral' is used for any l-type sounds, while the term 'rhotic' refers to any r-type sound; laterals and rhotics are often referred to as 'liquids'.)

Q51	Copy the following hypothetical segment inventory and draw lines that separate (a) [−son] from [+son], (b) [−approx] from [+approx] and (c) [+cons] from [−cons].

p	t	k	ʔ
b	d	g	
f	s	x	h
v	z	ɣ	
m	n	ŋ	
	lr		
w	j		
i	a	u	

Q52	In English, certain segments may appear after [sp, st, sk] in the same syllable. Characterize them with the help of a single distinctive feature, on the basis of the following data.

skɪp	spreɪ	stjuː	əˈspaɪə
stɔp	skjuːd	skləˈrəʊsɪs	skræp
skwɒd	spreɪn	spjuː	streɪt
stæk	strɔː	ˈsplɛndɪd	skʌl

The difference between vowels and glides like [j,w] is commonly assumed to be a matter of phonological structure, rather than of phonological content. That is, [u] is different from a labialvelar approximant [w] not because these two segments have different features, but because they occupy different positions in the syllable: the peak of the syllable for [u], and the margin, usually the onset, for [w]. Chomsky and Halle (1968) used the feature [±syllabic] to express this difference. In later work, syllabicity of segments is expressed directly in a representation that includes syllable structure. We will use the feature informally to refer to the difference between 'syllabic' (i.e. occupying the syllable peak) and 'non-syllabic' segments.

6.4.2   Laryngeal features

There are three laryngeal features, [±voice], [±spread glottis] and [±constricted glottis].

1. [±voice]. [+voice] are segments for which the vocal cords are close enough together to allow vibration, while for [−voice] this is not the case. Thus, [+voice] are vowels (e.g. [i,ʌ,ɛ̃,aɪ]), sonorant consonants (e.g. [m,ɲ, l,r,ʀ,w], voiced obstruents (e.g. [b,z,ɣ,dʒ] and [ɦ]), while [−voice] are voiceless obstruents [(e.g. [p,θ,ʃ,ts,h]).

2. [±spread glottis]. [+spread] segments have a vocal cord configuration that produces audible friction in the glottis, while [−spread] segments lack such a configuration. Thus, aspirated segments like [pʰ,kʷʰ] and [h,ɦ] are [+spread], while other segments are [−spread].

3. [±constricted glottis]. For [+constr] segments the vocal cords are tense and drawn together, while for [−constr] segments this is not the case. Thus [ʔ], laryngealized vowels (e.g. [ṵ]), and laryngealized sonorant consonants (e.g. [m̰]), glottalized obstruents (e.g. preglottalized [ʔp] or ejective [p']) are [+constr]. So are implosives ([ɓ,ɗ,ɠ]). Other segments are [−constr].

Q53   American English [p,t,k] are accompanied by a glottal closure when appearing in the syllable coda, as in *sit, atlas, popcorn, duckpond*. What feature specification do these plosives acquire in this context?

Q54   In Southern Oromo, a rule of i-ᴇᴘᴇɴᴛʜᴇꜱɪꜱ inserts [i] between the ejectives [t', tʃ'] and a following [t,n], as shown in (1a). However, [ʔ], [ɗ] and [t] do not trigger the rule, but undergo other changes that are not relevant here, as shown in (1b,c,d) (Lloret 1995). What combination of features distinguishes the [t'] from the three consonants that do not trigger i-ᴇᴘᴇɴᴛʜᴇꜱɪꜱ?

(1)	a.	fit'-na	fit'ina	'we finish'
	b.	aʔ-na	aːna	'we push'
	c.	feːɗ-ta	feːtːa	'you want'
	d.	bit-ta	bitːa	'you buy'

6.4.3 Manner features

There are four manner features, [±continuant], [±nasal], [±strident] and [±lateral].

1. [±continuant]. [+cont] segments lack a central occlusion in the vocal tract, while [−cont] segments are produced with such an occlusion. Thus, plosives (e.g. [p,d,g]), nasal consonants (e.g. [m,ŋ]), affricates (e.g. [tʃ]) and laterals (e.g. [l]) are [−cont], other segments are [+cont]. Some languages apparently treat laterals as [+cont], which is phonetically understandable in the sense that while these segments have a central occlusion, they have a lateral aperture.

2. [±nasal]. [+nas] segments (e.g. [m,n,ŋ]) are produced with the velum ('soft palate') lowered, [−nas] segments have the velum in its closed (raised) position. Nasal consonants and nasalized vowels are [+nas], other segments are [−nas].

3. [±strident]. [±strident] is relevant for obstruents only, and refers to a type of friction. [+strident] segments cause a noisier kind of friction than [−strident] segments. [+strident] voiceless fricatives are [f,s,ʃ,χ], [−strident] ones are [θ,ç,x]. Together with [CORONAL] (section 6.2), the feature can be used to capture sibilants ([s,z,ʃ,ʒ,tʃ,dʒ]), needed for a correct description of the context for English I-INSERTION. Languages for which a contrast between [f,v] and [ɸ,β] has been reported include Ewe and Venda (Ladefoged and Maddieson 1996: 140). The name *Ewe*, [èβè], forms a minimal pair with the word for 'two', [èvè], in that language, while English contrasts [s,z] with [θ,ð], as in *sigh, xi* (the Greek letter ξ, [zaɪ]), *thigh, thy*. The feature's other task is to distinguish plosives from affricates, both of which are [−son, −cont]. Such contrasts are common, as in German [tɔl] 'mad' vs [tsɔl] 'import duty', English [taɪm] *time* vs [tʃaɪm] *chime*, or Corsican ['ɟalu] 'freeze+1SG' vs ['dʒalu] 'yellow'. The representation of affricates is controversial. A widely supported view, however, is that they are [+strident] plosives (Rubach 1984; Clements 1999). For one thing, it is at least suggestive that affricates typically have strident friction after the release of the closure, as in [pf,ts,tʃ,kχ] rather than [pɸ,tθ,cç,kx].

Q55	In Scottish English, [i, e, a, o, u, ʌ, ʌi] are pronounced as long [iː, eː, aː, oː, uː, ʌː, ae] in open syllables. The long vowels (including [ae]) also appear before certain consonants. Characterize the class of consonants before which the long vowels appear. This regularity, described in Aitken (1981, 1984), has become known as Aitken's Law.

raeð	*writhe*	mʌil	*mile*
nʌin	*nine*	beːʒ	*beige*
tiːz	*tease*	rod	*road*
lʌːv	*love*	kaːr	*car*
liθ	*Leith*	hom	*home*
tiː	*tea*	lʌif	*life*
pis	*peace*	fud	*food*
mel	*mail*	raʃ	*rash*
fae.ər	*fire*	boːr	*boar*

Q56	In Turkish, the [±voice] contrast in obstruents is neutralized in the syllable coda in favour of the voiceless member, as shown in (1) (after Kim 1997).

(1)

UR	Objective	Plural	
ip	ipi	ipler	'rope'
dib	dibi	dipler	'bottom'
at	atɯ	atlar	'horse'
ad	adɯ	atlar	'name'
køk	køki	køkler	'root'
gøg	gøgi	gøkler	'sky'
diʃ	diʃi	diʃler	'tooth'
kɯz	kɯzɯ	kɯzlar	'daughter'
deniz	denizi	denizler	'sea'
satʃ	satʃɯ	satʃlar	'hair'
aːdʒ	aːdʒɯ	aːtʃlar	'tree'

1. Which obstruents are devoiced?
2. Can the group of obstruents that is subject to the neutralization be characterized as a natural class?

4. [±lateral]. [+lat] segments have a central tongue contact in the oral cavity with one or both sides of the tongue being held away from the roof of the mouth, allowing the air to escape there, like alveolar [l] and prepalatal [ʎ]. Other sounds are [−lat]. A lateral escape of the air is also possible for obstruents, like the lateral fricatives [ɬ] (voiceless) and [ɮ] (voiced) and the lateral affricates [tɬ] and [dɮ].

6.4.4 Ambiguity and nonspecification

In this section we further illustrate the kind of reasoning by which featural analyses of segments are arrived at. As you will recall from section 6.2, the first and foremost motivation for the definition of a feature is that it allows natural classes to be referred to. The aim of the exercises in this chapter so far has been to show this. It is possible, of course, that there is conflicting evidence for the inclusion or exclusion of a particular segment in a natural class. This is the case for [l], which behaves ambiguously vis-à-vis the feature [±cont]. We will conclude that languages may differ in the feature value of [continuant] for [l]. Second, it is to be expected that certain (classes of) segments are not specified for all features. That is, features may be **irrelevant** for certain segments. Thus, vowels will not be specified for [±lat], simply because those segments cannot be differentiated with the help of this feature. Less obviously, it appears that [h] does not participate in rules referring to [±cont]. In the section that follows, we will argue that laryngeal segments are not specified for either manner or place features.

The ambiguous behaviour of [l]

If you did Q55 correctly, you will have drawn the conclusion that in Scottish English, [l] is [−continuant]. In other languages, however, the same segment may have to be analysed as [+continuant]. In Frisian, vowels are nasalized before [n] in the same syllable, provided a [+cont] consonant follows. The [n] itself is subsequently lost (Tiersma 1985). From the data in (1), which consist of infinitival verb forms prefixed with [in-] or [oən-], it is clear that the [l] must be [+cont]: the group of consonants that does not allow the change to go through are [p,t,k,g,n], while the consonants that do allow it are [s,f,j,ʋ,r,l].

(1) in-pɑkə   impɑkə   'to wrap up'
     oən-trɛkə   oəntrɛkə   'to take to heart'
     oən-komə   oəŋkomə   'to arrive'
     ingɪən   iŋgɪən   'to enter'
     oən-nɪmə   oənnɪmə   'to accept'
     oən-stɪən   oə̃stɪən   'to please'
     in-fɔlə   ĩfɔlə   'to fall in'
     in-jaːn   ĩjaːn   'to give in'
     in-ʋɛ̃jə   ĩʋɛ̃jə   'to live with one's parents'
     oən-ropə   oə̃ropə   'to call'
     in-lɪzə   ĩlɪzə   'to preserve'

The feature specification of laryngeals

The Frisian rule of NASALIZATION may also give us an indication about another question that concerns the feature [continuant]. The laryngeal consonants are [−cons, −son]. If we take the definitions of these features seriously, this means that [h,ʔ] have a constriction in the larynx, but have no constriction in the vocal tract, and thus do not have the sort of constriction that sonorants like [j] have. That is, they do not have a constriction in the vocal tract that is at least as narrow as used by fricatives. The question therefore arises whether it makes sense to want to specify [h,ʔ] for manner features or for place features, since after all, if there is no stricture, how could we specify either its manner or place? While this makes good phonetic sense, the first question is whether languages make reference to any manner or place features of glottal consonants. For example, we might find rules that refer to sets of the type '[h] and other (classes of) [+continuant] segments'. One such set is 'all vowels, the approximants [l,r,j,w] and all fricatives, including [h]', which would be the class [+cont]; another is '[l,r,j,w] and all fricatives, including [h]', which would be the class [+cont, −syl]. As we have just seen, Frisian NASALIZATION is a rule referring to the class continuant consonants, but, interestingly, [h] is not among them, as shown in (2). If [h] were specified for manner features, that is, if [h] were [+continuant], we would expect the rule of nasalization to apply before it. Since nasalization does not apply before [h], we have to conclude that this segment is not specified for manner features and hence cannot be considered [+continuant].

(2)   inhɛljə   'to hold in'
       oənhɪərə   'to listen to'

A Dutch assimilation rule points to the same conclusion. PROGRESSIVE DEVOICING devoices fricatives after obstruents, as shown in (3).

(3)   zeː   'sea'   ɔp seː   'at sea'
       ʒur'naːl   'journal'   dɪt ʃurnaːl   'this journal'
       vyːr   'fire'   'kɑmpfyːr   'campfire'
       ɣɑs   'gas'   dɪt xɑs   'this gas'

The class of voiced fricatives could be referred to by [−son, +cont]. Clearly, if [h] is [+cont], this consonant would be included in that natural class. As it happens, the Dutch glottal fricative is frequently voiced. This voiced [ɦ] shows up after obstruents, too: *stadhuis* 'town hall' may be pronounced [stɑt'ɦœys] as well as [stɑt'hœys] (Rietveld and Loman 1985). This means that Dutch [ɦ] is not subject to PROGRESSIVE DEVOICING, and that it therefore cannot be [+cont]. We now have evidence from two languages that [h] is not specified for continuancy. With McCarthy (1988) we will assume therefore that laryngeal segments are not specified either for manner or for place features.

6.5   PLACE FEATURES

In the previous section, a set of binary features was introduced which are capable of specifying the major class, the state of the glottis and the manner of articulation of consonants. In this section we deal with the features used to specify the place of articulation of consonants and the tongue position of vowels. Among the place features, there are four univalent features specifying the major areas of articulation. These are the features [LABIAL], [CORONAL], [DORSAL] and [RADICAL]: a segment either has the feature or it does not. This implies that, just as laryngeal segments are not specified for a number of features (those specifying either manner or place of articulation), not all segments will be specified for all the place features: a consonant which is not coronal will not have the feature [CORONAL]. Binary place features will be used to characterize the place distinction **within** a major articulator area. The feature [±round], for example, will be used to specify segments that are articulated with the help of the lips, i.e. are [LABIAL]. Segments whose articulation does not involve any activity of the lips will thus be neither [+round] nor [−round]: they have no specification for that feature.

6.5.1   Labial

[LABIAL] segments are articulated with the lips, like [f,p,m], or – in the case of vowels – are formed with lip rounding, like [y,o,œ]. Segments that are [LABIAL] may be specified for [±round].

1.   [±round]. [+round] segments have lip rounding, like [pʷ,tʷ,o,u,ɔ]; [−round] segments do not. In rare cases, unrounded and rounded labial segments

contrast, as in Margi, Nambakaengo and Kilivila (Senft 1986). Labialized segments like [tʷ] will be discussed further in Chapter 13.

6.5.2   Coronal

[CORONAL] segments are articulated with a raised crown of the tongue, i.e. a raised tip and/or blade, ranging from a dental [θ] to a prepalatal [j]. Examples of [CORONAL] segments are [t,z,l,θ,j,ʃ,ɲ,r]. [CORONAL] segments are further specified for the features [±anterior] and [±distributed], and in the case of coronal fricatives and affricates also for [±strident].

1. [±anterior]. For [+ant] segments, the crown articulates with the alveolar ridge or somewhere further forward, while for [−ant] segments, the crown articulates with a point behind the alveolar ridge. Thus, [t,s,θ] are [+ant], while prepalatal or postalveolar and retroflex consonants (e.g. [ʃ,ʒ,ɲ,c,j] and [ʈ,ɖ,ʂ,ɳ,ɭ]) are [−ant].

2. [±distributed]. Segments that are [+distr] are produced with a constriction that extends for a relatively great distance along the vocal tract, while for [−distr] segments this is not the case. Thus, consonants produced with the tip of the tongue (**apical** consonants like British English [t,d,n]) are [−distr], as are [s,z] (Clements 1985). Blade-articulated (**laminal**) consonants like [ʃ,tʃ,ʒ]) are [+distr]. Dental consonants like [θ,ð,l̪,t̪] are also [+distr], because even where it is only the tip that touches the front teeth, the blade is close to the alveolar ridge and in fact contributes to the acoustic effect. Retroflex consonants are [−distr]: the tip articulates with the part of the palate immediately behind the alveolar ridge. Australian languages frequently have a four-way opposition, utilizing the four possibilities given by these features. Four coronal stops and nasals contrast in Kayardild, for instance, as shown in (4) (Evans 1995).[2]

(4)

	(Lamino-) dental	(Apico-) alveolar	(Lamino-) prepalatal	Retroflex
	t̪, n̪	t, n	c, ɲ	ʈ, ɳ
Ant	+	+	−	−
Distr	+	−	+	−

6.5.3   Dorsal

[DORSAL] sounds are articulated with bunched dorsum: [k,g,ɣ,ŋ] (velars), as well as [ç,k̟] (fronted velars) and uvulars (e.g. [χ,q]). In addition, all vowels are [DORSAL].

[2] This predicts that no language contrasts dental stops, which are [+ant, +distr], with laminally produced alveolar stops, which are also [+ant, +distr], which would seem to be correct.

[DORSAL] segments are further specified for a set of features that specify just where the bunch of the tongue body is located, the **tongue body features**.

1. [±high]. Segments that are [+high] raise the dorsum to a position close to the roof of the mouth, while [−high] segments do not. Thus, [+high] segments are [i, ɪ, y, ʏ, ʊ, ɯ, u], as well as [ç], and [k, ɡ, x, ɣ, ŋ], while [χ, e, o, a] are [−high], for instance.

2. [±low]. [+low] segments have the bunched dorsum low in the mouth, while [−low] segments do not. Thus, [+low] segments are [a, ɛː, ɔː], for instance.

3. [±back]. [+back] segments have the bunch of the tongue positioned in the centre or further back, while [−back] segments have the bunch in the front. Thus, [+back] segments are velar and uvular consonants (e.g. [k, ɣ, χ]) and vowels like [u, ə ,o, ʌ, ɑ], while [−back] segments are fronted velars like [k̟] and [ç], and vowels like [i,y,ø,ɛ]. It is emphasized that [ç], although classed with the palatal consonants [c,j,ɲ] in the IPA chart (i.e. with the [CORONAL] consonants), is interpreted as a fronted velar, i.e. a [DORSAL] consonant. Many languages have [ç] and [x] in complementary distribution depending on the backness of the preceding or following vowel. For instance, Greek ['çeri] 'hand' begins with the same phoneme as ['xari] 'charm' (cf. Q38).

4. [±tense]. [+tense] vowels like [i,e,a,o,u] are produced with a more peripheral and somewhat closer tongue position than their [−tense] counterparts [ɪ, ɛ, ɑ, ɛ, ʊ]. The feature is only relevant if the language has vocalic oppositions like [i–ɪ], [y–ʏ], [u–ʊ], etc. It is commonly used in Germanic languages, which have contrasts like English [suːt] *suit* – [sʊt] *soot* and German ['miːtə] 'rental fee' – ['mɪtə] 'middle'. The features [±Advanced Tongue Root; ATR], used for instance in the description of the West African language Akan (Lindau 1978), and [±Retracted Tongue Root; RTR], used for instance in the description of the Tungusic languages of Siberia (Li 1996), may be seen as phonetic variants of this phonological feature. [+ATR] involves a forward position of the tongue body, with concomitant enlargement of the pharynx, while [+RTR] involves a retraction and lowering of the tongue body, with concomitant narrowing of the pharynx. Akan has four plain vowels and five [+ATR] vowels, three of the former type occurring in [−ATR] [ɛbʊɔ] 'stone', and three of the latter in [+ATR] [ebuo] 'nest'. Baiyinna Orochen has nine plain and nine [+RTR] vowels, and [−RTR] [oloː] 'to cook', for instance, contrasts with [+RTR] [ɔlɔː] 'to wade'. The features [±tense], [±ATR] and [±RTR], while phonetically somewhat different, appear never to co-occur in the same language (cf. Halle and Clements 1983: 7; Ladefoged and Maddieson 1996: 300).

6.5.4 Radical

[RADICAL] (also [PHARYNGEAL]) sounds are articulated with the root of the tongue. A voiceless fricative [ħ] occurs in many varieties of Arabic, as does a pharyngeal approximant [ʕ]. See Ladefoged and Maddieson (1997) for more information.

6.6 SOME EXAMPLES

Table 6.1 contains feature values for a number of representative consonants. Notice that many segments have more than one place feature, and are technically 'complex'. A round vowel like [u] is [LABIAL, +round] as well as [DORSAL, +back, +high], while a labialized [t] is both [CORONAL] and [LABIAL]. In Chapter 13 we will further discuss the representation of complex consonants.

A seven-vowel system like that of Italian comes out as in (5). It is illustrated in (6).

(5)

	[−back] [−round]	[+back] [−round]	[+back] [+round]
[+high, −low]	i		u
[−high, −low]	e		o
[−high, +low]	ɛ	a	ɔ

(6)

milːe	'thousand'			puɲːo	'fist'
seta	'silk'			sole	'sun'
sɛmpre	'always'	skala	'stairs'	fɔka	'seal'

As observed above, in many Germanic languages, the vowels divide into a lax set and a tense set. Standard German has the vowel system in (7), where the lax vowel is given on the left of each cell. Examples are given in (8). The bracketed vowel [æː] has merged with [eː] in the speech of many speakers. Note that [ɛ,ɔ] are the lax counterparts of [eː,oː] in German and Dutch.

(7)

	[−back] [−round]	[−back] [+round]	[+back] [−round]	[+back] [+round]
[+high, −low]	ɪ, iː	ʏ, yː		ʊ, uː
[−high, −low]	ɛ, eː	œ, øː		ɔ, oː
[−high, +low]	(æː)		a, aː	

(8)

Lax					
mɪtə	'centre'	hʏlə	'cover'		fʊks	'fox'
dɛkə	'blanket'	hœlə	'hell'		hɔlts	'wood'
				katsə	'cat'

Table 6.1

Feature specifications of 23 representative consonants for 16 features. Binary features are specified as + or −, while the presence of a unary feature is indicated by √. Blanks indicate that the consonant is not specified for the feature. The value of the feature [continuant] for [l] varies across languages

	p	t̪	t	pf	tʃ	kʰ	b	f	θ	s	ʃ	ç	x	v	ɣ	m	ɳ	ŋ	r	l	j	w	h
cons	+	+	+	+	+	+	+	+	+	+	+	+	+	+	+	+	+	+	+	+	−	−	−
son	−	−	−	−	−	−	−	−	−	−	−	−	−	−	−	+	+	+	+	+	+	+	−
approx	−	−	−	−	−	−	−	−	−	−	−	−	−	−	−	−	−	−	+	+	+	+	−
cont	−	−	−	−	−	−	−	+	+	+	+	+	+	+	+	−	−	−	+	?	+	+	
nas	−	−	−	−	−	−	−	−	−	−	−	−	−	−	−	+	+	+	−	−	−	−	
lat	−	−	−	−	−	−	−	−	−	−	−	−	−	−	−	−	−	−	−	+	−	−	
voice	−	−	−	−	−	−	+	−	−	−	−	−	−	+	+	+	+	+	+	+	+	+	−
spread	−	−	−	−	−	+	−	−	−	−	−	−	−						−	−	−	−	+
LABIAL	√			√			√	√						√		√						√	
COR		√	√		√				√	√	√						√		√	√			
distr		+	−		+				+	−	+						−		−	−			
ant		+	+		−				+	+	−						−		+	+			
strid	−	−	−	+	+	−	−	+	−	+	+	−	−	+	−								
DORSAL						√						√	√		√			√			√	√	
high						+						+	+		+			+			+	+	
back						+						−	+		+			+			−	+	

Tense						
diːnst	'service'	myːdə	'tired'		guːt	'good'
meːr	'more'	ʃøːn	'nice'		roːt	'red'
(bæːr)	'bear'			raːm 'cream'		

There are languages that contrast four vowel heights without employing a tense–lax contrast, of which Danish and Imonda are examples. The tongue-height features [±high] and [±low] cannot characterize such systems. Of the four theoretically possible combinations, the specification *[+high, +low] must be ruled out, because it is contradictory: the body of the tongue cannot simultaneously be raised and lowered. The Imonda vowel system is given in (9) (Seiler 1985). Clements and Hume (1995) present a feature framework that can account for such four-height systems (as well as for five-height systems, which have also been reported to exist).

(9)

	Front unrounded	Back unrounded	Back rounded
High	i		u
High mid	e		o
Low mid	ɛ	ə	ɔ
Low	æ	a	ɒ

6.7   REDUNDANT VS CONTRASTIVE FEATURES

Frequently, feature specifications are predictable. This predictability is in part a consequence of the incompatibility of particular feature specifications. For instance, as we have seen in the previous section, the presence of [+low] in the specification of a vowel predicts that it will be [−high]: the tongue cannot be raised and lowered at the same time. The same goes for [+high]: it predicts [−low]. In large measure, however, the predictability is language-specific, and results from the fact that not all languages use the phonological possibilities to the full. Take the Turkish vowel system, for instance. This language employs all the combinations of [±back] and [±round], but only has two distinctive vowel heights, as shown in (10), with examples in (11).

(10)

	[−back] [−round]	[−back] [+round]	[+back] [−round]	[+back] [+round]
[+high]	i	y	ɯ	u
[−high]	e	ø	a	o

(11)

diʃ	'tooth'	gyl	'rose'	kɯz	'daughter'	tuz	'salt'
kep	'cap'	gøl	'lake'	at	'horse'	son	'end'

In this system the feature [±low] is entirely **redundant**, as one of its values, [+low], does not appear to be used at all. In other inventories, both values of a feature may occur, but one value may be predictable from other features. In the Italian vowel system (5), for instance, [+round] predicts [+back]: all round vowels in this language are back. (This absence of front rounded vowels, incidentally, is a characteristic that Italian has in common with most languages in the world.) Or again, while in many languages obstruents come in pairs contrasting for [±voice], like [p]–[b], [s]–[z], etc., sonorant segments like [m,l,r] are usually always voiced, with the result that in those languages [+son] predicts [+voice]. This means that while in the class of obstruents the feature [±voice] is **contrastive** (or **distinctive**), [±voice] is redundant in sonorants: they are predictably [+voice].

A large body of work, often referred to as **Underspecification Theory**, has been devoted to the question of whether redundant features should be included in the underlying representation of morphemes, and if not, when they should be supplied. Just as in the case of the nonspecification of manner and place features in glottal consonants (see section 6.4.4), arguments for or against underspecification have been based on the simplifying effect that the absence of a feature has on the formulation of phonological generalizations. We give one example here, from Steriade (1987). If we assume that [l] is [+cont] in Latin, [±lateral] is distinctive in Latin within the class of liquids, [l,r], or [+approx, +cons]. In the class of nasals and obstruents ([−approx]) as well as in the class of glides and vowels ([−cons]), the feature is redundant. Steriade (1987) proposes that only contrastive features are specified in underlying representations. This means that [r] is marked as [−lat] and [l] as [+lat], but that in no other segment is there a specification for [±lat]. This assumption allows for an interesting description of the distribution of the alternants *-aris* and *-alis* of the adjectival suffix. Consider the forms in (12).

(12) a. *nav-alis*   'naval'
          crimin-alis   'criminal
       b. *sol-aris*   'solar'
          milit-aris   'military'
       c. *flor-alis*   'floral'

The forms in (12a,b) show that the alternation depends on the presence of the feature [+lat] in the base: if the base contains [+lat], the form *-aris* is used, otherwise *-alis*. If we assume the underlying form of the suffix to be [alis], the [+lat] [l] is seen to change into [−lat] [r] after a base containing [+lat]. (Such processes are known as **dissimilations**.) But now consider (12c). Although the base contains [+lat], the suffix is *alis*. It is here that the underlying [−lat] specification of [r] comes in useful. Because other nonlateral sounds, like [t] of *militaris*, are not specified as [−lat], Steriade's proposal allows us to say that the last specification for [lat] in the base determines the specification for [lat] of the first consonant in the suffix. This is shown in (13).

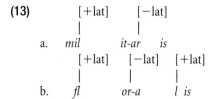

(13)

        [+lat]   [−lat]

a. *mil*   *it-ar*   *is*

        [+lat]   [−lat] [+lat]

b. *fl*   *or-a*   *l is*

This particular conception of underspecification, in which features are specified only in segments that contrast for the feature concerned, is known as **contrastive underspecification**. The topic of underspecification is closely related to one's view of how segments are represented; it is taken up again in Chapter 12, after we have presented a hierarchical representation of the distinctive features introduced in this chapter. There, it will appear that it is in fact more useful to include in underlying representations only one of the two feature specifications of contrastive features.

Q57   In Corsican, some vowels are nasalized before a nasal consonant in the same syllable (Agostini 1995). How would you characterize the class of vowels that undergo this nasalization?

'printʃipe	'prince'
'ãŋku	'also'
'põnte	'bridge'
'fuŋgu	'mushroom'
'kõntu	'account'
funda'mẽntu	'foundation'

Q58   In Bengali, there is an optional rule which deletes [r] before certain consonants, allowing the consonant to geminate. Characterize the class of consonants that trigger r-DELETION on the basis of the following data (Hayes and Lahiri 1991).

Input	Output	Gloss
barʃa	baʃʃa	'rainy season'
miṯʰu-r ʃari	miṯʰu-ʃʃari	'Mithu's sari'
ram-er bari	ram-er bari	'Ram's house'
ram-er ʈaka	ram-eʈ ʈaka	'Ram's money'
fon-korbo	fon-korbo	'will telephone'
ʃundor dɔrdʒa	ʃundod dɔddʒa	'beautiful door'
bɔrdi	bɔddi	'elder sister'
bʰorti	bʰotti	'full'
kor-lo	kol-lo	'do-3rd FUT.'
kor-ṯ o	koṯ-ṯo	'do-3rd PAST'
matʃʰ-er nɑːk	matʃʰ-en nɑːk	'fish's nose'
matʃʰ-er matʰa	matʃʰ-er matʰa	'fish head'

Q59 A number of nouns in the Dutch dialect of Wehl form their plurals by changing the last full vowel of the stem, a process known as UMLAUT (Haan 1996). What feature is involved in this process?

Singular	*Plural*	
zɔk	zœk	'sock'
ɣrɔːt	ɣrœːt	'fishbone'
vʊs	vʏs	'fox'
hoːp	høːp	'heap'

Q60 In Luganda, [r] and [l] occur in complementary distribution (Chesswas 1963).

olubiri	'palace enclosure'	akalulu	'vote'
liɲɲa	'climb'	eŋgiri	'warthog'
ssaffaali	'safari'	eŋkula	'rhinoceros'
eraŋg	'dye'	akasaale	'arrow'
akasolja	'roof'	olumuli	'reed'
kampala	'Kampala'	liiri	'silk'
omulere	'flute'	akabonero	'sign'
omulenzi	'boy'	weeraba	'goodbye'
luma	'to hurt'	lje	'my (poss. Class V)'

1. What determines their distribution? List the contexts in which each allophone occurs.
2. Which of these two contexts is statable in terms of distinctive features?
3. Which of the segments would you choose as the underlying one? Please motivate your answer.

Q61 Use minimal numbers of distinctive features to characterize the five natural segment classes within the segment inventory of Telugu.

p	pʰ	t	tʰ	tʃ	ʈ	ʈʰ	k	kʰ
b	bɦ	d	dɦ	dʒ	ɖ	ɖɦ	g	gɦ
		s			ʂ			
m		n			ɳ			
		l	r		ɭ			
w			j					
i	e	a	o	u				

1. pʰ bɦ tʰ dɦ tʃ ɖɦ kʰ gɦ
2. t tʰ d dɦ tʃ dʒ ʈ ʈʰ ɖ ɖɦ
3. b bɦ m
4. w j i e a o u
5. a o

Q62 Use minimal numbers of distinctive features to characterize the five natural segment classes within the segment inventory of Amharic (Hayward and Hayward 1992).

```
              t   t'  tʷ'      c   c'      k   kʷ  kʷ'
 b   bʷ       d                ɟ           g   gʷ
 f   fʷ       s   s'           ʃ                        h   hʷ
              z                ʒ
 m   mʷ       n                ɲ           ŋ
              l   r
 w                             j
 i   ɯ   u
 e   ɤ   o
         a
```

1. f fʷ s s' z ʃ ʒ
2. t' tʷ' c' kʷ' s'
3. c c' ɟ ʃ ʒ
4. n ɲ
5. u o

6.8 CONCLUSION

Segments can be analysed into collections of univalent and binary features. A successful feature analysis will characterize the segmental contrasts that are used in the languages of the world, while it will additionally allow natural feature classes, groups of segments that figure in phonological grammars, to be referred to. We have seen that segments may be unspecified for certain features, either because the feature is irrelevant for the class of segments concerned, like [±strident] in the case of vowels, or because the feature is univalent and the segment does not have it, like [LABIAL] in the case of [t]. We have also made a distinction between contrastive and redundant features, where the former are features that, in some class of segments in some language, characterize contrasts, like [±voice] in a language with voiced and voiceless obstruents, and the latter are not, like [±voice] in a language that only has voiceless obstruents and voiced sonorant consonants and vowels. It is often assumed that redundant features do not appear in underlying representations.

In Chapter 12, we will see that segments are not simply lists of features. Because features tend to be active in specific groups, such as the place features or the laryngeal features, the assumption has generally been made that features are grouped into constituents.

SPE. A case study:
the diminutive suffix in Dutch

7.1 INTRODUCTION

Phonological rules are formal expressions that describe changes in the phonological representations of words. As a result of the application of a phonological rule, a segment may be inserted or deleted, or one or more of its feature values may be changed (to mention the most frequent types). In this chapter, we first deal with the formal notation for writing the rules introduced by Chomsky and Halle (1968) (*SPE*). Next, we will see that the assumption that rules are ordered, whereby the output of one rule serves as the input to the next, allows for simple phonological generalizations. After that, we will apply the *SPE* theory to the alternations in the diminutive suffix in two varieties of Dutch. A number of ordered rules will appear to be necessary to derive the morpheme alternants of the diminutive suffix in Standard Dutch, historically a western variety. We then consider diminutive formation in Sittard Dutch, a south-eastern variety, which has a different underlying form for the suffix as well as a number of different rules that are needed to derive the morpheme alternants. Moreover, some of the rules that they have in common will have to be ordered differently to obtain the correct results.[1]

7.2 *SPE* REPRESENTATIONS AND RULES

In the representation proposed by *SPE*, segments are lists of feature specifications. Such a list is also referred to as a **feature matrix**. In the original proposal, all features were binary, and there were no dependencies between features. Strictly speaking, therefore, (1a) is the *SPE* feature matrix of an apical [t]. In (1b), we give the representation with the univalent place feature [CORONAL], which was introduced in Chapter 6. (In this book, representations with binary major place features, as in (1a), will not be used.) Note that the status of an expression like '[t]' is that of a shorthand notation for the corresponding feature matrix.

---

[1] The description for Standard Dutch is based on Gussenhoven (1978). For treatments of the diminutive formation in (standard and non-standard) Dutch, see van der Berg (1975), Trommelen (1983), Booij (1984), van der Hulst (1984), Hamans (1985), Nijen Twilhaar (1990), Wetzels (1990), Haan (1996) and van de Weijer (2002).

A morpheme is represented as a string of feature matrices. The beginnings and ends of morphemes are indicated by **boundary symbols**. What may, with hindsight, be seen as puzzling is that the only boundaries recognized by *SPE* are morphosyntactic boundaries. The symbol + was included in representations at the boundaries of word-internal morphemes (**morpheme boundary**), while # served as the **word boundary**. Thus, (2) is the representation of the word *pens*. In much of the literature, word-internal morpheme boundaries are represented by means of a dash, as in [pɛn-z] *pens*, rather than with +.

(1) a.
$$\begin{bmatrix} +\text{cons} \\ -\text{son} \\ -\text{voice} \\ -\text{spread} \\ -\text{constr} \\ -\text{cont} \\ -\text{nas} \\ -\text{lat} \\ +\text{cor} \\ +\text{ant} \\ -\text{distr} \\ -\text{round} \\ -\text{high} \\ -\text{low} \\ -\text{tense} \end{bmatrix}$$

b.
$$\begin{bmatrix} +\text{cons} \\ -\text{son} \\ -\text{voice} \\ -\text{spread} \\ -\text{constr} \\ -\text{cont} \\ -\text{nas} \\ -\text{strid} \\ -\text{lat} \\ \text{CORONAL} \\ +\text{ant} \\ -\text{distr} \end{bmatrix}$$

(2)

$$\#\begin{bmatrix} -\text{syl} \\ +\text{cons} \\ -\text{son} \\ -\text{voice} \\ -\text{spread} \\ -\text{constr} \\ -\text{cont} \\ -\text{nas} \\ -\text{lat} \\ \text{LAB} \\ -\text{round} \\ +\text{distr} \end{bmatrix} \begin{bmatrix} +\text{syl} \\ -\text{cons} \\ +\text{son} \\ +\text{voice} \\ -\text{spread} \\ -\text{constr} \\ +\text{cont} \\ -\text{nas} \\ -\text{lat} \\ \text{DORSAL} \\ -\text{back} \\ -\text{low} \\ -\text{high} \\ -\text{tense} \end{bmatrix} \begin{bmatrix} -\text{syl} \\ +\text{cons} \\ +\text{son} \\ +\text{voice} \\ -\text{spread} \\ -\text{constr} \\ -\text{cont} \\ +\text{nas} \\ -\text{lat} \\ \text{COR} \\ +\text{ant} \\ -\text{distr} \end{bmatrix} + \begin{bmatrix} -\text{syl} \\ +\text{cons} \\ -\text{son} \\ +\text{voice} \\ -\text{spread} \\ -\text{constr} \\ +\text{cont} \\ -\text{nas} \\ -\text{lat} \\ \text{COR} \\ +\text{ant} \\ -\text{distr} \end{bmatrix}\#$$

Sentences are represented as strings of words. The position in *SPE* was one in which the morphology and syntax preceded the phonology: only when the words are inserted into the sentence will the phonological rules be called upon to make the necessary adjustments. In (3), a 'shorthand' representation is given of the sentence *Pens leak*.

(3)   #pɛn+z##liːk#

The general format of an *SPE* rule is as given in (4).

(4)

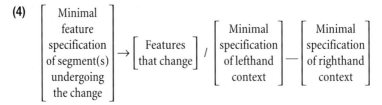

$$\begin{bmatrix} \text{Minimal} \\ \text{feature} \\ \text{specification} \\ \text{of segment(s)} \\ \text{undergoing} \\ \text{the change} \end{bmatrix} \rightarrow \begin{bmatrix} \text{Features} \\ \text{that change} \end{bmatrix} / \begin{bmatrix} \text{Minimal} \\ \text{specification} \\ \text{of lefthand} \\ \text{context} \end{bmatrix} - \begin{bmatrix} \text{Minimal} \\ \text{specification} \\ \text{of righthand} \\ \text{context} \end{bmatrix}$$

The information to the left of the arrow is the FOCUS of the change, that between the arrow and the slash is the STRUCTURAL CHANGE (SC), while the information to the right of the slash is the CONTEXT. The focus plus the context is known as the STRUCTURAL DESCRIPTION (SD). Rules are assumed to apply *within* words, and if a rule is to apply across word boundaries, the SD needs to include the symbol #. Rules are assumed to apply across +-boundaries, even if no + is specified. (If a rule applies *only* at a +-boundary, this must of course be included in the SC.) Rules written in this format were standard in phonological work from the late 1960s until the late 1970s, when the representations of Autosegmental Phonology introduced new ways of formulating rules (cf. Chapters 10 and 11).

To illustrate, we give (5) as the rule that devoices voiced obstruents at the word-end in Dutch.

(5)   FINAL DEVOICING $[-\text{son}] \rightarrow [-\text{voice}] / \_\_ \#$

The rule scans the feature matrices from left to right for the presence of $[-\text{son}]$; then, if it finds one, it checks whether there is a # on the right, and if there is, it specifies – as the value of the feature [voice] in the matrix with $[-\text{son}]$. In many cases, the obstruent will already *be* $[-\text{voice}]$. The rule is then said to apply **vacuously**: the SD is satisfied, but application of the rule does not bring about a difference. The reason for doing it this way, of course, is that the rule can be written with fewer terms than if we were to add the feature $[+\text{voice}]$ to the focus of the rule.

The obstruent undergoing rule (5) frequently appears in word-final position. However, sometimes an obstruent needs to be devoiced that is not adjacent to the word boundary. For instance, when the 3sg suffix [t] is attached to the verb stem [leːz] 'read', the surface result is not *[leːzt], but [leːst]. In the *SPE* representations, this means that we must express in the rule that other obstruents may intervene between the obstruent to be devoiced and the word end. This is done by adding the term 'C$_0$' before the #. The C itself is shorthand for $[-\text{syll}]$. (The symbol V is similarly used as a shorthand for $[+\text{syll}, -\text{cons}]$, i.e. a 'true vowel'.) The subscripted number n means 'n or more' (instances of the symbol), just as a superscripted digit means 'n or less'. The term 'C$_0$' therefore translates as 'zero or more consonants', and has the effect of allowing rules to ignore consonants in the positions in which it is used. Our rule therefore now looks like (6).

(6)   FINAL DEVOICING $[-\text{son}] \rightarrow [-\text{voice}] / \_\_ C_0 \#$

Version (6) would be able to apply twice in the same word. When shifting through the form from left to right, the rule will find that its SD is in fact met in a form like [leːz-t]. Similarly, it is met twice in a case like [hoːvd] 'head', whose singular and plural forms are [hoːft] and ['hoːvdən], respectively. The first focus is [v], when [d] corresponds to C_0, and the second is [d], when C_0 corresponds to no consonant.

> **Q63** The Dutch past participle is formed by prefixing [χə] and suffixing [d] to the verb stem. The suffix shows up in its underlying form when the inflectional suffix [ə] is added, as in [χə + vʏl + d + ə] 'filled-PARTIC-OBL', but otherwise shows up as [t]. In the case of a verb stem like [sχʏd], the uninflected [χə + sχʏd + d] may be formed, and is pronounced [χəsχʏt]. Does rule (6) apply to both underlying [d]s in this last form? Motivate your answer.

7.2.1   Reference to the syllable

Dutch FINAL DEVOICING applies to obstruents in the syllable coda, not just to the smaller category of word-final obstruents. This is clear from the way speakers of Dutch treat English words like *Sidney* ['sɪdni], *business* ['bɪznɪs]: when they are used as loans, English syllable-final [d,z] are replaced with [t,s], respectively (Booij 1995). Venneman (1972), Hooper (1976) and Kahn (1976) (re)introduced the syllable in phonological representation. Reference to the syllable makes it possible to give a formulation of FINAL DEVOICING which takes these additional facts into account. This is done in (7), where the σ-labelled parenthesis is used to indicate the syllable boundary. In Chapter 11 we will deal more extensively with the syllable in the structural descriptions of rules.

(7)   FINAL DEVOICING $[-son] \rightarrow [-voice] / \_\_ C_0)_\sigma$

7.2.2   The brace

A notational device that has been widely discredited as a theoretical element, but which is often used out of convenience, is the **brace**. The brace notation is used to express a disjunction between two or more terms ('either … or'), and is thus found in rules that are partly identical. Again, when no reference to the syllable is made, the syllable-final context can usually be captured by saying 'before a consonant or the word-end'. (Even this characterization frequently fails to capture the right context, as explained in Chapters 11 and 16.) Rule (8), for instance, nasalizes vowels before a nasal followed by another consonant or the word-end. Rule (8) would change French [bɔn] 'good-MASC' and [bɔnte] 'goodness' into [bɔ̃n] and [bɔ̃nte], respectively.

(8) $V \rightarrow [+nas] / \_ [+nas] \begin{Bmatrix} C \\ \# \end{Bmatrix}$

> **Q64** The symbol Ø is used to the left of the arrow in the case of insertion, and to the right of the arrow in the case of deletion. What would be the prose version of (1), for instance? And of (2)?
>
> (1) $Ø \rightarrow ə / V\_\_ r\#$
> (2) $r \rightarrow Ø / \_\_ \begin{Bmatrix} C \\ \# \end{Bmatrix}$

7.2.3   Variable feature values

To express assimilations, feature values need to be made to agree. For instance, in
Turkish, high vowels in suffixes agree for [back] and [round] with the preceding
vowel in the word, as shown in (9).

(9) | Nominative | Possessive | Gloss |
|---|---|---|
| køj | køjy | 'village' |
| kep | kepi | 'cap' |
| at | atɯ | 'horse' |
| son | sonu | 'end' |

A rule to achieve this would use **variable feature values**, expressed with the help of
Greek letters. Rule (10) says that high vowels agree in backness and roundness with
the preceding vowel: α could be $-$ or $+$, and so could β, independently.

(10) $$\begin{bmatrix} +\text{syll} \\ +\text{high} \end{bmatrix} \rightarrow \begin{bmatrix} \alpha\text{back} \\ \beta\text{round} \end{bmatrix} / \begin{bmatrix} \alpha\text{back} \\ \beta\text{round} \end{bmatrix} C_0 -$$

> **Q65**   Write out the four readings of (10).

7.2.4   Parentheses

The **parenthesis notation** is used to include optional elements in rules. Dutch
has a rule of REGRESSIVE VOICING which applies within words as well as across word
boundaries. Within words, it applies to [lif-də] 'dear-ness, love' to form [livdə],
and across words it applies in [lif ##diːr] 'dear animal' to form [liv diːr]. Since *SPE*
assumes that every word that leaves the morphology has #s around it, two #s need
to be specified in the SD. However, because the rule also applies within words, they
need to be put in parentheses to indicate that they may, but need not, be present in
the representation, as shown in (11).

(11) $[-\text{son}] \rightarrow [+\text{voice}] /$ ___ $(\#\#) \begin{bmatrix} +\text{voice} \\ -\text{cont} \\ -\text{son} \end{bmatrix}$

7.2.5   The transformational rule format

The focus of the rule format illustrated above is confined to only a single segment.
However, there are processes that affect more than one segment. For example, METATHESIS
is a process that switches round two segments, as can be seen in the Old English word
for *grass*, which varied between [græs] and [gærs]. To be able to refer to changes
involving more than one segment, the **transformational rule format** was used. It lists
the relevant string of segments and boundaries to the left of the arrow, and repeats that
string, with the SC, to the right of the arrow. The segments of the context are not literally
reproduced, but identified with the help of digits. Rule (12) says: 'Delete a coronal

nasal before a consonant or at the word-end, and nasalize the vowel that precedes it'. It would change French [bɔn] and [bɔnte] into [bɔ̃] and [bɔ̃te], respectively.

$$
(12) \quad [+\text{syll}] \begin{bmatrix} +\text{cons} \\ +\text{nas} \\ \text{COR} \end{bmatrix} \left\{ \begin{array}{l} \# \rightarrow 1 \\ C \quad [+\text{nas}] \quad \emptyset \quad 3 \end{array} \right.
$$
$$
\quad\quad 1 \quad\quad 2 \quad\quad 3
$$

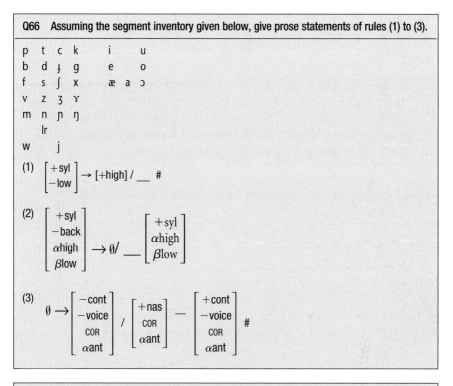

Q66 Assuming the segment inventory given below, give prose statements of rules (1) to (3).

p	t	c	k		i		u
b	d	ɟ	g		e		o
f	s	ʃ	x		æ	a	ɔ
v	z	ʒ	ɣ				
m	n	ɲ	ŋ				
	lr						
w		j					

(1) $\begin{bmatrix} +\text{syl} \\ -\text{low} \end{bmatrix} \rightarrow [+\text{high}] \,/\, \underline{\quad} \, \#$

(2) $\begin{bmatrix} +\text{syl} \\ -\text{back} \\ \alpha\text{high} \\ \beta\text{low} \end{bmatrix} \rightarrow \emptyset \,/\, \underline{\quad} \begin{bmatrix} +\text{syl} \\ \alpha\text{high} \\ \beta\text{low} \end{bmatrix}$

(3) $\emptyset \rightarrow \begin{bmatrix} -\text{cont} \\ -\text{voice} \\ \text{COR} \\ \alpha\text{ant} \end{bmatrix} \,/\, \begin{bmatrix} +\text{nas} \\ \text{COR} \\ \alpha\text{ant} \end{bmatrix} - \begin{bmatrix} +\text{cont} \\ -\text{voice} \\ \text{COR} \\ \alpha\text{ant} \end{bmatrix} \#$

Q67 Assuming the segment inventory given in the previous question, write formal rules:

1. Obstruents are voiceless after word-internal or word-external obstruents.
2. An [ə] is inserted between [r,l] and a labial obstruent in the same word.
3. Suffix-initial vowels are front if the preceding syllable contains [i], and back if the preceding syllable contains [u].

7.3 LINEAR ORDER

Obviously, if in some language there were only one rule, its input would consist of the lexical representation of the forms that meet its structural description (the underlying representation, UR), while its output would correspond to the actual pronunciation (the surface representation, SR). Languages generally have more than one rule, and the question therefore arises of how phonological rules apply: in sequence or simultaneously? Let us assume, for the sake of argument, that rules apply simultaneously to the underlying representation. Any rule would always scan the underlying representation to see if its structural description was met, and if it was, the change would be made. This mode of application is known as **simultaneous rule ordering**. Another possibility would be that the output of one rule is taken as the input of another rule. In this situation, you would have to know in which order the rules applied. This option is known as **linear rule ordering**. How do we decide between these two possibilities? As always, the answer depends on which theory provides the more economical description of the facts. Of course, the ordering of two rules is relevant only if the order in which they apply makes a difference for the forms that are produced.

Q68 In many varieties of Dutch, coda clusters consisting of a liquid and a consonant other than [t,d] are broken up by [ə], causing [kɛrk] 'church' and [kɑlf] 'calf' to be [kɛrək] and [kɑləf] on the surface, respectively. They also have a rule deleting [n] after [ə], if these segments occur in the same syllable. Demonstrate that the order in which n-DELETION and ə-INSERTION apply makes a difference for the SR of a word like [vaːrn] 'fern'.

Q69 The following are the underlying forms of a number of words in Tonkawa (from Phelps 1975).

netale-oʔ	'he licks it'
we-netale-oʔ	'he licks them'
netale-n-oʔ	'he is licking it'
we-netale-n-oʔ	'he is licking them'
picena-oʔ	'he cuts it'
we-picena-oʔ	'he cuts them'
picena-n-oʔ	'he is cutting it'
we-picena-n-oʔ	'he is cutting them'

1. Identify the underlying forms of the morphemes for 'lick', 'cut', '3rd-sg-SUBJ', '3rd-sg-OBJ', '3rd-pl-OBJ', and the 'PROGRESSIVE' (cf. English *to be* [Verb]-*ing*). (NB: One of these does not have a phonological form in Tonkawa).
2. Tonkawa has the rules CONTRACTION and TRUNCATION:
    (i)   CONTRACTION V → Ø / # CVC __ CV
    (ii) TRUNCATION V → Ø / V __
    Give derivations (i.e. underlying forms, rule applications, surface forms) of 'he licks it', 'he is cutting them' and 'he cuts them'.

There are many pairs of rules that do not interact, like Tonkawa CONTRACTION and TRUNCATION in the previous question. Such rules are unordered. In order to show that it is the sequential application of phonological rules that provides the simpler description, we will consider two rules of English, both of which apply to the plurals of nouns. As you may remember, the plural suffix of English has three alternants. After [s,z,ʃ,ʒ,tʃ,dʒ], the alternant [ɪz] is used; after voiceless segments other than [s,ʃ,tʃ], [s] occurs, while elsewhere [z] is used, which we argued in Chapter 5 is also the underlying form of the morpheme. The plurals of [bʌs], [pɛn] and [bʊk] (*bus, pen, book*) are, respectively, [bʌsɪz], [pɛnz] and [bʊks]. Recall that we need two rules: one that inserts [ɪ] between the stem and the suffix if the stem ends in [s,z,ʃ,ʒ] (I-INSERTION), and one that devoices [z] after voiceless segments (DEVOICING). We repeat this derivation in (13).

(13)		bʌs-z	pɛn-z	bʊk-z
	I-INSERTION	bʌsɪz	*(n.a.)*	*(n.a.)*
	DEVOICING	*(n.a.)*	*(n.a.)*	bʊks
		bʌsɪz	pɛnz	bʊks

Which theory allows us to write the simpler rules, the simultaneous-ordering theory or the linear-ordering theory? For the formulation of I-INSERTION, it would not make any difference which theory we adopted, because under either theory the rule applies to the underlying form. This is necessarily so under a simultaneous mode of application, and in an ordered mode of application, it would simply be ordered first. This rule is given in (14).

(14) I-INSERTION $\emptyset \rightarrow \text{I} / [+\text{strident}] \_\_ + z$

Now consider the second rule, DEVOICING. In a simultaneous-ordering theory, we would have to make sure that it does not devoice the [z] in cases like [bʌs-z]. That is, the rule needs to express 'devoice [z] after all voiceless segments except [s,ʃ,tʃ], i.e. after [p,t,k,f,θ]'. However, [p,t,k,f,θ] do not form a natural class: phonological rules do **not** typically refer to this group of sounds. Indeed, in the theory of distinctive features it cannot be characterized without the suspect 'either ... or' braces, and even then it must be assumed that [tʃ] is really a sequence of [t] and [ʃ]. This clumsy formulation is given in (15). It says: 'after a voiceless obstruent which is either [−strid] (i.e. [θ]) or [LABIAL] (i.e. [p,f]) or [−cont] (i.e. [p,t,k])'. Incidentally, [tʃ] is also included by [−cont], of course, which is why we needed to assume that this affricate is a sequence of [−cont] [t] and [+cont] [ʃ] quite against the intuition of native speakers, who consider [tʃ] a single consonant.

(15)
$$\text{DEVOICING} \ [-\text{son}] \rightarrow [-\text{voice}] / \begin{bmatrix} -\text{voice} \\ \left\{ \begin{matrix} [-\text{strident}] \\ [\text{LABIAL}] \\ [-\text{cont}] \end{matrix} \right\} \end{bmatrix} \_\_ \ \#$$

Now consider the other option. If DEVOICING is allowed to apply to the output of I-INSERTION, we could simplify (15) to (16). This is because at the time that DEVOICING gets to apply to [bʌsɪz] (the output of I-INSERTION), the [z] no longer appears after a voiceless segment, but after [+voice] [ɪ].

(16) DEVOICING $[-\text{son}] \rightarrow [-\text{voice}] / [-\text{voice}] \_\_ \#$

This example is representative of the difference between the two modes of application. The assumption that rules apply to the output of other rules allows us to formulate phonological rules as simple generalizations, while an assumption that rules always apply to the underlying form forces us to repeat information already stated in other rules.

The theory of linear rule ordering also assumes that the order of rules is constant. That is, if two rules apply in the order A−B to one form, they cannot apply in the order B−A to the next. The ordering is also **transitive**. This means that if there are three rules A, B and C, where rules A and B apply in the order A−B and rules B and C apply in the order B−C, then rules A and C necessarily apply in the order A−C.

7.4 DIMINUTIVES IN DUTCH

The remainder of this chapter illustrates the *SPE* rule-based model on the basis of diminutive formation in varieties of Dutch. We deal with Standard Dutch and with a variant of the dialect of Sittard and Geleen. In addition, data from other dialects, including Utrecht Dutch, are dealt with in the questions.

There are a number of phonological rules that all varieties of Dutch share. For the purposes of diminutive formation, there are three such variety-neutral rules: FINAL DEVOICING, PALATALIZATION and DEGEMINATION.

7.4.1 Final devoicing

Recall that in Dutch, no voiced obstruents can appear in the coda, a constraint which we referred to earlier as FINAL DEVOICING. For instance, underlying [bɔrd] 'plate' only appears with its [d] in the plural ['bɔrdən], its singular form being [bɔrt]. Because any underlying obstruents in the words to be discussed in this chapter appear in coda position in the diminutive form, we will represent all coda obstruents as voiceless in these data.

7.4.2 Palatalization

The articulatory contact for the coronals [t,s,n] is between the tip and/or blade of the tongue and the alveolar ridge, the sides making a complete closure with the gums. When these consonants appear before [j], the contact is between the forward part of the front of the tongue, i.e. the zone behind the blade, and the palatal area immediately behind the alveolar ridge. Thus, instead of alveolar, these coronal consonants are prepalatal in this context, and PALATALIZATION (17) thus assimilates [t,s,n] to their [−anterior] counterparts [c,ʃ,ɲ]. For instance, before the pronoun [jə] 'you', the verbal forms [eːt] 'eat', [lɑs] 'weld', [kɑn] 'can' are pronounced [eːc], [lɑʃ], [kɑɲ]. The [j] itself tends to be absorbed by the preceding consonant in what is sometimes referred to as a COALESCENT ASSIMILATION process. Thus, 'eat you' ('are you eating?') is [eːcjə] or [eːcə]. The coronal appproximant [l], which is articulated with the tip touching the alveolar ridge, does not undergo the rule. PALATALIZATION may affect more than one consonant. For instance, in [lɪnt] 'ribbon' both [n] and [t] will become prepalatal before [j], as in [lɪɲcə]. In Chapter 12 we will see that this can be achieved in a single operation in a 'nonlinear' representation of segments, in which the place features for [n] and [t] would be specified only once for both segments. In the 'linear' *SPE* representation, each segment is separately specified for the place features, and we therefore need to include the term 'C$_0$' (i.e. 'ignoring any following consonant(s)') in the rule to make sure the focus can be [n] if [t] follows (as well as [t,n,s] when ## follows). As will be clear, the rule can apply across word boundaries. (The use of a transformational format would also be possible.)

(17) PALATALIZATION $\begin{bmatrix} -\text{approx} \\ \text{COR} \end{bmatrix} \rightarrow [-\text{ant}] \: / \_\_ \: C_0 \: (\#\#) \: [-\text{ant}]$

In Sittard Dutch and the dialects further to the south, the (pre-)palatal segments that result from the rule also appear in underlying representations, as in [lɛɲc] 'ribbon' and [mɑɲ] 'basket' (Schelberg 1979). In such cases, there is no reason to assume that a [j] follows these segments, either in the underlying representation or on the surface. Because the segments derived by PALATALIZATION are not distinct from the underlying segments, we will assume that [j] deletes after the application of PALATALIZATION in Sittard Dutch, and we will make the same assumption for Standard Dutch.

7.4.3   Degemination

DEGEMINATION forbids the occurrence of a sequence of identical [+cons] segments (cf. Q53). It applies, for instance, to the past tense of the verb [heːt] 'be called', which consists of the verb stem and the suffix [tə]. The result is [heːtə], with one [t], which form is homophonous with the inflected form of the adjective [heːt], which consists of the stem and the suffix [ə]. We give the rule in (18), in a formulation that will allow it to apply both within and across word boundaries.

(18) DEGEMINATION $\begin{array}{ccc} [+\text{cons}] & (\#\#) & [+\text{cons}] \\ 1 & 2 & 3 \end{array} \rightarrow \emptyset \: 2 \: 3$ (Condition: 1 = 3)

7.5   STANDARD DUTCH

In Standard Dutch, the diminutive suffix has five alternants: bisyllabic [əcə], illustrated in (19a), and the four monosyllables [cə] (19b), [kjə] (19c), [pjə] (19d) and [jə] (19e).

(19)		*Stem*	*Diminutive*	
	a.	bɑl	bɑləcə	'ball'
	b.	ɛi	ɛicə	'egg'
	c.	koːnəŋ	koːnəŋkjə	'king'
	d.	raːm	raːmpjə	'frame'
	e.	rɔk	rɔkjə	'skirt'

A reasonable strategy is to take the alternant appearing after vowels to be the underlying form (cf. (19b)). Before PALATALIZATION, this alternant [cə] is [tjə]. Next, in order to obtain the bisyllabic form of (19a), we need to insert [ə] after some nouns. Third, in order to get [jə], we need to delete [t]. Fourth, [pjə] and [kjə] can be produced by a rule that changes the place of articulation of [t] to that of a preceding consonant. We will call these rules ə-INSERTION, t-DELETION and PLACE ASSIMILATION, respectively. The data in (20a) illustrate ə-INSERTION.

(20) a. slaŋ-tjə   slaŋətjə   'snake'

bɔm-tjə   bɔmətjə   'bomb'

pɑn-tjə   pɑnətjə   'pot'

bɑl-tjə   bɑlətjə   'ball'

snɔr-tjə   snɔrətjə   'moustache'

b. rɔk   rɔkjə   'skirt'

kraːχ   kraːχjə   'collar'

c. raːm   raːmpjə   'frame'

oːr   oːrtjə   'ear'

koːnəŋ   koːnəŋkjə   'king'

All the stems in (20a) end in a sonorant consonant, in contrast to those in (20b). The insertion of schwa thus appears to be triggered by the value of [±son] of the stem-final consonant. However, no schwa is inserted after the stems in (20c), which also end in a sonorant consonant. A further requirement, therefore, is that the vowel in the last syllable should be [−tense]. The (nonmarginal) monophthongs of Standard Dutch are given in (21). The five lax vowels are given on the left of each cell, and the seven tense monophthongs on the right. Dutch also has the diphthongs [ɛi,œy,ʌu], which end in [+tense] second elements [i,y,u] and thus are correctly exempted from the rule.

(21)

	[−back] [−round]	[−back] [+round]	[+back] [−round]	[+back] [+round]
[+high, −low]	ɪ, i	ʏ, y		u
[−high, −low]	ɛ, eː	øː		ɔ, oː
[−high, +low]			ɑ, aː	

If we assume that the vowel [ə] is neither tense nor lax, and the feature [±tense] is therefore irrelevant for this segment, we can formulate the rule as in (22). In Chapter 15, we will see that there is the additional condition that the last syllable should be the head of a foot, a fact which we will ignore here.

(22)   ə-INSERTION $\emptyset \rightarrow ə / [-\text{tense}] \begin{bmatrix} +\text{cons} \\ +\text{son} \end{bmatrix} + \_\_ X]_{\text{DIM}}$

We must specify in the rule that [tjə], indicated as X, represents the diminutive suffix, because the rule does not apply to similar segment strings arising in different morphological contexts. Thus, [lɑm-tə] 'lame-ness', or the word sequence [kɑm-t jə] 'comb-3SG your', are not subject to the rule.

We move on to the alternant [jə], which appears in the data in (23). The forms in (23b) have undergone PALATALIZATION of [s] before [j], after [t] was deleted.

(23) a. lɑp-tjə   lɑpjə   'cloth'

drœyf-tjə   drœyfjə   'grape'

kraːχ-tjə   kraːχjə   'collar'

rɔk-tjə   rɔkjə   'skirt'

b. faːs-tjə   faːʃə   'vase'

pɑs-tjə   pɑʃə   'step'

The observation to be made here is that [jə] appears after obstruents. What we need, then, is t-DELETION, as given in (24). Again, since [t]s are not deleted in comparable phonological contexts arising elsewhere, reference to the suffix is included in the rule's SD.

(24) t-DELETION $t \rightarrow \emptyset \: / \: [-son] + \underline{} \: jə]_{DIM}$

A complication arises in the case of stems that end in [t]. In the data in (25a,b) the stem-final [t] is itself preceded by an obstruent. As shown, both the [t] of the stem and the [t] of the suffix are deleted in such cases. (In (25), we see the effect of PALATALIZATION in the word for 'fist' on [sj], which sequence arises after the deletion of both [t]s, as well as on [nt] in the word for 'ribbon'.)

(25) a.   bɔχt-tjə   bɔχjə   'bend'
           kɑft-tjə   kɑfjə   'book cover'
      b.   fœyst-tjə   fœyʃə   'fist'
      c.   lɪnt-tjə   lɪɲɕə   'ribbon'

In order to get rid of stem-final [t] before [tjə], we invoke DEGEMINATION (18). The derivation in (26) shows how (18) and (24) delete both [t]s in [bɔχt + tjə]. In forms like [lɪɲɕə] (25c), in which a stem-final [t] appears after a sonorant, we see why DEGEMINATION needs to precede t-DELETION, also as shown in (26).

(26)   bɔχt-tjə   rɔk-tjə   lɪnt-tjə
      DEGEMINATION (18)   bɔχ∅ tjə   (n.a.)   lɪn∅ tjə
      t-DELETION (24)   bɔχ ∅jə   rɔk ∅jə   (n.a.)

Last, we need to account for the assimilation of [t] to [p,k]. Some nouns undergoing PLACE ASSIMILATION are given in (27). Evidently, [t] assimilates to the place of articulation of the stem-final nasal. (Since tense vowels are not allowed before [ŋ] in Dutch words, we can only show the assimilation of [t] to [k] after an unstressed syllable.) If we formulate the rule as in (28), where 'αPLACE' stands for all the features specifying the place of articulation, it will apply vacuously to [n-tjə], as in [sxun-tjə].

(27) raːm-tjə   raːmpjə   'window'
      beːzəm-tjə   beːzəmpjə   'broom'
      koːnəŋ-tjə   koːnəŋkjə   'king'

(28) PLACE ASSIMILATION $t \rightarrow [\alpha PLACE] \: / \: \begin{bmatrix} +nas \\ \alpha PLACE \end{bmatrix} + \underline{} \: jə]_{DIM}$

Representative derivations are given in (29). (We will use a dash for 'nonapplication' from now on.)

(29)	ɛi-tjə	raːm-tjə	bɔm-tjə	lɪnt-tjə	bɔχt-tjə	lɑp-tjə
ə-INSERTION (22)	–	–	bɔm-ətjə	–	–	–
DEGEMINATION (18)	–	–	–	lɪn∅ tjə	bɔχ∅-tjə	–
t-DELETION (24)	–	–	–	–	bɔχ-∅jə	lɑp∅jə
PLACE ASSIMILATION (28)	–	raːm-pjə	–	vac.	–	–
PALATALIZATION (17)	ɛicə	–	bɔməcə	lɪɲɕə	–	–
Output	ɛicə	raːmpjə	bɔməcə	lɪɲɕə	bɔχjə	lɑpjə

Q70

---

1. What is the diminutive form of [flɑm]? Give the derivation of this form. Demonstrate that ə-INSERTION needs to apply before PLACE ASSIMILATION.
2. What is the diminutive form of [feːst] 'party'? Give the derivation of this form. Demonstrate that DEGEMINATION should apply before t-DELETION.
3. The diminutive of [hɛmt] (*hemd* 'shirt') is [hɛmpjə]. Give the derivation of this form. Show that PLACE ASSIMILATION is crucially ordered after DEGEMINATION.

7.6 THE DIALECT OF SITTARD

The phonology of diminutive formation in the dialect of Sittard differs in a number of respects from the same morphological process in the standard language. Table 7.1 gives a comparative survey of 33 etymologically related words. First, as can be seen in [ɛikə] (item 1), the basic form of the suffix would appear to be [-kə] rather than [-cə]. The alternant [cə] does occur, though, as in [tɛɲcə] (item 13). Second, Sittard has no ə-INSERTION. All the Sittard forms that correspond to diminutive forms that have inserted schwas in the standard language appear without schwa in Sittard (cf. items 7, 17, 18, 19, 23, 24). Third, Sittard has UMLAUT, a rule which fronts stressed vowels preceding the suffix in the stem (for instance items 2–5). Fourth, an alternant [-skə] appears in, for instance, [ʃlɛŋskə] (item 7).

Taking our cue from the alternants appearing after vowels, we will assume that [kə] is the underlying form. First, we will take care of UMLAUT. The requirement appears to be that the last stressed (nonschwa) vowel of the stem should be front. The monophthongs of Sittard Dutch are given in (30). Whenever the last full vowel of the stem is [+back], the diminutive has the [−back] counterpart, as can be seen in items 2, 3, 4, 5, 8, 9, 11, 25. Because in [kʊmˈkʊmər] (item 11) the umlauted vowel is followed by an unstressed syllable in the stem, provision has been made for an optional schwa-containing syllable in the formulation in (31).

(30)		[−back] [−round]	[−back] [+round]	[+back] [−round]	[+back] [+round]
	[+high, −low]	ɪ, i, iː	ʏ, y, yː		ʊ, u, uː
	[−high, −low]	eː	øː		oː
	[−high, +low]	ɛ, ɛː	œ, œː	ɑ, aː	ɔ, ɔː

(31) SITTARD UMLAUT $V \rightarrow [-back] / \_\_ (C_0 \, ə) \, C_0 + kə]_{\text{DIM}}$

Table 7.1
Noun stems and diminutive forms in Standard Dutch and the dialect of Sittard

Gloss		Standard Dutch		Sittard	
1.	'egg'	ɛi	ɛicə	ɛi	ɛikə
2.	'rag'	lɑp	lɑpjə	lɑp	lɛpkə
3.	'grape'	drœyf	drœyfjə	druːf	dryːfkə
4.	'collar'	kraːχ	kraːχjə	kraːx	krɛːçskə
5.	'skirt'	rɔk	rɔkjə	rɔk	rœkskə
6.	'king'	koːnəŋ	koːnəŋkjə	køːnəŋ	køːnəŋskə
7.	'snake'	slɑŋ	slɑŋəcə	ʃlɑŋ	ʃlɛŋskə
8.	'needle'	naːlt	naːlcə	nɔːʎ	nœːʎkə
9.	'chair'	stul	stulcə	ʃtɔul	ʃtœylkə
10.	'adventure'	aːvənˈtyːr	aːvənˈtyːrcə	aːvənˈtyːr	aːvənˈtyːrkə
11.	'cucumber'	kɔmˈkɔmər	kɔmˈkɔmərcə	kʊmˈkʊmər	kʊmˈkʏmərkə
12.	'evening'	aːvənt	aːvəɲcə	ɔːvənt	œːvəɲcə
13.	'aunt'	tɑntə	tɑntəcə	tɑnt	tɛɲcə
14.	'side'	kɑnt	kɑɲcə	kɑɲc	kɛɲcə
15.	'ribbon'	lɪnl	lɪɲcə	lɛɲc	lɛɲcə
16.	'basket'	mɑnt	mɑɲcə	mɑɲ	mɛɲcə
17.	'flame'	flɑm	flɑməcə	vlɑm	vlɛmkə
18.	'bomb'	bɔm	bɔməcə	bʊm	bʏmkə
19.	'pot'	pɑn	pɑnəcə	pɑn	pɛŋkə
20.	'thumb'	dœym	dœympjə	duːm	dyːmkə
21.	'broom'	beːzəm	beːzəmpjə	bɛsəm	bɛsəmkə
22.	'frame'	raːm	raːmpjə	raːm	rɛːmkə
23.	'ball'	bɑl	bɑləcə	bɑl	bɛlkə
24.	'moustache'	snɔr	snɔrəcə	ʃnɔr	ʃnœrkə
25.	'ear'	oːr	oːrcə	oːr	øːrkə
26.	'shoe'	sχun	sχuɲcə	ʃoːn	ʃøːŋkə
27.	'vase'	faːs	faːʃə	vaːs	vɛːskə
28.	'step'	pɑs	pɑʃə	pɑs	pɛskə
29.	'cover'	kɑft	kɑfjə	kɑf	kɛfkə
30.	'fist'	fœyst	fœyʃə	vuːs	vyːskə
31.	'curve'	bɔχt	bɔχjə	bɔx	bœçskə
32.	'foot'	fut	fucə	vɔut	vœycə
33.	'plate'	bɔrt	bɔrcə	bɔrt	bœrcə

The data for [kraːx], [rɔk] and [ʃlɑŋ] (items 4, 5, 7) suggest that there is a rule inserting [s] between the stem and the suffix, if the stem ends in a dorsal consonant. S-INSERTION is given in (32).

(32)   SITTARD S-INSERTION $\emptyset \rightarrow s \,/ \begin{bmatrix} -\text{syll} \\ \text{DORSAL} \end{bmatrix} + \underline{\quad} \text{kə]}_{\text{DIM}}$

Next, forms like [œːvəɲcə, lɛɲcə, mɛɲcə] (items 12, 15, 16) suggest that there is a rule changing the [k] of the suffix into [c] after stem-final [t,c,ɲ], which we will refer to as k-FRONTING, given in (33). The feature that distinguishes these coronal consonants from [s] is [−cont], and the requirement is therefore that the last consonant of the stem should be a noncontinuant coronal. The dorsal [k] then acquires the features [COR] and [−ant], causing it to be [c]. Here, the assumption is that when [k] acquires [CORONAL], it loses [DORSAL].

(33)   SITTARD k-FRONTING $k \rightarrow \begin{bmatrix} \text{COR} \\ -\text{ant} \end{bmatrix} / \begin{bmatrix} \text{COR} \\ -\text{cont} \end{bmatrix} + \underline{\quad} \text{ə]}_{\text{DIM}}$

Q71   Sittard has two coronal laterals, [l] and [ʎ], occurring in the words for 'chair' and 'needle'. Would you class these segments as [+cont] or [−cont]? Hint: Consider the behaviour of k-FRONTING.

How are the three rules discussed so far ordered? First, UMLAUT does not interfere with the other two rules. It is triggered by the suffix, and its result, the front vowel, cannot make a difference to the structural description of any of the other rules. We will apply it as the first rule in our derivation. At first sight, rules (32) and (33) would also appear to be unordered, since they apply in mutually exclusive contexts: (32) applies if the stem ends in a velar consonant, and (33) applies if the stem ends in a coronal consonant. They are, however, indirectly ordered, because both rules are ordered with respect to an assimilation rule we have not considered so far. Consider items 19 and 29, repeated in (34), whose stems end in [n]. Importantly, [n] does not trigger k-FRONTING.

(34)   pɑn   pɛŋkə   *pɛɲcə
         ʃoːn   ʃøːŋkə   *ʃøːɲcə

The assimilation rule is needed to take [n] to [ŋ] before [k], creating [pɛŋkə], from [pɛn-kə]. This rule crucially intervenes between (32) and (33). On the one hand, we do not want [pɛn-kə] to undergo k-FRONTING, as shown in (34), on the other hand, we do not wish to subject [pɛn-kə] to s-INSERTION (*[pɛŋskə]). In other words, we first need to apply s-INSERTION, then change the [n] of the stem into [ŋ], and then apply k-FRONTING. The derivation of the diminutive form of 'pot' is given in (35), together with those of 'snake' and 'basket'.

(35)	pɑn-kə	ʃlɑŋ-kə	mɑɲ-kə
UMLAUT (31)	pɛn-kə	ʃlɛŋ-kə	mɛɲ-kə
S-INSERTION (32)	–	ʃlɛŋ-ske	–
n-ASSIMILATION	pɛŋ-kə	–	–
k-FRONTING (33)	–	–	mɛɲ-cə
Output	pɛŋkə	ʃlɛŋskə	mɛɲcə

As explained above, Sittard shares PALATALIZATION and DEGEMINATION with Standard Dutch. However, DEGEMINATION is ordered later than it is in Standard Dutch. First, it must be ordered after S-INSERTION (32), in order to prevent DEGEMINATION from removing the final [k] of [rɔk], which would produce the incorrect *[rœkə] (item 5). Second, DEGEMINATION must come after k-FRONTING (33), since the output of k-FRONTING is subject to DEGEMINATION in a case like [lɛɲc-kə] ([lɛɲc-kə] → [lɛɲc-cə] → [lɛɲcə] (item 15). And finally, PALATALIZATION must be ordered before DEGEMINATION as shown by in a form like [tɛɲc-cə], which is produced after k-FRONTING (item 13). This ordering is illustrated in (36). Observe that Sittard treats [c] like any other consonant: [cc] is reduced to [c], just as [tt] would be reduced to [t]. That is, [c] is not a cluster [cj] in Sittard.

(36)	rɔk-kə	lɛɲc-kə	tɑnt-kə
UMLAUT (31)	rœk-kə	*vac.*	tɛnt-kə
S-INSERTION (32)	rœk-skə	–	–
n-ASSIMILATION		–	–
k-FRONTING (33)	–	lɛɲc-cə	tɛnt-cə
PALATALIZATION (17)	–	*vac.*	tɛɲc-cə
DEGEMINATION (18)	–	lɛɲ-cə	tɛɲ-cə
Output	rœkskə	lɛɲcə	tɛɲcə

Q72	In the dialect of Wehl, ə-INSERTION applies in a somewhat different set of contexts than in the standard language, as shown in the following data (Haan 1996). What is the difference?				
	Standard		*Wehl*		
a.	snɔr	snɔrəcə	snɔr	snɣrəcə	'moustache'
b.	pɑn	pɑnəcə	pɑn	pɛnəkə	'pot'
c.	kɑm	kɑməcə	kɑm	kɛmkə	'comb'
d.	slɑŋ	slɑŋəcə	slɑŋ	slɛŋskə	'snake'
e.	stɑl	stɑləcə	stɑl	stɛləkə	'stable (noun)'

Q73   The underlying form of the diminutive suffix in the dialect of Utrecht is [ti]. Representative noun stems and diminutive forms are listed below (van den Berg 1975).

a.	ɛi	ɛiχi	'egg'
b.	lɑp	lɑpi	'rag'
c.	drœyf	drœyfi	'grape'
d.	kraːχ	kraːχi	'collar'
e.	rɔk	rɔki	'skirt'
f.	koːnəŋ	koːnəŋki	'king'
g.	slɑŋ	slɑŋəχi	'snake'
h.	naːlt	naːltsi	'needle'
i.	stul	stultsi	'chair'
j.	mɑnt	mɑntsi	'basket'
k.	bɔm	bɔməχi	'bomb'
l.	pɑn	pɑnəχi	'pot'
m.	beːzəm	beːzəmpi	'broom'
n.	raːm	raːmpi	'frame'
o.	bɑl	bɑləχi	'ball'
p.	snɔr	snɔrəχi	'moustache'
q.	oːr	oːrtsi	'ear'
r.	sχun	sχuntsi	'shoe'
s.	pɑs	pɑsi	'step'
t.	kɑft	kɑfi	'cover'
u.	bɔχt	bɔχi	'bend'
v.	fut	futsi	'foot'
w.	bɔrt	bɔrtsi	'plate'

1. List the alternants of the diminutive suffix.
2. Of the rules in the derivation in (29), identify the ones that exist in the dialect of Utrecht (with replacement of [(t)jə] by [(t)i] where appropriate).
3. Two additional rules are needed to account for the alternations in the diminutive suffix. Determine the ordering of each of these two rules relative to the rules Utrecht shares with the standard language. Formulate these rules, using symbols for segments rather than distinctive features. (Hint: their formulation can be very simple if they are ordered right.)
4. Show the derivation of items a, e, k, n, u, v and w, using the presentational format of (29).

Q74   In Sittard Dutch, a diminutive form like [bɛɲcə] could be derived from six possible stems. What are they? Why isn't [bɛn] among them?

Q75 In many respects, the Brabant variety of Dutch as spoken in Alphen is similar to Sittard Dutch. First, the phonological form of the diminutive suffix after vowels is [kə], as can be seen in the word for 'egg', [aikə]. Moreover, s-INSERTION applies just as in Sittard. However, like Standard Dutch, it has ə-INSERTION, and lacks UMLAUT. A rule which neither Sittard nor Standard Dutch has is VOWEL LAXING, which in effect shortens the last vowel of the stem.

VOWEL LAXING V → [−tense] / __ C_0 + kə] $_{DIM}$

1. Determine the order in which VOWEL LAXING, s-INSERTION and ə-INSERTION are applied, on the basis of the data below.

2. Give derivations of items d, i and j.

a.	lɑp	lɑpkə	'cloth'
b.	krɔːx	krɔxskə	'collar'
c.	koːnəŋ	koːnəŋskə	'king'
d.	slɑŋ	slɑŋəskə	'snake'
e.	vlɑm	vlɑməkə	'flame'
f.	pɑn	pɑnəkə	'pot'
g.	dœːm	dœmkə	'thumb'
h.	bɪsəm	bɪsəmkə	'broom'
i.	snɔr	snɔrəkə	'moustache'
j.	oːr	ɔrkə	'ear'

7.7 CONCLUSION

The comparison between Standard and Sittard Dutch diminutive formation, together with the data in the questions, has shown that different varieties of a language may have different underlying forms for what is functionally the same morpheme. Thus, the standard language has [tjə], Sittard and Alphen have [kə], and Utrecht has [ti] as the UR for the diminutive suffix. Also, the sets of phonological rules they have may only be partly identical, as illustrated by the fact that Alphen and Sittard both have s-INSERTION, while Alphen has ə-INSERTION and VOWEL LAXING, which rules Sittard lacks, while conversely Sittard has UMLAUT, which is absent in Alphen. Varieties may also have the same rules, but apply them in different orders, as was the case with DEGEMINATION and PALATALIZATION in Standard Dutch and Sittard Dutch. Finally, varieties may also differ in having the same rule, or what can be seen as the same rule, but have slightly different versions of it, one having a wider SD (Structural Description) than the other. This was the case with ə-INSERTION, which applies after sonorants in the standard language, but after coronal sonorants in the dialect of Wehl.

These differences in a sense reflect the way in which phonological change is accounted for in a derivational grammar. First, rules may expand their SDs, and come to apply to wider sets of forms. Second, new rules may be added to the grammar, causing the difference between the URs and the SRs to be increased. Third, rules may come to be reordered, causing different outputs to be produced. And fourth, URs may be changed, a process known as **restructuring**, causing the distance between the URs and the SRs to be decreased. These theoretical implications were investigated in Kiparsky (1968, 1988) and King (1969).

In the model of Optimality Theory, phonological change must be understood as either of two things. First, it can result from the reranking of constraints, which in current OT are seen as universal. Second, it can be seen as restructuring, i.e. as the listing of a different UR, something known in OT as **lexicon optimization**. We will not work these comments out any further in this course (but see Holt 2003). In the next chapter we will discuss the issue of rule ordering from the *SPE* perspective, which has led to the recognition of four possible types of rule interaction. Subsequently, we will consider the question how these interactions translate into the OT perspective, where ordered rules have been replaced by ranked constraints.

8

Transparency and opacity
with rules and constraints

8.1 INTRODUCTION

A number of questions raised by rule ordering have preoccupied many a phonologist over the years. Are there general principles that predict the order in which rules apply? Are there rule orders that are more natural or more expected than others? The work on these questions has led to the recognition of four types of rule interaction, in addition to the notions of opacity and transparency.

In this chapter, we first discuss the Elsewhere Condition, a convention that allows us to omit exceptions from a general rule, and then exemplify the descriptive effects of the four types of rule interaction. We then discuss opacity, both from a rule-based and a constraint-based perspective, and point out that opacity is a problem for OT, where all markedness constraints are surface constraints. We will consider four solutions that have been proposed in OT to handle opacity. We discuss Sympathy Theory, Comparative Markedness and Stratal OT and show why they are not successful. We finish the chapter with a discussion of OT with candidate chains.

8.2 EXTRINSIC AND INTRINSIC ORDERING

Is the order in which rules apply predictable from any properties of the rules concerned? If it is, no ordering statement would be necessary: the rule order is said to be **intrinsic**. If the order is not given by the theory, and an explicit ordering statement of the type *'Rule X applies before Rule Y'* is necessary, the rule order is **extrinsic**. The issue of intrinsic rule order occupied many phonologists in the 1970s, but the search for the principles that exhaustively govern the order in which rules apply is generally considered to have been unsuccessful (Kenstowicz and Kisseberth 1977). A principle that has stood the test of time is the ELSEWHERE CONDITION. This is really a principle governing the application of rules in general, and has been invoked in morphology as well as phonology. What it says is that when one rule applies to a subset of the forms that another rule applies to, the general rule is blocked from applying to that subset. So it is not just a principle governing **order**, but also application as such, in the sense that only one of the two rules will be allowed to apply. A morphological example will make it clear why this is a useful principle.

Take the English morphological rules given in (1) and (2). Rule (1) says: '*Attach the suffix [z] to noun stems in order to form the plural*', and rule (2) says: '*Attach the suffix [ən] to the noun stem* ox *in order to form the plural*'.

(1) $[[\quad]_N z]_{PLUR}$

(2) $[[ɔks]_N ən]_{PLUR}$

In order to prevent the formation of *oxes*, we must either stipulate that (2) applies before (1), or add to (1) the clause '*except in the case of* [ɔks]'. The ELSEWHERE CONDITION makes either move unnecessary: because (2) applies to a subset of the contexts specified by (1), it automatically blocks (1). It will be clear that this principle saves us from having to add all sorts of exception clauses to general rules. A Finnish phonological example, from Kiparsky (1973a), is given in (3).

(3)

Underlying	*Derived*	
menek	mene	'go'
menek alas	mene alas	'go down'
menek pois	menep pois	'go away'
menek kotiin	menek kotiin	'go home'

Word-final [k] in Finnish is deleted, unless a consonant follows, in which case the [k] assimilates to that consonant, creating a geminate. The k-ASSIMILATION rule is given in (4). The rule at issue is k-DELETION. Without the ELSEWHERE CONDITION, we would have to state this rule as (5), which explicitly specifies the context '*either when followed by a vowel or by pause*', i.e. '*except when a C follows*'.

(4) k-ASSIMILATION $\quad \begin{matrix} k\ \#\ C \\ 1\ 2\ 3 \end{matrix} \rightarrow 3\ 2\ 3$

(5) k-DELETION $k \rightarrow \emptyset\ /\ \_\_\ \#\left\{\begin{matrix} V \\ pause \end{matrix}\right\}$

If we were to formulate k-DELETION as (6), the ELSEWHERE CONDITION would ensure that it would only apply if (4) did **not** apply. Rule (4) applies to a proper subset of the forms to which (6) is applicable, and therefore applies first, blocking (6). As a result, (6) cannot apply to [menek pois]. Also, (6) will not apply to [k] in [menek kotiin], which after all was input to rule (4). In this form, (4) assimilated the 'original' [k] of [menek] to the [k] of [kotiin]. Although it applied vacuously, it did apply, thereby blocking (6).

(6) k-DELETION $k \rightarrow \emptyset\ /\ \_\_\ \#$

A widely quoted argument for *extrinsic* ordering is based on a case of dialectal variation in Canadian English (Joos 1942). The difference between the two dialects concerned can be described as resulting from different orderings of the same two rules, FLAPPING and PRE-FORTIS CLIPPING (the terms are from Wells 1982). The first rule, given in (7), causes a [t,d] to be pronounced as an alveolar tap before reduced syllables, as in ['sɪɾi] *city*, ['bɛɾɾ] *better*. Note that [ɾ] is voiced. The second rule (8) shortens vowels and sonorant consonants preceding voiceless segments. As a result of this rule, the [iː] in [biːd] *bead* is longer than that in [biːt] *beat*, the [ɛn] in [tɛnz] *tens* is longer than the [ɛn] in [tɛns] *tense*, and the [iː] in ['tiːzɪŋ] *teasing* is longer that in ['liːsɪŋ] *leasing*. (More adequate statements of these rules are possible, but not necessary for the point at issue.) We will use an ad hoc feature [±long].

(7) FLAPPING $[t,d] \rightarrow ɾ \,/\, [-cons]$ ___ $\begin{bmatrix} V \\ -stress \end{bmatrix}$

(8) PRE-FORTIS CLIPPING $[+voice] \rightarrow [-long] \,/\,$ ___ $[-voice]$

In some dialects, these rules apply in the order FLAPPING – PRE-FORTIS CLIPPING. That is, the words *rider* ('someone who rides') and *writer* ('someone who writes') are homophones, both being pronounced ['raɪɾər], while *ride* and *write* are [raɪd] and [rʌɪt] (where [ʌɪ] represents a shortened [aɪ].) This is shown in (9).

(9)		'raɪd-ər	'raɪt-ər	raɪd	raɪt
	Rule (7)	ɾ	ɾ	*(n.a.)*	*(n.a.)*
	Rule (8)	*(n.a.)*	*(n.a.)*	*(n.a.)*	ʌɪ
	Output	'raɪɾər	'raɪɾər	raɪd	rʌɪt

In most Canadian speech, however, the pronunciations of these same words are [raɪɾər], [rʌɪɾər], [raɪd] and [rʌɪt]. This situation is obtained if we reverse the order of the rules, as shown in (10).

(10)		'raɪd-ər	'raɪt-ər	raɪd	raɪt
	Rule (8)	*(n.a.)*	ʌɪ	*(n.a.)*	ʌɪ
	Rule (7)	ɾ	ɾ	*(n.a.)*	*(n.a.)*
	Output	'raɪɾər	'rʌɪɾər	raɪd	rʌɪt

Clearly, if dialects can differ depending on the order in which two rules apply, it cannot be the case that rule ordering is predictable.

8.3   FEEDING, COUNTERFEEDING, BLEEDING, COUNTERBLEEDING

Early attempts to find universal principles governing the order in which rules apply led to a categorization of **rule interactions** (Kiparsky 1968). The idea was that certain rule orderings were more natural or expected than others, and that phonological change could in part be explained by assuming that in the course of time rules tend to reorder so that they come to have natural orders. While the principles have been abandoned, the terms used to refer to the different types of interaction have acquired wide currency. Four types will be distinguished. In every case two rules are assumed, which will be referred to as rule A and rule B.

8.3.1   Feeding order

If Rule A increases the number of the forms to which rule B can apply, the order A−B is a feeding order. The British English data in (11) illustrate PREGLOTTALIZATION, given in (12), which rule glottalizes voiceless plosives in the coda.

(11)   *Underlying*   *Derived*
        lʊkt   lʊˀkt   *looked*
        kæts   kæˀts   *cats*
        hɪnts   hɪnˀts   *hints*
        kæmpgraʊnd   kæmˀpgraʊnd   *campground*

(12)   PREGLOTTALIZATION

$$\begin{bmatrix} -\text{cont} \\ -\text{voice} \end{bmatrix} \rightarrow [+\text{constr}] \, / \, [+\text{voice}] \underline{\quad} \, (\# \, \#) \, C$$

Now consider the data in (13). In the first and second columns, we see that between a nasal and a voiceless fricative in the same syllable a voiceless plosive is inserted, whose place of articulation is that of the preceding nasal. As shown in the third column, this rule of FORTIS PLOSIVE INSERTION (14) applies before (12), and thus causes words like *prince*, which underlyingly end in a nasal consonant followed by a fricative, to be input to rule (12). That is, (14) feeds (12).

(13)   *Underlying*   *Fortis stop*   *Preglottalization*
        prɪns   prɪnts   prɪnˀts   *prince*
        lɛnθ   lɛnkθ   lɛnˀkθ   *length*
        wɔːmθ   wɔːmpθ   wɔːmˀpθ   *warmth*

(14)   FORTIS STOP INSERTION

$$\emptyset \rightarrow \begin{bmatrix} -\text{cont} \\ -\text{voice} \\ \alpha\text{PLACE} \end{bmatrix} / \left(\ldots \begin{bmatrix} C \\ +\text{nas} \\ \alpha\text{PLACE} \end{bmatrix} - \begin{bmatrix} C \\ +\text{cont} \\ -\text{voice} \end{bmatrix} \ldots \right) \sigma$$

8.3.2   Counterfeeding order

If Rule A increases the number of the forms to which rule B can apply, the order B−A is a counterfeeding order. The French feminine adjectival suffix is [ə]. The language has a rule that deletes word-final [ə], which is given as ə -DELETION in (15). The language also has FINAL CONSONANT DELETION (16), which deletes certain word-final consonants in contexts other than before a vowel or glide, causing [pətit] to be pronounced [pəti] in the context concerned. FINAL CONSONANT DELETION applies before ə-DELETION. If the rules applied in the opposite (feeding) order, ə-DELETION would cause the feminine alternant of 'little' to be homophonous with the masculine form. In other words, the rules apply in counterfeeding order, as illustrated in (17) for the forms for 'little nephew' and 'little niece'.

(15) ə-DELETION ə → Ø/ __ #

(16) FINAL CONSONANT DELETION C → Ø/ __ # # [+ cons]

(17)

	pətit nəvø	pətit-ə njɛs
Rule (16)	Ø	*(n.a.)*
Rule (15)	*(n.a.)*	Ø
	pəti nəvø	pətit njɛs

8.3.3 Bleeding order

If Rule A decreases the number of the forms to which rule B can apply, the order A−B is a bleeding order. This type of interaction, in which Rule A prevents Rule B from applying to particular forms, occurs in the derivation of the English plural. In Chapter 7, it was shown that I-INSERTION prevents DEVOICING from applying to a form like [bʌs-z] by separating the final [z] from the stem-final obstruent. In (18), this interaction is shown. That is, I-INSERTION bleeds DEVOICING.

(18)

	bæk-z	kɪs-z	aɪ-z
I-INSERTION	*(n.a.)*	I	*(n.a.)*
DEVOICING	S	*(n.a.)*	*(n.a.)*
	bæks	kɪsɪz	aɪz

Thus, when two rules A and B are in a counterfeeding order, the application of rule A *does not increase* the number of forms to which rule B can apply. When they are in a bleeding order, rule A actually *decreases* the number of forms to which rule B can apply.

8.3.4 Counterbleeding order

If Rule A decreases the number of the forms to which rule B can apply, the order B–A is a counterbleeding order. If two rules can apply to the underlying form, this order enables both rules actually to do so. In the Kaatsheuvel dialect of Dutch, [ə] is inserted between the noun stem and the diminutive suffix, if the stem ends in a lax vowel followed by a sonorant consonant. Thus we find it in (19a), but not in (19b), which stem ends in an obstruent, or in (19c), which stem has a tense vowel. The rule of ə-INSERTION is given in (20). Here, X is a free variable, and represents whatever shape the diminutive suffix has.

(19)

a.	snɔr-kə	snɔrəkə	'moustache'
	hɑl-kə	hɑləkə	'hall'
	kɑm-kə	kɑməkə	'comb'
b.	lɑp-kə	lɑpkə	'cloth'
	mʏs-kə	mʏskə	'sparrow'
c.	raːm-kə	raːmkə	'window'

(20) ə-INSERTION $\emptyset \rightarrow ə\,/\,[-\text{tense}]\begin{bmatrix} +\text{cons} \\ +\text{son} \end{bmatrix} + \underline{\quad} \, X]_{\text{DIM}}$

Kaatsheuvel also has a rule which inserts [s] between the dimunitive suffix [kə] and a stem-final dorsal consonant. Thus, s-INSERTION (21) breaks up a sequence of two dorsal consonants, as in [bɑkskə], from [bɑk- kə] 'tray', [maːxske], from [maːx-kə] 'stomach'.

(21) s-INSERTION $\emptyset \rightarrow s\,/\,\begin{bmatrix} +\text{cons} \\ \text{DORSAL} \end{bmatrix} + \underline{\quad} \, \text{kə]}_{\text{DIM}}$

If we want to know how these two rules interact, we need to consider the diminutive form of a word like [slɑŋ] 'snake', which satisfies both rules. Let us suppose – contrary to fact – that it is *[slɑŋəkə]. In order to obtain this form, we would have to apply ə-INSERTION first, so as to destroy the context of the two adjacent dorsal consonants. This would be a bleeding order. The correct form, however, is [slɑŋəskə]. That is, we need to apply the rules in a counterbleeding order: first (21), then (20).

(22)

	bɑk-kə	slɑŋ-kə	snɔr-kə
Rule (21)	s	s	*(n. a.)*
Rule (20)	*(n.a.)*	ə	ə
	bɑkskə	slɑŋəskə	snɔrəkə

Q76 Mwera has three rules, given as (1), (2) and (3) below. Two noun stems in Mwera are [gomo] 'lip' and [kuja] 'cape bean'. The plural is formed by prefixing a nasal consonant, whose underlying form is [n]. The plural surface forms are [ŋomo] and [ŋguja]. The following three rules derive the surface forms (Kenstowicz and Kisseberth 1977: 157).

(1) $\begin{bmatrix} -\text{son} \\ -\text{cont} \\ +\text{voice} \end{bmatrix} \rightarrow \emptyset\,/\,[+\text{nas}] \underline{\quad}$

(2) $\begin{bmatrix} -\text{son} \\ -\text{cont} \end{bmatrix} \rightarrow [+\text{voice}]\,/\,\begin{bmatrix} -\text{syl} \\ +\text{nas} \end{bmatrix} \underline{\quad}$

(3) $\begin{bmatrix} -\text{syl} \\ +\text{nas} \end{bmatrix} \rightarrow [\alpha\text{PLACE features}]\,/\,\underline{\quad}\begin{bmatrix} -\text{cont} \\ \alpha\text{PLACE features} \end{bmatrix}$

1. Suggest suitable names for these rules.
2. Please show that of the six possible orders that these rules could have, only one is correct.

Q77 Dutch has a number of rules affecting the feature [±voice] in obstruents. In order to derive the surface forms in the second column from the underlying forms in the first, four rules are required: DEGEMINATION, FINAL DEVOICING, PROGRESSIVE DEVOICING and REGRESSIVE VOICING. The first two can be formalized as follows:

$$\text{DEGEMINATION} \quad \begin{array}{ccc} [+cons] & (\#) & [+cons] \\ 1 & 2 & 3 \end{array} \quad \rightarrow \emptyset\ 2\ 3$$

Condition: 1 = 3

FINAL DEVOICING $[-son] \rightarrow [-voice] / \_\_ C_0 \#$

Underlying	Derived	Gloss
a. laːt#blujər	laːdblujər	'late developer'
b. bad#bruk	badbruk	'bathing trunks'
c. kʌud#vyːr	kʌutfyːr	'gangrene'
d. ʋand#teːχəl	ʋanteːχəl	'wall tile'
e. leːz#fʌut	leːsfʌut	'reading error'
f. lup#zœyvər	lupsœyvər	'very pure'
g. boːt#tɔχt	boːtɔχt	'boat trip'
h. kaːz#zaːk	kaːsaːk	'cheese shop'
i. kɔp#bal	kɔbal	'header' (football)
j. χʌud#dɛlvər	χʌudɛlvər	'prospector'
k. χʌud#koːrts	χʌutkoːrts	'gold fever'
l. krab#sχaːv	krapsχaːf	'scraper'
m. leːz#brɪl	leːzbrɪl	'reading glasses'
n. hɛis#balk	hɛizbalk	'hoisting beam'

1. Determine what the other two rules should do, and how the four rules should be ordered.
2. Give formal notations of PROGRESSIVE DEVOICING and REGRESSIVE VOICING.
3. Give the derivations of items d, f, h, i, m.

Q78 The river *Linge* [lɪŋə] flows not far from Kaatsheuvel. What would you expect the diminutive form to be?

Q79 In (10), the order in which FLAPPING and PRE-FORTIS CLIPPING are applied to *rider* and *writer* in mainstream Canadian English results in different surface forms for these two words. What type of rule order is this?

8.4 TRANSPARENCY AND OPACITY: RULES AND CONSTRAINTS

Which of the rule orderings discussed in the previous section are the more natural, or more expected? The answer depends to some extent on the perspective that is taken. Kiparsky (1968) has argued that historical change could in part be explained by assuming that over time rules tend to re-order so as to maximize their application. If rule A feeds rule B, the number of forms to which rule B can apply is increased, because rule A supplies additional forms to rule B, as was the case for PREGLOTTALIZATION discussed above. As a result, rule B can be maximally applied. Obviously, in a counterfeeding order, rule B will not be supplied with additional forms to which it can apply, as illustrated for FRENCH FINAL CONSONANT DELETION in 8.3.2. Similarly, if rule A *does not remove* forms to which rule B can potentially apply (B–A: a bleeding order), the opposite order, a counterbleeding, allows rule B to apply maximally. Thus, on the basis of the principle of **maximal rule application**, feeding and counterbleeding are the natural rule orders. Whereas there was general consensus that feeding was more natural than counterfeeding, there was disagreement as to whether bleeding or counterbleeding should be considered more natural (or less 'marked').

But what determines what is 'marked'? From the perspective of rule maximization, feeding and counterbleeding are the unmarked rule orders, but an alternative perspective was that rules are more natural when their application is transparent on the surface. From the point of view of **maximal rule transparency**, bleeding and feeding are the natural orders. To see this, two more cases of counterfeeding and counterbleeding rule orders are presented.

In Gran Canarian Spanish (Oftedal 1985), the voiced stops /b, d, g/ are subject to SPIRANTIZATION when they are in intervocalic position and are realized as [β, ð, ɣ], respectively. Additionally, VOICING causes intervocalic voiceless stops [p, t, k] to be realized as voiced [b, d, g], as illustrated in (23).

(23) UR   SPIRANTIZATION
      /roba/   [roβa]   'he/she steals'
      /nada/   [naða]   'nothing'
      /la gana/   [la ɣana]   'the appetite'

      UR   VOICING
      /tipiko/   [tibigo]   'typical'
      /la kama/   [la gama]   'the bed'
      /una tjɛnda/   [una djɛnda]   'a shop'

A counterfeeding application of SPIRANTIZATION followed by VOICING straightforwardly generates the correct surface forms. However, from a surface perspective, the voiced plosive in [la gama] 'the bed' does not make good sense, given the existence of SPIRANTIZATION. By this rule, intervocalic /g/ surfaces as [ɣ], and yet [g] does occur in intervocalic position in surface forms like [la gama].

Or again, Slovak (Rubach 2000) has a diminutive suffix /æ/ which triggers PALATALIZATION of a preceding stem-final coronal, as in *páňa* /pan+æ/ [paɲæ] 'master (dimin.)'. A further process of æ-BACKING backs underlying /æ/ to [a] after non-labials, by which [paɲæ] becomes surface [paɲa]. So, when the diminutive suffix /æ/ is preceded by a labial consonant, as in *holúbä* /holub+æ/ [holubæ] 'pigeon (dimin.)', neither rule applies. In traditional rule terminology, this is an example of a counterbleeding rule order: PALATALIZATION must be applied before æ-BACKING to prevent /pan+æ/ from surfacing as incorrect *[pana]. From the perspective of maximal rule application, the counterbleeding rule order is natural, since it makes PALATALIZATION maximally applicable, but from a surface perspective it is not natural, since it makes PALATALIZATION a non-transparent rule. This is because the surface form [paɲa] has a palatalized consonant in the absence of the front vowel that causes the palatalization. In other words, something happens, but it is unclear (opaque, not transparent) *why* it does. For a counterfeeding rule order, things are exactly the other way round: something does *not* happen ([la gama] surfacing from /la kama/ instead of turning into [la ɣama]), but it is not clear why it does not. So, both counterfeeding and counterbleeding rule orders lead to surface opacity (i.e. to rules that are not transparent). Counterbleeding is often referred to as **over-application** and counterfeeding as **under-application** of rules.

In the next section we will show that opaque rule interactions (counterfeeding and counterbleeding rule orders) are problematic for OT and review four solutions that have been proposed in OT to deal with opacity.

8.5 OPACITY AND OT: FOUR SOLUTIONS

8.5.1 Counterfeeding opacity and Comparative markedness

OT has no problems in accounting for feeding (transparent) rule orders, but cannot handle counterfeeding (opaque) rule orders. This is illustrated for Gran Canarian Spanish in tableau (25), where we have used the two faithfulness constraints and the two markedness constraints listed in (24).

(24) IDENT(VOICE): A consonant in the output has the same 'voice' specification as in the input.
IDENT(CONT): A consonant in the output has the same 'continuant' specification as in the input.
VOICING: No voiceless intervocalic plosive.
SPIRANTIZATION: No voiced intervocalic plosive.

(25a)

/la gana/	VOICING	IDENT(VOICE)	SPIRANTIZATION	IDENT(CONT)
[la gana]			*!	
[la kana]	*!	*		
☞ [la ɣana]				*

(25b)

/la kama/	VOICING	IDENT(VOICE)	SPIRANTIZATION	IDENT(CONT)
[la gama]		*	*!	
[la kama]	*!			
☞ [la ɣama]		*		*

Tableau (25a) shows that, in order for SPIRANTIZATION to take place, the constraint SPIRANTIZATION must dominate IDENT(CONT). If it does not, the first output candidate will be selected as optimal. Similarly, as shown in (25b), to produce voiced intervocalic plosives, VOICING must dominate IDENT(VOICE). This ranking, however, incorrectly predicts that /la kama/ is optimally realized as [la ɣama] rather than as actual [la gama].

Q80 Show that the ranking of VOICING » IDENT(VOICE) below SPIRANTIZATION » IDENT(CONT) does not produce the correct results either. What is the incorrect result of this ranking for the intervocalic plosives?

Tableaux (25a) and (25b) thus show that OT can describe a feeding rule order for SPIRANTIZATION and VOICING, but cannot account for a counterfeeding interaction between them. As it happens, counterfeeding situations involving SPIRANTIZATION and VOICING are quite common. The same counterfeeding situation we gave for Gran Canarian Spanish can be observed in Sardinian (Bolognesi 1998) and Corsican (Gurevich 2004). Kaye (1975) proposed a functional motivation for counterfeeding opacity: keeping intact lexical contrasts and thus *avoiding neutralization*. Indeed, if SPIRANTIZATION and VOICING were to stand in a feeding relationship in Gran Canarian Spanish, the surface forms for minimal pairs like /nata/ [nada] 'cream' and /nada/ [naða] or /ropa/ [roba] 'clothes' and /roba/ [roβa] would be realized identically as [naða] and [roβa] respectively, and the underlying contrast would be neutralized on the surface. In fact, Gurevich (2004) observes in her study of 230 similar processes in a corpus of 153 languages that in the majority of cases (92%) they tend be non-neutralizing. Incidentally, this contrast preserving tendency is not only problematic for OT, but also for rule-based theory. Hale and Reiss (2008: 14) state: 'Opaque rules are not surface true, rules that are not surface true are harder to learn, failure to learn aspects of the ambient language constitutes a diachronic change, therefore, languages are more likely to lose a given instance of opacity than to gain one.' Now, if the unmarked rule order is a feeding rule order (Kiparsky 1982), it is not easy to understand why in the majority of cases a counterfeeding ordering between SPIRANTIZATION and VOICING is attested.

In OT, markedness constraints cannot refer to the input form and thus cannot refer to lexical contrasts. They evaluate candidates without looking at other candidates. **Comparative Markedness** (McCarthy 2003) in a way permits an indirect peek at underlying forms by introducing an output candidate that is identical to the underlying form.

Here is how it works. Markedness constraints no longer evaluate output candidates by themselves, but instead compare them with another output candidate. This special candidate is the most faithful, or fully faithful, candidate (FFC), which, in fact, is the underlying form as it would show up unaltered on the surface. Two situations can arise. In one case, the candidate that is evaluated contains a markedness violation that is also present in the FFC ('old' violation) and in the other case it does not ('new' violation). In order to be able to carry out this evaluation, each markedness constraint is split up in $^{N(EW)}$Markedness and $^{O(LD)}$Markedness. For the interaction between spirantization and voicing this means that we now have four constraints at our disposal, ^{N}Spirantization, ^{O}Spirantization, ^{N}Voicing and ^{O}Voicing. By ranking ^{O}Spirantization and ^{O}Voicing above the faithfulness constraints Ident(voice) and Ident(cont), counterfeeding Gran Canarian Spanish can now be described, as illustrated in tableau (26), where the FFC is given just below the underlying form.

(26a)

/la gana/	^{O}Spir	^{O}Voi	Ident(voice)	Ident(cont)	^{N}Spir	^{N}Voi
FFC [la gana]						
[la gana]	*!					
[la kana]			*!			*
☞ [la ɣana]				*		

(26b)

/la kama/	^{O}Spir	^{O}Voi	Ident(voice)	Ident(cont)	^{N}Spir	^{N}Voi
FFC [la kama]						
☞ [la gama]			*		*	
[la kama]		*!				
[la ɣama]			*	*!		

The crucial difference between tableau (26b) and tableau (25b) is that the output candidate [la gama] for /la kama/ does not violate ^{O}Spirantization, but low-ranked ^{N}Spirantization. It thus appears that Comparative Markedness, just as rules, can describe counterfeeding opacity, and can even provide a reasonable answer to the question why counterfeeding opacity is not uncommon. It allows us to keep lexical contrasts intact, by judging or evaluating 'derived' markedness differently from 'underlying' or 'lexical' markedness. In the next section, we will discuss Sympathy

Theory, given that Comparative Markedness, as we will show, is unable to account for counterbleeding opacity.

8.5.2   Counterbleeding opacity and Sympathy Theory

A counterbleeding rule order of Palatalization and æ-Backing leads to a palatalized consonant in Slovak [paɲa] for underlying /pan+æ/ 'master (dimin.)', which palatalized consonant is not transparent from a surface perspective. Tableau (28), where the faithfulness and markedness constraints in (27) are used, shows that counterbleeding opacity is as problematic for OT as counterfeeding opacity.

(27)   Ident(back): A vowel in the output has the same value for the feature 'back' as in the input.
Ident(anterior): A consonant in the output has the same value for the feature 'anterior' as in the input.
Palatalization: No non-palatalized coronal consonants before a front vowel.
æ-Backing: No [æ] after non-labials.

(28)

/pan+æ/	æ-Backing	Ident(back)	Palatalization	Ident(anterior)
panæ	*!		*	
paɲæ	*!			*
☞ pana		*		
paɲa		*		*!

Tableau (28) shows that the third output candidate is incorrectly selected as optimal instead of the actual Slovak form [paɲa].

> **Q81**   Show that a ranking æ-Backing » Ident(back) below Palatalization » Ident(anterior) is not helpful in obtaining a counterbleeding relationship between Palatalization and æ-Backing.

Before proceeding with Sympathy Theory, let us first explain why Comparative Markedness is unable to deal with counterbleeding opacity. In tableau (28), there is only one output candidate, the first one, [panæ], which satisfies both the faithfulness constraints and which, therefore, is the fully faithful candidate. Neither the optimal third output candidate nor the fourth output candidate, the one that should be optimal, violates any of the markedness constraints. This means that there is simply no ranking of the constraints æ-Backing and Palatalization, even if split up into Old and New versions, that could possibly result in [paɲa] becoming optimal over [pana].

Sympathy Theory (McCarthy 1999, 2002), just like Comparative Markedness, allows inspection of output candidates by comparing them with another output candidate. The output candidate to which other candidates are compared this time is not the underlying form disguised as the fully faithful candidate, but a judiciously selected candidate. A faithfulness constraint, the selector (marked ★), selects an output candidate, called the sympathetic candidate (marked ⊛). All other output candidates are required to look as much as possible like the sympathetic candidate and are checked whether they have the same faithfulness violations.

A Sympathy analysis for Slovak counterbleeding opacity (Rubach 2000) runs as follows. For the analysis to work, the selector, as you will work out in the next question, has to be the constraint IDENT(BACK). There are two output candidates in tableau (28) that do not violate this faithfulness constraint: the first two. Of these two, the second ([paɲæ]) is better than the first ([panæ]), as it does not violate PALATALIZATION. Therefore, [paɲæ] is selected as the sympathetic candidate. The constraint ⊛CUMUL evaluates whether all output candidates have the same faithfulness violations as the sympathetic candidate. As illustrated in (29), this identifies the correct output candidate, [paɲa], as optimal, given that the first and third output candidates do not have the sympathetic candidate's faithfulness violation of IDENT(ANTERIOR). The constraint ⊛CUMUL needs to be crucially ranked above IDENT(ANTERIOR). If not, [pana] would still be incorrectly the optimal output candidate.

(29)

/pan+æ/	æ-BACKING	ID (BACK) SELECTOR ★	PALATALIZATION	⊛CUMUL	ID(ANTERIOR)
panæ	*!		*	*	
paɲæ ⊛	*!				*
pana		*		*!	
☞ paɲa		*			*

Q82 Show that with IDENT(ANTERIOR) as the selector the third output candidate incorrectly becomes both the sympathetic as well as the optimal output candidate.

Sympathy Theory can thus, just as rules, describe counterbleeding opacity. Can it also deal with counterfeeding opacity? The short answer is no. To see why, we have repeated in (30) tableau (25b).

(30)

/la kama/	VOICING	IDENT(VOICE)	SPIRANTIZATION	IDENT(CONT)
[la gama]		*	*!	
[la kama]	*!			
☞ [la ɣama]		*		*

There are two faithfulness constraints that can serve as the selector for the sympathetic candidate. If IDENT(VOICE) were the selector, [la kama] would be the sympathetic candidate, as it is the only output candidate that does not violate IDENT(VOICE). However, the constraint ⊛CUMUL would have no effect at all, given that [la kama] itself has no faithfulness violations. If, by way of contrast, IDENT(CONT) were the selector, the choice for the sympathetic candidate would be between [la gama] and [la kama], of which two candidates [la gama] is the more harmonic given the ranking in (30) and thus the sympathetic candidate. The constraint ⊛CUMUL, this time, would signal a violation for [la kama], as it does not have the same faithfulness violation for IDENT(VOICE) as sympathetic [la gama]. However, ⊛CUMUL would remain silent for [la ɣama], which has the same, that is accumulates, [la gama]'s IDENT(VOICE) violation.

In this section, we have seen that Comparative Markedness does not work for counterbleeding opacity. We have briefly discussed Sympathy Theory and illustrated how it can handle counterbleeding opacity, but also why it cannot deal with counterfeeding opacity. Before turning to OT with candidate chains (a solution for opacity that can deal with both counterfeeding and counterbleeding in the same way), we will first briefly discuss Stratal OT.

8.5.3 Opacity and Stratal OT

In Chapter 9, we will see that there are good reasons to assume that, besides the underlying and the surface representation, there is an intermediate level of representation: the lexical representation. That idea has also been implemented in OT and is generally known as **Stratal OT**. Without going into the details, the basic idea is straightforward. The underlying form passes through a constraint hierarchy and yields an optimal intermediate output form. This form then is input to a second constraint hierarchy, potentially different from the first, and produces the optimal surface form (Booij 1997), Rubach (2000), Bermúdez-Otero (forthcoming) among others). For counterbleeding, opaque Slovak PALATALIZATION, Rubach (2000) has proposed the following analysis. In the first constraint hierarchy, the order of the constraints æ-BACKING and IDENT(BACK) is the opposite to that in tableau (28) above. This is illustrated in (31), where the optimal output candidate now becomes the second output candidate, [paɲæ], instead of [pana].

(31)

/pan+æ/	IDENT(BACK)	æ-BACKING	PALATALIZATION	IDENT(ANTERIOR)
panæ		*	*!	
☞paɲæ		*		*
pana	*!			
paɲa	*!			*

This optimal intermediate output form [paɲæ] is then input to a second constraint hierarchy, where the order of the constraints æ-BACKING and ID (BACK) is inverted, as illustrated in (32).

(32)

/paɲæ/	æ-Backing	Ident(back)	Palatalization	Ident(anterior)
panæ	*!		*	*
paɲæ	*!			
pana		*		*!
☞ paɲa		*		

The result of this two-level approach is that correct [paɲa] is selected as the optimal output form for underlying /pan+æ/.

> Q83   Provide a Stratal OT analysis of counterfeeding Gran Canarian. Hint: the relative ranking of Voicing and Ident(voice) and of Spirantization and Ident(cont) will need to be different at both levels. Hint: start by making Spirantization happen at the first level, but not Voicing.

In this section, we have briefly discussed Stratal OT. All the OT solutions that we have discussed up to now seem arbitrary. For Stratal OT there is some arbitrary switching around of constraints at the different levels. Why would Spirantization and Voicing be operative at different levels, where at first sight they seem to be identical in their application? In the terminology of lexical and post-lexical phonology to be discussed in the next chapter, they would both be considered to belong to the post-lexical component of the grammar, given that they apply across word boundaries and given that Spirantization produces a novel segment, [ɣ], that is a segment not belonging to the underlying consonant inventory of Gran Canarian Spanish. In addition, Comparative Markedness and Sympathy Theory are complementary theories, one for counterfeeding and the other one for counterbleeding. Even for the more theory-oriented phonologist, two theories for opacity would seem over the top. Moreover, both theories seem to put a rather heavy burden on the language-acquiring child, who will need to detect what the order of the New and Old Markedness constraints is and which Faithfulness constraint is going to be the selector. In the next section, we will briefly discuss a fourth solution to opacity: OT with candidate chains, which can deal with counterfeeding and counterbleeding in the same way.

8.5.4 Counterfeeding and counterbleeding opacity in OT with candidate chains

Looking back again at counterfeeding opacity in Gran Canarian Spanish, what one really wants to say is that it is all right for /la kama/ to change into [la gama], but that it should not further change into [la ɣama]. Similarly, for counterbleeding Slovak, that /pan+æ/ should *first* change to [paɲæ] and *then* to [paɲa], but not *directly* from /pan+æ/ to [pana]. To achieve this, it is necessary to keep track of the derivational history by which an input form changes into an output candidate. Standard OT cannot do that, as markedness constraints are output constraints and can refer neither to the input nor to the way input and output are connected. **OT with candidate chains** allows us to do precisely that. Evaluation does not take into account every possible candidate, but instead evaluates well-formed chains connecting a given input to an output. An output candidate is a chain of forms connecting input to output. The first member of every candidate chain is a fully faithful parse, violating none of the faithfulness constraints. Each successive form in a chain adds one faithfulness violation, and has to be more harmonic than the preceding form. Successive forms in a chain are required to accumulate all of the faithfulness violations of preceding forms. In short, a candidate chain is literally a series of forms that step-wise give up faithfulness in order to improve on markedness. In (33), we illustrate the candidate chains for Slovak /pan+æ/, where we have indicated below the candidate chain the faithfulness violations incurred by its successive forms.

(33)

1 /pan+æ/	\<panæ\>	No Faithfulness Violations	[panæ]
2 /pan+æ/	\<panæ\>	\<paɲæ\> ID(ANT)	[paɲæ]
3 /pan+æ/	\<panæ\>	\<pana\> ID(BACK)	[pana]
4 /pan+æ/	\<panæ\>	\<paɲæ\>, \<paɲa\> ID(ANT) ID(ANT) ID(BACK)	[paɲa]

All four chains start with the fully faithful parse and chains 2 and 3 each have one more form in which one faithfulness constraint is violated, respectively IDENT(ANTERIOR) and IDENT(BACK), and both improve on markedness; chain 2 on PALATALIZATION and 3 on æ-BACKING. The last chain has three forms and gradually improves on both PALATALIZATION and æ-BACKING. The second form in that chain violates IDENT(ANTERIOR). The third form accumulates that faithfulness violation and adds a violation of IDENT(BACK).

How can we implement the idea that /pan+æ/ should *first* change to [paɲæ] and *then* to [paɲa], but not *directly* from /pan+æ/ to [pana]? This is done by imposing some order in which faithfulness constraints may be violated in chains. For both counterfeeding and counterbleeding opacity, a new type of constraint is used, PREC(EDENCE), which has the form PREC (A, B), where A and B are faithfulness constraints. The constraint is violated when a violation of B is not preceded by a violation of A in a candidate chain, or when a violation of B is followed by a violation of A (McCarthy 2007). For Slovak, the constraint PREC (ID (ANT), ID (BACK)) can be used, as illustrated in (34).

(34)

/pan+æ/	æ-BACKING	IDENT(BACK)	PREC Id(ANT), Id(BACK)	PAL	ID(ANT)
1 /pan+æ/ <panæ> [panæ]	*!			*	
2 /pan+æ/ <panæ>, <paɲæ> [paɲæ]	*!				*
3 /pan+æ/ <panæ>, <pana> [pana]		*	*!		
4 ☞ /pan+æ/ <panæ>, <paɲæ>, <paɲa> [paɲa]		*			*

In (34), we have listed the output candidates in the first column, as usual, but added the input form and the chain connecting input to output. The constraint PREC(ID(ANT), ID(BACK)) is violated, whenever a violation of IDENT(BACK) is not preceded by a violation of IDENT(ANTERIOR). Candidate chain (33/34-1) has no faithfulness violations, so the constraint PREC (ID(ANT), ID(BACK)) is not relevant in the evaluation. The candidate chain (33/34-2), with output [paɲæ], has a violation of ID(ANTERIOR), but given that there is no violation of of ID(BACK) in that chain, the PREC constraint is again irrelevant for its evaluation. The third chain, (33/34-3), has a violation of ID(BACK), its only faithfulness violation, but, since that violation is not preceded by a violation of ID(ANTERIOR), it therefore incurs a violation of the PREC constraint. Candidate chain (33/34-4) has a violation of both faithfulness constraints, but in the order required by the PREC constraint, the violation of ID(BACK) is indeed preceded by a violation of IDENT(ANTERIOR).

In (35), we have provided the relevant candidate chains for counterfeeding Gran Canarian Spanish.

(35)

1 /la gana/	<la gana>	No FAITHFULNESS VIOLATIONS	[la gana]
2 /la gana/	<la gana>	**<lakana> ID(VOICE)	[la kana]
3 /la gana/	<la gana>	<la ɣana> ID(CONT)	[la ɣana]
4 /la kama/	<la kama>	<la gama> ID(VOICE)	[la gama]
5 /la kama/	<la kama>		[la kama]
6 /la kama/	<la kama>	<la gama>, <la ɣama> ID(VOICE) ID(VOICE) ID(CONT)	[la ɣama]

All these output candidate chains, except chain 2, are well-formed, since they gradually give up faithfulness and improve by one markedness step at a time. The second chain has a violation of IDENT(VOICE), but does not become less marked, but more marked, as it entails a violation of higher-ranked VOICING. The second output candidate in (35) is therefore ruled out from evaluation as it does not arise through a well-formed chain, which has been indicated by the double asterisk. Strictly speaking it should not be included for the evaluation, but, for clarity's sake, we will present it in tableau (36).

For Gran Canarian Spanish, we use the precedence constraint PREC (ID (CONT), ID (VOICE)), which is violated if a violation of ID(VOICE) is not preceded by a violation of ID(CONT), or if a violation of ID(VOICE) is followed by a violation of ID(CONT).

(36a)

/la gana/	VOICING	ID(VOICE)	PREC ID(CONT), ID(VOICE)	SPIRANT	ID(CONT)
1 /la gana/ \<la gana\> [la gana]				*!	
2 /la gana/ \<la gana\>, **\<la kana\> [la kana]	*!	*	*		
3 /la gana/ \<la gana\>, \<la ɣana\> ☞ [la ɣana]					*

(36b)

/la kama/	VOICING	ID(VOICE)	PREC ID(CONT), ID(VOICE)	SPIRANT	ID(CONT)
4 /la kama/ \<la kama\>, \<la gama\> ☞ [la gama]		*	*	*	
5 /la kama/ \<la kama\> [la kama]	*!				
6 /la kama/ \<la kama, la gama, la ɣama\> [la ɣama]		*	* *!		*

The constraint PREC (ID (CONT), ID (VOICE)) does not play a role in the evaluation of /la gana/, but only for /la kama/. In chain 4, the violation of ID (VOICE) in the second form is not preceded by a violation of ID (CONT), hence the violation mark. Similarly, for chain 6, the violation of ID (VOICE) is not preceded by a violation of ID (CONT), but, moreover, the violation of ID (VOICE) is followed by a violation of ID (CONT), and therefore there are two violations of the PREC constraint.

In this section, we have briefly illustrated how OT with candidate chains allows us to describe both counterfeeding and counterbleeding opacity with PREC constraints. An obvious improvement for OT is that counterfeeding and counterbleeding opacity are dealt with by a single theory, instead of two, Comparative Markedness and Sympathy. A further advantage of candidate chains is that it greatly reduces the number of possible output candidates. Only well-formed chains, determined by the constraint ranking of the language, enter the competition rather than an unlimited set of output forms, as in the original model described in Chapter 4. Contrariwise, in order to describe opacity some 'extrinsically' imposed order on the way an input form may be connected to an output is built back into the theory, in the form of PRECEDENCE constraints. If the set of constraints is truly universal, as we mentioned in Chapter 4, this implies that all the PRECEDENCE constraints required to describe all possible opaque interactions have to be part of that set.

8.6   CONCLUSION

In this chapter we have discussed and exemplified four possible types of rule interaction: feeding, counterfeeding, bleeding and counterbleeding. We established that counterfeeding and counterbleeding lead to opaque phonological surface forms—forms that contradict some phonological rule of the language, either by showing the effect of the rule where there is no longer any context for it (counterbleeding), or by not showing the effect where the context is present (counterfeeding).

We have also seen that OT has a special problem in accounting for opaque forms, given that markedness constraints intend to say something about surface forms, and are therefore inherently 'transparent'. We have reviewed four solutions that have been proposed within OT to deal with opacity. Comparative Markedness and Sympathy Theory have been proposed to describe counterfeeding and counterbleeding opacity, respectively, but these theories come at considerable cost. All markedness constraints have to be split up in New and Old versions in the case of Comparative Markedness, and in Sympathy Theory it is not obvious how to choose the faithfulness constraint that serves as the selector for the 'sympathetic' candidate. Stratal OT would appear to require some arbitrary ranking reversals at the different strata (or 'levels'). Finally, OT with candidate chains may appear to be the most attractive of the four proposals, as it can describe both counterfeeding and counterbleeding opacity, even if this comes at the cost of introducing a large family of PRECEDENCE constraints.

The basic observation made in Chapter 4 was that one of the goals of phonological theory is to account for the fact that morphemes may be pronounced differently depending upon their environment. When we compared rule-based and constraint-based descriptions, we argued that OT is to be preferred, given that it does not run into the duplication problem—the necessity of stating the same generalization both in a phonological rule and in a constraint, a problem inherent in rule-based descriptions. Also, OT was argued to be able to express directly how any new input forms from any donor language are brought in line with the structural demands of the recipient language. Systematic modifications in pronunciation thus seemed to be taken care of by OT. In this chapter, we have seen that OT can deal with opacity, a common fact of life in the phonologies of languages, only by introducing additional machinery that does not always seem well motivated.

Perhaps this is the point where we should step back and briefly evaluate the phonological enterprise. Since *SPE*, theoretical phonology has had a two-fold research agenda. One of these focused on representations, and has led to the introduction of moras, syllables, feet, and more, as we will show later in this book. The second has focused on levels of representation and how these are connected. While the first focus has led to exciting insights, the second focus on the phonological research agenda leaves us wondering what went wrong. Without much ado, a speaker of Gran Canarian Spanish will take a sound sequence [la gama] to refer to a representation /la kama/, just as he will take a sound sequence [la ɣama] to refer to a representation /la gama/. But none of the theories that we have discussed would appear to explain convincingly that what at some level must be /la kama/ or /pan+æ/ gets to be [la gama] and [paɲa] in actual pronunciation. Whether rule-based or constraint-based, all input-output models appear to have a speaker orientation in common, which perspective might be too narrow. There have been proposals that take the opposite perspective (Boersma 1998, Smolensky 1996, Kager 1999). Progress in this area could come from research into the way language production and perception is dealt with in real life, the language user's brain. Such research is now conducted both by psycholinguists on the basis of various behavioural tasks and neurocognitive scientists on the basis of the time course and localization of brain activity associated with producing and perceiving speech. Clearly, more research is required before phonological theory can claim to be psychologically real.

The next chapter is concerned with an issue that is relatively independent of the issue of how to describe phonological adjustments. It concerns the question of whether two levels of representation—one for underlying representations and one for surface representations—suffice to explain what we know about the pronunciation of languages.

Levels of representation

9.1 INTRODUCTION

In this chapter, we consider the question of how many phonological representations a word has. So far we have postulated two levels of representation, an underlying one and a surface one, a position that was motivated in Chapter 5. It can be argued, however, that this two-level model does not account for the intuitions of native speakers about the pronunciation of the words of their language. In brief, the underlying representation would seem to be too abstract, while the surface representation appears to be too detailed (cf. Schane 1971). This unsatisfactory state of affairs has come to an end with the advent of Lexical Phonology, which theory postulates an intermediate level of representation known as the **lexical representation**. Not only does it correspond to native speaker intuitions, it will also be shown to have a number of interesting properties. After dealing with the lexical representation, we turn our attention to the relation between the surface representation and the physical pronunciation of the words. We will see that languages may differ in the way they realize identical surface representations. Such language-specific realizations of phonological elements are accounted for by rules of **phonetic implementation**.

9.2 DEFINING AN INTERMEDIATE LEVEL OF REPRESENTATION

If you look up the pronunciation of a word in a dictionary, you will find it is normally given in **phonemic transcription**. In this type of transcription, an English word like *pin* is transcribed [pɪn], not [pʰɪn]. This is because the segment [pʰ] is an allophonic variant of the phoneme /p/, and as such has no place in a phonemic transcription. Clearly, the dictionary's phonemic transcription defines a level of representation which is more abstract than the surface level. However, it does not correspond with the underlying representation either. The pronunciation of *looked*, for instance, would be given as [lʊkt], not as [lʊkd]. The form that is given incorporates the output of a devoicing rule that makes obstruents voiceless after voiceless obstruents. That is, the phonemic transcription apparently corresponds to a level of representation which is somewhere between the underlying level and the surface level.

It might at first sight be reasonable to suppose that the intermediate level corresponds to the output of all rules that produce existing segments, which were called 'neutralization rules' in Chapter 5, while all rules that produce novel segments, or 'allophonic rules', would then apply to the intermediate representation so as to produce the more detailed surface representation. This would put all the rules that produce phonemes, or existing segments, in a different compartment of the grammar from all the rules that produce allophones, or novel segments. While this assumption is almost correct, there is still something not quite right. This is because there are rules whose output is a mix of existing and novel segments. Not all rules allow themselves to be characterized as either 'neutralizing' or 'allophonic'. Some rules are both: depending on the input, they produce either an already existing segment or a novel segment. For instance, Dutch has a rule that voices plosives before [b,d], called REGRESSIVE VOICING. (It applies to all obstruents, as shown in Q77, but we will ignore the fricatives here.) The language has the three voiceless plosives [p,t,k], each of which can appear before /b,d/. REGRESSIVE VOICING thus produces the voiced plosives [b,d,g]. Dutch has oppositions between /p/ and /b/, as in [pɑk] 'parcel' – [bɑk] 'tray', and /t/ and /d/, as in [tɑk] 'branch' – [dɑk] 'roof', but there is no contrast /k/–/g/. Therefore, the output of REGRESSIVE VOICING is partly phonemic, viz. when /p,t/ are voiced to /b,d/, and partly allophonic, viz. when /k/ is voiced to [g]. In (1), the first column gives the underlying representations, while the third column gives the results of REGRESSIVE VOICING.

(1)	*Underlying*	*Phonemic*	*Surface*	*Gloss*
	ɔp dun	ɔb dun	[ɔb dun]	'put on'
	œyt braːk	œyd braːk	[œyd braːk]	'breakout'
	zɑk buk	zɑk buk	[zɑg buk]	'pocket book'

It should be clear that it would not be very clever to maintain a distinction between rules that produce existing segments and rules that produce novel segments, for this would mean that we would have to split REGRESSIVE VOICING, given in (2), into two subrules, one to produce the existing segments /b,d/, the 'neutralizing' part of the rule, shown in (3a), and a second to produce the novel [g], the 'allophonic' part, shown in (3b). (We formulate the rules so that they voice all obstruents.)

(2) REGRESSIVE VOICING $[-\text{son}] \rightarrow [+\text{voice}] \,/ \,\underline{\quad}\, (\#\#) \begin{bmatrix} -\text{son} \\ -\text{cont} \\ +\text{voice} \end{bmatrix}$

(3) a. REGR. p,t-VOICING $\begin{bmatrix} -\text{son} \\ \left\{ \begin{matrix} [\text{COR}] \\ [\text{LAB}] \end{matrix} \right\} \end{bmatrix} \rightarrow [+\text{voice}] \,/ \,\underline{\quad}\, (\#\#) \begin{bmatrix} -\text{son} \\ \left\{ \begin{matrix} [\text{COR}] \\ [\text{LAB}] \end{matrix} \right\} \end{bmatrix}$

b. REGR. k-VOICING $\begin{bmatrix} -\text{son} \\ \text{DORSAL} \end{bmatrix} \rightarrow [+\text{voice}] \,/ \,\underline{\quad}\, (\#\#) \begin{bmatrix} -\text{son} \\ \left\{ \begin{matrix} [\text{COR}] \\ [\text{LAB}] \end{matrix} \right\} \end{bmatrix}$

Rule (2) converts the underlying forms in the first column in (1) into the forms in the third column, which seems just right. There is no reasonable case for maintaining an intermediate representation of the type illustrated in the second column in (1), which gives the intermediate representations that would result if we were to split (2) up into (3a), the neutralizing rule that produces /p,t/, and (3b), the allophonic rule that produces [g].

Halle (1959) used the above argument, which he made on the basis of a similar case of undesirable rule duplication in Russian, to argue that the notion of the 'Structuralist Phoneme', which was a cornerstone of phonological theory as it existed before the advent of 'Generative Phonology', was misguided. American Structuralists – phonologists like Zellig S. Harris, Charles F. Hockett and W. Freeman Twaddell, whose work was superseded by the Generativists of the late 1950s and 1960s, like Morris Halle, Noam Chomsky and Paul Postal – held that the underlying representation was transferred into an intermediate, **phonemic** representation, which in its turn was transformed by rules into an **allophonic** surface representation. The notion **phoneme** is based on the existence of a **surface contrast**. The (entirely reasonable and valid) idea was that whenever a **minimal pair** could be formed, i.e. a pair of words whose members differ by one segment only, like English *lock – rock*, or *beat – boot*, the two segments responsible for the difference must belong to different phonemes. So the above two minimal pairs are evidence for the existence of the phoneme categories /l/ $\sim$ /r/ and /iː/ $\sim$ /uː/ in English. What made their theory problematic, however, was the additional premiss that a segment could only belong to **one** phoneme. So once a /t/ had been set up in a language on the basis of some minimal pair in which the segment [t] contrasts with some other segment, any occurrence of [t] in any other word, regardless of context, also belonged to the phoneme /t/. This premise has been referred to as 'Once a phoneme, always a phoneme.' Adherence to this principle leads inevitably to the sort of undesirable splits in generalizations that we have seen in the case of Dutch REGRESSIVE VOICING. Since [d] belongs to the phoneme /d/, a conclusion based on minimal pairs in which it contrasts with [t] in the onset, [d] must also be assumed to represent /d/ when it occurs in the coda before a voiced plosive, as in the word for 'breakout' in (1). Since the same reasoning does not apply to [g], the position encapsulated in 'Once a phoneme always a phoneme' implies the recognition of an undesirable representational level illustrated in the second column of (1).

So we are back at square one. It is still the case that dictionaries give phonemic transcriptions, and that untrained speakers of English will maintain that [pʰɪn] and [spɪn] contain the same consonant [p]. It is reasonable to assume that their judgement is based on some (psychologically real) representation, here one that corresponds to a derivational stage **before** ASPIRATION. But equally, they will maintain that the final consonant in *looked* is not the same as that in *begged*: in *looked* a [t] occurs, but in *begged* a [d]. This judgement is evidently based on a representation that arises **after** the application of DEVOICING. Halle's argument makes it clear that there is no place for the Structuralist Phoneme in phonological theory. It does not, of course, rule out the existence of **any** intermediate representation. The answer to the question of what the appropriate intermediate level is has been provided by the theory of Lexical Phonology.

9.3   LEXICAL PHONOLOGY

The crucial assumption made by Lexical Phonology is that some of the phonological generalizations of a language are stated in the lexicon, the morphological module which incorporates the semantic, phonological and morphological information of the language's morphemes, while others are stated outside it. That is, a distinction is drawn between **lexical phonological rules** and **postlexical phonological rules**, the latter applying after the words have been inserted into the sentence (Kiparsky 1982, 1985; Mohanan 1986). In (4), a number of the distinguishing properties are listed.

(4)	*Lexical rules*	*Postlexical rules*
	a. May refer to morphological labels	Cannot refer to morphological labels
	b. May have exceptions	Cannot have exceptions
	c. Structure-preserving	Need not be structure-preserving
	d. Accessible to native-speaker intuition	Not easily accessible to native-speaker intuition
	e. Cannot apply across word boundaries	May apply across word boundaries
	f. Must precede all postlexical rules	Must follow all lexical rules

We discuss each of these properties in the following sections.

9.3.1   Reference to morphological labels

Since lexical rules apply inside the lexicon and postlexical rules do not, the former, but not the latter, have access to category labels like 'N(oun)', 'V(erb)', etc. For example, there is a rule in Dutch that deletes word-final [n] after [ə], as shown in (5).

(5)	*Underlying*	*Surface*	*Gloss*
	$[[lo{:}p]_V + \partial n]_{Inf}$	lo:pə	'to walk'
	$[[za{:}k]_N + \partial n]_{Pl}$	za:kə	'things'
	$[te{:}k\partial n]_N$	te:kə	'sign'
	$[[te{:}k\partial n]_V + \partial n]_{Inf}$	te:kənə	'to draw'
	$[o{:}p\partial n]_{Adj}$	o:pə	'open'

When [ən] occurs finally in a verb stem, however, no deletion takes place (Koefoed 1979; Trommelen and Zonneveld 1983). This is shown in (6).

(6)	*Underlying*	*Surface*	*Gloss*
	$[te{:}k\partial n]_V$	te:kən	'draw'
	$[o{:}p\partial n]_V$	o:pən	'open'

n-DELETION (7) thus distinguishes between the words for 'a sign' and 'to draw', or between the adjective 'open' and the verb 'to open'. Such a condition can only be put on a lexical rule. Once a word has left the lexicon and has been inserted in syntactic structure, category labels are removed, and postlexical rules therefore cannot refer to them.

(7)   n-DELETION $n \rightarrow \emptyset / \vartheta \_]_X$

Condition: X ≠ Verb

9.3.2   Exceptions

Lexical rules, but not postlexical rules, have access to the lexicon, and as such can tell which word they are dealing with. A rule that has exceptions, therefore, cannot be a postlexical rule. To return to the example of n-DELETION (7) above: ['hɛidən] 'heathen' and ['krɪstən] 'Christian' are exceptional in not undergoing the rule. The entries of these words are assumed to be provided with the information 'Not subject to (7)'. Similarly, English has a rule of TRISYLLABIC LAXING, which laxes a vowel in the antepenultimate syllable of words derived with suffixes like -*ity*. Examples are given in (8). However, the words *nicety* and *obesity* (cf. *nice, obese*) exceptionally have [aɪ, iː] in the antepenultimate syllable, rather than the expected lax [ɪ, ɛ].

(8)   *Tense*   *Lax*
      div[ai]*ne*   *div*[ɪ]*nity*
      v[ei]*n*   *v*[æ]*nity*
      ser[iː]*ne*   *ser*[ɛ]*nity*

While postlexical rules cannot have exceptions, lexical rules could either have exceptions or be exceptionless. For instance, English has a rule deleting [n] after [m] at the end of the word (Kiparsky 1985). This rule must be lexical, because it needs information about the status of the word *before* inflectional endings are added. Thus, it applies in column 1 in (9), and in column 2, where the words have been provided with inflectional endings, but not in column 3, where [n] is not final in the word. This lexical n-deletion rule is exceptionless: there are no words in English that end in [mn].

(9)   *Stem*   *Inflected form*   *Derived form*
      dam[∅]   *dam*[∅]*ed, dam*[∅]*ing, dam*[∅]   *dam*[n]*ation*
      colum[∅]   *colum*[∅]*s, colum*[∅]   *colum*[n]*ar*
      hym[∅]   *hym*[∅]*s, hym*[∅]*ing, hym*[∅]   *hym*[n]*al*

9.3.3   Structure preservation

Lexical rules are structure-preserving in the sense that their output is confined to segments that already exist in underlying representations. The idea is that there is a **lexical inventory** of vowels, consonants and tones which is smaller than the inventory observable in surface representation. For example, since in the underlying representation of English words there is no need to distinguish aspirated from unaspirated plosives, this distinction being allophonic in English, the rule that creates aspirated plosives must be postlexical. The segments [pʰ, tʰ, kʰ] are novel segments, i.e. not included in the English lexical segment inventory.

Structure preservation is not an exceptionless property of lexical rules. A number of varieties of English have rules that apply before the affixation of inflectional endings and must for that reason be lexical, like the rule that deletes [n] in words like *autumn*, discussed above. The point is that many of such rules produce novel segments (Harris 1994: 28). An example is the Scottish rule lengthening word-final vowels (as well as vowels before [+voice, +cont] segments) (Aitken's Law cf. Q55). Unexpectedly, the inflectional suffix [d] of the past and past participle is ignored in the context of the rule, which makes the rule a lexical rule. This is shown in (10). But the product of the rule is a novel segment.

(10)   *Uninflected stem*   *Past tense form*
     fid   *feed*   fri:d   *freed*
     tʌid   *tide*   taed   *tied*
     sʌid   *side*   saed   *sighed*
     fud   *food*   su:d   *sued*

Interestingly, there is evidence that when a novel sound is produced by a lexical rule, it may be made available for inclusion in lexical representations. Thus, some speakers pronounce *concise* and *scythe* with [ae], even though in Scottish English these words end in [s] and [θ], respectively (Aitken 1984). Clearly, developmental stages in which all occurrences of a novel segment are produced by a lexical rule must be expected to occur, if it is assumed that at least some lexical rules historically start out as postlexical rules.

9.3.4   Native-speaker intuitions

Native speakers would appear to make reference to the lexical representation when determining whether two phonetically different sounds are the same sound or two different sounds: their judgements refer to the lexical segment inventory. For instance, native speakers of English regard the second segment in *stop* and the first segment of *top* as the same sound, even though they are phonetically different, which fits with the assumption that ASPIRATION is a postlexical rule. Likewise, phonetically identical sounds that were neutralized by a postlexical rule will typically be looked upon as different sounds. As a result of the American English process of FLAPPING, the intervocalic consonants in *Adam* and *atom* are phonetically identical in all styles except the most formal ones (['ærəm]), but native speakers nevertheless consider them different consonants. By contrast, when a lexical rule neutralizes an underlying opposition, the intuition of the native speaker tends to conform to its output.

9.3.5   Application across word boundaries

Because lexical rules apply in the lexicon, their structural description can never be determined by elements taken from different words. A rule that applies across word boundaries, therefore, must be a postlexical rule. Dutch REGRESSIVE VOICING (2) is a postlexical rule for this reason.

Q84

---

1. What do you think is the lexical representation form of 'breakout' in (1)?
2. Do you think that Dutch REGRESSIVE VOICING has exceptions?
3. What would native speakers of Dutch say is the last consonant of the prefix in [œyd-bra:k]?

9.3.6   Lexical rules apply before postlexical rules

The final distinguishing property listed in (4) is once more a necessary consequence of the lexical phonology model. Words get inserted into postlexical structures in their lexical representations, i.e. after all lexical rules have applied. It follows that if we know that a rule is postlexical, a rule that must apply after it must also be postlexical, and thus display all the postlexical properties listed in (4).

9.4   PHONOLOGICAL INFORMATION IN THE LEXICON

All phonological rules may refer to phonological information. The phonological information available in the lexicon is not confined to segments. Syllable and foot structure also exist in the lexicon of Dutch and English (Booij 1988; Inkelas 1989). Evidence for this position is provided by morphological processes that are sensitive to the syllable structure or the stress of the base. For example, the English comparative and superlative suffixes [[ ]$_{Adj}$ ər] and [[ ]$_{Adj}$ əst] require that the base should not exceed a binary foot. Therefore, the formation is allowed with the adjectives in (11a), but not with those in (11b).

(11)   a.   *white*   (waɪt)$_F$ (waɪtər)$_F$
             noble   (nəʊbl)$_F$ (nəʊblər)$_F$
             silly   (sɪli)$_F$ (sɪliər)$_F$
         b.   *beautiful*   (bjuːtəfl)$_F$ *(bjuːtəflər)$_F$
             manifest   (mænə)$_F$(fest)$_F$ *(mænə)$_F$(festər)$_F$
             serene   sə(riːn)$_F$ *sə(riːnər)$_F$

An interesting illustration of the point that lexical rules may refer to both morphological structure and phonological structure is provided by FINAL DEVOICING in two varieties of German. In Low German, a term covering the varieties of German spoken in the northern half of the country, this process applies to syllable-final obstruents, as shown in the second column of (12) (Venneman 1972). The requirement that the obstruent should occur in the coda also holds for High German, but this variety requires in addition that in positions before sonorants the obstruent should be morpheme-final. As a result, the examples in (12b), in which the obstruent is both syllable- and stem-final, show devoicing in both varieties, but differences appear in the case of such words as *Adler* 'eagle', where an obstruent is syllable-final, but not stem-final, as shown in (12c).[1]

(12)   *Underlying*   *Low German*   *High German*   *Gloss*
     a.   kɪnd   kɪnt   kɪnt   'child'
          kɪnd-ɪʃ   kɪn.dɪʃ   kɪn.dɪʃ   'childish'

[1] Rubach (1990) provides an account of the High German data based on resyllabification. Giegerich (1992) assumes that the varieties or styles with voiced plosives in words like *Adler* place the plosive in onset position. This solution implies that clusters that are ill-formed word-initially (*[dl, gm]) are often well-formed word-internally. In fact, the opposite sometimes occurs, since edges may allow 'extra' elements. A case in point is French [ps], which can be an onset in *psychologie*, but not in *capsule* (cf. Selkirk 1982).

b. kɪnd-lɪç   kɪnt.lɪç   kɪnt.lɪç   'childlike'

     taːg-lɪç   teːk.lɪç   teːk.lɪç   'daily'

c. vaːgnəʀ   vaːk.nəʀ   vaːg.nəʀ   'Wagner'

     magmaː   mak.maː   mag.maː   'magma'

     aːdlər   aːt.lər   aːd.lər   'eagle'

     ɔrdn-ʊŋ   ɔrt.nʊŋ   ɔrd.nʊŋ   'order'

Q85

The Korean lexical consonant inventory is given in (1).

(1)

Labial	Cor [+ant]	Cor [−ant]	Dorsal	Lar
p	t	tʃ	k	
pʰ	tʰ	tʃʰ	kʰ	h
p'	t'	tʃ'	k'	
	s			
	s'			
m	n		ŋ	
	l			

Before [i], [t,tʰ,t',s,s',n,l] are prepalatal by a rule of PALATALIZATION: [c,cʰ,c',ç,ç',ɲ,ʎ], as shown in (2), causing surface syllables like *[si] to be ill-formed. In addition, there is a rule PLAIN PLOSIVE VOICING, which voices [p,t,tʃ,k] between sonorant segments.

(2)

kaps-i	kapçi	'price + NOMINATIVE'
sikan	çigan	'time'
k'ini	k'iɲi	'meal'
pɯtʰi	pɯcʰi	'endure'
tʰi	cʰi	'dust'
kaksi	kakçi	'bride'
mati	maɟi	'knot

A rule of AFFRICATION causes coronal plosives to become affricates before [i], if [i] forms part of a suffix. Thus, [t,tʰ] are replaced with [tʃ, tʃʰ] in the contexts shown in (3a). ([t'] happens not to occur stem-finally). The affricates [tʃ, tʃʰ] also appear in underlying representation, as shown in (3b) (after Kiparsky 1993).

(3) a.

patʰ-i	patʃʰi	'field + NOMINATIVE'
kut-i	kudʒi	'harden + ADV'
kjɯtʰ-i	kjɯtʃʰi	'side + NOMINATIVE'

     b.

tʃip	tʃip	'house'
tʃitʃɯ	tʃidʒɯ	'tear (IMP)'
tʃɯtʃ-i	tʃɯdʒi	'milk + NOMINATIVE'

1. Is PLAIN PLOSIVE VOICING a structure-preserving rule?
2. Is AFFRICATION a structure-preserving rule?
3. There is no rule that changes [t] into [ɟ], and no rule that changes [t] into [dʒ]. How do you explain the forms for 'knot' in (2) and 'harden + ADV' in (3a)?
4. Mention three properties of AFFRICATION that are consistent with its status as a lexical rule.

Q86

French has a rule of VOWEL NASALIZATION, which nasalizes a vowel before a [n] in the same syllable (Tranel 1981). After VOWEL NASALIZATION, a rule of n-DELETION deletes [n] if it appears in the coda after a nasalized vowel. This is illustrated in (1), where the feminine forms were created by suffixing the stem with [ə]. (The nasal vowel [ɛ̃] is the reflex of underlying [i,y,e]; please ignore the variation between [e] and [ɛ].)

(1)
Stem		Masc.	Fem.	Derivation	
plɛn	'full'	plɛ̃	plɛnə	plenitydə	'fullness'
bryn	'brown'	brɛ̃	brynə	brynɛ	'brownish'
fin	'fine'	fɛ̃	finə	finɛs	'fineness'
bɔn	'good'	bɔ̃	bɔnə	bɔnifije	'make good'
roman	'Romance'	romã	romanə	romanist	'scholar of Romance'

There is a third rule, ə-DELETION, which deletes foot-final [ə] except in the most formal styles, causing the feminine forms in (1) to be [plɛn, bryn, fin, bɔn, roman] on the surface.

1. Give formal notations of the three rules, referring to syllable and foot boundaries as in example (7) in section 7.2.1.
2. Show the derivation of the masculine and feminine forms for 'fine'.
3. Before a consonant-initial noun, the feminine indefinite article is [yn], as in [yn fam] 'a woman'; before a vowel-initial feminine word like [e.ro.in] 'heroine', the indefinite article [yn] is divided over two syllables, as in [y.ne.ro.in] 'a heroine'. The masculine form of the indefinite article is [ɛ̃] before consonant-initial nouns, as in [ɛ̃ garsɔ̃] and [ɛn] before vowel-initial nouns, where the [n] is syllabified with the noun-initial vowel, as in [ɛ̃.nɔm] 'a man'. How would you account for the preservation of the [n] in the masculine indefinite article?
4. Why must n-DELETION be postlexical?
5. In some contexts, word-final [ə] is preserved, as in [bãdə dɛsine] 'strip cartoon'. Is ə-DELETION a lexical or a postlexical rule?
6. *Citroën* is pronounced [sitroɛn]. Why can this fact be used as an argument for the assumption that VOWEL NASALIZATION is a lexical rule?
7. There are many words like [ɔ̃də] 'wave', which only ever have a nasalized vowel, never an oral vowel plus [n]. What would you assume as the underlying form of the word for 'wave'?

9.5 CONTROVERSIAL PROPERTIES OF LEXICAL RULES

Two further properties have been claimed to distinguish lexical from postlexical rules. However, they do not appear to have the same fairly unexceptional status as the properties mentioned in (4), and have therefore been disputed (Halle and Kenstowicz 1991; Kiparsky 1993). One of these is the property of **cyclicity**, the application of a rule to internal constituents of derived words in addition to the application to the derived word itself, which has been thought to be an exclusive and necessary property of lexical rules. It will briefly be illustrated in Chapter 15. The second is NON-DERIVED ENVIRONMENT BLOCKING. This is the phenomenon that many lexical rules would appear to skip underived words, i.e. to apply only to forms that are derived. For instance, English TRISYLLABIC LAXING applies to derived forms like ['vænəti] *vanity*, [də'vɪnəti] *divinity*, but not to underived forms like *ivory* ['aɪvəri] *['ɪvəri], *nightingale* ['naitɪŋgeɪl] *['nɪtɪŋgeɪl]. Accordingly, it has been proposed that lexical rules can only apply to derived forms (e.g. the STRICT CYCLE CONDITION of Mascaró 1976). However, many cases have been presented in which structure-preserving rules apply to all occurrences of a morpheme, derived or underived (e.g. Hyman 1970; Kenstowicz and Kisseberth 1979: 77).

Q87   In Dutch, all obstruents are devoiced in the coda. As we saw in Chapter 5, this rule is responsible for the alternation between singular forms and plural forms like [pɑt] 'toad (Sing)' and [pɑdə]. Does the rule show the effect of NON-DERIVED ENVIRONMENT BLOCKING?

Q88   In Northern Irish English, all occurrences of [ɛː] can be derived from [iə] (Harris 1994). Some alternations are shown below.

[iə]	[ɛː]	[iə]	[ɛː]
fate	*day*	*station*	*pay them*
made	*stayed*	*same*	*say more*
raise	*rays*	*fail*	*daily*
baby	*playful*		

1. Is the rule that produces [ɛː] a lexical rule?
2. Is it a neutralization rule?
3. Is it structure-preserving?
4. Does it show the effect of NON-DERIVED ENVIRONMENT BLOCKING?

9.6   BEYOND THE SURFACE REPRESENTATION

In summary, the phonological grammar advocated by Lexical Phonology can be schematized as in (13).

(13)

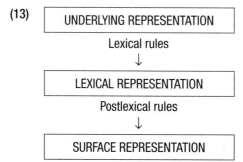

UNDERLYING REPRESENTATION

Lexical rules
↓

LEXICAL REPRESENTATION

Postlexical rules
↓

SURFACE REPRESENTATION

The surface phonological representation which is produced by the grammar contains all the information the articulators require in order to do the work of pronouncing the linguistic expressions concerned. In other words, it is a fully specified phonological representation. Converting that cognitive representation into the physiological actions that constitute the articulation of the expression is the task of the **phonetic implementation rules**. The diagram in (13) can therefore be completed as in (14).

(14)

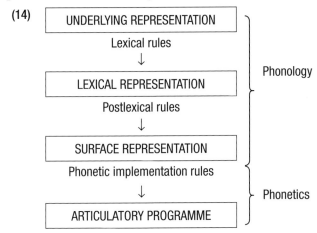

9.6.1 Phonetic implementation

The phonological surface representation which ultimately results from the phonological grammar consists of some configuration of phonological features and structures. The representation is discrete, in the sense that any feature or structural configuration is there or is not there. The translation of this discrete representation into quantitative physiological activity, the articulatory actions discussed in Chapter 2, is taken care of by rules of **phonetic implementation** (Pierrehumbert 1980, 1990; Keating 1990). It used to be thought that such rules were universal, and that for that reason anything that was language-specific needed to be given a place in the language's phonology. Everyday experience tells us that this is an improbable position. For one thing, the same phonological syllable is usually pronounced somewhat differently by speakers of different languages. For instance, [kis] will typically be pronounced with a somewhat more fronted [k] in French than in either Spanish or Dutch, while [s] will have lower frequency friction in Dutch than in either French or Spanish. Second, speakers of the same language may fine-tune the articulation of certain segments in order to signal the social group they belong to. As a result, we can often form a fair idea of the speaker's social background on the basis of the precise quality of their vowels, say. But even though speakers can fine-tune their articulations with great precision, postulating ever more discrete phonological features to capture segmental differences which never appear to be used contrastively in any language would defeat the phonological enterprise, which is to account for the fact that the phonologies of the world's languages are formally constrained and can be described with the help of a small, or at the least a finite, set of discrete elements. The detailed intra- and interlanguage variation in the implementation of the phonological representation, therefore, is to be accounted for in the phonetic implementation.

Q89　In New York City English, BATH-raising raises and diphthongizes [æ] to [ɛə] or [ɪə]. The rule applies in a number of phonological contexts, among which is 'when a nasal follows in the same syllable'. It thus fails in *family* [fæ.mə.li], but applies in *damn* [dɪəm]. Moreover, it applies in underived major-class stems, so that the stressed minor-class auxiliary *can* has [æ], while the noun *can* (*of beer*) has [ɪə]. Likewise, *swam* (a derived past tense of *swim*) has [æ], while *ham* has [ɪə].

1.　Is BATH-raising a rule of phonetic implementation, a postlexical phonological rule or a lexical phonological rule? Motivate your answer.
2.　English *swan* [swɔn] used to have an unrounded [a] in the oldest stages of the language. The [w] caused [a] to have liprounding, after which it was interpreted as [ɔ], unless a velar consonant followed. This also took place in words like *quality*, which were borrowed from Norman French with an unrounded [a] after the invasion of 1066. However, the [a] in present-day words with [wa] doesn't acquire this rounding, as shown by *aquatic* [əˈkwætɪk], and there is thus no productive rule of [a]-rounding today. How could you show that BATH-raising is productive? Hint: Think of a New York school child learning a foreign language.

9.6.2　Models of implementation

In a widely adopted view, phonetic implementation involves the translation of a phonological feature into a target for the designated articulatory parameter. For instance, the feature [−cont] triggers the formation of an oral closure at the location specified by the place features. A feature like [+nasal] will trigger an opening of the velum for the segment specified for that feature, while [−nasal] will do the opposite. The different targets of the same articulatory parameter will be connected up by transitions known as **interpolations**. Thus, the movement of the velum from a raised to a lowered position constitutes the interpolation between two phonologically specified target positions. This view of phonetic implementation implies two things. One, phonetic implementation rules do not themselves add or remove phonological features: the only thing they can do is translate features into articulations. Second, segments that have no specification for a particular feature may be in the path of an interpolation between two segments that do. For instance, Cohn (1990) shows that the nasalization of the vowel in American English words like *den, room, sung* should be described in just that way. The nasalization starts early in the vowel and progressively increases to reach full velic opening at the end of the vowel. This is shown graphically in (15a), where the graph represents the nasal airflow, or – indirectly – the degree to which the velum is lowered. Cohn argues that in (15a) the vowel has no specification for the feature [nasal], and that its nasality results from the interpolation between the [−nasal] specification of the preceding consonant and the [+nasal] specification of the following consonant. By contrast, in words like *camp, dent, sink*, the velum opens fully right at the start of the vowel, and closes fairly suddenly at the moment when the oral contact for the voiceless plosive is made. In fact, the nasal consonant disappears before a voiceless plosive in the coda, so that the nasality of the vowel can be seen as the transfer of that feature from the deleted [m,n,ŋ]. This is shown in (15b). (The voiceless plosive is accompanied by a glottal closure by an independent rule of GLOTTALIZATION.) The opposite pattern to (15a) is found in words like *mood, Ned*, where the nasality 'cline' runs in the opposite direction, as shown in (15c). Thus, only in (15b) does the nasality of the vowel result from a [+nasal] feature on the vowel, which is supplied by a phonological rule nasalizing vowels before a sequence of a **tautosyllabic** (i.e. occurring in the same syllable) nasal and plosive.

(15)   a.   b.   c.

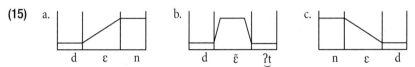

An alternative view holds that phonological features are translated into **gestures**. That is, instead of defining the beginning and end-points of articulatory movements, the elements in a gestural model are the articulatory movements themselves (Zsiga 1997). Under this view, the phonological features in the syllable [dɛn] are translated into a laryngeal gesture (voicing), two tongue tip gestures (one for [d] and one for [n]), a tongue body gesture (palatal wide, to produce the quality of [ɛ]), and a velic closing and a velic opening gesture. Their timings are governed first by the order of the segments and second by the more detailed, language-specific instructions. If the opening gesture of the velum is initiated at the same time as the tongue tip closing gesture, there will be some nasalization during the last part of the vowel: the velum opens immediately the gesture is started, while it will take the tongue tip some time actually to reach the alveolar ridge and, with the rims of the tongue, make the alveolar closure. In a language that allows a greater degree of nasalization, the velic opening gesture is extended so that it starts earlier.

The developers of the gestural model had originally intended the gestures to be the phonological features encoding the pronunciation of words in the lexicon (Browman and Goldstein 1989). A problem with this very 'phonetic' view of phonological representations is that it makes it difficult to state the contrasts a language employs. It would, for instance, be impossible to say whether the nasalization during a vowel was contrastive or allophonic. A related assumption was that phonological adjustments arose from extending the duration of gestures, such that gestures come to overlap (as in the hypothetical case of the nasalization of prenasal vowels noted above). This, however, makes it impossible to distinguish between phonological, i.e. categorical effects (which typically cause gestures to disappear or be reordered) and gradient phonetic effects (which can be very adequately expressed by adjusting the durations of gestures). The gestural model is thus better suited for dealing with the phonetic implementation than for encoding underlying forms.

Recently, phonetic implementation has been thought of less as the construction of an acoustic signal on the basis of gesture-based or target-based interpretations of phonological features than as the probabilistic selection of auditory representations remembered by the speaker, known as 'exemplars'. Speakers appear to modify the pronunciation of specific words on the basis of the pronunciation of other speakers whom they recently heard pronounce those words. These word-by-word adjustments suggest that we store detailed phonetic information about individual words. A well-known argument for the fact that we store minimal information about a word's phonology is that we cannot usually say what any word of our language, *piano* say, sounded like when we first heard it, and are typically unable to say whether the speaker was male or female, adult or child or what its pitch pattern or speech tempo was (Halle 1985). That may be true, but apparently we do remember the last time we heard it! Tacitly or overtly, we remember a great deal about speakers and they way they said things, and we may use that information during our own speech production. There is no conflict between the two facts, however, since one refers to our grammar, our knowledge of contrasts and the structures they are embedded in, while the other refers to how we pronounced them (Pierrehumbert 2002). Models of phonetic implementation that are based on word-based phonetic knowledge are known as 'exemplar models'.

9.6.3 Deciding between phonology and phonetic implementation

It is not always obvious whether a particular generalization should be accounted for in the phonology or in the phonetic implementation. A reasonable assumption would be that if the output of the rule crucially feeds into another rule, the regularity must be phonological. An example may clarify this point. In many varieties of British English, including Received Pronunciation (RP), there is a tendency to insert a voiceless plosive between a nasal and a following fricative, if they belong to the same syllable. As a result, a word like *sense* is pronounced as if it was the plural of *cent*, i.e. as [sɛnts] rather than [sɛns]. At first sight, there would appear to be two possible ways of accounting for this process. First, it might result from the details of phonetic implementation. For [n], there is an alveolar closure and the velum is lowered. To get to [s], the alveolar closure must be gradually released while the velum must be raised. The occurrence of the [t] will now depend on the precise timing of these two articulatory gestures: if the velum is raised before the alveolar closure is released, an oral stop will come to exist between the moment the velic closure is made and the alveolar closure is released. (The vocal cords will typically stop vibrating once the velic closure is made, and the stop therefore is voiceless.) This entirely plausible account would not appear to be right in the case of RP. As it happens, this insertion of [t] creates the context for a phonological process which glottalizes voiceless stops in the coda of the syllable. If the insertion of the voiceless stop in *sense* is recorded in the phonological representation, we should expect it to trigger PREGLOTTALIZATION. The fact that such inserted stops do trigger PREGLOTTALIZATION, just as do underlying stops, implies that VOICELESS STOP INSERTION must be a phonological process in RP. Incidentally, a preglottalized [t] also occurs in words like *sensitive, concert*, which is explained by the fact that [s] in this type of word belongs to the first as well as to the second syllable. (This type of **ambisyllabic** consonant will be examined in Chapter 11.)

Q90 Would you expect *sense* and *cents* to be homophonous in British English?

By contrast, the equivalent process in American English is an instance of phonetic implementation (Ohala 1986). The first syllable in a word like *teamster* or *sensitive* may well be followed by an intrusive voiceless stop, but it does not feed into the phonology of the language: these syllables appear to be longer than syllables closed by a voiceless stop would be in the same context. Also, words like *sense* and *cents* are distinct. *Cents* has a categorically nasalized vowel, as well as a glottal stop ([sɛ̃ʔts] (see (15b)), while *sense* has a partially nasal vowel, and no glottal stop, a pronunciation corresponding to (15a): [sɛ̃n(t)s]). Thus, in an *SPE*-type description, the British English situation is captured by (16), while the American English situation is best described by some such instruction as in (17).

(16) BrE STOP INSERTION $\emptyset \rightarrow \begin{bmatrix} -\text{cont} \\ -\text{voice} \\ \alpha\text{PLACE} \end{bmatrix} / \sigma \ [\dots \begin{bmatrix} +\text{nas} \\ \alpha\text{PLACE} \end{bmatrix} - \begin{bmatrix} -\text{son} \\ +\text{cont} \end{bmatrix} \dots] \sigma$

(17) AmE STOP INSERTION (Implementation): When realizing an intraword sequence [+nas]-[−son, +cont] before an unstressed syllable, time the velic closure for [s] just before or at the moment of the release of the alveolar closure for [n].

Q91 Before voiced obstruents, vowels are longer than before voiceless obstruents. Languages vary in the amount of lengthening before voiced obstruents. The difference in French ([vid] 'empty' vs [vit] 'quickly') is much smaller than in English ([biːd] *bead* vs [biːt] *beat*), for instance. How would you account for this lengthening before voiced obstruents?

Q92 English [s] before [ʃ], as in *stocks shelves, trace shapes*, often assimilates to a consonant that is indistinguishable from [ʃ], but is also frequently pronounced as a fricative that gradually moves from [s] to [ʃ] (Holst and Nolan 1995). How would you characterize these two situations in terms of the rule typology discussed in this chapter?

9.7 CONCLUSION

We have shown that Lexical Phonology provides a satisfactory answer to the problem of the definition of a level of representation between the underlying representation and the surface representation. Instead of drawing the dividing line between rules of neutralization and rules of allophony, it assumes that phonology exists in two separate components in the grammar. One part resides in the lexicon, where it can refer to information present in the lexicon, which is, first, morphological information, and second, the set of lexical phonological segments and structures. The other part is outside the lexicon, where morphological information is no longer available and segments can be produced that do not form part of the lexical segment inventory. A number of properties that can be associated with lexical rules contribute to the coherence and explanatory power of this distinction between lexical and postlexical rules.

Postlexical rules must be distinguished not only from lexical rules but also from phonetic implementation rules. While postlexical rules are phonological rules, and can therefore only manipulate the phonological elements that representations consist of (features, segments, moras, etc.), phonetic implementation rules can only translate the phonological representation into actions of the articulators. The effect of phonetic implementation rules may resemble the effect of phonological rules, and in practice it is not always easy to tell when a rule is phonological.

It might be thought that if lexical rules can be sensitive to morphological information, postlexical rules will be able to refer to syntactic information. There is strong evidence against this assumption. Rather, it would appear that postlexical rules refer to representations that are part of a phonological constituent structure, known as the **prosodic hierarchy**. The theory of Prosodic Phonology, to be discussed in Chapter 16, provides an answer to the question of what that constituent structure is and how it might be related to syntactic structure.

10

Representing tone

10.1 INTRODUCTION

As explained in Chapter 2, **tone languages** use pitch contrasts to keep words apart, in the same way that languages use vowel and consonant contrasts for this purpose. Mandarin, for instance, has four lexically contrastive pitch patterns. In (1a,b,c,d) these pitch patterns are illustrated with four words that minimally differ for tone, a 'minimal quadruplet'. In (1e) a fifth word is given, which has the same tone as (1d) but has a different consonant, and so forms a minimal pair with (1d). Other languages that use tone contrasts for lexical purposes can be found in south-east Asia, Africa and the Americas.

(1)
a. ḅaa   b. ḅaa   c. ḅaa   d. ḅaa   e. maa
       'eight'   'pull up (grass)'   'grasp'   'father'   'scold'

Many languages, like most Austronesian and Indo-European languages, do not use tone contrasts for the specification of their morphemes. Instead, tone patterns are independently meaningful: they add a discourse meaning to the expression. Thus, in English, the same expression, *Jonathan* for instance, will sound as an answer to a question in (2a), as a question in (2b), and as a reminder or a question in (2c). This use of pitch is known as **intonation**.

(2)
a. Jonathan b. Jonathan   c.   Jonathan

In this chapter, we will be concerned with the question of how pitch is represented in phonological structure. We will see that the information about linguistic pitch is represented in terms of tones, and that tones, on the one hand, and vowels and consonants, on the other, are arranged on separate, parallel structural **tiers**. We will consider various arguments for this **autosegmental** status of tone. On the basis of data from African languages, we will show that the tonal patterns of words can be insightfully described in a two-tier model. We will discuss the way the tones are associated with the other elements in the phonological representation on the basis of Goldsmith's ASSOCIATION CONVENTION and the NO CROSSING CONSTRAINT. A second argument will be based on the phenomenon that vowels may be deleted but their tone be preserved, a phenomenon known as **stability**. We discuss the phonetic implementation of tones before turning to intonation. Finally, we will introduce and discuss the status of the OBLIGATORY CONTOUR PRINCIPLE.

10.2   THE INADEQUACY OF A LINEAR MODEL

Until the 1970s, it was assumed that segments form a single layer of structure, a single string of feature matrices. This **linear** conception of segmental structure, in which every segment is a self-contained list of features, makes it impossible to represent aspects of pronunciation that characterize more than one segment as a single feature. However, languages frequently treat particular aspects of pronunciation, notably tone, nasality and tongue-body features, as if they belonged to whole sequences of segments. For instance, if a tone language were to have words whose syllables were either all high-toned or all low-toned, then it would make sense to say that each word of the language either had the feature [+hightone] ('H') or [−hightone] ('L'). In the *SPE* representation of feature matrices, we would not be able to express this generalization: every segment, or at least every vowel, would have to be specified for [±hightone]. If we did that, the question arises why the words of this language either have consistent strings of [+hightone] specifications or consistent strings of [−hightone] specifications, without ever mixing these in the same word. We can of course construct a grammar that demands this consistency, through the introduction of some constraint family that requires that all the segments in a word have the same specification for feature X. However, the same effect would be obtained if feature X could underlyingly specify the word and that some algorithm would see to it that it were distributed over all the relevant segments. This will allow us to express directly that words are either high-toned or low-toned. That is, if we could represent the tonal features and the other features as two separate strings, we would be able to have different numbers of entities in the two strings, which would allow us to say that a word consisted of six segments, say, but of only one tone. We show the difference for a hypothetical high-toned word [ta ta] in (3): (3a) gives the linear *SPE* situation (where [a] stands for the rest of the distinctive features in that matrix) and (3b), or equivalently (3c), gives the representation with two parallel strings.

(3)   a. $t \begin{bmatrix} a \\ +\text{hightone} \end{bmatrix} t \begin{bmatrix} a \\ +\text{hightone} \end{bmatrix}$ b.   ta ta   c.   ta ta
                                                                       [+hightone]   H

Goldsmith (1976) characterized the *SPE* position as a theory that adheres to the ABSOLUTE SLICING HYPOTHESIS: the phonological representation of a word is given by making a number of clean cuts along its time axis, each slice so produced being a segment. The representation which he argued should be adopted instead is one in which the cuts for different features may be made in different places. Because this procedure will lead to one or more strings of features in addition to the string of (depleted) feature matrices, he used the term **autosegment** to refer to any feature that had come to be removed from the others, while the separate strings of autosegments and depleted feature matrices are known as **tiers**.

10.3 WORD-BASED TONE PATTERNS

If, regardless of the number of syllables, the words of a language were either entirely high-toned or entirely low-toned, a situation briefly considered in the previous section, it would obviously be economical to specify each word once either for low tone or for high tone. Put differently, we would wish to say that the language had two **tone melodies**, H and L, and that each word had either the one or the other. A somewhat more complex case is presented by Etung. A syllable in an Etung word has high, low, falling or rising tone. Importantly, however, there are certain constraints on the distribution of the tones: not all tones can appear on all syllables. The symbols used in the transcription of tone are given in the first column of (4), and the tonal representations in the third.

(4)	ˊ	high tone	H
	ˋ	low tone	L
	ˆ	falling tone	HL
	ˇ	rising tone	LH
	᷈	falling-rising tone	HLH
	᷉	rising-falling tone	LHL

In (5a,b,c), we list actual words of one syllable, two syllables and three syllables, respectively. Notice that **level** tones (i.e. high tone and low tone) may occur on all syllables, but that **contour** tones (falling tone and rising tone) only appear on monosyllables and on the final syllable of disyllabic words. Moreover, if a syllable has the same tone as the preceding syllable, all following syllables have that tone. Thus, the words in (5a,b,c) are all fine, while those in (5d,e,f) are all bad. In (5d), we see that contour tones must be final, in (5e) we see that contour tones cannot appear in words of more than two syllables, while in (5f) we see that in words of three syllables, the first two cannot have the same tone if the third has a different tone.

(5)	a.	monosyllabic words	kpá, kpè, nâ, nǒ
	b.	disyllabic words	óbá, èkát, òbô, ódà, ábǒ
	c.	trisyllabic words	ékúé, ókpùgà, bìsóŋé, édìmbá
	d.	disyllabic	*âbó, *ǎbó
	e.	trisyllabic	*ábìmbâ, *ábîmbà, *âbîmbà, *àbìmbǎ, . . .
	f.	trisyllabic	*ábímbà, *àbìmbá

Leben (1973) argued that such distributional facts can be captured by assuming that tones are not chosen per syllable, but per word, and that, moreover, these tone patterns are independent of the vowels and consonants. These Etung tone patterns are given in (6). Importantly, the tonal tier and the segmental tier are unassociated in the lexicon: the point is that all and only the well-formed lexical patterns of (5) can be derived by an association algorithm, so that we account for the ungrammaticality of the forms in (5d,e,f). To achieve this, Goldsmith (1976) provided the ASSOCIATION CONVENTION (7). The timing of an autosegment with the rest of the representation is expressed with the help of an association line. The phonological element with which the tone associates is known as the **tone-bearing unit**, or TBU. It is usually either the syllable or the mora (whereby long vowels count for two moras).

(6) A word has one of the six patterns L, H, LH, HL, LHL, HLH
(7) ASSOCIATION CONVENTION (AC)
    a. Associate tones and TBUs left-to-right, one-to-one
    b. Associate left-over TBUs with the last tone
    c. Associate left-over tones with the last TBU

In (8) a number of examples have been worked out. In (8a) the number of tones and the number of TBUs is equal, and one-to-one association is all we need to do (clause (7a)). In (8b,c), there are fewer tones than there are syllables. According to clause (7b), we must now associate the last tone with the left-over syllable(s), an operation known as **spreading**. Notice that this causes the same tone to be associated with more than one TBU. In (8d), there are more tones than there are TBUs. The last TBU receives the left-over tone (clause (7c)), causing this TBU to be associated with a contour tone.

(8) *Lexical representations*

	a. edimba	b. bisoŋe	c. ekue	d. obo
	HLH	LH	H	LHL
(7a)				
	edimba	bisoŋe	ekue	obo
	∣ ∣ ∣	∣ ∣	∣	∣ ∣
	H L H	L H	H	L HL
(7b)				
		bisoŋe	ekue	
		∣ V	V	
		L H	H	
(7c)				

obo
∣ ⋀
L HL

édìmbá	bìsóŋé	ékúé	òbô
'pot'	'wife'	'forest'	'arm'

Etung has no falling-rising or rising-falling words of the type * nǎ or *nȁ. Apparently, there is a limit to the number of tones that can associate with a TBU in this language.

This No Crowding Constraint, which appears to be quite common in languages generally, is given in (9).

(9) No Crowding Constraint   * TBU

/|\
T T T

The above description accounts elegantly for the distribution of the four surface tone types (high, low, falling, rising) of Etung. If we were to elevate those surface tone types to features inside a segmental feature matrix, a description would result that would consist of a series of arbitrary facts. In (10), this alternative is made explicit. This cumbersome description should be compared to the simple autosegmental alternative consisting of (6), (7) and (9).

(10) a.   A syllable has one of the four tones High, Low, Fall, Rise.
b.   Fall and Rise never occur on a nonfinal syllable.
c.   Words of more than two syllables never have a Fall or a Rise.
d.   Words of more than two syllables never have the same tone on the first n syllables if the nth+1 syllable has a different tone.

The TBU may be defined differently for different languages. In some languages the syllable is the TBU, so that long vowels count as one TBU. In other languages, the mora is the TBU, in which case long vowels are two TBUs, and sonorant consonants in the syllable rhyme may be TBUs.

10.3.1   Language-specific associations

The Association Convention (7) is not an obligatory procedure in tone languages. For one thing, there may be language-particular rules which override it. In Kikuyu, the association proceeds from the second TBU in the word, rather than the first. The word in (12), which means 'way of releasing oneself quickly', is made up of the morphemes in (11). The verb root extension [aŋg] 'quickly' is toneless. The association of the tones contributed by the various morphemes proceeds as predicted by (7), with the last H spreading to the left-over TBUs, except that instead of associating to the first TBU, the first tone associates with the second TBU. Subsequently, the first empty TBU is associated with the first tone, as shown in (12) (Clements and Ford 1979). An interrupted association line represents an instruction to establish the association concerned.

(11)   mo   e   rɛk+aŋg   eriɛ
L   H   L   H
CLASS PREFIX   REFLEXIVE   allow+quickly   NOUN SUFFIX

(12)   mo   e   rɛ   ka   ŋg eriɛ
\ / / / |/
L H L   H

> **Q93**   The Kikuyu words for 'firewood' and 'tree' are [ròkǒ] and [mòtǒ].
>
> 1. What are the underlying tone patterns of these words?
> 2. In Tharaka, a related Bantu language spoken in Kenya, these words have the same underlying tone patterns, but are realized as [ròkó] and [mòtó]. How would you describe this difference between Kikuyu and Tharaka?
> 3. The Tharaka word for 'way of releasing oneself quickly' is made up of the same morphemes and the same tones as in (11). How will it be realized in Tharaka? Show the representation.

Thus, languages may have specific constraints on associations of particular tones. For instance, Hyman and Ngunga (1994) show that the TBU which the (first) tone associates with may be determined by the morphological class in Ciyao. Even in languages like Etung, whose word tonal patterns are evidently governed by the ASSOCIATION CONVENTION (7), there may be exceptional patterns that cannot so be accounted for. Likewise, there is no universal requirement that tones should always spread to empty TBUs. Pulleyblank (1986) shows that in Tiv, noninitial TBUs may remain unspecified for tone until a point in the derivation when they receive a default L. Neither need it be the case that left-over tones always form contours on the last TBU. Languages may not tolerate contouring at all, obeying an even more restrictive constraint than (9).

> **Q94**   Zulu (Laughren 1984) obeys a more restrictive constraint than the No CROWDING CONSTRAINT (9), since no contour tones may appear on short vowels at all. Zulu words behave either like Kikuyu words or like Etung words. That is, every word is lexically specified as to whether association starts with the first or the second TBU. In Natal Coast Zulu, the word for 'chiefs' consists of two morphemes, /ama/ and /kosi/, both of which have underlying HL. The first morpheme is specified for association to start with the first TBU, the second for association to start with the second TBU. After this initial association, the rest of the derivation is taken care of by the ASSOCIATION CONVENTION in (7).
>
> 1. How will the word [amakosi] be realized?
> 2. Why is the realization not [ámà kòsî]?

While the ASSOCIATION CONVENTION in (7) may be seen as representing an unmarked procedure, evidently languages may decide to introduce language-particular instructions or choose to have representations that deviate from its predictions. The only uncontroversially universal aspect to autosegmental representations is the No CROSSING CONSTRAINT, given in (13). It is an inalienable feature of the autosegmental representation: if it did not hold, the order of the autosegments on different tiers could change relative to the orders on other tiers. The constraint in (13) is there to prevent such order changes.

(13)   No CROSSING CONSTRAINT: Association lines do not cross.

In this section, the autosegmental representations of tones was argued for on the basis of distributional restrictions that they are subject to in various languages.

10.4 STABILITY

There is another argument for the autosegmental representation of tone, which Goldsmith (1976) refers to as the **stability** of tones. Sometimes, a vowel is deleted, but the tone it had remains, showing up on an adjacent vowel. In (14) some examples are given from Etsakọ, in which a nonhigh vowel is deleted before another vowel (Elimelech 1976). When the final vowel of the stem is deleted, its tone shows up on the next vowel, where it creates a contour. If the tone of the deleted vowel is the same as the tone on the following vowel, however, nothing happens. In Etsakọ, reduplication of the noun has the meaning 'every'.

(14) ìkpà   'cup'   ìkpìkpà   'every cup'
      ówà   'house'   ówŏwà   'every house'
      ɔ̀yɛ̀dɛ́   'banana'   ɔ̀yɛ̀dɔ́yɛ̀dɛ́   'every banana'

It is of course *possible* to describe these facts in a theory in which all features are contained in segment-size matrices. We could, for example, assume the feature analysis of the low, high, falling and rising tones in (15) and write (16) to account for the tone changes. In prose, (16) says that a word-final vowel is deleted before a word-initial vowel, and if it has a different tone from the word-initial vowel of the next word, the tone on the word-initial vowel becomes rising if it was high and falling if it was low. While it correctly describes the situation, it presents the facts as arbitrary: we could just as easily write a rule with $[-\text{contour}]$ rather than $[+\text{contour}]$, but that rule would not describe any actual language data.

(15)

	Low ˋ	High ´	Fall ˆ	Rise ˇ
Hightone	−	+	−	+
Contour	−	−	+	+

$$(16) \quad \begin{bmatrix} +\text{syl} \\ \left\langle \begin{matrix} \alpha\,\text{hightone} \\ -\text{contour} \end{matrix} \right\rangle \end{bmatrix} \; ^{\#} \; \begin{bmatrix} +\text{syl} \\ \left\langle \begin{matrix} -\alpha\,\text{hightone} \\ -\text{contour} \end{matrix} \right\rangle \end{bmatrix} \rightarrow \emptyset \; 2 \; {}^{<[+\text{contour}]>}$$

$$\qquad\quad 1 \qquad\qquad 2 \qquad 3 \qquad\qquad 1 \qquad\qquad 3$$

The autosegmental representation allows us to express the fact that it is only the vowel, not its tone, that is deleted. By reassociating the stranded tone to the next vowel, we accurately express the tonal adjustments. In (18b) a rise is produced, in (18c) a fall, while in (18a) no tonal change is predicted. Associating the same feature more than once to a structural element is meaningless, and the two identical tones are automatically reduced to one by a convention known as the TWIN SISTER CONVENTION (see (17), Clements and Keyser 1983).

(17)   TWIN SISTER CONVENTION

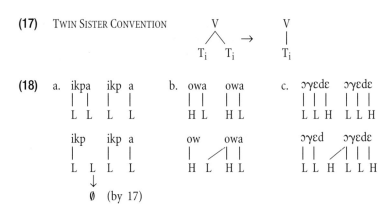

10.5   PHONETIC IMPLEMENTATION OF TONE

The description of the pronunciation of tones follows the target-and-interpolation model outlined in section 9.6.2. A tone's pronunciation is thus a target with some F0 (its 'scaling') occurring at some point in the segment string (its 'phonetic alignment') (Pierrehumbert 1980). In Mandarin, whose four lexical tone patterns given in (1) will have tonal representations much as in (19), the end of the syllable provides the approximate phonetic alignment point of its last tone's target (Xu 2006). The bracketed H in the Low tone only shows up when another Low tone follows and at the end of a phrase (see Duanmu 2000: 221). A sequence of a Low tone, a High tone and a Falling tone, therefore, will be pronounced as shown by the solid line in panel (a) of Figure 10.1, where the filled dots represent the targets of the Low tone (1st syllable), the High tone (2nd syllable) and two tones of the Falling tone (3rd syllable). This means that the High tone comes out as a rising pitch movement through the second syllable. However, this pitch contour is distinct from the pitch contour for the Rising tone in the same context, whose two targets are indicated by the open circles. The rising movement is located late in the second syllable, instead of covering the entire syllable. In panel (b),

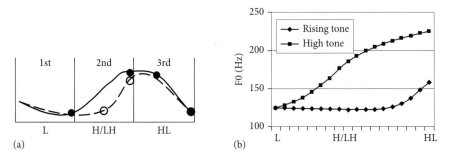

Figure 10.1
Theoretical Mandarin Chinese pitch contours of High tone and Rising tone between Low tone and Falling tone (panel (a)), and actual pitch contours of High tone (■) and Rising tone (♦) after low tone and before falling tone, averaged over 27 tokens (panel (b), from Chen 2008).

the averaged measured contours are shown for the second syllable in emphatic speech. In this speech style, the high target of the rising tone may in fact be located in the next syllable. This may happen in other languages, too, and is known as 'peak delay'.

(19) a. baa   b. baa   c. baa   c. baa
          V || | ||
          H   LH   L(H)   HL

          High   *Rising*   *Low*   *Falling*

10.6 INTONATION

The description of intonation contours goes along the same lines (Ladd 2008, Gussenhoven 2004). Intonation languages only provide tonal representations postlexically. These tones are independent morphemes, whose meanings are somewhat vague, having to do with whether you are giving the listener some information or are asking for some, but no attempt to define them will be made here. A distinction is made between tones that are associated with the primary stressed syllables of some words and tones that are located at the edges of larger domains. The former are **pitch accents**, while the latter are known as **boundary tones**. Like word melodies, pitch accents may consist of one or more tones, but only one of them associates with a stressed syllable. Intonation contours are not word-based, as the tonal melodies are in tone languages, even though the pitch accents are associated to specific words, known as **accented** words. Intonation contours generally ignore word boundaries, and many syllables can be spanned by the F0 interpolations. In Figure 10.2, the pitch contour

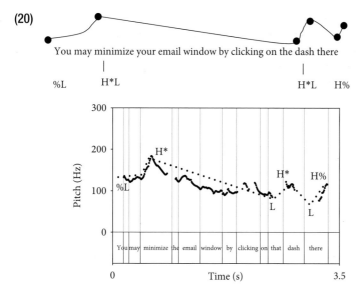

Figure 10.2
Pitch curve of a British English utterance of You may minimize your email window by clicking on the dash there, *spoken with H*L on* min- *and on* dash *and an initial %L and final H%.*

and speech waveform is given of *You may MINimize your email window by clicking on the DASH there*, spoken with falling pitch accents on *min-* and *dash*, and with low and high boundary tones at the beginning and end, respectively. The pitch accent H*L thus occurs twice, and the sentence begins with %L, an initial boundary tone, and ends with H%, a final boundary tone. As expected, the targets of the boundary tones are aligned at the beginning and at the end of the Intonational Phrase (for this constituent, see also section 16.5.2). The target of the starred tone, H* or L*, tends to occur in the accented syllable. For multi-tonal pitch accents like H*L and L*H, the target of the second tone is aligned rightmost, so as to occur just before the target of the H* or L* of the next pitch accent. This is illustrated in (20) for the intonation contour in Figure 10.2, where the target of the L of H*L of *min-* occurs just before *dash*. As a result, the stretch *–nimize your email window by clicking on the* lies along the interpolation between the targets of H* and L of the first H*L. In the case of a last pitch accent in an Intonational Phrase, the second tone is pronounced leftmost, causing a steeper fall in H*L and a steeper rise in L*H. Thus, in (20), the last fall covers only *–ash* plus a number of immediately following segments, and this is true even if we added some unaccented words after *dash*, as in *the DASH you can see there*, as shown in (21). In short, if we know where the Intonational Phrase begins and ends and where the accented syllables are, we know enough to say where the tonal targets are located.

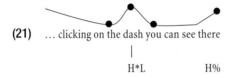

(21)   … clicking on the dash you can see there

H*L   H%

Q95   Describe the F0 pattern that will occur on *John* if the sentence *Has JOHN?* is pronounced with the intonation contour %L H*L H%. Give a representation with tones and targets of the way shown in (20) and (21).

10.7   THE OBLIGATORY CONTOUR PRINCIPLE

The success of the autosegmental account of the word tone patterns in languages like Etung depends in part on the decision not to represent the tone of each syllable as a separate tone in the representation. Crucially, adjacent syllables with the same tone need not each be specified separately for tone, since the same tone can associate with more syllables through spreading. Considerations like these have led to the assumption that identical tones cannot be adjacent in the same word. This restriction on representations goes by the name of the OBLIGATORY CONTOUR PRINCIPLE (OCP), formulated by Goldsmith (1976) with reference to Leben (1973) as (22), which forbids the occurrence of identical adjacent tones in the same morpheme.

(22)   OBLIGATORY CONTOUR PRINCIPLE: * V   V
                                             | |
                                             T$_i$ T$_i$

Another argument for the OCP is that rules changing or deleting tones usually delete whole strings of what on the surface appear to be sequences of identical tones. If we assume that the string of identical surface tones is in reality a single, multiply associated tone, a ready explanation is found for this phenomenon. Example (23), from Odden (1986), comes from Shona. The 'associative prefix' [né] 'with' lowers any consecutive H-tones to low. Clearly, if these words have only one H, rule (24) can change that H into L, thus accounting for these data, as shown in (25).

(23) mbwá   'dog'
      hóvé   'fish'
      mbúndúdzí   'army worms'

(24) H → L / $\begin{array}{c} \text{H} \\ | \\ \text{ne} \end{array}$ ___

(25) ne-mbundudzi →   ne-mbundudzi
      | ↘↓ | ↘↓
      H   H   H   L

By contrast, if each of the three syllables of 'army worms' were to have its own H, a more complicated analysis results. We must apply a rule deleting H after [né] provided the following tone is also H (which rule will apply more than once to the same word in a case like 'army worms'), then change the remaining H-tone into L, and third, spread that L back to the preceding toneless syllables. Clearly, having a single H-tone in the representation makes life a lot simpler!

> **Q96** How does the derivation of 'every cup' proceed if, as argued by Leben (1978), Etsakǫ obeys the OCP? Would there still be a need for the operation of the Twin Sister Convention?

10.7.1 Violating the OCP

The OCP cannot be a universally obeyed constraint. For one thing, languages like Etung frequently have exceptional patterns. For instance, words with surface melodies HHL and LLH do exist, like [ŋgárè] 'pepper'. Such words must either be assumed to have underlying melodies like HHL, *contra* the OCP, or to have a single H tone **prelinked** in the lexicon *contra* the AC. In the latter option, the SR of 'pepper' would look like (26) (Odden 1986).

(26) ngare
      ∨ |
      H L

While prelinking of tones would appear to be able to save the OCP in Etung, representations that violate the OCP do appear to be necessary in some languages.

One indication for the separate representation of adjacent identical tones in a word is their realization: if they are pronounced at different pitch heights, it is reasonable to assume that each pitch target results from a separate tone. A case in point is found in Dinka (Andersen 1987). Dinka syllables may have L, H or the contour HL. Examples are [tḭːk] 'woman', [bá̰ɲ] 'chief', [tṵ̀ŋ] 'horns'. Like many tone languages, Dinka has a phonetic implementation rule of downstep which causes a H after a L to be lowered relative to an earlier H. Any following H has the same pitch as the preceding (lowered) H, and if there is another L, a further downstep of a following H will take place. In (27), the word [lɔ̰ːk] is pronounced with downstepped H because of the preceding L. However, downstep also occurs on the phrase-final syllable with H tone after a H tone. The pitch of the final H in (25) is just what it would have been if L had preceded it. The bisyllabic word for 'here', therefore, must be assumed to have two separate Hs. In the transcription, downstepped tones have been marked with !. The numerical transcription of the pitch contour which results from the phonological representation uses 0 for the highest pitch, 1 for the next highest pitch, etc. The difference between H and L is 2, and downstep lowers the pitch by 1.

(27)   c-a̰ mḛt lɔːk nḭːn ḛtḛːn
      | | | | | |
      H L !H H H!H
      0 2 1   1   1 2
      'when did you wash the child here?'
      PERF-2sg child wash+PARTICIPLE when here

As we have seen in section 10.6, languages frequently have boundary tones, and the downstep on the final H of Dinka is possibly caused by the interaction between a final L-boundary tone and the H on the final syllable. This is shown in (28): an implementation rule will realize the final HL% after H as a downstepped H.[1]

(28)   ḛt ḛːn   ]
      | |
      H H   L%
      0 1

There are further facts that suggest that sequences of identical tones must be allowed to occur in Dinka. L-tones can be downstepped, too. L-tones are downstepped after

---

[1] There is a possible way round the conclusion that disyllabic high-toned words have two consecutive Hs. It is possible to assume that they have HL on the first syllable and H on the second. This is because the contrast between the HL contour and H is neutralized in positions before H. The first syllable is pronounced just like H, as if L was deleted, while the second is pronounced high in pre-phrase-final position and downstepped H in phrase-final position. Thus, in the more elaborate representation [HL H], the OCP is not violated.

L, provided no H-tone follows in the same phrase. This is shown for a sentence with six consecutive L tones, after an H-tone in (29) and in a context without any H-tone in (30). The two syllables of the words [tà:ŋ-dù̱] 'your spear' in (29) and [àn̰ɔ̰ŋ] 'DEF-have' in (30) show the same pattern as any two L-toned syllables separated by a word boundary, and each therefore must have its own L.

(29) rjɛ::m a̰-tɔ ɛ ta:ŋ-du̱ to̱k

    | | | | | | |

    H   L !L !L !L   !L !L

    0   2 3 4 5   6 7

'there is blood on your spear'
blood DEF-be on spear-2sg mouth

(30) a̰nɔŋ lɛc ɛ cwa̱:r

    | | | | |

    L !L !L !L !L

'he has the teeth of a lion'
DEF+have teeth of thief+ERGATIVE

The downstepping pattern contrasts with a level contour before a H-tone. In (31), a word with H-tones has been added to the L-toned sentence, and here no downstepping occurs in the low-toned words, not even for the L-tones that are far removed from the H. This suggests that the whole of the pitch contour before the first H is the realization of a single L-tone. The example shows that the difference between a representation with a single L and one with multiple Ls is meaningful: it distinguishes between a level low stretch and a contour that descends syllable by syllable. In order to account for the representation in (31), we must assume a postlexical rule merging adjacent L-tones before H.

(31)
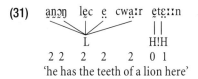

    a̰nɔŋ lɛc ɛ cwa̱:r ɛtɛ̰::n

                             | |

              L   H!H

    2 2   2 2   2   0 1

'he has the teeth of a lion here'

Q97	The majority of Mende words have the tone patterns illustrated below:
one syllable:	kɔ́ 'war', kpà 'debt', mbû 'owl', mbǎ 'rice', mbâ 'companion'
two syllables:	pɛ́lɛ́ 'house', njàhâ 'woman', ŋgílà 'dog', fàndé 'cotton', bɛ̀lɛ̀ 'trousers'
three syllables:	kpàkàlì 'tripod chair', félàmà 'junction', ndàvúlá 'sling', nìkílì 'groundnut', háwáná 'waistline'

1. What are the underlying tone patterns of Mende?
2. Does Mende, like Etung, obey the No Crowding Constraint?
3. Give the tonal representations of the words for 'woman' and 'tripod chair'.

Q98 In Kipare, an utterance-final H is downstepped, as shown in (1a) (Odden 1986).

(1) a. ìpa ꜜŋgá   'machete'
    b. ìpáŋgá lédì   'good machete'

Assume that the end of the utterance has a boundary L%, which causes the downstep on the final H. When L-tones precede the final H, a frequent, though not obligatory, pronunciation is one in which the final (downstepped) H spreads leftward to all the L-toned TBUs. (2a) shows the pronunciation without the spreading, (2b) the pronunciation with.

(2) a. nìfínìkìrè màyèmbè màèꜜðá   'I covered long hoes'
    b. nìfíꜜníkíre᷄ máyémbé máéðá

Although it is optional, the spreading of the final H shown in (2b) is always to all possible TBUs. That is, it is not possible to pronounce the sentence with spreading of H to only some of the words that are pronounced with low pitch in (2a). What does this suggest about the representation of the L-toned words before H spreads?

Q99 West Greenlandic is a nontonal language, which has a phrase-final boundary melody HL and an utterance-final H. At the utterance end, these tones come together to form the melody HLH. The timing of these boundary tones varies, as illustrated in the following data (Rischel 1974; Nagano-Madsen 1993). Assume that the preceding unmarked syllables are unspecified for tone, and are pronounced with middish pitch.

a. akívàrá   'I answered him'
b. atâːsíq   'one'
c. akívǎː   'he answered him'
d. úvàŋá   'I'
e. uvàŋàlú   'and I'
f. uvaŋátːǎː   'I, too'

1. Assuming that the TBU in West Greenlandic is the vowel, with long vowels and diphthongs counting as two TBUs, show the structure of the expressions in a, b, c. Show long vowels with double symbols (i.e. [aː] as [aa]).
2. State the direction of association.

Yes–no questions end in the same melody, but are distinguished from Declaratives by the lengthening of the final syllable. In particular, short vowels become long, long vowels become overlong (i.e. count as three TBUs), and diphthongs have a first element corresponding to a long vowel. This is shown in the following data:

Declarative		Interrogative	
g. takuʷâːná	'he saw me'	takuʷáːnǎː	'did he see me?'
h. takúʷìᶨúk	'you saw him'	takuʷíᶨǔːk	'did you see him?'
i. tsigúʷǎː	'he takes that'	tsiguʷã̌ːː	'did he take that?'
j. apírài̯	'he asked them'	apirâːí	'did he ask them?'

3. Are these data compatible with your account of the association of HLH? Give the autosegmental representations of the Declarative and Interrogative forms of 'he asked them'.
4. The penultimate vowel of the Interrogative form in (g) is fully high-toned. What extra assumption must be made to account for this fact?

10.8   CONCLUSION

Goldsmith's thesis (1976) represented a breakthrough in our conception of phono-logical representations. While the idea that speech is to be represented as a number of parallel tiers of elements was not new, and had in particular been advocated by a group of British phonologists who worked in association with J.R. Firth (e.g. Palmer 1970), the intellectual environment in which Goldsmith did his research ensured that its impact went well beyond the question of how to represent tone. Autosegmental phonology soon came to be applied to segmental duration, as we will see in the next chapter, as well as to phonological features like [±nasal] and [±ATR], and eventually led to what is now known as Feature Geometry (Chapters 12 and 13). At about the same time, beginning with the work of Liberman and Prince (1977) (Chapter 14), the representation of stress underwent an evolution which, together with the renewed appreciation of the role of syllabic structure (Kahn 1976; see Chapter 11), led to the introduction of prosodic structure in phonology and ultimately to what we now know as Prosodic Phonology (Chapter 16). The *SPE* model of phonological representation, with its strict sequential arrangement of segments and boundaries, came to be known as a **linear** model, while the new conceptions came to be collectively referred to as **nonlinear** phonology.

Between the segment and the syllable

11.1 INTRODUCTION

In this chapter we will consider the way in which segments are organized into syllables. The syllable dominates the segments only indirectly. That is, between the syllable and the segment a further level of structure is commonly assumed. One view of this intermediate level of structure is that of the CV tier. Two of the roles this tier is required to fulfil are first, the representation of segmental duration and second, the designation of the syllabicity of the segment, i.e. whether it occurs in the peak or, alternatively, in the onset or coda. In a sense, then, the topic of Chapter 10 is continued, but instead of tone we now consider segmental duration as a candidate for autosegmental representation. The arguments for the CV tier will be reviewed and illustrated in section 11.4. There is, however, an alternative representation for these aspects of phonological structure. One reason for including the syllable in phonological structure is that it forms the domain to which stress is assigned: it is the structural element that can be either stressed or unstressed. In many languages the 'stressability' of a syllable appears to be influenced by the contents of its rhyme: broadly speaking, single (short) vowels behave differently from other syllables. Accordingly, the mora is taken to be the intermediate level of structure that allows the distinction between such light (or monomoraic) and heavy (or bimoraic) syllables to be expressed. It is generally seen as a representation that makes the CV tier superfluous, the idea being that all the roles that have been claimed for it can be fulfilled by other aspects in the phonological representation.

In addition to the behaviour of stress and the sequential restrictions that were referred to in Chapter 3, where *[ætk] was said to be an impossible syllable of English, the evidence for the syllable as a phonological constituent comes from the fact that it must be referred to by many phonological generalizations. Examples of such syllable-based generalizations are given in section 11.6. Finally, we consider the need for the ambisyllabic representation of certain consonants.

11.2 A SKELETAL TIER

In the previous chapter we have seen that tone is best represented as an independent string of segments. Another aspect of the pronunciation of words that appears to behave independently of the segments is segmental duration. A particularly clear example is provided by language games. One of these, called Ludikya, is reported by Clements (1986) for Luganda, and involves a reversal of the order of the syllables in the word. Luganda has both a vowel length contrast and a contrast between long and short consonants. Instead of by the length mark, we indicate long segments by doubling the symbol. The striking thing is that although the vowels and consonants move round in this game, the durational structure remains intact, as shown in (1).

(1) *Luganda*   *Ludikya*
     mukono   nokomu   'arm'
     mubinikilo   lokinibimu   'funnel'
     baana   naaba   'children'
     ɟɟuba   bbaɟu   'dove'
     kiwoɟɟolo   loɟowwoki   'butterfly'
     kubaɟɟa   ɟabakku   'to work in wood'

In order to be able to describe this process, the mutual independence of segmental duration and segmental quality needs to be expressed in the representation. Clements and Keyser (1983) propose that segments are not immediately associated to their syllables, but are dominated by structural positions, known as **(skeletal) slots**, which encode the segment durations. Consonants and vowels that are associated to single slots are short, while long vowels and geminate consonants are represented as being doubly linked to two slots. Additionally, they assume that there are two types, a C and a V, where the C represents a syllable margin (onset or coda) and V a syllable peak. That is, CV slots take over the role of the feature [±syllabic], in addition to providing a representation for segmental duration.

The CV slots are dominated by the syllable nodes, each syllable being represented by σ. For example, a language with a duration contrast for vowels as well as for consonants, like the Dravidian languages Malayalam and Tamil, would have representations like those in (2), which represent the Tamil words [paʈu, paːʈu, paʈːu, paːʈːu], respectively (Firth 1957; Mohanan 1986: 108). All four words consist of two syllables each and have the same string of segments; however, they differ in their segmental timing structure.

(2)

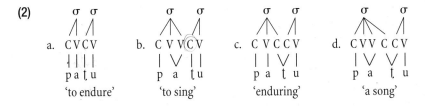

The CV representation allows us to characterize the Luganda word game Ludikya illustrated in (1). It involves a reversal of the phonological content of the syllables of each word, with the retention of the structure above the segments. This is shown in (3), where the top line gives the order of the segments in the Luganda word, while the bottom line gives the Ludikya version. Importantly, the strings of skeletal slots are identical in the two versions of each word.

(3)

In addition to providing a representation for the duration and syllabicity of segments, the CV tier has been motivated on the basis of other phenomena. These arguments involve the representation of morphemes in terms of CV templates, the use of C slots without associated segments or without association to the syllable node, and the description of compensatory lengthening as the spreading of segments to vacated slots. These arguments are discussed in section 11.4. Before considering them, we need to say a few things about syllabification.

11.3   SYLLABIFICATION: THE MAXIMUM ONSET PRINCIPLE

The syllabic affiliation of the C slots is largely predictable. The presence of the intervocalic consonant in the onset of the second syllable, rather than the coda of the first (cf. (2a,b)) is universal. That is, consonants prefer to form an onset rather than a coda, if they can legitimately do so. This is why Clements and Keyser assume that at best only the association of the V slot with a vowel is lexically given, but that the associations of the C slots with the syllable nodes can be derived by rule. The principle responsible for maximizing the onset is (4) (Kahn 1976).

(4)   MAXIMUM ONSET PRINCIPLE (MOP): First make the onset as long as it legitimately can be; then form a legitimate coda.

The MOP requires that a string like [tata] should be syllabified [ta.ta], rather than *[tat.a]. And if the language allows [st] onsets, then a string like [asta] will be [a.sta], rather than *[as.ta] or *[ast.a]. Of course, it is essential to keep in mind that, while the MOP is a universal principle, languages differ in the kinds of syllables they allow. For example, Dutch and English allow [st] in the onset, but Spanish does not. Application of (4) to a Spanish string [basta] will therefore yield [bas.ta], not *[ba.sta]. By the same token, German syllabifies *extra* as [ɛks.tra], but Dutch as [ɛk.stra], because Dutch does, but German does not have [st] onsets, even though it does have [ʃt] onsets. And since no geminates can appear in the onset, the geminate is divided over the coda of one and the onset of the next syllable (cf. (2c,d) above). The pronunciation of a glottal stop before a vowel in languages that don't have a glottal stop in the lexical inventory, as in English *How awful!*, is a sure sign that the vowel has no onset, at least not underlyingly.

Languages differ in the **syllabification domain**. In West Germanic languages, the syllabification domain tends to be the word, or rather, the phonological constituent to be introduced in Chapter 16 as the phonological word. For instance, the English *see Morton* is not homophonous with *seem Orton*, the first syllable being [siː] in the first phrase and [siːm] in the second, which difference will have an effect on the duration of [iː], in particular. Other languages may have larger domains, like French, which syllabifies across words and where *petit ami* 'little friend' and *petit tamis* 'little sieve' are both [pə.ti.ta.mi], or smaller domains, like Japanese, where certain suffixes will not syllabify with the stem, as shown by /a.ni/ 'brother' and /an.i/ 'easy going'. In the Japanese case, the corresponding phonetic difference is very clear, because the onset nasal is coronal, but the coda nasal more likely to be velar or uvular. That is, /a.ni/ is pronounced [ani], and /an.i/ [aŋʔi]. More generally, prefixes in German do not syllabify with the stem, as in *Verein* [fɛrʔain] 'club', where *Ver-* is a prefix.

11.3.1 The sonority profile

The segmental composition of onsets and codas show striking similarities across different languages. If you were to bet on the type of consonant that could occupy the second position in a CC onset in some unknown language, your chances of winning would be well served by opting for a glide like [j] or [w]. And if your bet concerned the first consonant, you would be well-advised to go for [p], [t] or [k]. Venneman (1972) described these tendencies in terms of a number of syllable 'laws'. Much of the regularity is captured by the SONORITY PROFILE, given in (5).

(5)   SONORITY PROFILE: The sonority of a syllable increases from the beginning of the syllable onwards, and decreases from the beginning of the peak onwards.

Intuitively, sonority is related to the overall acoustic energy of segments. In (6), the classes of segments that are usually distinguished along this dimension are listed in the order of increasing sonority.

(6)   SONORITY SCALE: Obstruents – Nasals – Liquids ([l,r], etc.) – Glides ([w,j], etc.) – Vowels

Thus, the observation is that any onset that reverses the direction of increasing sonority, like [mk-] or [wl-], is less common than one that does not, like [pn-] or [ml-]. Conversely, any rhyme that increases the sonority from left to right, like [-lj], is disfavoured. Violations of the sonority profile are indeed rare. Swedish has syllables like [bærj] 'mountain', while Dutch has syllables like [ʋrɪŋ] 'wring', where the first consonant is a labial glide. In addition, Clements (1990) observes that in the onset large sonority differences are preferred over small ones, making [pj-] a better onset than [lj-], while in the rhyme small sonority differences are preferred over large ones, making [-j] a better coda than [-t]. Apparently, syllables prefer to start with a bang and end with a whimper. Because the beginning of the syllable is maximally salient as a result, catching the listener's attention when it should, the reason for this state of affairs is probably perceptual.

The preference of onsets with increasing sonority will lead to syllabifications of intervocalic sequences of consonants as in [akla] as [a.kla]. That is, in a language that allows CC onsets, [alka] will typically come out as [al.ka], and not as *[a.lka] but [akla] as [a.kla].

There is an interesting consequence of the observation by Clements (1990) that syllables, to repeat the phrase, start with a bang and end with a whimper. Syllables tend to group in words so that the sonority of the end of one syllable is greater than that of the beginning of the next, favouring a whimper-bang transition over a bang-whimper one. In languages without complex onsets or codas, [al.ka] will therefore be a more likely structure than [ak.la]. This tendency was earlier described as the SYLLABLE CONTACT LAW by Venneman (1972). So also when considering the relation between syllables, the tendency is to maximize the bang at the beginning.

Sonority can be defined in terms of the features introduced in Chapter 6 (Clements 1990). The four consonantal sonority classes of (6) are so characterized by the features [±cons], [±son], [±approx]. To distinguish vowels from glides, the syllabicity needs to be called upon.

> **Q100**   What do the English words *stigma*, *comrade* and *Daphne* have in common?

11.4   ARGUMENTS FOR THE CV TIER

In this section we consider three types of argument that have been made for the inclusion of segmental timing slots in phonological representation. Later in this chapter, we will see that the role of these timing slots is in part better served by a more economical representation, that of the mora.

11.4.1   The templatic use of the CV tier

The independent status of the CV tier was first proposed in McCarthy (1985a). It was inspired by the fact that certain morphemes in Arabic appear to be specified in terms of strings of consonant and vowel positions, or skeletal slots, referred to as **templates**. The morphology of the Arabic verb includes a number of derivational morphemes ('conjugations'), which are not just expressed by particular affixes, but also by different templates. In some cases there is no affix, so that conjugations can differ only in the CV template they have. The verbal root consists only of consonants, usually three. The vowels in such verbal forms represent the third type of morpheme, which corresponds to verbal aspect or voice. In (7), some of these morphemes are listed. A verbal form, then, consists minimally of a verbal root (two or more consonants), a conjugation (a CV template) and a verbal aspect (one or more vowels).

(7)	ktb	'write'
	ħq	'be true'
	CVCVC	'Plain'
	CVCCVC	'Intensive'
	CVVCVC	'Influencing'
	a	'Active Perfective'
	ui	'Passive Perfective'

The corresponding forms for 'write' and 'be true' are given in (8), where the final [a] is the third person masculine singular. To derive these forms, it is necessary to assume that the consonants and vowels form separate tiers, and that the consonants associate with the Cs and the vowels with the Vs. Moreover, adjacent slots of the same type are filled by the same segment. That is, association is not one-to-one, but subject to the requirement that long vowels and geminate consonants are created where possible. This is shown in (9), where the third person suffix is not shown.[1]

(8)	Conjugation	Active		Passive	
	Plain	katab-a	'he wrote'	kutib-a	'it was written'
	Intensive	kattab-a	'he caused to write'	kuttib-a	'it was made to write'
	Influencing	kaatab-a	'he corresponded'	kuutib-a	'he was corresponded with'
	Plain	ḥaqq - a	'it is true'	–	
	Intensive	ḥaqqaq-a	'he realized st.'	ḥuqqiq-a	'it has been realized'
	Influencing	ḥaaqaq-a	'he contested sb.'s right'	ḥuuqiq-a	'his right was contested'

(9)

```
      k   t   b          k     t  b
      |   ∧   |          |     |  |
      C V C C V C        C V V  C V C
          ∨                ∨    |
          a                u    i
'he caused to write'   'he was corresponded with'
```

For the morpheme 'be true' we could either assume an underlying 'triliteral' root ([ḥqq]) or a 'biliteral' one ([ḥq]). If we assume that the direction of association is left to right, the form [ḥaqqaq-a], for instance, can be accounted for by the spreading of the [q] of a biliteral root, as shown in (10): the left-over C slots are filled by the spreading of the last consonant. There is strong evidence that this latter solution is correct. In verbal and nominal forms with three surface consonants, it is never the case that the first two consonants are identical, a rare exception being [dadan] 'plaything' (McCarthy 1985a: 146). This is explained if repetitions of the same consonant are produced by the left-to-right spreading of a rightmost consonant segment to empty C slots, as shown in (10). Thus, a constraint on the underlying form of Arabic roots is that there are no adjacent identical consonants. This constraint is evidently akin to the ban on sequences of identical tones discussed in the previous chapter, the OCP. This constraint, therefore, has come to be generalized to a ban on adjacency of identical phonological elements in general.

---

[1] The expected form *[ḥaqaq-a] 'it is true' is ruled out because of a general process deleting vowels in this context.

(10)

```
 ħ   q              ħ    q
 |  ╱╲              |   ╱╲
C V C C   V C      C V V C V C
   ╲___╱               ╲╱  |
     a                 u   i
'he realized s.t.'    'his right was contested'
```

Q101   A secret language based on Amharic uses the forms in the second column for the words in the first (McCarthy 1985b). The apostrophe indicates glottalization of the consonant; adjacent glottalized consonants are only marked once for glottalization.

	Amharic	Disguised form	Gloss
a.	gɪn	gainən	'but'
	mətt'a	mait'ət'	'come'
	kɪfu	kaifəf	'cruel'
	t'ətt'a	t'ait'ət'	'drink'
	hed	haidəd	'go'
	wəddədə	waidəd	'love'
b.	wərk'	wairk'ək'	'gold'
	təmara	taimrər	'learn'
	sɪgara	saigrər	'cigarette'
	səkkərə	saikrər	'drunkard'
	kəbad	kaibdəd	'difficult'
	wɪʃət	waiʃtət	'lie'

1. What is the difference between the Amharic words and the disguised words?
2. Which segments are preserved in the speech disguised forms and which are not?
3. What determines the number of (surface) consonants in the speech disguised forms?
4. Give an account of the formation of the speech disguised forms, employing a representation with a skeletal CV tier. Consider [ai] a single short vowel that associates with a single V slot.
5. How does your description of this secret language differ from Arabic verbal morphology?
6. Give the representations of the disguised forms for 'drink' and 'gold'.

Q102   Scottish Gaelic has a three-way length opposition for vowels, 'short', 'half-long' and 'fully long', as illustrated by [ʃĩn] 'we', [ʃiːnʲ] 'venison', [ʃiːːnʲ] 'to sing', or [tuɫ] 'to go', [uːɫ] 'apple', [suːːl] 'eye'. At most, two different vowel qualities may occur per syllable, as illustrated in [ĩan] 'John' and [ĩaːn] 'bird'. In addition to this constraint, there are these two facts:

a. Diphthongs are either half-long or fully long.
b. The distribution of the durations of two intrasyllabic vowel segments is 'short, short' (as in [ĩan]) or 'short, half-long' (as in [ĩaːn]), but never 'half-long, short' (*[ĩːan]) (Ternes 1973: 96).

How would you account for these facts?

11.4.2   Unfilled and unassociated slots

The slots in the CV skeleton are structural positions, which in the usual case dominate segmental material and are associated with a syllable node. By assuming that slots need not have an association with any segments and need not have an association with a syllable, their explanatory role can be extended. Clements and Keyser (1983) call on both these possibilities to account for the alternation between French morpheme-final consonants with ∅, known as LIAISON, and the phenomenon of *h-aspiré*.

The French definite article is [lə] (masc.) or [la] (fem.) for the singular, and [le] for the plural, as shown in (11a). When the noun begins with a vowel, the vowel of the singular definite article is deleted, while the plural is followed by an apparently inserted [z], as can be seen in (11b). In fact, many words appear to be have a consonant that only shows up before a vowel, like [pəti], which has a [t] in [pətit ami] 'little friend'. These potential consonants are called LIAISON consonants.

(11)		*Singular*	*Plural*	
	a.	lə bwa	le bwa	'wood'
		lə pa	le pa	'step'
		la karaf	le karaf	'carafe'
		la nчi	le nчi	'night'
	b.	l abe	lez abe	'priest'
		l ide	lez ide	'idea'

The loss of the vowel of the singular definite article is effected by ELISION (12), which deletes the final V slot of the definite article before V, causing its syllable node to be lost as well.

$$\textbf{(12)} \quad \text{ELISION} \quad \begin{matrix} \text{V} \\ | \\ [\ldots]_{\text{DEF}} \end{matrix} \quad \rightarrow \quad \emptyset/ \_\_ \text{V}$$

LIAISON is expressed in (13), which says that an onsetless syllable syllabifies any unsyllabified consonant appearing before that vowel.

$$\textbf{(13)} \quad \text{LIAISON} \quad \begin{matrix} \sigma \\ \diagup\text{-}\dashv \\ \text{C} \quad \text{V} \end{matrix}$$

These rules produce the correct results if the singular and plural forms of the article are represented as in (14a,b). The singular will lose its vowel before a V-initial word, while the unsyllabified final consonant in the plural will only be syllabified, and pronounced, before a V-initial word.

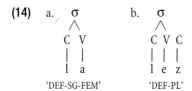

$$\textbf{(14)} \quad \text{a.} \quad \begin{matrix} \sigma \\ \diagup\diagdown \\ \text{C} \quad \text{V} \\ | \quad | \\ \text{l} \quad \text{a} \end{matrix} \qquad \text{b.} \quad \begin{matrix} \sigma \\ \diagup\diagdown \\ \text{C} \quad \text{V} \quad \text{C} \\ | \quad | \quad | \\ \text{l} \quad \text{e} \quad \text{z} \end{matrix}$$

'DEF-SG-FEM'   'DEF-PL'

Certain vowel-initial nouns appear to behave as if they began with a consonant: they take the preconsonantal alternants of the definite article, both in the singular and in the plural, as shown in (15). In order to account for the behaviour of words like 'hero' and 'hatred', their underlying forms are assumed to begin with an empty C, which is syllabified as an onset C just as any filled C would be. This is shown in (16b), which representation should be compared with (16a).

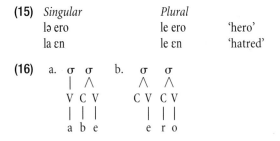

(15)   *Singular*   *Plural*
     lə ero   le ero   'hero'
     la ɛn   le ɛn   'hatred'

Thus the deletion of pre-V [a] in (17a), as well as its retention in the pre-C context of (17b), are readily accounted for. Likewise, the difference between the presence of the liaison [z] in 'the priests' (18a) and its absence in 'the heroes' (18b) is explained by the inability of the unsyllabified [z] to undergo LIAISON in (18b). This solution accurately expresses the fact that words with *h-aspiré* behave as if they began with a consonant, even though no surface consonant is observed. Also, it correctly characterizes both the distribution and the identity of the LIAISON consonant.

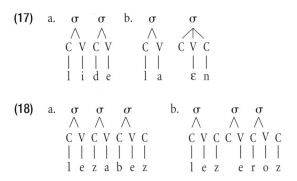

11.4.3 Compensatory lengthening

A final type of argument for the existence of the skeletal tier is the phenomenon of **compensatory lengthening**. Frequently, the loss of a segment is incomplete in the sense that the time it took before it was deleted is preserved in a neighbouring segment. The parent language of English and Frisian, which at one time constituted a West Germanic dialect sometimes referred to as Ingwaeonic, underwent a process of nasal loss before fricatives within the word. Prior to the loss of the nasal, the vowel before it was short, but a long vowel remains today. In (19), we give reconstructed (hypothetical) forms. The presence of the nasal is attested in Gothic texts, as well as in modern German. (Probably, the nasalization was also preserved on the vowel at first, and was lost later. We ignore this in the transcriptions.)

(19) gans   ga:s   'goose'
          fimf   fi:f   'five'
          tanθ   ta:θ   'tooth'
          munθ   mu:θ   'mouth'

The representation with the skeletal tier allows one to express the change as a retiming of the segments, as shown in (20). An additional measure, one which is triggered by the [−cons] segment associated with it, is a change of the vacated C slot into a V slot.

(20)

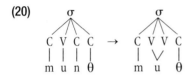

Compensatory lengthening can also be recognized in consonants that have come to occupy the syllable peak (**syllabic consonants**). The second syllable in English *bottle* ['bɔtl̩] consists purely of the consonant [l]: the release of the plosive [t] takes place through a lowering of the sides of the tongue, the tip retaining its contact (**lateral plosion**). Assuming that the duration of the syllabic [l] is no different from the duration of [əl], a less common but attested pronunciation, the syllabic consonant could be represented as in (21a). In Mandarin Chinese, retroflex syllabic consonants derive historically from the spreading of the onset consonant to the syllable peak, as in [tʂʐ̩] 'late' or [ʂʐ̩] 'wet'. In (21b) the voicing of the consonant will follow from a constraint that syllable peaks are voiced (Wiese 1986).

(21)   a. C V C V C   b. C V
                  | | | V   V
                  b ɔ t l   ʂ
                                         'wet'

Retiming of segments is a well-known feature of Bantu languages. Class prefixes like [ki] usually only show up in that form before consonant-initial stems. When the stem begins with a vowel, however, the close vowel turns into a glide while the vowel lengthens. Consider the Luganda examples in (22), from Clements (1986).

(22) li + ato   lja:to   'boat'
          mu + iko   mwi:ko   'trowel'
          ki + uma   kju:ma   'metal object'
          mi + aka   mja:ka   'year'

If it is assumed that the resulting onset does not consist of two consonants, but of a single, complex consonant which is either labialized (in the case of retimed [u]) or palatalized (in the case of retimed [i]), the process can be described as in (23).

(23)

```
     σ              σ   σ            σ                  σ
     ∧              |   ∧            ∧⟍                 ∧
     C V   +   V  C  V     →     C  V  +  V   C  V
     | |          | |  |            ↖  ∨          | |
     l i          a  t  o         l  j  a      t  o
```

> **Q103** In Catalan, a word-initial high vowel turns into a glide when preceded by a stressed vowel, as in [kuntə'rajs'tɔriəs] *contará histories* 'he will tell stories' and [kətə'lawniβər'sal] *català universal* 'universal Catalan' (Hualde 1992). Assuming that the duration of the vowel plus glide is equivalent to that of a short vowel, how could you describe this process in CV phonology?

11.5　MORAS

It has been pointed out that the skeletal tier fails to account for two phenomena (Hayes 1989). One is that compensatory lengthening always occurs in the case of segments deleted from the rhyme, never in the case of segments deleted from the onset. This suggests that segments in the rhyme possess something that other segments do not possess. Second, it appears that many languages distinguish syllables on the basis of **quantity**, a property of syllables which is determined by the number of segments in the rhyme, again to the exclusion of their onset. As for the first objection, consider the fate of the onsets [kn-, gn-] in Middle English. When [k,g] were lost, and the English syllable no longer admitted onsets that consisted of [−cont] [+nas], there was no compensatory lengthening of any of the other segments in words like *knot* and *gnat*, now pronounced [nɔt] and [næt], not *[nːɔt] or *[nɔːt], etc.

　　Second, the location of the word stress frequently appears to be sensitive to the segmental composition of the rhyme, while the number of segments in the onset is irrelevant (barring a few exceptional and incidental instances). In Hawaiian, for instance, stress falls on the last syllable if it contains a long vowel, and on the penultimate syllable if the last is a short vowel, as illustrated by [na'naː] 'strut' and ['naːna] 'for him'. Significantly, a consonant in the rhyme is often counted as if it was a vowel. In Hopi, for instance, the stress falls on the first syllable if the rhyme contains a long vowel or a short vowel and a consonant, as shown in (24a), but on the second syllable if it contains a short vowel, as shown in (24b) (Jeanne 1982). That is, the consonant in the rhyme can determine the location of the stress in a way that a consonant in the onset cannot.

(24)　a.　'qøq.tø.som.pi　　'headbands'
　　　　　'soː.ja　　　　　　'planting stick'
　　　b.　qø.'tø.som.pi　　'headband'
　　　　　ko.'jo.ŋo　　　　　'turkey'

In order to capture the difference in status between segments in the rhyme and segments in the onset, the mora has been proposed as an intermediate level of structure between segments and the syllable (Hyman 1985; Hayes 1989). The prosodically 'active' status of a segment can then be expressed by giving it moraic status, while 'inactive' segments are not entitled to their own mora. A language that has no vowel-length distinction and does not allow a coda will have only syllables with one mora. A language with a vowel-length distinction has both monomoraic and bimoraic syllables. The term **weight** is used to refer to the opposition between monomoraic (or **light**) and bimoraic (or **heavy**) syllables. Onset consonants are nonmoraic, and in the representation of Hayes (1989) are attached directly to the syllable node. Postvocalic consonants may or may not be moraic. They are moraic in Hopi, where the stress rule treats the coda consonant on the same basis as the second half of a long vowel. Because vowels are always moraic, but coda consonants may or may not be, Hayes assumes that languages may or may not apply the rule of WEIGHT-BY-POSITION, by which a postvocalic consonant is assigned a mora. In (25), some syllable types are represented. As will be clear, (25a,c) are light syllables, while (25b,d) are heavy syllables.

(25)

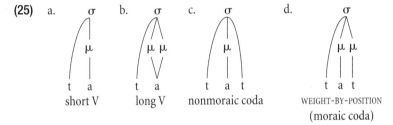

Geminate consonants must be moraic in order to express their duration. The Italian distinction between [fato] 'fate' and [fatːo] 'fact' is expressed by representing the nongeminate as an onset consonant, and the geminate as a consonant that is attached to a mora in the first syllable and as a weightless onset in the second, as shown in (26). Languages with intervocalic geminate consonants are predicted to have WEIGHT-BY-POSITION.

(26)

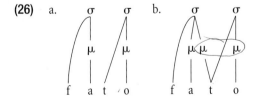

Although it is not uncommon for languages to allow the last syllable of the word to have three moras, languages that generally allow their rhymes to have three moras are rare. That is, if a language has WEIGHT-BY-POSITION, usually only the first consonant after a short vowel is moraic, while the next consonant or any consonant after a long vowel is nonmoraic. Languages that have three degrees of vowel length, like Dinka, and languages that allow a geminate to follow a long vowel have trimoraic syllables. Such syllables are called **superheavy**. Tamil, as we saw in (2), is an example of a language with geminates after long vowels. The moraic representations of those four structures is given in (27), where (27a) has a light, (27b,c) a heavy and (27d) a superheavy first syllable.

(27)

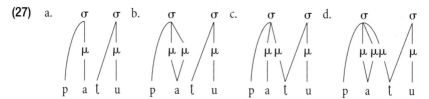

Since trimoraic languages are rare, it is common for long vowels to be banned before geminates. For instance, in Koya, while words like [aːnd] 'female power', [manasuːrku] 'men', [meːnduːli] 'back', in which long vowels appear before a coda consonant, are fine, as are short vowels before a geminate, as in [pɪkːa] 'cup', a form like *[puːtːi] is ill-formed. In fact, when such a combination arises as a result of morphological concatenation, the vowel is shortened, as shown in (28).

(28)   keː – tː – oːɳɖa   [ketːoːɳɖa]   'he told'
       oː – tː – oːɳɖu   [otːoːɳɖu]   'he brought'

The restriction is explained if the Koya rhyme is restricted to two moras, where the second can either be the second half of a long vowel or a consonant, additional consonants being nonmoraic. Since geminates cannot be nonmoraic, they require the vowel before them to be short (Tyler 1969).

Q104   Word stress in Koya falls on every long syllable and every closed syllable in the word, and the language therefore has WEIGHT-BY-POSITION (Tyler 1969). Koya does not have complex onsets. Give the moraic-cum-syllabic representations of the words [pɪkːa], [manasuːrku] and [beske] 'when'.

Q105   The syllable structure of Tera is CV(X), where X can be V or C. Except at the end of the sentence, word-final [ə] is deleted unless the preceding syllable has a long vowel or when it is immediately preceded by two consonants. Thus the words in the first column are subject to the rule, but not those in the third (Newman 1970). ([mb] and [nd] are single consonants.)

ə deleted		ə retained	
sədə	'snake'	pərsə	'horse'
wurə	'tomorrow'	meːnə	'today'
mbukə	'to throw at'	xənndə	'nose'

1.   What determines if [ə] is deleted?
2.   Does Tera have WEIGHT-BY-POSITION? Motivate your answer.

Q106 The following words show the position of the main stress in a number of words in Lenakel (Hayes 1995).

'napuk	'song'
tɨ'komkom	'branches'
natjakamwap'keːn	'you two will be jealous'
rɨme'tjaːw	'he arrived'
tupʷalu'kaluk	'lungs'

Does Lenakel have WEIGHT-BY-POSITION? Motivate your answer.

Q107 Here are some examples of a word game in Bakwiri (from Hombert 1986). (Bakwiri is a tone language and tones are marked in the usual way; it has prenasalized stops: [mb], [nd] and [ŋg].)

	Bakwiri	Word game	
a.	mɔ̀kɔ́	kɔ̀mɔ́	'plantain'
b.	lówá	wáló	'excrement'
c.	kóndì	ndíkò	'rice'
d.	ìŋɔ́	ŋɔ́ʔì	'throat'
e.	éʔèè	zéʔèè	'it is not'
f.	lùùŋgá	ŋgàálú	'stomach'
g.	lìòβá	βààljó	'door'

1. What is the general rule for forming word game words? Apply your rule to the hypothetical form [ndàkóó].
2. Bakwiri syllable structure is (C)V(V), where VV may be filled by one vowel, or by two different vowels. Give relevant examples.
3. Why isn't the game form for 'door' *[βààljó]?
4. Why do you think there are glottal stops in the words for 'it is not' and 'throat'?

Q108 Kisanga, another tone language, has the syllable structure (C)V(V). In a children's language game called Kinshingelo, sentences (a) and (b) are pronounced as (c) and (d), respectively (Coupez 1969).

a. óbé múkʷèːtù tʷâjáː kú múkólá
   'you, my friend, come with me to the river'

b. bâːnábákàɟí bâː mú kóːŋgò bǎːtèmʷâː kúdímá
   'the Congolese women love to cultivate the land'

c. béó mútùːkʷè jâtʷáː kú múláko

d. bâːnábáɟiká bâː mú ŋgóːkò bǎːmʷàtêː kúmádí

Argue that this language game provides evidence for the existence in Kisanga of: the word; the syllable; the tonal tier; a timing tier.

> **Q109** Tagalog has a denominal formation meaning 'an imitation of' (Schachter and
> Otanes 1972). The formation involves the reduplication of the noun and the
> suffixation of [an], as shown below. Syllable onsets in Tagalog are C or CC,
> where – at least in the native vocabulary – the C in second position is either [j] or
> [w]. The syllable may have a coda, which is obligatory in word-final position. In
> addition to many other consonants, [h] and [ʔ] can occur at the end of the word,
> but these consonants do not appear word-internally in the coda. Vowel length is
> in general unpredictable, except in word-final position, where vowels are always
> long. This can be seen in the forms in both columns. However, vowel length in
> 'imitation of' forms is subject to further restrictions.

	Base		Derived form	
a.	baːhaːj	'house'	bahajbahaːjaːn	'doll house'
b.	libruːh	'book'	libruːlibruːhaːn	'imitation book'
c.	paːriːʔ	'priest'	pariːpariːʔaːn	'pretended priest'
d.	bulaklaːk	'flower'	bulaklakbulaklaːkaːn	'artificial flower'
e.	kabaːjuːh	'horse'	kabajuːkabajuːhaːn	'imitation horse'
f.	daːhoːn	'leaf'	dahondahoːnaːn	'imitation leaf'

> 1. There are two generalizations to be made about vowel duration in 'imitation of'
>   formations. The first concerns syllables that are not stem-final. What is it?
> 2. The second generalization concerns stem-final (but not word-final) syllables. What
>   is it?
> 3. Is the second generalization more easily expressed in terms of a moraic representation
>   or a CV representation? Motivate your answer.

11.6 SYLLABLE-BASED GENERALIZATIONS

In this section we consider the role of the syllable in the SD of phonological
generalizations. It is very common for consonants to be pronounced differently
depending on their position in the syllable. Thus, as was explained in Chapter 5,
British English [l] is accompanied by velarization whenever it appears in the coda,
as shown in (29). Observe that [lj-] is a legitimate onset, occurring word-initially in
a word like *lure* [ljʊə], for instance.

(29) *In onset*

[laɪ]	*lie*	*In rhyme*	
[lʊk]	*look*	[hɔːɫ]	*hall*
['væli]	*valley*	[kɪɫt]	*kilt*
[ɪ'tæljən]	*Italian*	['mɪɫdjuː]	*mildew*
		['mɔrəɫ]	*moral*

The need to include syllable structure in phonological representations was demonstrated most clearly by Kahn (1976), who showed that in many cases the context of a rule could only be expressed in segmental terms at the cost of fairly baroque specifications. In the case of l-VELARIZATION, we would have to state that it applied 'before all consonants except [j] and at the word end'. Obviously, this approach does not yield a natural class. It would not be possible either to derive the nonvelarized allophone from an underlying velarized [ł], as in that case we would have to state the context as 'before all vowels and [j]'. Again, this is not a natural class, since [w] is excluded. Reference to the syllable makes it possible to formulate the context as in (30).

(30)   l-VELARIZATION l → ł / $_\sigma(\ldots V \quad C \ldots)_\sigma$
$$\qquad\qquad\qquad\qquad\qquad\qquad\qquad | \atop \underline{}$$

Many other examples can be given of consonants having different allophones depending on whether they appear in the onset or the rhyme. Thus, the Dutch labial approximant is labiodental [ʋ] in the onset and rounded bilabial [β] in the coda in the varieties spoken in the northern half of the Dutch language area,[2] as shown in (31). Again, neither the generalization 'in the coda' nor the generalization 'in the onset' can be expressed directly. Since Dutch allows [ʋr-] onsets, the onset happens to be equivalent to 'before a vowel or [r]', while the coda must be captured by 'before a consonant other than [r] or a word boundary'. Such SDs clearly look arbitrary, and fail to express just what it is that governs the allophony.

(31)

In onset		*In rhyme*	
[leː'ʋɪn]	'lioness'	[leːβ]	'lion'
[ʋreːt]	'cruel'	[χeːβt]	'yawn + 3SG'
['kleːʋaŋ]	'scimitar'	['lyβtə]	'lull'

---

[2] Dutch is spoken in the north-western half of Belgium and in the Netherlands. Many English-language publications use the word 'Flemish' when referring to Dutch as spoken in Belgium.

Q110 In Bugotu (Solomon Islands), vowels can be long or short. Any two vowels in either order can form a diphthong, such as [ao], [io], as inferred from the data in Kennedy (2008). It has a reduplicative prefix whose phonological form depends on the base, as illustrated in (1a, b, c, d). The full stop indicates a syllable boundary and a dash indicates that the unreduplicated form is not used. The language has undominated NoCODA, and a form like *[kal.ka.lu] would therefore be ungrammatical.

(1)	a.	ka.lu	-	kau.ka.lu	"to stir up'
		ka.ve	'grandmother'	kae.ka.ve	'to be old, of woman'
		pa.ŋa	-	paa.pa.ŋa	'to pant'
		lo.po	'be in a roll'	loo.lo.po	'to fold'
		po.no.ti	'to close'	poo.po.no.ti	'to to patch'
	b.	koa	-	koa.koa	'fornication, to sin'
		mee	'to be foolish'	mee.mee	'to be importunate'
		rei.ŋa	'to look'	rei.rei.ŋa	'appearance"
	c.	a.θo	'cord, rope'	a.θoa.θo	'to signal'
		i.li	'to totter'	i.lii.li	'to be drunk'
		u.do.lu	'to be gathered'	u.dou.do.lu	(*no gloss available*)
	d.	ou	-	ou.ou	'to cough'
		ao	-	ao.ao	'crow, bird'
		iu	'dog'	(mane) iu-iu	'loafer'

The prefix has a segmentless structure of two moras which is filled with a copy of the segments from the base, left-to-right. Unparsed segments are deleted. The underlying form of [kau.ka.lu] thus is as in (2a) and that of [poo.po.no.ti] in (2b).

(2) a.   b.

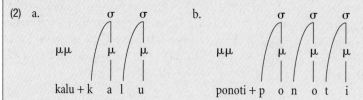

1. Show the autosegmental surface representation of [kau.ka.lu].
2. DEP(σ) bans the addition of syllable nodes, MAX(μ) bans the deletion of moras, and ONSET requires that syllables have onsets. Draw a tableau with these three constraints and (2a) as input. Assume moraic-cum-syllabic representations of [kau.ka.lu], [*au.ka.lu], *[a.lu.ka.lu], *[ka.ka.lu] and *[ka.lu.ka.lu] as candidate outputs. Do these constraints have to be ranked to make [kau.ka.lu] the winner?
3. The tableau you drew up for question 2 explains why [a.θoa.θo] is better than *[a.θa.θo] and *[a.θo.a.θo], but not why it is better than *[θoo.a.θo]. Show these four candidates in a tableau and propose a constraint which is violated by *[θoo.a.θo], but not by [a.θoa.θo]. Does your constraint have to be ranked with the other three?
4. What would be the reduplicated form of a hypothetical loanword [ko.kao]?

11.7   POST-MOP SYLLABIFICATION RULES

The Maximum Onset Principle (4) introduced in section 11.3, together with the specification of a syllabification domain within which it is applicable, suffices to explain the syllable structure of many languages. Other languages have additional syllabification rules. The motivation for these additional rules is that consonants which from one point of view appear to be in the coda would seem to act as onset consonants of the following syllable when viewed from a different perspective. Somewhat crudely, we might say that there are two possible approaches to this situation. It is possible to redo the initial MOP-driven syllabification after a derivation or cliticization, so that what appeared as a coda consonant at one level of representation appears as an onset consonant at another, a description known as **resyllabification**. If the first syllabification was V.CCV, as shown in (32b), the second would be (32c). Other descriptions will go on the assumption that the MOP is a persistent principle and that additional syllabification rules must respect existing syllabification. The new syllabification is 'added' to the old, and as a result a consonant may simultaneously belong to the coda of one syllable and to the onset of the next: such consonants are said to be **ambisyllabic**. As stressed by Kahn, the latter position is more restrictive, in that it limits the number of possible syllabifications. In the hypothetical situation (32), the syllabification required by the MOP would be V.CCV, and only the first C can be ambisyllabic (32a), since the No Crossing Constraint rules out the ambisyllabicity of a second C. By contrast, in a resyllabification analysis, there is no principled limit to the number of consonants that can be resyllabified. Starting out with (32b), we could change that into (32c), but there is no reason why a further resyllabification could not change that to VCC.V (not shown). In this section, we will argue that ambisyllabicity is in fact a necessary representation on the basis of Kahn's description of (American) English FLAPPING. In Chapter 16 we will see why some phonologists nevertheless object to ambisyllabic representations. There we will also point out that those objections should not be taken too seriously.

(32)   a. σ   σ   b. σ   σ   c. σ   σ

   V   C   C   V   V   C   C   V   V   C   C   V

11.7.1   Ambisyllabicity in English

English has two post-MOP syllabification rules. LIAISON, which applies across word boundaries, causes a word-final consonant to be in the onset of a following vowel-initial word. This is shown in (33). The rule only applies across word boundaries, because word-internally onsets will have been created by the MOP. As a result of (33), a consonant like [v] in *five* is **both** syllable-final **and** syllable-initial. After the application of LIAISON, the word-initial vowel can no longer be preceded by a glottal stop.

(33)   LIAISON   σ   σ

      C   V

(34)	faɪv ɛgz	[v]	*five eggs*
	oʊld ɪŋglɪʃ	[d]	*Old English*
	saʊθ æfrəkə	[θ]	*South Africa*

The other rule is RIGHT CAPTURE, which causes the first consonant of a weak syllable to serve as a (final) coda consonant of a preceding syllable.[3] That is, it is a syllabification rule which applies within the domain of the foot. As explained in Chapter 14, the English foot is left-dominant, in which the weak syllable(s) typically have [ə,ɪ,ʊ] or, especially word-finally, [i,oʊ]. Note that other vowels are string and, therefore, define a foot. Foot-based RIGHT CAPTURE, given in (35), spreads an onset consonant to a preceding syllable, where it forms part of its coda.

(35)   RIGHT CAPTURE   (...σ   σ ...) F

                              C

As a result of (35), the [p] in a word like *happy* will be the final consonant of the first syllable and the first consonant of the second syllable. As in the case of MOP, we must make the assumption that the resultant coda is a well-formed coda of English. That is, RIGHT CAPTURE cannot create a syllable *[bɛdf] in ['bɛdfərd] *Bedford*, even though this word is a single foot. Examples of words in which consonants become ambisyllabic by (35) are given in (36). In (36a), the rule applies after an open syllable, in (36b,c) it applies after a closed syllable, while (36d) shows that the left-hand syllable may be unstressed.

(36)	a.	'sɪti	[t]	*city*
	b.	'kɑnsərt	[s]	*concert*
	c.	'kʌntri	[t]	*country*
	d.	ə'sperəgəs	[r], [g]	*asparagus*

As pointed out by Kahn (1976), American English FLAPPING, the rule that causes certain instances of intervocalic [t,d] to be pronounced as an alveolar flap, provides evidence that ambisyllabic consonants are a natural class. FLAPPING applies in what are at first sight two entirely unrelated contexts. In (37), the contexts in which the rule applies are compared with a context in which it does not. The curious generalization that emerges is that FLAPPING applies when the right-hand vowel is in the next word, or is in a weak syllable in the same word.

(37)	FLAPPING applies		No FLAPPING		FLAPPING applies	
	['leɪtər]	*later*	['leɪtɛks]	*latex*	['leɪt ɛks]	*late ex*
	['hɪtɪŋ]	*hitting*	['hɪtaɪt]	*Hittite*	[hɪt 'aɪk]	*hit Ike*
	['sɪti]	*city*	['sætaɪər]	*satire*	['naɪt aʊl]	*night owl*

---

[3] This rule was originally seen as one that applied only if the left-hand syllable was open (Kahn 1976, Clements and Keyser 1983). The more general formulation in (35) was proposed and motivated in Gussenhoven (1986).

The unifying element of the contexts in which FLAPPING applies is ambisyllabicity. LIAISON and RIGHT CAPTURE, which can both be motivated on independent grounds (cf. also Gussenhoven 1986, Rubach 1996), provide the appropriate representations for rule (38), which simply says 'Flap [t,d] when they are ambisyllabic'.

$$\sigma\ \sigma$$
$$\vee$$
(38) FLAPPING $[t,d] \rightarrow [\mathfrak{r}] /$ C
$$|$$
$$[-cons] \quad \underline{\quad}$$

Neither the linear theory of *SPE* nor the resyllabification theory yields an elegant account of these facts. In a linear theory, we would arrive at (38), after Kahn (1976), where the angled brackets indicate mutually dependent terms.

(39) FLAPPING $[t,d] \rightarrow [\mathfrak{r}] / [-cons] \underline{\quad} <\#\#>_a \begin{bmatrix} +syl \\ < -stress >_b \end{bmatrix}$

Condition: if not a, then b

In addition to the awkward condition 'within the word, the following vowel must be unstressed', we also need to stipulate that in slow, deliberate speech styles, in which rules like LIAISON do not apply, word-final [t,d] will not be flapped. This will make it necessary to add a second condition: 'In unconnected speech, not a.' Clearly, the ambisyllabic representation is superior to a linear analysis without syllable structure. It is also superior to a resyllabification theory, such as offered by Selkirk (1982). Selkirk assumes that FLAPPING applies to coda consonants. In order for this account to go through, there must be no LIAISON (in order to keep final [t,d] in coda position), while RIGHT CAPTURE must be replaced with a rule that delinks the initial onset consonant of a weak syllable and moves it into the coda of a preceding syllable, so that *get $ Anne, get $ it* and *gett$ing* are syllabified as indicated by $. The disadvantages of this analysis are, first, that real coda consonants, like [d] in *Too bad!* or [t] in *The lot*, are characterized as flapped, a claim which requires independent evidence. Second, an explanation is required for the fact that [t,d] in 'real' flapping contexts are neutralized (cf. *bidder – bitter*), but contrast in the 'real' coda (*bid – bit*). Third, the claim that weak syllables in words like *city* or *sadder* are onsetless is difficult to square with the general finding that onsetless syllables may be pronounced with a preceding [ʔ]. Moreover, as was observed above, there is the general drawback that the resyllabification option will have to be constrained, since it would otherwise freely allow changes of onsets into codas and vice versa.

In moraic structure, ambisyllabic consonants have an association with the last mora of the syllable it closes and one with the onset of the next, as shown in (40a) for *Old English*. It is an interesting fact that languages do not appear to contrast ambisyllabic and geminate consonants, which suggests that they be represented identically within words (van der Hulst 1985). For English, this assumption leads to (40b) as the representation of *city*. For English, we are assuming that unstressed syllables have only one mora.

(40) a.   b.

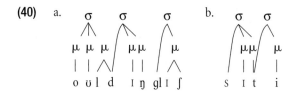

Q111 In some dialects of Spanish (Harris 1983), [r] and [l] are realized as [j] in certain positions, as illustrated in (1).

(1)   *revolver*   [rɛvɔjvɛj]   'revolver'
     carta   [kajta]   'card'
     papel   [papɛj]   'paper'
     calor   [kalɔj]   'heat'

Give an account in *SPE* theory as well as in a theory that can refer to the syllable, and argue that the latter is superior.

Q112 British English (RP) [r] can be realized either as a flap [ɾ] or an approximant [ɹ] in the expressions in columns I and III, but in those in column II only an approximant realization is available (Rubach 1996).

I	II	III
courage	*courageous*	*for example*
very	*reduce*	*for instance*
baron	*red*	*the other end*
laurel	*bright*	

Argue that these data support the existence of ambisyllabic consonants in English.

11.8   CONCLUSION

In this chapter we have seen that segmental duration can be accounted for by assuming that there is an independent tier of skeletal slots which constitutes an intermediate level of structure between the segments and the syllable. Moreover, by differentiating between C slots and V slots, the feature [±syllabic] can be dispensed with. In addition, the elements on this tier serve to define the morphemes for verb aspect in Arabic. By allowing C slots to be unsyllabified, it also appeared possible to account for French LIAISON, while an empty C slot could be used to account for *h-aspiré* in French. However, a distinction must be made between segments that determine the status of the syllable with respect to foot assignment and cause compensatory durational effects on the one hand, and those that do not on the other. The mora serves to represent this special prosodic status of these segments. The moraic theory predicts that compensatory effects and sensitivity to stress rules go hand in hand in any

> **Q113** The structure of the syllable rhyme of Brazilian Portuguese (BP) is V(X), where X
> can be C or V. BP has the nasals [m,n,ɲ]. The [ɲ] distinguishes itself from the other
> nasals in a number of respects. First, while [m,n] can appear word-initially, as shown
> in (1a,b), [ɲ] cannot, as shown in (1c), where V stands for any vowel (Wetzels 1997b).

(1) a.   'mɔvel   'mobile'
     b.   'nɔrti   'north'
     c.   *ɲV...

Second, although diphthongs are freely formed out of consecutive vowels before other nasals
(2a,b), they do not occur before [ɲ]. Instead, the two vowels are divided over two syllables (2c,d).

(2) a.   'rei.nu   'kingdom'
     b.   an.'dai.mu   'stage'
     c   fu.'iɲa   *'fuiɲa   'weasel'
     d.   ra'iɲa   *'raiɲa   'queen'

Third, while [m,n] tolerate a consonant immediately before them (3a,b,c,d), [ɲ] does not (3e).

(3) a.   a'dornu   'ornament'
     b.   'arma   'weapon'
     c.   'alma   'soul'
     d.   vulne'ravel   'vulnerable'
     e.   *VrɲV, *VlɲV

The three differences between [ɲ] on the one hand and [m,n] on the other can be explained
if [ɲ] is incorporated differently in syllable structure from [m,n].

1.   What is this structural difference?

BP has a rule of VOWEL NASALIZATION which causes a stressed vowel to be nasalized before a
nasal, as shown in (4a,b). Unstressed vowels remain oral before nasal consonants, as shown
in (4c,d). However, before [ɲ], vowels are always nasalized, as shown in (4e,f).

(4) a.   'sĩnu   'bell'
     b.   'kãma   'bed'
     c.   bo'nɛka   'doll'
     d.   kuma'ri   'chili'
     e.   a'rãɲa   'spider'
     f.   dĩ'ɲeiru   'money'

It is possible to account for the nasalization of stressed vowels before [m,n] and the lack of
nasalization of unstressed vowels before [m,n] by assuming that in stressed syllables consonants
like [m,n] are incorporated differently in syllable structure than in unstressed syllables.

2.   What is that assumption?
3.   What is – under that assumption – the correct generalization for VOWEL NASALIZATION?
4.   How does your solution account for the fact that before [ɲ] both stressed and unstressed
     vowels are nasalized?

one language. It is usually assumed that the mora tier should replace, rather than supplement, the CV tier.

In this chapter we have also seen that the syllable plays an active role in the SDs of phonological rules, which often appear sensitive to whether a consonant is in the coda or in the onset. Additionally, it has been shown that ambisyllabicity is a form of representation required for the descripiton of a number of processes. Before moving on to the constituent above the syllable, the foot, in the next two chapters we will consider the segment-internal structure, and show how it plays a role in the characterization of a wide variety of phonological processes.

Feature geometry

12.1 INTRODUCTION

We have seen that tone and segmental duration must be autosegmentalized in order to account for a number of phonological phenomena. In this chapter, we will continue this theme. We will replace the matrix comprising the remaining distinctive features with a hierarchical configuration of these features. We will begin by considering a number of arguments for replacing the unstructured list of laryngeal, manner and place features with a **feature tree**. The main advantage of this 'autosegmentalized' representation is that features or particular groups of features can spread to neighbouring segments, which greatly improves the description of assimilation processes. Moreover, the assumption made in Chapter 6 that not all segments are specified for all features appears to have interesting consequences in the new model. Some of these will be discussed in this chapter, while others will be discussed in Chapter 13, which continues this topic.

12.2 TWO PROPERTIES OF ASSIMILATIONS

Assimilations frequently show a non-arbitrary relationship between the structural description and the structural change. Time and again, rules appear to transfer a specific feature or group of features from one segment to a neighbouring segment. However, the representation we introduced in Chapter 7 is incapable of expressing this relationship. To illustrate the problem, consider once more the Dutch rule of REGRESSIVE VOICING, which voices obstruents before [b,d]. Rule (1) might be said to be a natural rule in the sense that voiced segments cause preceding segments to be voiced. It would be very strange if Dutch had a rule which caused segments to become voiceless before [b,d]. The problem with the *SPE* notation, however, is that it is in fact as easy to write a rule or constraint that describes such an implausible process (cf. (2)) as it is to write a perfectly ordinary rule like (1). That is, the notation represents a theory which cannot distinguish between the impossible and the commonplace.[1]

---

[1] This is not to suggest that dissimilation processes are in general impossible. What is implausible is that a dissimilation rule like (2) would ever be needed to describe a phonological process.

(1)   REGRESSIVE VOICING $[-\text{son}] \rightarrow [+\text{voice}] /$ __(##) $\begin{bmatrix} -\text{son} \\ -\text{cont} \\ +\text{voice} \end{bmatrix}$

(2)   IMPLAUSIBLE RULE $[+\text{son}] \rightarrow [-\text{voice}] /$ __(##) $\begin{bmatrix} -\text{son} \\ -\text{cont} \\ +\text{voice} \end{bmatrix}$

What would be an elegant way of expressing the fact that assimilations involve the adoption of a feature by one segment from another? First, we might think of a copying operation. This would produce a non-arbitrary result in that only features and feature values that are present in the context can be copied. However, as we have seen in Chapter 10, phonologies show a pervasive dislike of sequences of identical features (the OCP), and it would obviously be a bad idea to design a theory of rules whose essence it is to violate the OCP. A better solution would be to find a representation which would allow segments to *share* the same feature(s), much in the way successive TBUs can be associated with the same tone.

There is a second striking fact about assimilations. Commonly, the same *groups* of features appear to be transferred from one segment to the next. For example, many languages have processes that transfer the features specifying a consonant's place of articulation to a preceding nasal consonant. Since the features in the matrix are unstructured, it is impossible to express that the feature groupings we find in the processes of so many languages are in fact natural groups of features. That is, in a theory without a feature tree, an unnatural feature group like [LABIAL, ±son] can be as easily expressed as a natural one like [±voice, ±spread, ±constr].

The solution to both problems is known as **feature geometry**. The problem of the grouping of features is solved by representing segments as trees, in which the nodes represent features and feature groups. The assimilation problem is solved by assuming that a single node may be part of more than one tree. We will first introduce the feature tree. Then, in section 12.5, we turn to the ways in which one feature tree (i.e. segment) can interact with an adjacent feature tree.

12.3   NATURAL FEATURE CLASSES

As was observed above, assimilations of place involve the transfer of a collection of features. Many languages have rules assimilating nasal consonants to the place of articulation of the following consonant. For instance, Hindi, which has the underlying nasals [m,n,ɳ], assimilates the place of articulation of nasal consonants to that of a following consonant within the word. Word-internally, sequences like *[nk], *[ɳt] or *[mt] are therefore ill-formed. As a result of NASAL ASSIMILATION, a prefix like [sam] 'together' shows alternations of the type illustrated in (3) (Ohala 1983). Clearly, the place features must be accessible as a group in order to express this phonological process: the assimilation involves the transfer of all the place features, including dependent ones like [±anterior], as shown by the words for 'equilibrium' and 'movement'.

(3)
aːkaːr	'shape'	samaːkaːr	'homophonous'
kiːrtan	'devotional singing'	saŋkiːrtan	'collective devotional singing'
toːl	'measure'	santoːl	'equilibrium'
calan	'conduct'	saɲcalan	'movement'
naːd	'sound'	sannaːd	'consonance'

There are also processes that transfer a subgroup of the place features. English CORONAL ASSIMILATION assimilates [t,d,n,l] in place of articulation to the following coronal consonant. That is, before [θ,ð] they are dental, before [t,d,n,l] they remain alveolar, and before [ɹ], which in English has a postalveolar place of articulation, they are postalveolar. Recall that the feature values for the segments concerned are as given in (4). The data in (5) illustrate that the values of the features [anterior] and [distributed] are **together** passed on to the preceding [−cont, +cor] segment (Clements 1985).[2]

(4)
	Cor	Ant	Distr
θ, ð, n̪	+	+	+
t,d,n,l	+	+	−
ɹ, t̠	+	−	−

(5)
ɪn̪ ɹəʊm	*in Rome*
ɔːl̪ ðɛə	*all there*
ɪn̪ θɜːsk	*in Thirsk*
t̠ɹaɪ	*try*
gɛt̠ ɹɛd	*get red*
wɪd̪θ	*width*

Of course, single features are also frequently transferred from one segment to the next. Consider the Old English data in Chapter 5 (Q38) which showed that the [−back] [ç] appeared after [−back] vowels, and [+back] [x] appeared after [+back] vowels. This process is understandable if we assume that the vowel transfers the value for the feature [back] (but no other features) to the following dorsal fricative. Just as phonological processes are seen as evidence for the existence of natural segment classes (any group of segments referred to by a process), so a **natural feature class** can be defined as a group of features that is manipulated (i.e. transferred, deleted or inserted) by some phonological process.

12.4   BUILDING A TREE

So far, the assumption has been that the representation of a segment is an unstructured list of features. Spelt out in full, the representation of [t] would be as in (6a). What rules like Hindi NASAL PLACE ASSIMILATION suggest is that the representation

---

[2] This rule should arguably be seen as a rule of phonetic implementation (Hayes 1992).

must be as in (6b). Further, on the basis of processes like that illustrated in (5) we would seem to need a representation like that in (6c).

(6)

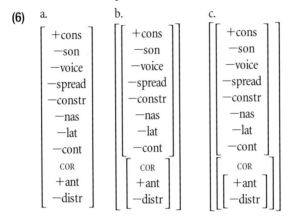

What this means, of course, is that the segment is not a single constituent, but has internal structure. Such constituency is conventionally represented by means of a tree diagram. The development of **feature trees** (or **feature geometry**) is mainly due to Clements (1985), Sagey (1986) and McCarthy (1988).

12.4.1 The place node

The node dominating the place features is called the PLACE node. Within this constituent there are four **articulator nodes** corresponding to the univalent features [LABIAL], [CORONAL], [DORSAL], [RADICAL]. Each of these four nodes dominates subconstituents corresponding to their relevant features. Thus, the [LABIAL] node dominates [±round] and [±distr], the [CORONAL] node dominates [±ant] and [±distr] and the [DORSAL] node dominates [±back], [±high] and [±low]. This representation of the PLACE node is given in (7). With the help of this representation, processes can refer to the constituent [LABIAL, distr, round], but not to the nonconstituent [high, ant], for instance. We will assume that the position of [±tense] will be under [RAD], assuming it is equivalent to [±ATR].

(7)

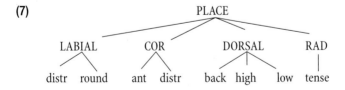

Q114
1. Which constituent is transferred from a consonant to a preceding [t,d,n,l] by English CORONAL ASSIMILATION?
2. Which constituent is transferred from a consonant to a preceding nasal by Hindi NASAL ASSIMILATION?

12.4.2 The laryngeal node

What other natural feature classes are there besides place features? Lass (1976: 145ff.) has argued that the laryngeal segments [h,ʔ] have no supralaryngeal specification at all. He based his case on the frequently observed phenomenon that obstruents sometimes appear to lose all their supralaryngeal information. Consider the London English data in (8), which are representative of this kind of process. In certain contexts, preglottalized plosives are pronounced as [ʔ]. (The variation between preglottalized plosives and glottal stops is stylistic, i.e. both pronunciations may be heard from the same speaker.)

(8)	pɪʔktʃə	or	pɪʔtʃə	*picture*
	mɪiʔt wɪljəm	or	mɪiʔ wɪljəm	*meet William*
	nɪʔk næʔks	or	nɪʔ næʔks	*knick-knacks*
	nɔʔt næʊ	or	nɔʔ næʊ	*not now*
	kɪiʔp smaɪlɪŋ	or	kɪiʔ smaɪlɪŋ	*keep smiling*

In New World Spanish, [s] has been lost in coda position. That is, the plural of [klase] 'class', which in Peninsular Spanish is [klases], is [klasɛ]. (The [ɛ] arises from a separate process which is not relevant here.) However, the [s] has not left without a trace: an [h]-like offglide can be heard after the plural in careful speech. Similarly, voiceless sonorants have arisen word-internally after the loss of the oral articulation of [s], as shown in (9).

(9)	*Stage I*	*Stage II*	
	mismo	miĭmo *or* mimmo	'same'
	fosforo	fosforo	'match'

Both processes could be described if, following Lass, we assume that laryngeal and supralaryngeal features are separate constituents. Under that assumption, both the English and the Spanish data would receive the same description: deletion of the supralaryngeal constituent. In the case of English, this would leave [+constr, −voice, −spread] behind, i.e. [ʔ], and in the case of Spanish it would leave [−constr, −voice, −spread] behind, i.e. a voiceless interval at that point in the word. Thus, such orphaned laryngeal features generally end up as [ʔ] and [h], respectively.

To express Lass's proposal in our feature tree, we need to assume that segments consist of two main parts: the laryngeal and the supralaryngeal constituent. The dominating node is referred to as the ROOT node. If we want to ensure that segments that have only one of these constituents can be specified for the major class features ([±cons] and [±son]), these features must be present in either of these constituents. Following McCarthy (1988), we assume they make up the root node. This decision can safely be made, since no processes have been reported that transfer [±cons] or [±son] from one segment to the next. This means that our tree now looks like (10). We will treat the feature [±approx] as a manner feature.

(10)

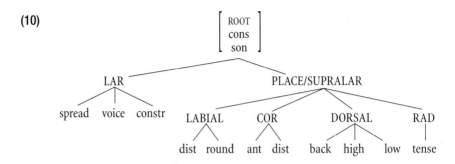

12.4.3 The supralaryngeal node

In the preceding sections, we have been able to establish a constituent structure for the major class features, the laryngeal features and the place features. What remains to be determined is the location of the manner features [±nas], [±cont] and [±lat]. Do they form a third constituent, or are they located inside the PLACE/SUPRALAR constituent? We will argue that [continuant] is indeed located in the right-hand branch of (10) on the basis of an assimilation process changing [h] to [ç] in Frisian (Tiersma 1985). Recall that [h,ʔ] are not specified for [+cont], and that this was the explanation for the fact that it did not trigger NASALIZATION. This rule nasalizes a vowel before [n], provided a [+cont] consonant follows. In (11a) the effect of the rule is illustrated, while (11b) shows that [h] does not trigger it (cf. Chapter 6).

(11)		*Underlying*	*Surface*	
	a.	in-jaːn	ĩjaːn	'to give in'
		oən-fliənə	oə̃fliənə	'to attack'
	b.	in-hɛljə	inhɛljə	'to hold in'
		oən-hiərə	oənhiərə	'to listen to'

The southern variety of Frisian has a rule of DIPHTHONG SHIFT, which – among other vocalic changes – turns [iə] into [jɛ]. When this [j] appears after [h], it assimilates [h] to [ç]. This rule can be used to decide which constituent, the laryngeal or the supralaryngeal constituent, accommodates the feature [continuant]. If this feature is part of the same constituent as the PLACE/SUPRALAR node, the assimilation rule will transfer the [+cont] of [j], along with its place features, to [h]. This would predict that after the assimilation, [ç] will trigger NASALIZATION. However, if [+cont] is not in the PLACE/SUPRALAR constituent and the place features can transfer without bringing [+cont] along with them, the prediction is that [ç] will not trigger NASALIZATION, because it would still lack a specification for [continuant], like [h]. The data in (12) show that the first assumption is correct: the new [ç] triggers NASALIZATION, and must therefore be [+cont]. This segment is now [−son, −cons, +spread, −voice] (which is what [h] contributes), as well as [+cont, −lat, −nas, COR, −ant] (which is what [j] contributes).[3]

---

[3] Well-formedness rules must change the segment into [+cons], because it now has a constriction causing friction.

(12)	Underlying	Northern	Southern	
	in-hɪəkjə	inhɪəkjə	īçjɛkjə	'to hook in'
	oən-hɪərə	oənhɪərə	oə̄çjɛrə̄	'to listen to'

When Frisian [h] is transformed to [ç], it acquires place and manner features from another segment, but it does not itself lose any place or manner features, because it did not have any. Segments other than [h,ɦ,ʔ] do of course have manner and place features. The location of manner features in the PLACE/SUPRALAR constituent in (10) predicts that segments can lose these features, while acquiring new ones from a neighbouring segment. Such a transfer should be possible independently of the laryngeal features. This can indeed be shown for the lateral consonants of Klamath. In addition to a voiced [l], Klamath has a glottalized [l'] and a voiceless [l̥]. When appearing after [n], the lateral consonant transfers its lateral articulation to the preceding segment, but **without** its laryngeal features, which remain behind as [ʔ] and [h], as shown in (13). This suggests that there is a constituent in the feature tree that contains manner but not the laryngeal features. Since the new segment is not [+nas], this Klamath process suggests that the PLACE/SUPRALAR node of (10) contains [±lat] (because it is transferred from the second to the first segment) as well as [±nas] (because it is deleted from the second segment).

(13) [nl'] → [lʔ]
      [nl̥] → [lh]

While it is clear that the manner features are inside the supralaryngeal constituent, it is also clear that the manner features cannot be under the PLACE node. In Hindi, as in many other languages, it is just the consonant's place node that is transferred to a preceding nasal, not its [−nas] specification. From the node labelled PLACE/SUPRALAR in (10), we must therefore split off the PLACE node. Since there have been no reports of processes that transfer [±nas], [±cont], [±lat], [±strid], [±approx], *en bloc*, from one segment to the next, these features are not grouped in a manner constituent, but rather form separate terminal nodes dominated by SUPRALAR, as shown in (14).

(14)

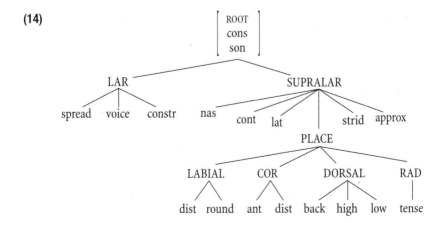

Single manner features can be shown to transfer independently to neighbouring segments. Processes that transfer [+nas] are widely attested. (We have seen examples of this in American English and Frisian here and in earlier chapters.) Transfer of [±cont] is much rarer. In American English, forms like [gɪbm] for *given*, [hiːd̩n] for *heathen*, [bɪdnəs] for *business* and [wʌdnt] for *wasn't* occur (Bailey 1985: 63). No case has been made for the transfer of [±strid], [±lat] or [±approx]. There are many proposals that modify the structure of (14); however, this structure is one that is widely used, and may be seen as a 'consensus' tree (Broe 1992).

12.5 SPREADING AND DELINKING

The structure of the tree introduced in the previous section explains *what* must be made accessible to phonological rules, i.e. what the natural feature classes are. In this section, we will deal with the way features or subconstituents of the segment tree spread or delink. In our representation, segments are arranged from left to right, which is the usual metaphor for the order from 'early' to 'late'. Along this time axis, the segment trees are arranged much in the way the records in an old-fashioned jukebox are arranged: a row of parallel disks, where a disk represents a segment. Each disk defines a plane in which some instantiation of the feature tree is to be found. If you were to take out a disk to look at its right or left face, you would see some version of (14). This is known as an **end view**.

How can a node of some segment be dominated by the appropriate node of an adjacent segment? Imagine two adjacent segments S1 and S2. Now mentally draw a line from the [±nas] node of S1 to the [±nas] node of S2, and a line from the SUPRALAR node of S1 to the SUPRALAR node of S2. The lines you have just drawn are, of course, **tiers**. All corresponding nodes form tiers in this way, so that we can talk about the 'nasal tier', the 'supralaryngeal tier', the 'root tier', etc. Evidently, tiers are adjacent if no tier intervenes between them. This is the case with the node PLACE and the immediately dominating SUPRALARYNGEAL node, for instance: no node intervenes between them. Two adjacent tiers define a **plane**.

Q115

Draw two feature trees in pencil, next to each other. Draw all tiers. Now erase all pencil lines that are 'behind' the planes nearest to you. As you will realize, your picture shows three dimensions.

We can now draw, in some plane, an **association line** from any node to the immediately dominating node in an adjacent segment. That is, from the [LABIAL] node of S1 we can draw an association line to the PLACE node of S2, and from the PLACE node of S1 to the SUPRALARYNGEAL node of S2, and so on. This **spreading** of nodes in the feature tree is entirely comparable with the spreading of tones, or with the association of one vowel to two moras.

> **Q116** Can you draw an association line from the PLACE node of S1 to the ROOT node of S2? If not, why not?

In Hindi PLACE ASSIMILATION, the PLACE node of the right-hand segment associates with the SUPRALARYNGEAL node of the left-hand segment. This is shown in (15) by the interrupted association line. Notice that there is something wrong now: what was an [n] is now specified for two sets of place features. What we need to do is remove the original PLACE constituent. This operation is known as **delinking**, and is symbolized by '='. Delinked nodes are deleted.

(15)

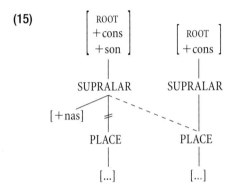

12.5.1 Writing rules

It would be a very daunting prospect indeed if all rules were to be formulated by drawing these elaborate three-dimensional pictures. What we would need to do is draw just those elements in the configuration that are involved in the spreading and delinking, and make sure that the appropriate contextual conditions are expressed. We will do this in an adaptation of a notation proposed by Clements (1985). The adaptation consists in separating out two aspects in the rule. First, the Structural Change (SC) is identified: which node spreads to the appropriate dominating node in the adjacent segment (with or without subsequent delinking of the original association line in that segment)? This is shown by specifying two tiers, one of which immediately dominates the other, together with the corresponding nodes of two adjacent segments. To express the assimilation, it shows either an association towards the left – **regressive assimilation** – or one towards the right – **progressive assimilation**. In (16) these are the supralaryngeal tier and the PLACE tier, while the right-hand place node is specified as the spreading one. Second, the Structural Description (SD) specifies what phonological properties the two segments concerned must have for the change to go through. These properties (features, usually) are simply listed below the two segments concerned. In not specifying the SD in the tree itself, we express the fact that the tree was motivated on the basis of natural feature classes that are actually manipulated by phonological processes. By contrast, features in the SD merely condition those processes.

The rule in (16) thus reads as follows: the PLACE node of any consonant spreads to (the supralaryngeal node of) a nasal on the left, while the PLACE node of the latter is delinked. Observe that in our interpretation of Clements's display, the upper and lower tier are always adjacent. The higher node label (here: SUPRALAR) is therefore redundant.

(16)   NASAL ASSIMILATION

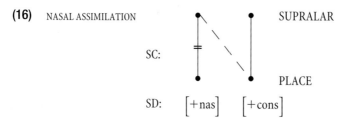

SC:

SUPRALAR

PLACE

SD: $\begin{bmatrix} +\text{nas} \end{bmatrix}$ $\begin{bmatrix} +\text{cons} \end{bmatrix}$

Similarly, English CORONAL ASSIMILATION is given in (17): 'Spread the coronal node (with all the features it dominates) to a noncontinuant coronal on the left.'

(17)   CORONAL ASSIMILATION

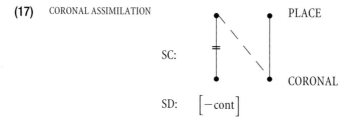

PLACE

SC:

CORONAL

SD: $\begin{bmatrix} -\text{cont} \end{bmatrix}$

Q117	We saw in Chapter 6 that distinctive features were phonetically non-abstract in the sense that they can be defined in terms of phonetic concepts. Would you say that natural feature classes are phonetically abstract?

Q118	English has an optional rule assimilating [t,d,n] to the place of articulation of following velar and labial plosives and nasals, as shown in the data below. Formulate this English PLACE ASSIMILATION in the display format.

θɪn	θɪm bʊk	*thin book*
ðæt	ðæk kʌp	*that cup*
gʊd	gʊb bɔɪ	*good boy*
tɛn	tɛm maɪlz	*ten miles*
ðæt	ðæt naɪt	*that night*

12.6   IMPLICATIONS OF UNDERSPECIFICATION

In a number of ways, the proposal to represent the phonological content of segments as a feature tree has led to more insightful formulations of phonological rules. As explained in Chapter 6, two assumptions have been made here. One is that not all segments have all nodes. Thus, laryngeal segments have no supralaryngeal node, and the place node has only those articulator nodes that positively specify the place of articulation of the segment, which implies, for instance, that [t] does not have a labial, dorsal or radical node (Sagey 1986, McCarthy 1988). Second, it has been assumed that predictable information is absent in underlying representation, and is supplied by **default rules** which apply at the end of the derivation. Below, a number of advantages of such underspecification in feature trees are briefly outlined.

12.6.1   Default rules

The decision to leave predictable features unspecified may have a simplifying effect on the formulation of rules that neutralize contrasts to some neutral, 'default' realization. Let us take (Low) German FINAL DEVOICING as an example. As we have seen in Chapter 6, the expected laryngeal feature specification for obstruents is [−voice, −spread, −constr]. Let us assume that these values are filled in before the phonetic implementation rules start their work if no other value is specified, causing all obstruents without laryngeal specification to be voiceless, unglottalized and unaspirated. FINAL DEVOICING neutralizes the distinction between voiced and voiceless obstruents in the coda (cf. the uninflected and genitive forms of 'variegated', [bunt – buntəs], and 'union', [bunt – bundəs]). If a default rule were assumed for German which supplies the value [−voice] to obstruents in the coda, FINAL DEVOICING could consist of a rule delinking the laryngeal node in coda position. In (18), we formulate this version of the rule.

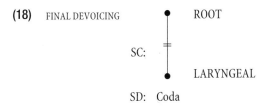

(18)   FINAL DEVOICING   • ROOT

SC:

   • LARYNGEAL

SD: Coda

A separate question is whether voiceless obstruents in a language like German can be left unspecified for the feature [−voice] in the lexicon. Even though [±voice] is contrastive for obstruents in German, which has contrasts like [pain] 'pain' – [bain] 'leg', it would be possible to leave voiceless obstruents unspecified, while specifying voiced obstruents as [+voice]. The voiceless obstruents then only acquire their [−voice] specification at the end of the derivation, or, if the feature needs to be referred to by some rule, as early as it is needed. This would be the assumption made in the theory of **Radical Underspecification** (Kiparsky 1982, 1993, Archangeli 1988), which, as its name suggests, goes one step further than the theory of Contrastive Underspecification, which was briefly discussed in Chapter 6. In Radical Underspecification, only one value of a feature is ever lexically specified. A survey of the issues is provided by Roca (1994: ch. 2) and Steriade (1995). In the next chapter, we will discuss a number of further instances in which underspecification would appear to facilitate the application of rules.

Q119 Two northern dialects of British English each have a postlexical assimilation rule affecting consonant sequences across word boundaries (Wells 1982, Kerswill 1987). Neither rule occurs in the standard accent (RP).

1. Give *SPE* formulations of the two rules.
2. Explain why it would not be possible to assume that a default rule supplies the feature [−voice] to English voiceless obstruents at the end of the derivation.

	RP	Yorkshire	Durham
white blouse	[tb]	[tb]	[db]
wide shot	[dʃ]	[tʃ]	[dʃ]
ripe beans	[pb]	[pb]	[bb]
drab conditions	[bk]	[pk]	[bk]
black velvet	[kv]	[kv]	[gv]
five votes	[vv]	[vv]	[vv]
rough boys	[fb]	[fb]	[vb]
this village	[sv]	[sv]	[zv]
bad joke	[ddʒ]	[ddʒ]	[ddʒ]
live performance	[vp]	[fp]	[vp]
Bradford	[df]	[tf]	[df]
that night	[tn]	[tn]	[dn]
at last	[tl]	[tl]	[dl]
all true	[lt]	[lt]	[lt]
in Spain	[ns]	[ns]	[ns]

Q120 In Klamath, the underlying consonant pairs listed in the first column are pronounced as in the second column (cf. the data in (13); after Halle and Clements 1983). Demonstrate that two ordered rules are sufficient to derive the outputs correctly. Assume that voiced sonorant consonants are unspecified for [+voice], and that a default rule supplies this feature to unspecified sonorants at the end of the derivation. Also assume that if a geminate arises as a result of a spreading operation, the two original feature trees merge under a single ROOT node. State in prose what these two rules should accomplish. Formulate the rules in autosegmental display notation. (Hint: Draw partial trees of a typical sequence like [nl'] before and after the change. Also draw a feature tree of [ll] after the merger under a single ROOT node.)

Underlying	Derived
nl	ll
n!	lh
nl'	l?
l!	lh
ll'	l?

Q121 In Brao, voiced, voiceless unaspirated, voiceless aspirated and preglottalized voiced plosives are contrastive in the onset, as illustrated by [dɑk] 'walk (verb)', [truː] 'fish', [tʰun] 'season', [ʔɗuːr] 'type of flute' (the last may vary with an implosive [ɗ]). In the coda, the only plosives that can occur are voiceless unaspirated, as illustrated by [ɲeːt] 'drink (verb)' (Keller 1993).

1.	Provide the full laryngeal feature specifications for the four types of initial plosive.
2.	Which features could be supplied by default rules?
3.	What underlying laryngeal feature specification would you assume for the coda plosives?

12.7 CONCLUSION

If the representation of a segment consists of a self-contained list of features, it is impossible to express that, frequently, sequences of segments share particular features, a phenomenon known as assimilation. Also, the fact that such assimilations often involve specific groups of features, such as the features specifying the place of articulation, cannot be expressed. If, by contrast, the features are arranged in a constituent structure, or feature tree, with each constituent defining a tier, it does become possible for two adjacent segments to share the same feature. Also, because the feature tree can group features under a single constituent node, it will be possible for groups of features to be transferred, or spread, to an adjacent segment.

Exploiting the feature tree

13.1   INTRODUCTION

In this chapter, we continue our discussion of the feature tree. Two main topics will be dealt with. One concerns the opportunity that is afforded by the underspecification of features – and hence, the absence of particular nodes in the representations of segments – to characterize long-distance assimilations. Particularly relevant in this context are word-based restrictions on the distribution of certain features, such as is seen in Vowel Harmony, for instance. We will see that the solution to characterizing these distributional restrictions is reminiscent of the description of the lexical tone patterns of languages like Etung and Mende, discussed in Chapter 10. The second topic concerns the representation of complex segments. We will deal with the three types of complex segment recognized in Chapter 2. Also, we will return to the question of the representation of palatal and palatoalveolar segments, like [tʃ] and [j], and argue that they, too, are complex segments.

13.2   LONG-DISTANCE ASSIMILATION

It would be reasonable to expect that assimilations only occur between immediately adjacent segments. For instance, we would not expect to find a language in which the initial consonant of a word assimilates in place of articulation to the coda consonant of the second syllable. However, it is in fact not unusual to find cases in which an articulator node spreads to the dominating node of an apparently non-adjacent segment. If the NO CROSSING CONSTRAINT introduced in Chapter 10 is valid in the segment tree, then this can mean only one thing: the intervening segment or segments must lack the node concerned. Long-distance processes of this kind have accordingly been used as evidence for underspecification. As an example, consider the Russian data in (1) (Kiparsky 1985). Sequences of obstruents in Russian, whether or not separated by a word boundary, agree in voicing with the rightmost one. This is shown in (1a). As shown in (1b), however, it does not appear to be the case that the obstruents must be strictly adjacent: a sonorant consonant may intervene.

(1) a. ɡorod-k-a   gorotka   'little town (genitive)'
             mtsensk bɨl   mtsenzg bɨl   'it was Mtsensk'
         b. iz mtsensk-a   is mtsenska   'from Mtsensk'
             ot mzd-ɨ   od mzdɨ   'from the bribe'

Russian devoices final obstruents, which rule is assumed to apply before the assimilation of voice illustrated above. The spreading feature can accordingly be assumed to be [+voice]. RUSSIAN VOICING ASSIMILATION is given in (2). The feature [+voice] spreads left and any original specification for [voice] is lost through delinking. This spreading may take place more than once, to deal with sequences of obstruents.

(2)   RUSSIAN VOICING ASSIMILATION

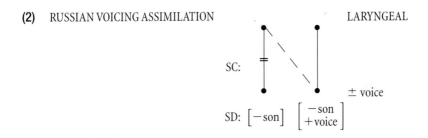

However, the spreading of [+voice] from the rightmost obstruent to a non-adjacent obstruent can only proceed if sonorants do not have a specification for [±voice] in the underlying representation. This is shown in (3), which shows that the assimilation goes right through an intervening sonorant consonant. The subsequent specification of the feature [+voice] in sonorant segments is achieved by a default rule: Russian does not contrast voiced and voiceless sonorants.

(3)

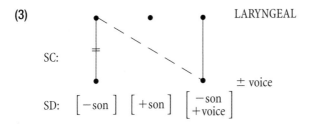

It has also been assumed that certain segments in principle refuse to bear certain nodes. As we have seen above, laryngeal segments are a case in point. Consequently, we can safely spread supralaryngeal nodes across [h, ʔ], since these segments cannot bear such a node. The fact that nasalization processes frequently spread through laryngeal segments to vowels in adjacent syllables is often assumed to receive an explanation in this assumption.

Another oft-cited case of long-distance spreading relies on the absence of a CORONAL node in noncoronal (labial and dorsal) segments. Sanskrit RETROFLEXION turns alveolar [n] into retroflex [ɳ] after [ʈ,ʂ,ɳ,ɽ]. Retroflex consonants are contrastively [−ant, −distr], as shown in (4) (Steriade 1987, Kenstowicz 1994a).

(4)		Alveolar			Retroflex				Prepalatal		
		t	s	n	ʈ	ʂ	ɳ	ɽ	c	ʃ	ɲ
ant		+	+	+	−	−	−	−	−	−	−
distr		−	−	−	−	−	−	−	+	+	+

We would at first sight expect the rule to be blocked by any consonant other than [n]. However, noncoronal consonants as well as vowels may freely intervene between context and focus, as shown in the first column of (5). By contrast, there may **not** be a coronal consonant other than [n] between target and focus, as shown in the second column of (5). (Underlyingly voiceless obstruents are shown as voiced between sonorant segments.)

(5)
		Applies		*Blocked*	
-na	'present'	ɪʂ-ɳa	'seek'	mr̥d-na	'be gracious'
-na	'pass. partic.'	puːɽ-ɳa	'fill'	bhug-na	'bend'
-aːna	'middle partic.'	puɽ-áːɳa	'fill'	marɟ-aːna	'wipe'
		kʂubh-áːɳa	'quake'	kʂved-aːna	'hum'
-mːana	'middle partic.'	kr̥p-a-máːɳa	'lament'	kr̥t-a-maːna	'cut'

The rule to accomplish this is given in (6). It relies crucially on the absence of a coronal node between the two segments. If there is a coronal node, the nasal cannot be reached, as the spreading association line would cross the association line between the coronal node and the PLACE node, as shown in (7).

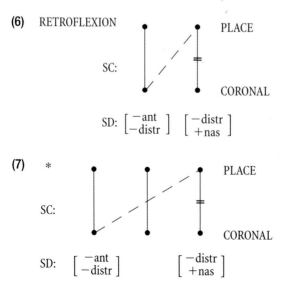

(6) RETROFLEXION

SC: PLACE ... CORONAL

$$\text{SD:} \begin{bmatrix} -\text{ant} \\ -\text{distr} \end{bmatrix} \quad \begin{bmatrix} -\text{distr} \\ +\text{nas} \end{bmatrix}$$

(7) *

SC: PLACE ... CORONAL

$$\text{SD:} \begin{bmatrix} -\text{ant} \\ -\text{distr} \end{bmatrix} \quad \begin{bmatrix} -\text{distr} \\ +\text{nas} \end{bmatrix}$$

Q122 In Sundanese, nasalization of vowels is predictable as a result of a phonological rule, NASALIZATION. Consider the following data (Robins 1957, Cohn 1990).

/siar/	[siar]	'seek'
/mawur/	[mãwur]	'spread (Active)'
/paŋliŋ/	[paŋliŋ]	'unrecognizable'
/ŋajak/	[ŋãjak]	'sift (Active)'
/ŋatur/	[ŋãtur]	'arrange (Active)'
/kana/	[kanã]	'for the purpose'
/tiʔis/	[tiʔis]	'relax in a cool place'
/niʔis/	[nĩʔis]	'relax in a cool place (Active)'
/mahal/	[mãhãl]	'expensive'
/caŋra/	[caŋra]	'very nice weather'
/ŋarahɨtan/	[ŋãrahɨtan]	'wound (Active)'
/ɲaho/	[ɲãhõ]	'know (Active)'
/ɲiar/	[ɲĩãr]	'seek (Active)'

1. Give a prose statement of NASALIZATION.
2. Argue on the basis of these data that the feature tree for laryngeals does not include a supralaryngeal node.

Q123 Stem-initial obstruents in Bakairí, a language whose syllable structure is (C)V, are realized as voiceless plosives, unless preceded by a vowel, when they are voiced (Wetzels 1997b). This is shown by [təkə] 'bow', [tə-dəka-ge] 'have a bow'.
A stem-internal obstruent, however, can be voiced or voiceless, as shown by [itubi] 'skin', [ədəpigɔ] 'heat'.

1. Assume that stem-initial obstruents are unspecified for [±voice] in underlying representations. Which two default rules must be assumed?

The distribution of stem-internal obstruents is not free. If stem-initial consonants are not counted, there can be only one voiceless obstruent in the stem, which must be either the first or the second obstruent (again, not counting any stem-initial consonant). Thus, while [təkə] 'bow', [ədəpigɔ] 'heat' and [ʊdɔdɔ] 'jaguar' are fine, forms like *[itupi], *[titupi], *[idebiko] are impossible. This state of affairs can be captured by assuming that Bakairí stems have a limited number of [±voice] melodies, much in the way that Etung has a limited number of tone melodies.

2. Assuming that [−son] segments are the [±voice]-bearing segments, which [±voice] melodies would you assume? Would the feature spread?
3. How are [ʊdɔdɔ] and [ədəpigɔ] accounted for?
4. Give the underlying forms of [təkə] 'bow' and [tədəkage] 'have a bow', indicating obstruents unspecified for voice with capital letters P, T, K. Illustrate the association of [±voice] melodies and the effects of the default rules.
5. In [kɔnɔpiɔ] 'little bird', the voiceless [p] is the third consonant of the stem. Why isn't this form ungrammatical?

13.2.1 Vowel harmony

Vowel harmony can be seen as a subclass of long-distance assimilation. Many languages exclude certain combinations of vowels in the word (for a survey, see van der Hulst and van de Weijer 1995). For instance, a Finnish word containing one of the back vowels [u,o,a] must not contain any of the front counterparts [y,œ,æ]. Thus, possible words are [mitæ] 'what', [suomi] 'Finland', [talo] 'house', while *[tymo] and *[tumæ] are ill-formed. Since the vowels must apparently agree for the feature [±back], Finnish represents a case of Back Harmony. Languages may also display Round Harmony, Height Harmony and ATR-Harmony. An example is Akan, in which the four [+ATR] vowels [i,e,o,u] must not co-occur with any of their [−ATR] counterparts [ɪ,ɛ,ɔ,ʊ]. This situation is reminiscent of the restriction on tonal patterns in Ewe and Etung discussed in Chapter 10. Specifically, it would be reasonable to assume that, underlyingly, backness in Finnish and ATR-ness in Akan are properties of the word, rather than of the individual vowels. Thus, underlyingly, the vowels of a Finnish word like [pysæhtyæ] 'to stop' would be unspecified for [±back]. Instead, the word appears in the lexicon with a 'floating' feature [−back] (8a), which associates to the DORSAL nodes of all the vowels, as shown in (8b), which is equivalent to (8c). (In (8a,b) the underspecification for [±back] is indicated by the capital letters. Thus, [A] could be [æ] or [a], etc.) Notice that there is little point in assuming a particular direction of association, as there is only one feature to be associated. The important advantage of the lexical representation in (8a) is that the mutual exclusion of [+back] and [−back] vowels in the same word is naturally accounted for.

(8)   a. pUsAhtUA   b. pUsAhtUA   c. [pysæhtyæ]
         [−back]   ＼↓↙
                          [−back]

The vowel systems of languages with vowel harmony frequently have one or more vowels which do not contrast for the harmony feature of the language. Thus, in addition to the two sets of four vowels mentioned above, Akan has a [−ATR] [ɑ], for which there is no [+ATR] counterpart *[a]. Similarly, Finnish has the two [−back] vowels [i,e], for which there are no [+back] counterparts *[ɯ,ɤ]. Depending on the language, such noncontrasting vowels behave in either of two ways. They may be **opaque**, in which case they stop the spreading of the feature with the opposite value and, moreover, impose their value on any following vowels. Alternatively, they are **transparent**, in which case they allow the spreading of the harmony feature to go right through them. Opaque vowels thus block and impose harmony, while transparent vowels neither undergo nor impose it (Gafos and Dye 2011). Akan [ɑ] is an opaque vowel, while Finnish [i,e] are transparent vowels.

As shown by Clements (1981), the autosegmental model has no problem in characterizing the behaviour of opaque vowels. If we assume that the floating feature only spreads to vowels that are unspecified for the harmony feature, we predict that the spreading is stopped by any vowel that already has a specification. Akan words are made up of a root, which is marked either [+ATR] or [−ATR], plus a number of prefixes and suffixes. If the word contains only nonlow vowels, all the vowels agree with the feature value of the root, as illustrated by [e-bu-o] 'nest', which contains the [+ATR] root [bu], and [ɛ-bʊ-ɔ] 'stone', which contains the [−ATR] root [bʊ]. However, [ɑ] may occur in combination with either [+ATR] or [−ATR] vowels, as shown by the disyllabic roots [pɪrɑ] 'to sweep', [jɑrɪ] 'to be sick', [bɪsɑ] 'to ask' and [kɑrɪ] 'to weigh', where the last two are 'disharmonic' (Clements 1981). Their lexical representations are given in (9).[1]

(9)   a. pIrA   b. jArI   c. bIsA   d. kArI
        ＼| ＼/   ／ | | ＼
      [−ATR]   [−ATR]   [+ATR][−ATR]   [−ATR][+ATR]

Disharmonic roots will have prefixes and suffixes that surface with opposite values for [ATR]: the floating [+ATR] feature and the associated feature of [ɑ] will each spread to their 'half' of the word, as shown in (10), where (10a,b) are equivalent to (10c,d), respectively.

(10)   a.   O - bIsA - I   b. O - kArI - I
              ／   ／   ＼| ＼|
           [+ATR][−ATR]   [−ATR][+ATR]

       c. [o-bisɑ-ɪ]   d. [ɔ-kɑri-i]

Q124   Akan does not have words with [+ATR] vowels on both sides of [ɑ]. Does the above account explain this?

By contrast, the behaviour of transparent vowels has been problematic for the autosegmental model. It would be reasonable to want to represent transparent vowels as underspecified for the harmony feature of the language, so that they can let the spreading feature through. Recall, however, that the solution to the problem of vowel harmony was to leave the **harmonizing** vowels unspecified for the harmonizing feature. So how can a Back Harmony rule, for instance, distinguish between harmonizing and transparent vowels during its search for empty DORSAL nodes in vowels? It might be thought that the solution lies in underspecifying transparent vowels even further, and leaving the entire DORSAL node out. This might work in the case of languages that have only one transparent vowel, but not in the case of Finnish, which has two transparent vowels, [i] and [e], which contrast for a feature which in the consensus model is present on the DORSAL node: [±high]. One solution that has been proposed is to appeal to a constraint banning the ill-formed vowels concerned. For Finnish, the constraint would be (11), according to which back unrounded vowels like [ɯ] and [ɤ] are disallowed. The idea is that rules are prevented from producing the structure concerned, but that their working is otherwise unimpeded. This case may serve as a further argument for abandoning rule-based descriptions in favour of constraint-based ones.

---

[1] The vowel [ɑ] has a number of allophones, which we have not indicated.

(11)

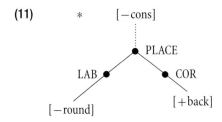

Q125   The Finnish word game Siansaksa ('Pig German') produces the forms in the second column for the Finnish forms in the first (Vago 1988).

a.	saksalaisia hæty:tet:i:n	hæksælæisiæ satu:tet:i:n
	'the Germans were attacked'	
b.	tyk:æ:n urheilusta	uk:a:n tyrheilystæ
	'I like sports'	
c.	otsansa hies:æ	hitsansa oes:a
	'in the sweat of his brow'	
d.	pitæ: kalasta	kata: pilasta
	'likes fish'	

1. Give an analysis of Siansaksa.
2. Does your analysis account for the fact that the first word in the game form in (a) is not *[hæsælæisiæ]?
3. Does your analysis account for the fact that the second form in the game form in (a) is not *[saty:tet:i:n]?
4. Does your analysis account for the fact that in (c) the first word in the game form is not *[hitsænsæ]?

13.3   COMPLEX SEGMENTS

Unlike **simplex** segments, **complex** segments have more than one specification either for place of articulation or a manner feature. Three types of complex segment can be distinguished.

1. **Complex place segments.** A complex place segment has more than one articulator node, and more than one articulator therefore participates in realizing the constriction specified by the manner features in the root. That is, a **double articulation** is produced. Examples are [gb], [kp] and [ŋm], all of which are labial-dorsal. English [w] is a labial-dorsal approximant. Labial-coronal [pt] occurs in Bura and Margi. In section 13.3.2 we will propose that prepalatal and palatoalveolar consonants like [j], [tʃ] and [c] are coronal-dorsal. In (12), an example is given of a segment with a labial as well as a coronal node. Of course, above the PLACE node the segment looks just like a simplex segment. This is

an end-view: the two articulator nodes lie in the segment plane, and are thus phonologically simultaneous.

(12)

2. **Manner-contour segments.** Manner-contour segments have a sequence of differently valued occurrences of the same manner feature. For example, prenasalized stops like [mb, nd, ŋg] are [+nas] as well as [−nas]. Since [±nasal] defines a feature-plane, this can only be represented by arranging the two specifications in sequence, and a side-view of such a segment would look like (13).

(13)
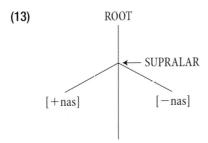

A second type of manner-contour segment has been claimed by Lombardi (1990), among others, for affricates, like German [ts] as in [tsuː] 'closed' or English [tʃ] as in [tʃuː] *chew*. In this view, affricates have a sequence of [−cont][+cont], instead of being simplex segments that are characterized by [+strid], to distinguish them from [−strid] plosives. The most important argument for the view that affricates are complex is that they are pronounced as complex segments, a closure followed by a narrowing causing friction. A second argument might be that affricates may have fricative portions that would be characterized as [−strid] if the friction constituted a segment by itself. In such cases, it may not be clear what the value of [strid] should be. However, there is also evidence that affricates function as strident plosives and are simply [−cont]. If they were (also) specified as [+cont], they would be expected to pattern with fricatives, but this appears not to be the case. For instance, the Polish fricative [s] is assimilated to [ʃ] by a following [tʃ], as in [ɔʃtʃe] 'thistle+SG,LOCATIVE', from [ɔstʃe], but the affricate [ts] is unaffected, as in [ɔtstʃe] 'vinager+SG,LOCATIVE', *[ɔtʃtʃe] (Rubach 1984, Kim 2001; see also Q56). Of course, under either analysis, affricates are single segments, and we will leave the question whether they are simplex or complex undecided.

3. **Secondary articulations**. Consonants with a secondary articulation have two place specifications: one to indicate the location of the manner of articulation, and one to indicate a simultaneous vocalic articulation. That is, while the segment is [+cons], and can have any configuration of manner features, it has an additional component specifying a vowel-like gesture of either the lips or the tongue body. A secondary articulation like labialization can combine with a labial, a coronal or a dorsal segment. The labialized segments [pʷ], [mʷ], [tʷ], [nʷ], [kʷ] and [ŋʷ] are only some of the contrastively labialized segments of Nambakaengo. Similar freedom of combination can be shown to exist for palatalization, velarization and pharyngealization. As explained in Chapters 4 and 10, there is however a strong tendency not to combine identical place specifications. While segments like [xʷ], [χʷ] are relatively common, labialized labials are rare. (Velarized velars have not been reported; indeed, it is not clear how such segments could be different from plain velars.)

Clearly, the representation of secondary-articulation segments will involve the addition of a place node, and in having more than one place node, these segments resemble complex-place segments. However, unlike what we find to be the case in complex-place segments, the two place specifications of secondary-articulation segments differ in manner of articulation. To indicate which of the place features specifies the secondary articulation and which specifies the consonantal place, it is customary to mark either the consonantal place or the vocalic place with some diacritic, as has been done in (14), which shows a partial representation of [pⁱ]. In Clements and Hume (1995), a less arbitrary solution to this problem is offered. In this proposal, the feature tree includes a vocalic place node in addition to a consonantal place node, each of which dominates the articulator nodes Labial, Coronal, Dorsal and Radical. A feature like Coronal is interpreted as a front articulation in the case of vowels, and as a coronal pronunciation for consonants, while Dorsal is used to characterize back vowels or dorsal consonants. A separate node is used to specify the degree of opening of vowels. A further discussion of this important proposal is beyond the scope of this chapter (cf. Clements and Hume 1995, Kenstowicz 1994a).

(14)

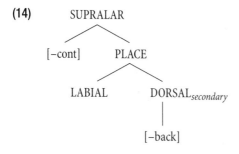

The two place nodes in a segment with secondary articulation are not sequenced in time. Although in the IPA symbols the superscripts indicating labialization, velarization, etc. conventionally appear to the right of the consonant symbol, the two components of a secondary articulation segment are phonologically simultaneous. That is, a side-view would show a straight line.

> **Q126** There have been no reports of complex segments like [px] or [dŋ]. How do the representations assumed above account for this?

13.3.1 Evidence for complex segments

Complex segments are single segments, and as such distinct from sequences of segments in having a single root node, a representational difference which we would expect to see reflected in the behaviour of complex segments. For instance, a manner-contour segment like [mb] should not be treated as if it were a sequence of [m] and [b], while a palatalized [tʲ] should not be treated as if it were [t] followed by [j]. An obvious place to look for such single-segment behaviour is the way they are incorporated in syllable structure. At first sight, we might be tempted always to regard phonetic sequences like [mb] or [nd] as sequences of phonological segments. However, the fact that in Bakwiri, for example, these are the only phonetic sequences ever to appear prevocalically is a strong indication that [mb], [nd], [ŋg] are single segments in this language, as this analysis will allow us to restrict its syllable structure to CV: it explains why no other combinations of consonants ever occur. Under the alternative analysis with CC onsets, an explanation would have to be found for the peculiar restriction that only sequences of nasal plus homorganic plosive can fill CC onsets, even though clusters like [st-] or [pj-] are fairly common in other languages. Another conceivable alternative is equally unattractive. If we assumed that the syllable

> **Q127** In Ewe, verb stems reduplicate to form a present participle, noun or adjective. Determine what segments of the verb stem are reduplicated. Why do these data (from Sagey 1986: 86) demonstrate that Ewe has compound-place segments and an affricate?
>
> | Stem | Gloss | Derivation | Gloss |
> |------|-------|------------|-------|
> | fo | 'to beat' | fofo | 'beating' |
> | zo | 'to walk' | zozo | 'walking' |
> | aha + no | 'liquor + drink' | ahanono | 'liquor-drinking' |
> | fja | 'to burn' | fafja | 'burning' |
> | bja | 'to ask' | babja | 'asking' |
> | fle | 'to buy' | feflee | 'buying' |
> | ɲra | 'to rave' | ɲaɲrala | 'a raver' |
> | kplo | 'to lead' | kpokplo | 'leading' |
> | avo + sja | 'cloth + to dry' | avosasja | 'cloth-drying' |
> | tsi | 'to grow' | tsitsi | 'grown up' |
> | gbla | 'to exert oneself' | gbagblam | 'exerting oneself' |

structure was CV(C), [limba] would be syllabified [lim.ba] rather than [li.mba], while a word like [mbila] would be [m.bi.la], with a syllabic [m]. This analysis can be empirically excluded on the basis of the word game that appeared in Q107, in which the syllables of disyllabic words are inverted (Hombert 1973, 1986), as shown in (15). Clearly, if the language were to allow codas we would expect the syllable structure of the word for 'rice' to be *[kón.dì], and the inverted form to be *[dìkón]. This, however, is not the correct game form.

(15)   *Word*   *Game form*
        mòkò   kòmò   'plantain'
        lòwá   wálò   'excrement'
        kwéli   likwè   'falling'
        kòndi   ndìkò   'rice'

13.3.2   The representation of palatals and palatoalveolars

Since in the consensus model (Broe 1992), roundness requires a labial articulator node and tongue body specification requires a dorsal articulator node, round vowels have two articulator nodes. Segments like [y,ø,u] are therefore complex, i.e. labial-dorsal. Thus, the place specification of the segment [u] is identical to that of the labial-dorsal approximant [w], as well as to that of the labial-dorsal plosive [gb]. But while the assumptions made so far correctly characterize [u] and [w] as a natural class, they fail to characterize [i] and [j] as having the same place of articulation. The assumption that [i,j] and [u,w] form natural classes is supported by processes in a number of languages which have alternations between [i] and [j] as well as between [u] and [w]. In such cases, [i,u] appear in the syllable peak, while [j,w] appear elsewhere. Our treatment so far has assigned the feature [CORONAL] to palatoalveolars and (pre)palatals like [j], but [DORSAL] to vowels, including front vowels like [i]. Not only does this make it impossible to describe alternations between [i] and [j] as involving a difference in position in syllable structure, it also fails to account for a number of effects [i] and [j] have in common (Bhat 1978, Lahiri and Evers 1991).

1. The segment [j] triggers fronting of velars, just like [i] (and possibly other front vowels). For instance, French [kjɔsk] 'kiosk' has the same [ḵ] as does [ki] 'who'. The fronting is easily explained for [i], which is [DORSAL,−back]. But why should [j], a coronal, have the same effect?

2. In many languages, [ḵ] before [i] has changed into prepalatal (i.e. [CORONAL]) [c], and from there into palato-alveolar [tʃ]. Taking this route, Latin [kiːwiˈtaːtem] and [ˈkirkaː] ended up as [tʃitˈta] 'city' and [ˈtʃirka] 'approximately' in Italian. If [i] is [DORSAL], how can it affect a dorsal consonant so as to become a coronal consonant?

3. Many languages, of which Japanese is an example, have processes that change [t,s] into [tʃ,ʃ] before [i], as in [sitimi], pronounced [ʃitʃimi],

'pepper'. [tʃ,ʃ] are coronal. If [i] is [DORSAL], then why don't we get dorsal [çiǩimi] instead?

Beginning with Keating (1987), many researchers have analysed segments like [j] as compound-place segments with both a coronal and a dorsal articulator. In this view, [j,i] both have the structure as in (16). With Jacobs (1989) and Jacobs and van de Weijer (1992), we assume that the palatoalveolars [ʃ,ʒ,tʃ,dʒ] are also coronal-dorsal. This view is supported by articulatory data, in the sense that all these segments involve articulations between the forward part of the tongue and a section of the palate stretching some 2 cm back from the alveolar ridge. These data have been obtained with the help of X-ray pictures with side-views of the tongue, as well as with the help of electropalatography, a technique for recording contact areas of the roof of the mouth (Recasens et al. 1995).

(16)

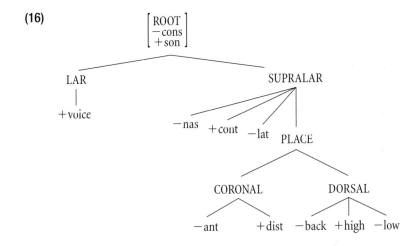

This feature analysis easily accounts for all three observations above. First, French VELAR FRONTING of [k] to [ǩ] in the environment of [i,j] can be accounted for as spreading of the [±back] node of [j] and front vowels to the dorsal node of the velar. This is shown in (17), where the [−back] feature of [i,j] will associate with the dorsal node of [k]. (Depending on the language, the rule may have to be constrained to prevent other front vowels from triggering it.)

(17) VELAR FRONTING

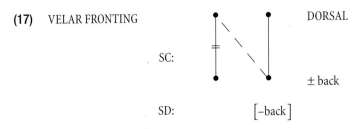

This analysis also accounts for the occurrence of [ç] instead of velar [x] in the environment of [j] and front vowels, as in Greek ['çilia] 'thousand' versus [xo'ros] 'dance'. That is, the fronting of [x] to [ç] amounts to the replacement of [+back] with [−back] in the dorsal fricative.[2]

The assimilation of [k̟] to [c] or [tʃ] can be described as the spreading of the coronal-dorsal node of [j,i] to the SUPRALAR node of the velar, as shown in (18), where the left-hand segment, [k,g], receives the PLACE node of the following [i,j].

(18)

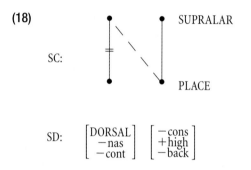

SUPRALAR

SC:

PLACE

SD: $\begin{bmatrix} \text{DORSAL} \\ -\text{nas} \\ -\text{cont} \end{bmatrix}$ $\begin{bmatrix} -\text{cons} \\ +\text{high} \\ -\text{back} \end{bmatrix}$

And, to complete the story, (19) describes the assimilation of [t,s] to [tʃ,ʃ] as the spreading of the PLACE node from [i,j] to the consonant. This analysis predicts that the coronal specification of [t,d,s,z] becomes [−ant,+distr], which is correct.

(19)

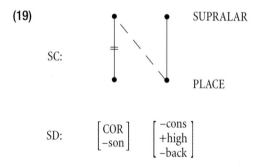

SUPRALAR

SC:

PLACE

SD: $\begin{bmatrix} \text{COR} \\ -\text{son} \end{bmatrix}$ $\begin{bmatrix} -\text{cons} \\ +\text{high} \\ -\text{back} \end{bmatrix}$

These spreading operations only account for the place assimilation. The manner features will in many cases be supplied. For instance, if the product of (18) is [c], nothing needs to be done, but if it is [tʃ], [+strid] needs to be added (cf. Kim 2001).

---

[2] The [ç] is classed as a complex coronal-dorsal by Keating (1987). In addition to making it impossible for [ʃ] to be coronal-dorsal, this characterization does not do justice to the more retracted articulatory contact for [ç] than for the palatoalveolars and [j]. Also, the implied suggestion that the fronting of [k] is a different process from the fronting of [x] has not, as far as we know, been confirmed.

13.3.3 Distinguishing among palatoalveolars

The coronal-dorsal representation of [ʃ,ʒ,tʃ,dʒ] would appear to offer a satisfactory description of these consonants, which are typically pronounced with the tongue tip raised towards, or articulating with, the alveolar ridge and a simultaneous raising of the tongue blade and forward part of the front towards the postalveolar area of the hard palate. The coronal node is responsible for specifying the first type of articulation, while the dorsal node is responsible for the second aspect. Of course, the coronal node can dominate a number of specifications for the features [±ant] and [±distr]. Even though different palatoalveolar consonants rarely contrast in the same language, the implicit prediction that there are different types of palatoalveolar consonants is certainly correct. First, a [−ant,+distr] articulation will have the blade articulating with the postalveolar region, while allowing the tongue tip to be behind the lower teeth. This is typically the tongue position for [j] and [i]. In the case of [+cons] segments, this type is sometimes referred to as 'prepalatal' or 'alveopalatal'. The obstruents are sometimes symbolized [ç,ʑ,tç,dʑ], particularly in the case of languages in which they contrast with other palatoalveolars. In Serbocroat, for instance, [tç] contrasts with [tʃ], for which the coronal contact is postalveolar or retroflex, i.e. [−ant,−distr], as shown by [tʃâːr] 'enchantment' – [tçâːr] 'profit'. (Both coronal-dorsal affricates are distinct from the coronal affricate [ts], as shown by ['tsŭriti] 'to leak' – [tçŭriti] 'to blow (of wind)' and [tsêh] 'guild, union' – [tʃêh] 'Czech man'.) Similarly, Polish contrasts retroflex [ʂ, tʂ] with alveopalatal [ç, tç], as in *proszę* [prɔʂɛ] 'please', *czas* [tʂas] 'time' versus *prosię* [prɔçɛ] 'piglet' and *ciasny* [tçasnɨ] 'tight'.

English [ʃ,ʒ,tʃ,dʒ] are [+ant,−distr]: in addition to the raised front and/or blade, there is an apical articulation with the alveolar ridge. This representation accounts for an apparent asymmetry in the application of CORONAL ASSIMILATION in English. Recall that this process causes coronal [t,d,n,l] to adopt the place of articulation of a following coronal consonant, so that the [t] of *that* is dental in *that thing*, alveolar in *that tin* and postalveolar in *that trip* (cf. p. 159). The apparent asymmetry is that before palatoalveolars the place of articulation of [t,d,n,l] remains unaffected. Even though the forward part of the front may show some anticipatory raising towards the hard palate, [t,d,n,l] retain their contact between the tip and the alveolar ridge, just as they do when a vowel follows, so that the location of the crown during [t] in *that egg* is the same as that during [t] in *that chore*, and the [n] in *keen officer* is no different from the [n] in *keen judge*.[3] Our analysis readily accounts for these data: [tʃ,dʒ] have a coronal node with [+ant,−distr], which explains the articulatory action of the tongue tip, in addition to a dorsal node with [−back], which explains the raising of the front of the tongue. Since it is only the coronal node that spreads

---

[3] Clements (1985) notes that the articulation of [t,d,n], but not of [l], changes before palatoalveolars. At least in British English, we believe there is no such distinction.

to a preceding [t,d,n,l], the effect on their place of articulation is entirely vacuous, these consonants already being [+ant,−distr]. By contrast, if we were to analyse palatoalveolars as simplex coronal segments, as was done in Chapter 6, they would have to be [−ant,+distr], which featural characterization would be necessary to explain the largely postalveolar place of articulation. This would incorrectly predict that CORONAL ASSIMILATION causes a considerable retraction of the place of articulation of [t,d,n,l] before palatoalveolars.

Q128   Tahltan has the following system of oral coronal [+cons] segments (Shaw 1991):

t	tɬ	tθ	ts	tʃ
d	dl	dð	dz	dʒ
t'	tɬ'	tθ'	ts'	tʃ'
	ɬ	θ	s	ʃ
	l	ð	z	ʒ

The dental, alveolar and palatoalveolar consonants in the last three columns are involved in a consonant harmony process of CORONAL HARMONY. Within the word, the rightmost consonant in this group determines the place of articulation of all other consonants in the same group. This is illustrated with [s] 'first person singular subject', and with [θi] 'first person dual subject' in the data below. The (a) examples show these suffixes in their unassimilated form, while the (b) examples show the effect of CORONAL HARMONY. The consonants in the first two columns above are transparent to CORONAL HARMONY: they neither trigger nor block the process. This is illustrated by the (c) examples.

	Underlying [s]		*Underlying* [θi]	
a.	ɛsk'aː	'I'm gutting fish'	dɛθigɪtɬ	'we threw it'
	ɛsdan	'I'm drinking'	θiːtθædi	'we ate it'
	sɛsrɛɬ	'I'm sleepy'	naθibaːtɬ	'we hung it'
b.	hudiʃtʃa	'I love them'	iʃitʃotɬ	'we blew it up'
	ɬɛnɛʃtʃuːʃ	'I'm folding it'	uʃidʒɛ	'we are called'
	ɛθduːθ	'I whipped him'	xas̱iːdɛts	'we plucked it'
	mɛθɛθɛq	'I'm wearing'	dɛs̱idzɛl	'we shouted'
c.	ɛdɛdɛθduːθ	'I whipped myself'	dɛs̱it'ʌs	'we are walking'
	jaʃtɬ'ɛtʃ	'I splashed it'	mɛʔɛʃit'otʃ	'we are breast-feeding'

1. How can we tell from these data that the two suffixes have different underlying forms?
2. What are the three place specifications of the consonants involved in CORONAL HARMONY?
3. Why is it impossible to view CORONAL HARMONY as the leftward spreading of a [CORONAL] node to consonants that are unspecified for [CORONAL]?
4. Is it possible to view CORONAL HARMONY as a rule that spreads a [CORONAL] node to consonants that have a [CORONAL] node, while skipping consonants that do not? Motivate your answer.

We summarize our feature analysis of coronal, coronal-dorsal and dorsal consonants in Table 13.1.

Table 13.1
Feature analysis of coronal, coronal-dorsal and dorsal consonants stands for the presence of a unary feature

	Coronal	Coronal-dorsal		Dorsal	
	Apical [t,s]	Prepalatal [i,j,ɲ,ʃ]	Eng. [ʃ,ʒ,tʃ,dʒ]	[kɕ]	[k,x]
Coronal	√	√	√		
Anterior	+	−	+		
Distributed	−	+	−		
Dorsal		√	√	√	√
Back		−	−	−	+

13.4 CONCLUSION

Many languages place restrictions on the combination of different values of the same phonological features in the word. Such word-based distributional restrictions include vowel harmony and consonant harmony, but also word-based distributional patterns of nasalization and obstruent voicing occur. The autosegmentalization of features, together with the underspecification of certain features in certain segments, allows us to describe these patterns with the help of many-to-one associations, a more insightful solution than is possible in a listed representation of features, as was usual in the linear theory of *SPE*. To account for transparent segments, however, a rule-based description will need to fall back on constraints. This was seen as an argument for abandoning the concept of rules that literally change one representation into another, and for adopting a theory like OT, which relies on constraints that simply tell us what surface representations must look like.

We also saw that the feature tree allows for a natural representation of complex segments. It was shown that, in addition to obviously complex segments like [mb], [kp] and [tʷ], palatal and palatoalveolar consonants can fruitfully be interpreted as (complex) CORONAL DORSAL segments, a type of representation that makes it possible to describe naturally various place assimilations involving palatal or palato-alveolar articulations.

Stress and feet

14.1 INTRODUCTION

This chapter discusses two conceptions in which word stress has been represented in phonological theory, first, by means of a feature [±stress] in a linear model and, second, by means of a structural position in a nonlinear model. After a brief description of the phonological nature of stress and of the notion of foot in section 14.2, section 14.3 discusses the way in which stress was accounted for in linear phonology. In section 14.4 we will provide an overview of the nonlinear metrical theory proposed by Hayes (1981) and show that it allows for a more principled way of accounting for the different stress patterns of the world's languages.

14.2 THE PHONOLOGICAL NATURE OF STRESS

It used to be thought that stress was realized by some phonetic parameter, much in the way that [CORONAL] is realized by a raising of the crown of the tongue. While at first, loudness was taken to be the relevant phonetic parameter, experiments by Fry (1955; 1958) showed that a number of different parameters were involved in creating the impression of stress in English, specifically duration, pitch variation and vowel quality. Beginning with Liberman and Prince (1977), it was realized that stress was not a phonological feature that was given some content by the phonetic implementation rules, as assumed in the linear theory of *SPE*, but a structural position. The structural position is the **foot**, which is a phonological constituent above the syllable and below the word. It is typically characterized by one strong and one weak syllable. As explained in Chapter 2, one of the feet in a word is the strong foot, and its strong syllable (its head) will typically be more prominent than the other feet, for instance because it attracts intonational tone or extra duration. This syllable has the main stress of the word, while the heads of the other feet are said to have secondary stress.

The question of how stress is realized depends on the question how a language chooses to use the structural position represented by the foot. English is a language that makes a very clear distinction between stressed and unstressed syllables. For one thing, only a subset of the vowels is allowed in the weak position of the foot: [ə,ɪ,i,ʊ], as in the final syllables of *villa*, *market*, *folly* and *fellow*.

Second, weak syllables are noticeably shorter than strong syllables, particularly in non-word-final position. Thus, in *Aberdeen*, which consists of the feet [æbə] and [diːn], the middle syllable is very much shorter than either the first or the third, both of which occur in the strong position of a foot. Third, the head of the foot is used as the association site for intonational tones. In a citation pronunciation, a pitch accent like H*L is associated with the strong foot (primary stress), while a weak foot (secondary stress) before a strong foot may also be associated with a pitch accent. In (1abc), an initial %L and a final L% boundary tone are assumed in each case.

(1)

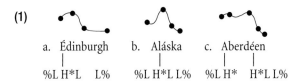

    a. Édinburgh   b. Aláska   c. Aberdéen
        | | | |
    %L H*L   L%   %L H*L L%   %L H*   H*L L%

14.2.1 Metrical feet and feet in poetry

The notion of the foot as used in metrical theory is similar, but not identical, to the foot known from metrical poetry. The essential aspect of the foot both in poetry and in stress theory is that it represents a kind of grouping of syllables into constituents. To illustrate this more clearly, let us consider Latin. Latin poetry was based on a quantitative rhythm (alternating heavy and light syllables). As explained in Chapter 11, a syllable is light if it has a short vowel and is not closed, while a syllable that ends in a consonant or has a long vowel is heavy. One of the best known meters is the dactylic hexameter, a verse line which consists of six dactylic feet. A dactylic foot is a group of syllables, possibly separated by word boundaries, that consists of one heavy syllable followed by two light syllables. Alternatively, two heavy syllables may constitute one foot. The opening verses of Virgil's *Aeneid* in (2), in which the metrical feet are indicated by parentheses, illustrate the dactylic hexameter. The stressed syllables, in bold, are ignored by the meter, which only cares about whether the syllable is light or heavy. Note that a word-final closed syllable counts as light if the following word starts with a vowel, which explains why *-mus* and *ab* in the first line are light, and why *-gus* in the second line is heavy.

(2)   (ārmă vĭ)(rūmquĕ că)(nō Trō)(iāe quī)(prīmŭs ă)(b ōrīs)

      (Ītălĭ)(ām fā)(tō prŏfŭ)(gūs, Lā)(vīnĭă)(vēnīt)

      (Līttŏră)…

      I sing about the man and his weapons who first from the shores of Troy

      To Italy, to the shores of Lavinia, came, driven by fate

In English poetry the rhythm is based on stress, that is, on alternating stressed and unstressed syllables. The most common meter is the iambic pentameter. Each verse line consists of five iambic feet. An iambic foot is a group of two syllables, again possibly separated by a word boundary, of which the first is weak (W) and the second strong (S). By way of optional variation, the first foot may be SW. Consider the opening lines of one of Shakespeare's famous sonnets in (3).

(3) S   W/ W   S/ W   S/ W S/   W   S
Shall I compare thee to a summer's day?
W   S/   W   S/ W   S/ W   S/ W   S
Thou art more lovely and more temperate.
W   S/   W   S/ W   S/ W   S/ W   S
Rough winds do shake the darling buds of May…

What we observe in (2) and (3) is that the S(trong) and W(eak) positions of feet in poetry need not coincide with stressed and stressless syllables, respectively. In fact, meters as well as languages vary in the extent to which they enforce such a one-to-one matching. For instance, as in (2), the word stress of *cano* is a weak position and the unstressed syllable [noː] is a strong position. In Latin this was quite common, whereas in English similar mismatches, as in the case of *thee to*, are allowed only in limited circumstances (see e.g. Kiparsky 1977, Hayes 1989).

In poetry the feet or the meter are used for esthetic reasons. In metrical stress theory, feet serve no such purpose, but represent the rhythmic structure of the word, in other words, its stress pattern. As such, they are intended to provide the descriptive units necessary to account for the stress patterns that may exist in the world's languages. Metrical theory is thus primarily concerned with the properties that govern the determination of the *location* of the stressed syllables in a word, whose phonetic realization may vary from language to language. Metrical theory is not one single theory, but rather consists of a number of alternative proposals. In the next section we will discuss the way in which word stress was represented in linear phonology.

14.3   STRESS AS AN ABSOLUTE PROPERTY OF SEGMENTS: LINEAR PHONOLOGY

As an example of how stress was accounted for in the linear phonological theory of *SPE*, let us continue our discussion of Latin. In Latin, monosyllabic words are stressed on the only syllable available. In words that have more than one syllable, the main stress is never on the final syllable. Thus, in bisyllabic words stress is always realized on the first of the two syllables. In words of three syllables or more, stress can either be on the prefinal (penultimate) or preprefinal (antepenultimate) syllable. In these cases the location of stress depends on the weight of the prefinal syllable. The minimal pairs in (4) illustrate that vowel length in Classical Latin is distinctive.

(4)
populus	'people'	*poːpulus*	'poplar tree'
malum	'misfortune'	*maːlum*	'apple'
liber	'book'	*liːber*	'free'
lego	'I read'	*leːgo*	'I appoint as delegate'
furor	'fury'	*fuːror*	'I steal'

Main stress was realized on the penultimate syllable if that syllable was heavy, otherwise main stress was realized on the antepenultimate syllable. Some examples are given in (5), where **l** and **h** stand for light and heavy.

(5)	a.	*mél*		b.	*lác*		
		'honey'			'milk'		
	c.	*má lum*		d.	*má: lum*		
		'misfortune'			'apple'		
	e.	*a mí: cum*		f.	*cá me ram*		
		l h			l l		
		'friend'			'(bed)room'		
	g.	*ár bo rem*		h.	*pe dés ter*		
		h l			l h		
		'tree'			'on foot'		

In (5a) and (5b) the main stress is on the only available syllable in the word. In the bisyllabic words, (5c) and (5d), stress is on the first syllable. The words in (5e–h) have three syllables. In (5e) the prefinal syllable is heavy because the vowel is long, and the main stress is therefore on the prefinal syllable. In (5h) the prefinal syllable is heavy because it is closed. Again, the main stress is on the prefinal syllable. In both (5f) and (5g) the prefinal syllable is light, and therefore the stress is on the preprefinal syllable.

The stress rules for Latin can be given in terms of the *SPE* formalism discussed in Chapter 7 as the three rules in (6), where $\breve{V}$ stands for a short and V either for a long or for a short vowel.

(6)	a.	$V \rightarrow [+\text{stress}] \;/\; \_\_ C_0 \breve{V} C_1 V C_0 \#$
	b.	$V \rightarrow [+\text{stress}] \;/\; \_\_ C_0 V C_0 \#$
	c.	$V \rightarrow [+\text{stress}] \;/\; \_\_ C_0 \#$

If applied in this order, rule (6a) is tried first, and only if its structural description is met – that is, if there is a word of more than two syllables with a prefinal light syllable – will it apply. It cannot apply if the word contains only one or two syllables, or if the word contains more than two syllables and the prefinal is heavy. In that case, rule (6b) is tried. This rule will apply in all remaining cases, unless the word has only one syllable. Rule (6c) will then provide monosyllabic words with main stress. The three rules in (6) can be collapsed as the single rule in (7), with the condition that the longest expansion of the rule is tried first, followed by the second longest, etc.

(7) $\quad V \rightarrow [+\text{stress}] \;/\; \_\_ C_0 ((\breve{V} C_1) V C_0) \#$

Secondary stresses in longer words, such as *liberàtiónem* 'liberation' can be accounted for by applying rule (8) as often as it can apply to a word. This has the effect that stresses are assigned to every syllable that is separated by one syllable from the following stressed syllable. This repeating action of a rule is called **iterative** rule application.

(8) $V \rightarrow [+stress]$ /   ___ $C_0 V C_0 V[+stress] C_0$ (iterative)

At the beginning of this chapter, we observed that a number of objections have been raised against this linear way of accounting for stress patterns. Here we note one more objection. The rules involved are purely descriptive. That is, although stress patterns that occur in natural languages can be described by rules similar to the ones in (6–8), there is no explanation for why the stress patterns are the way they are. The formalism allows in principle for all kinds of patterns that are never attested. Secondary stresses, for instance, typically alternate in a binary fashion. However, a rule assigning stress after every two, three, four or more syllables is not more or less marked than a rule like (8). This 'binary' aspect, which we might call the 'counting-by-two' aspect of stress rules, is something that is left unexplained in the linear framework. In the next section we will review the way in which metrical theory is more successful in providing a principled theory of stress patterns. To round off this section, let us illustrate the 'counting-by-two' aspect by giving the somewhat more complex stress system of Cairene Arabic (cf. McCarthy 1985, Hayes 1981, 1995, among others). In Cairene Arabic the main stress is on the final syllable, if that syllable is superheavy (ending in a long vowel plus one consonant, or a short vowel plus two consonants). If the final syllable is not superheavy, the main stress is realized on the penultimate syllable if heavy. If neither of these two conditions is met, main stress is realized on the penultimate or antepenultimate syllable depending on which of these two is separated by an even number of syllables from the rightmost, nonfinal heavy syllable in the word. If the word does not contain any heavy syllables at all, stress is realized on the syllable that is separated by an even number of syllables from the *beginning* of the word. Some examples are given in (9), where **sh** stands for superheavy.

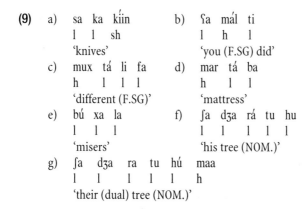

(9)   a)   sa ka kíin   b)   ʕa mál ti
            l   l   sh   l   h   l
            'knives'   'you (F.SG) did'

      c)   mux tá li fa   d)   mar tá ba
            h   l   l   l   h   l   l
            'different (F.SG)'   'mattress'

      e)   bú xa la   f)   ʃa dʒa rá tu hu
            l   l   l   l   l   l   l   l
            'misers'   'his tree (NOM.)'

      g)   ʃa dʒa ra tu hú maa
            l   l   l   l   l   h
            'their (dual) tree (NOM.)'

In (9a) the main stress is on the superheavy final syllable, and in (9b) it is on the prefinal heavy syllable. In (9c) and (9d) there is a nonfinal heavy syllable in the word and, being the only one, it is also the rightmost one. In (9c) main stress is on the antepenultimate syllable rather than on the penultimate syllable, because the syllable [ta] and not [li] is separated by an even (zero) number of syllables from the rightmost nonfinal heavy syllable [mux]. In (9d) main stress is on the penultimate syllable and not on the antepenultimate one, because the syllable [ta] is separated by an even number of syllables from the rightmost nonfinal heavy syllable, [mar]. In (9e–g), there are no nonfinal heavy syllables, so the main stress is determined by counting by two from the left edge of the word.

Q129	In Passamaquoddy (Stowell 1979, Dell and Vergnaud 1984, Hayes 1995), syllables with full vowels count as heavy and those with schwa as light. Formalize the stress rule in your own words.
a.	mekənutəsə́pənik	'those who must have been chosen'
b.	akənutəmákən	'story'
c.	luhkewínəwək	'workers'
d.	eləkiləkə́pən	'he was big'
e.	wəməsənə́mənəl	'he gets them'

14.4 STRESS AS RELATIVE PROMINENCE: NONLINEAR PHONOLOGY

14.4.1 A parametric theory of relative prominence

Hayes (1981), elaborating on Liberman and Prince (1977) and Halle and Vergnaud (1978), proposed a theory of stress that is an improvement upon the linear account in two respects. First of all, stress is no longer represented by means of a feature [±stress], but is essentially considered to be a strength relation between syllables. That is, stress is formally represented by using binary branching tree structures in which one node is **dominant** and the other **recessive**. The dominant node is stronger than its recessive sister node, and accordingly the nodes of such binary branching trees are labelled S(trong) and W(eak). Second, Hayes proposes to account for the different stress patterns in natural languages by a number of parameters. Each parameter represents two choices between which languages will choose. Hayes (1981) assumes the four parameters in (10).

(10) Right-dominant vs left-dominant
Bounded vs unbounded
Left to right vs right to left
Quantity-sensitive vs quantity-insensitive

We will briefly explain each of these parameters. The first parameter allows languages to vary in whether it is the right node or the left node in a binary branching tree structure that is dominant: in any one language, nodes are either labelled (WS) right-dominant or (SW) left-dominant.

The second parameter is necessary to describe the difference between **bounded** and **unbounded** languages. In bounded languages, the main stress is located at a fixed distance from the boundary of the word. In the unmarked case, main stress may be separated by one syllable from the right or left word boundary. In addition, secondary stresses are located at fixed intervals from other stresses. As we observed in section 14.3, secondary stresses are typically separated by one unstressed syllable. In unbounded stress systems, stresses cannot be located at a fixed distance in this way. Proto-Indo-European, for instance, had the following system. The leftmost heavy syllable, which might well be the last syllable in a long word, received the main stress. If a word did not contain a heavy syllable, the main stress was located on the first syllable (cf. Halle and Vergnaud, 1987). Tetouan Arabic is the mirror image. It has the main stress on the rightmost heavy syllable (which may well be the first syllable in a long word) or, if the word does not contain heavy syllables, on the penultimate syllable.

The primary stress in unbounded languages is thus pulled towards heavy syllables quite regardless of the distance that separates the heavy syllable from the edge of the word. In both Proto-Indo-European and Tetouan Arabic, [taː.ta.ta.ta.ta] will have the primary stress on the first and [ta.ta.ta.ta.taː] on the last syllable, and only when there is no heavy syllable, as in [ta.ta.ta.ta.ta], will the difference between the two languages come out. Bounded languages, by contrast, will not allow the primary stress to stray too far from the word's edge, and will place it on a light syllable if no heavy syllable is available. In Hayes' (1981) theory, this resolves as a difference in allowable foot size: bounded languages have maximally binary feet (cf. (11a)), while unbounded languages put no upper limit on the size of a foot. Technically, the distinction is derived by allowing unbounded languages to have S-nodes higher up in the foot tree (non-terminal S-nodes). In (11b,c), the nodes indicated by a dot can thus be labelled S, potentially allowing feet to grow without limit. A prediction of this account is that unbounded languages do not have the typical binary rhythm of secondary stresses in longer words.

(11)   (a) σ   σ   (b) σ   σ   σ   (c) σ   σ   σ   σ

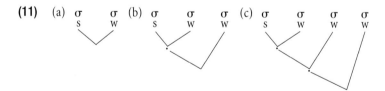

Bounded languages cannot have non-terminal S-nodes, and because, by stipulation, no language can have non-terminal (i.e. branching) W-nodes, the only way a four-syllable structure like (11c) can be parsed in a bounded language is as in (12). The two foot nodes will then be gathered up in a word tree to complete the prosodic structure of the word (see below).

(12)   σ   σ   σ   σ
        S   W   S   W

Languages can thus have unbounded stress systems if S nodes are not necessarily terminal nodes. In the remainder of this chapter we will focus on bounded stress systems. (See Prince (1985) for a proposal to describe unbounded stress systems by using bounded feet.)

Languages that have bounded stress systems may differ in whether the main stress (located at a fixed distance from the word boundary) occurs at the beginning or at the end of the word. To capture this difference, the third parameter in (10) is necessary, which allows foot construction to start either at the **right edge** or at the **left edge** of a word. A further difference among bounded stress systems, represented by the fourth parameter in (10), is related to the importance of the internal structure of the syllable when constructing feet. In one group of languages, the fact that a syllable is heavy or light does not influence the construction of feet. Languages of this kind are said to be **quantity-insensitive**. In another group of languages, the internal structure of the syllable has to be taken into account. In a **quantity-sensitive** language, a W node may not dominate a heavy syllable. For quantity-sensitive stress systems, metrical trees are built on the rhyme projection, where the distinction between heavy and light syllables can be formalized as a distinction between bimoraic versus monomoraic rhymes. In quantity-insensitive languages, trees are built on the syllable projection, where the difference between heavy and light syllables is not visible. If we disregard the direction parameter in (10), the following four basic bounded tree types are possible: quantity-insensitive, left-dominant (QI-ld), quantity-insensitive, right-dominant (QI-rd), quantity-sensitive, left-dominant (QS-ld), and quantity-sensitive, right-dominant (QS-rd). In the next section we will discuss each of these possibilities.

Q130   To what kind of input must a child be exposed in order to determine that stress in his or her language is

1.   sensitive to quantity?
2.   unbounded?

14.4.2   Four types of bounded stress system

We discuss the four types of bounded stress system identified above in the order QI-ld, QI-rd, QS-ld and QS-rd. Garawa is an example of a QI-ld stress system. Some data are given in (13) (see e.g. Furby 1974, Hayes 1981).

(13)   já.mi   pún.ɟa.la   wá.cim.pà.ŋu
       'eye'   'white'   'armpit'
       ká.ma.la.rìn.ɟi   já.ka.là.ka.làm.pa
       'wrist'   'loose'
       ŋán.ki.ri.kì.rim.pà.ji
       'fought with boomerangs'

Main stress is always on the initial syllable and secondary stress iterates in a binary fashion, i.e. occurs on every other syllable, from right to left. The rules in (14a) will produce the metrical structures in (14b).

(14a) Construct a QI-ld foot at the left-edge of the word
Assign QI-ld feet from right to left

(14b)

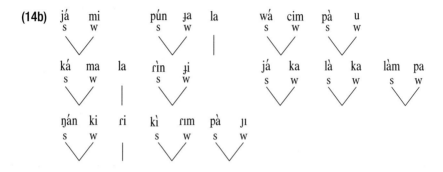

Notice that the third syllable in words with an odd number of syllables cannot be grouped with another syllable in a foot, and as a result, monosyllabic feet are constructed. In Hayes' (1981) theory, a monosyllabic foot is labelled neither W nor S, but interpreted as a stressed foot. Languages vary in their treatment of monosyllabic feet; sometimes they remain as such, and sometimes they are **destressed** (i.e., the foot is erased and the syllable it dominates attached to a preceding or following foot depending on whether the feet are left- or right-dominant). This is what must be assumed for Garawa also, given that the third syllable in these words does not have a secondary stress. The issue of monosyllabic feet will be taken up again in Chapter 15.

The rules in (14a) describe which syllables are stressed, but do not differentiate between the syllable with the main stress and the secondary stressed syllables. In Hayes (1981) this is accounted for by an extra layer of tree structure above the level of the feet, which is called the **word tree**. If, for Garawa, we group the feet into a left-dominant, unbounded word tree, the first syllable will be the only one dominated by a strong node and will therefore have main stress, as illustrated in (15) for some of the forms in (14). Henceforth, as in the metrical representations in (15), the feet are separated from the word tree by a horizontal line for reasons of clarity. As shown for [kámalaɾìnɟi] in (15), the destressed left-over syllable is attached to the foot on its left rather than to the foot on its right, given that feet in Garawa are left-dominant.

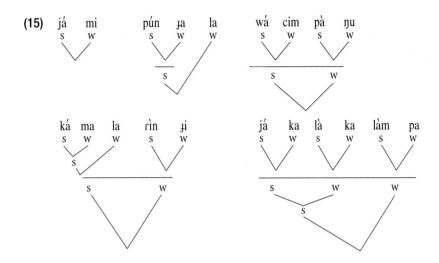

(15)

The stress pattern of Weri (see e.g. Boxwell and Boxwell 1966, Hayes 1981) can be described by assigning QI-rd feet from right to left followed by the construction of a right-dominant unbounded word tree, as illustrated in (16). In Weri, monosyllabic feet are not subject to destressing.

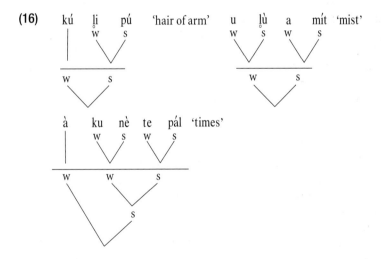

(16)

Classical Latin may serve to illustrate the QS-ld foot. In Latin polysyllabic words, as mentioned above, stress was never realized on the final syllable, but on either the penultimate or antepenultimate syllable. If stress is on the antepenultimate syllable, we may seem to need a ternary foot at the right edge of the word. However, in order to maintain the basic bounded foot types (maximally two syllables in a foot), Hayes (1981) uses the concept of **extrametricality**. At the periphery of a word – that is, at the right or left edge – a phonological constituent (syllable, segment, consonant, vowel, rhyme, mora, etc.) may be declared extrametrical, that is, be made invisible to the metrical tree construction rules. For Latin, a rule marking the final syllable extrametrical prior to QS-ld foot construction is needed, as illustrated in (17). In (17) we have indicated extrametrical syllables by angled brackets. Furthermore, in (17) we have only built one QS-ld foot, that is, QS-ld feet are not constructed iteratively in Latin. The main reason for this is that secondary stresses in Latin alternate in a binary fashion regardless of syllable weight. In a word like *vòluptátem* 'voluptuousness', secondary stress is on the initial syllable, although the second syllable is heavy. The same holds for a longer word like *lìberàtiónem*. This is accounted for by iterative assignment of QI-ld feet after the construction of a single QS-ld foot. Finally, a right-dominant, unbounded word tree is needed to promote the final foot to main stress.

(17)

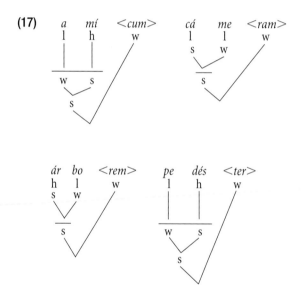

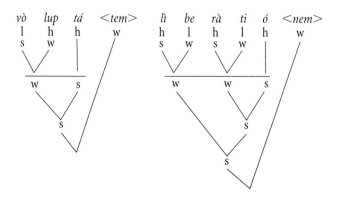

Three remarks on the derivations in (17) are in order. First, the initial monosyllabic feet in *amicum* and *pedester* wrongly predict that in those words there is secondary stress on the syllable preceding the main stress. Again, a destressing rule (not indicated in (17)) is necessary. Second, monosyllabic words like *mel* and *lac* (cf. (1) above) are stressed. The rule marking final syllables as extrametrical must therefore be blocked if it would render the entire stress domain extrametrical. Third, extrametrical syllables are adjoined as W nodes to the word tree.

The final foot type to consider is the QS-rd foot. In Hixkaryana (Derbyshire 1979, Hayes 1995) a weight distinction is made between closed and open syllables – that is, in the underlying representations no long vowels occur. As in Latin, the final syllable in polysyllabic words is never stressed, and we thus need a rule of final syllable extrametricality. The construction of QS-rd feet from left to right and a right-dominant unbounded word tree will produce the correct metrical structures as shown in (18).

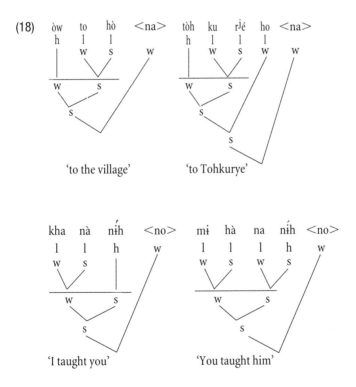

Given that the prefinal light syllable in [tohkur^jéhona] is not stressed, a rule destressing the prefinal light monosyllabic foot is necessary. After destressing, this syllable is adjoined as a weak member to the word tree, as illustrated in (18). It cannot be adjoined to the preceding foot, because in Hixkaryana the feet are right-dominant. We will return to this in the next chapter.

Q131 Icelandic (Árnason 1985) exhibits the following stress pattern in noncompound words. (Because the acute accent is also used as an orthographic diacritic in Icelandic, we indicate main stress with the help of a stress mark.)

'Jon	'John'
'tas.ka	'briefcase'
'höf.ð̄ing.jà	'chieftain (gen. pl.)'
'a.kva.rèl.la	'aquarelle'
'bi.o.grà.fi.à	'biography'

Propose an analysis.

Q132 Here are some examples of stress in Hopi (Jeanne 1978, Hayes 1981).

lés.ta.vi	'roof beam'
ko.jó.ŋo	'turkey'
me.ló:.ni	'melon'
pá:.wi.kʸa	'duck'
ca.qáp.ta	'disk'

Formalize the stress rules.

14.5   CONCLUSION

In this chapter we have discussed linear and nonlinear representations of stress. We have illustrated the four basic foot types for bounded stress systems with examples from Garawa, Weri, Classical Latin and Hixkaryana. The role of destressing rules has been discussed, and the concept of extrametricality has been motivated and illustrated for Latin and Hixkaryana. Furthermore, we have seen that the distinction between main stress and secondary stress is accounted for by a separate layer of metrical tree structure: the word tree. If we now compare the metrical theory advanced by Hayes (1981) to the previous linear account, then it is obvious that the objections raised above no longer hold. The 'counting-by-two' aspect is a direct result of the tree structures, and there is no longer a feature [stress]. The metrical trees express in a quite natural way that stress is a relative property of syllables in a word. However, it still is not clear why the trees are the way they are. That is, although a much more principled way of accounting for the possible different stress patterns in natural languages is available, it is still not clear why the patterns we find are in a way natural. This issue will be taken up in the next chapter.

Further constraining stress

15.1 INTRODUCTION

This chapter discusses Hayes' (1995) revised metrical theory on the basis of the stress patterns of the languages discussed in Chapter 14, and illustrates how stress can be accounted for in Optimality Theory. Section 15.2 discusses the three basic metrical units (the syllabic trochee, the iamb and the moraic trochee) of Hayes' (1995) stress theory. The notion of catalexis is introduced, and it is shown that compared with the analyses in the previous chapter destressing rules are no longer needed. After that, in section 15.3, foot-based segmental rules are briefly discussed. Section 15.4 addresses the relation between stress and morphology. Finally, section 15.5 shows how stress is accounted for in Optimality Theory.

15.2 IAMBIC AND TROCHAIC RHYTHM

In Hayes (1985, 1987) it is observed on the basis of typological research that of the four basic foot types discussed above, the QI-rd foot is quite rare. That is, the majority of QI languages use the QI-ld foot. Moreover, among QS languages, the most frequent foot type is QS-rd. In addition, in languages that do need the QS-ld foot, it never appears to be constructed iteratively. Hayes (1995) connects these facts with the results of perception experiments which show that listeners group sequences of even duration, like *ta-ta-ta-ta-ta-ta* ..., in a binary fashion with initial prominence, that is, *(táta) (táta)(táta)*, but group sequences of stimuli of unequal duration, like *ta-taa-ta-taa-ta-taa* ..., in a binary fashion with final prominence, that is, as *(tatáa) (tatáa) (tatáa)*, etc. Hayes terms the former grouping 'trochaic' and the latter 'iambic', and accordingly defines two fundamental laws of alternating rhythm: **trochaic rhythm** (even duration, initial prominence) and **iambic rhythm** (uneven duration, final prominence). He then proposes the foot inventory in (1), where bracketed grids are used instead of labelled trees: a bracketed grid (x .) is equivalent to a foot labelled SW, while (. x) is equivalent to a foot labelled WS. Also, in (1) the mora is used as a unit of syllable weight: a light syllable has one and a heavy syllable two moras (Chapter 11).

(1)

	(x .)
a. SYLLABIC TROCHEE:	σ σ
	(where σ is either l or h)
	(x .)
b. MORAIC TROCHEE:	μ μ
	(where μμ is either ll or h)
	(. x) (x)
c. IAMB:	μ σ or h

The foot types (1a) and (1c) do more or less the same descriptive work as the former QI-ld foot and the former QS-rd foot, respectively. The moraic trochee (1b) is designed, among other things, to account for stress systems that in Hayes (1981) were described with the QS-ld foot, although it is not equivalent to the QS-ld foot. As already mentioned in Chapter 14, metrical theory consists of a number of alternative proposals. Different foot inventories have been proposed by, among others, Jacobs (1990), Dresher and Lahiri (1991) and Kager (1993). Also, a different way of deriving metrical constituent structure has been proposed by Halle and Idsardi (1995).

Let us briefly consider how the languages discussed in Chapter 14 can be described with the Hayes (1995) foot inventory given in (1) above. The Garawa stress facts follow straightforwardly if we assign a syllabic trochee at the left edge followed by right-to-left assignment of syllabic trochees, as illustrated in (2). The word-tree construction rules discussed in Chapter 14 have been replaced in Hayes (1995) by a general rule, called the END RULE, which promotes either the first (END RULE INITIAL) or the last (END RULE FINAL) dominant position marked by an x to main stress status by adding an extra x to it on a superior layer of metrical structure. For Garawa we need the END RULE INITIAL (2b) in order to derive initial main stress. Notice that compared with the analysis in (14) and (15) in Chapter 14 no destressing is needed, given that left-over syllables are not footed by (1a).

(2)

	a. já mi	b. pún ɟa la	c. wá cim pà ŋu
SYLLABIC TROCHEE	(x .)	(x .)	(x .) (x .)
END RULE INITIAL	(x)	(x)	(x)

	d. ká ma la rìn ɟi	e. já ka làka làm pa
SYLLABIC TROCHEE	(x .) (x .)	(x .) (x .) (x .)
END RULE INITIAL	(x)	(x)

	f. ŋán ki ri kì rim pà ji
SYLLABIC TROCHEE	(x .) (x .) (x .)
END RULE INITIAL	(x)

Since no monosyllabic feet are allowed by the SYLLABIC TROCHEE, the question arises of what, in this new analysis, happens to languages like Weri, which do not destress monosyllabic feet. (A monosyllabic foot in systems with (1a) or a monomoraic foot in systems with either (1b) or (1c) is known as a **degenerate** foot.) For this former QI-rd system, we could use a syllabic trochee left to right to produce the alternating pattern, but we are left with the problem that the final syllable of words with an odd number of syllables will not be stressed. Also, words with an even number of syllables will be stressed incorrectly. Right-to-left syllabic trochee construction will always predict main stress on the penultimate syllable, which again is incorrect. It seems that the final syllable should form its own foot. This could be done by applying the END RULE FINAL twice: before and after iterative right-to-left syllabic trochee construction as illustrated in (3).

(3)

		a. kù ḷi pú	b. u ḷù a mít
END RULE FINAL		x)	x)
SYLLABIC TROCHEE		(x .)	(x .)
END RULE FINAL		(x)	(x)

		c. à ku nè te pál
END RULE FINAL		x)
SYLLABIC TROCHEE		(x .) (x .)
END RULE FINAL		(x)

An alternative solution would be to appeal to the notion **catalexis** (Kiparsky 1991), the opposite of extrametricality. Catalexis is the addition at the edge of a word of a prosodically relevant, though segmentally empty, constituent (syllable, mora or segment). A catalectic syllable is thus an abstract syllable at the end of a word, which is treated as a real syllable by the footing algorithm. This would mean that, for instance, [kuḷipu] and [uḷuamit] can be parsed as in (4) by right-to-left syllabic trochee assignment and the END RULE FINAL. In (4), catalectic syllables are indicated by square brackets.

(4)

	a. kù ḷi pú [σ]	b. u ḷù a mít [σ]
SYLLABIC TROCHEE	(x .) (x .)	(x .) (x .)
END RULE FINAL	(x)	(x)

The notion of catalexis has been proposed in order to completely eliminate degenerate feet, which Hayes (1995) still allows in very limited circumstances. We will not go into the implications of catalexis theory here, but refer for some discussion to Kager (1995) and Jacobs (1994). We conclude that former QI-ld straightforwardly translates into syllabic trochee assignment, whereas the former QI-rd stress systems require some reanalysis.

Let us next look at Hixkaryana. Final syllable extrametricality and left-to-right iambic construction followed by the END RULE FINAL produces the correct results, as demonstrated in (5).

(5)

	a. òw to hó \<na\>	b. tòh ku rʲé ho\<na\>
	h l l	h l l l
IAMB	(x) (. x)	(x) (. x)
END RULE FINAL	(x)	(x)

	c. kha nà nɨh \<no\>	d. mɨ hà na nɨh \<no\>
	l l h	l l l h
IAMB	(. x) (x)	(. x) (. x)
END RULE FINAL	(x)	(x)

Importantly, because the iamb construction rule does not allow a single light syllable to form a foot on its own, the prefinal light syllable in [tòhkur^jéhona] is skipped. This means that again, unlike the analysis presented in Chapter 14, no destressing rule is needed.

Let us finally look at Latin, previously QS-ld. Final syllable extrametricality, the construction of a moraic trochee at the right edge, followed by iterative left-to-right construction of syllabic trochees and the END RULE FINAL, produces the desired metrical structures, as illustrated below.

(6)

	a. *ár bo <rem>*	b. *cá me <ram>*	c. *pe dés <ter>*
	h l	l l	l h
MORAIC TROCHEE	(x)	(x .)	(x)
SYLLABIC TROCHEE			
END RULE FINAL	(x)	(x)	(x)

	e. *vò lup tá <tem>*		e. *lìbe rà ti ó <nem>*
	l h h		hl h l h
MORAIC TROCHEE	(x)		(x)
SYLLABIC TROCHEE	(x .)		(x .) (x .)
END RULE FINAL	(x)		(x)

By giving an extralinguistic, functional motivation to the formal elements of the descriptive vocabulary of metrical theory, we now have a more straightforward answer to the question raised at the end of Chapter 14: why is it that the stress patterns we find in the languages of the world are the way they are? In what way are they natural? The foot inventory in (1) is a direct translation of the basic ways in which people apparently group sequences of elements of even duration and sequences of elements of uneven duration.

We now return to Cairene Arabic, which we gave as an example of a language that has a rather complicated pattern of stress distribution. Its stress pattern cannot be covered by the descriptive framework discussed in Chapter 14, and requires special treatment. Consider the stress pattern in the words ʕamálti 'you (SG, FEM) did', martába 'mattress' and búxala 'misers'. If we treat the final syllable as extrametrical, the stress pattern of búxala suggests a left-dominant foot. However, using a left-dominant QS foot makes the wrong prediction for the stress in martába. The first heavy and the second light syllable should form a QS-ld foot, incorrectly predicting stress on the first syllable: *mártaba. If we were to use a QS-rd foot, the stressing in ʕamálti and martába comes out right, but now buxala is incorrectly predicted to be *buxála. Therefore, a special foot type was proposed, one in which a dominant node could be strong if and only if it was branching, that is, heavy. A rd-foot on ʕamál can therefore indeed be labelled WS, because the dominant node mál branches, whereas the rd-foot on buxa cannot labelled WS, given that its dominant node xa does not branch. In this situation, paradoxically, the rd foot will be labelled SW. It appears that, in the new model, an elegant description of these facts is possible. Quite simply, final mora extrametricality (which is suspended if this would make the entire final syllable extrametrical), left-to-right moraic trochee construction, followed by the END RULE FINAL, will derive the correct results.

(7)

	a. sa ka kíi \<n\>	b. ʕa mál ti
	l l h	l h l
MORAIC TROCHEE	(x .) (x)	(x)
END RULE FINAL	(x)	(x)

	c. mux tá li fa	d. mar tába
	h l l l	h l l
MORAIC TROCHEE	(x) (x .)	(x) (x .)
END RULE FINAL	(x)	(x)

	e. bú xa la	f. ʃa dʒa rátu hu
	l l l	l l l l l
MORAIC TROCHEE	(x .)	(x .) (x .)
END RULE FINAL	(x)	(x)

	g. ʃa dʒa ra tu hú ma \< a \>
	l l l l l l
MORAIC TROCHEE	(x .) (x .)(x .)
END RULE FINAL	(x)

In this section, we have discussed the refinements that led to the revised metrical theory of Hayes (1995). Three basic foot types are assumed which receive extralinguistic motivation. In the next section we will discuss the foot as a domain for phonological rules, and briefly investigate the relation between stress and morphology.

Q133 Turkish normally has stress on the final syllable. However, there is a class of words, including mainly loans and toponyms, where stress is never on the final syllable (Sezer 1983). Consider the examples below.

tor	na	ví	da	'screwdriver'
h	l	l	l	
lo	kán	ta		'restaurant'
l	h	l		
Wa	shíng	ton		place-name
l	h	h		
Án	ka	ra		place-name
h	l	l		
çi	ko	lá	ta	'chocolate'
l	l	l	l	

1. Determine whether this stress system is quantity-sensitive.
2. How can you account for the fact that stress is never on the final syllable?
3. The absence of secondary stresses suggests that foot assignment is not iterative. Determine whether a moraic trochee or an iamb is required to account for the stress facts.

> **Q134** In Italian, stress can be located on the final, penultimate or antepenultimate syllable. However, if the penult is heavy, stress never falls on the antepenult. Accordingly, loans with a prefinal heavy syllable and with stress on the antepenult are adapted. For instance, German [hámburk] is taken over as [ambúrgo] (cf. Sluyters 1990), which suggest a quantity-sensitive foot. Apparently, we must assume that Italian uses a moraic trochee.
>
> 1. How would you account for the existence of *corníce* 'corniche' by the side of *cálice* 'chalice', both of which have a light prefinal syllable?
> 2. Unexpectedly, stress can also fall on a final, light syllable, as in *cittá* 'city' and *colibrí* 'colibri'. How could you account for this?

> **Q135** Hayes (1995: 262) analyses Turkish nonfinal stress by constructing moraic trochees from right to left. The final foot is marked as extrametrical if a clash, i.e. a sequence of two adjacent (x)s, would otherwise arise. This alternative is illustrated in (1) with the metrical representation of *Washíngton*.
>
> (1) Wa   shíng   ton
> | h   h
>   (x)   <(x)>
>
> Demonstrate that the two analyses are not in fact equivalent by considering their predictions of the stress patterns of items (2) and (3).
>
> (2) In   di   ya   na   pó   lis
> | | h
>
> (3) Ús   kü   dar
>   h | h

15.3 FOOT-BASED RULES

15.3.1 Quantitative adjustments

As we have seen in section 15.2, iambic rhythm is typically applied to sequences of elements of uneven duration, whereas trochaic grouping typically concerns even duration. It may come as no surprise that languages with iambic rhythm tend to have segmental processes whose effect is to increase the durational unevenness. Consider again some of the Hixkaryana forms discussed in (5) above, repeated in (8).

(8)   a. òw to hó <na>   b. mɨ hà na nɨ́h <no>
                  h 1 1   1 1 1 h
    IAMB   (x) (. x)   (. x) (. x)
    END RULE FINAL   (x   )   (x   )

In (8), not all disyllabic feet are identical. For instance, in the last form the first foot is of even duration, whereas the second one is of uneven duration. Now, languages with iambic rhythm typically have rules that lengthen the vowel in the stressed syllable of the foot, rules that geminate the consonant after such a stressed vowel, causing the syllable to be closed, or rules that reduce the vowel in the unstressed syllable, thereby increasing the durational contrast within the foot. Hixkaryana has the first quantitative adjustment: a vowel in an open nonfinal syllable becomes lengthened if it occurs in the stressed position of a foot. This will change the forms in (8) into those in (9).

(9)		a. ów to hóː \<na\>	b. mi háː na nı́h \<no\>
		h l h	l h l h
IAMB		(x) (. x)	(. x) (. x)
END RULE FINAL		(x)	(x)

Strikingly, according to Hayes (1995), languages with trochaic rhythm lack rules of the kind mentioned above. However, not all foot-based rules are quantitative adjustment rules. In the next section it is shown that the foot can figure in the structural description of segmental phonological rules that are not directly related to optimizing the iambic rhythm. We illustrate the role of the foot in two lexical rules of Dutch.

15.3.2   Foot-based segmental rules

In this section we are concerned with the more general role of the foot in the structural description of phonological rules. Two lexical rules of Dutch will illustrate this role, ə-INSERTION in diminutives and PRE-r LENGTHENING.

In Chapter 8 we formulated the rule of ə-INSERTION as in (10).

$$(10) \quad \text{ə-INSERTION} \quad \emptyset \rightarrow \text{ə} / \ [-\text{tense}] \ \begin{bmatrix} +\text{cons} \\ +\text{son} \end{bmatrix} + \underline{\quad} \ \text{tjə]}_{\text{DIM}}$$

According to (10), schwa is inserted if the noun stem ends in a lax vowel followed by a sonorant consonant, as illustrated in (11). However, the schwa does not always appear when these conditions are met. In particular, the words in (12) fail to undergo the rule.

(11)	mɑn	'mɑnəcə	'man'
	bɔm	'bɔməcə	'bomb'
	'ʋɑndə̗lɪŋ	'ʋɑndə̗lɪŋəcə	'walk'
	'hoːri̗zɔn	'hoːri̗zɔnəcə	'horizon'

(12)	'meːdiəm	'meːdiəmpjə	'medium'
	'beːzəm	'beːzəmpjə	'broom'
	'paːlɪŋ	'paːlɪŋkjə	'eel'
	'ɑlbʏm	'ɑlbʏmpjə	'album'
	'seːsɑm	'seːsɑmpjə	'sesame'
	'saːrɔŋ	'saːrɔŋkjə	'sarong'

The words in (11) differ from those in (12) because their bases have final syllables with either primary or secondary stress. This suggests that the rule is prosodically conditioned. More specifically, in addition to the requirement that the stem-final syllable should have a rhyme that consists of a lax vowel and a sonorant consonant, it must be the head of a foot (Kooij 1982, Gussenhoven 1993). This version of the rule is shown in (13).

(13)   ə-INSERTION

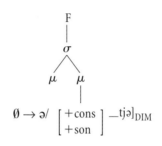

$$\emptyset \rightarrow \text{ə} / \begin{bmatrix} +\text{cons} \\ +\text{son} \end{bmatrix} \underline{\quad}\text{-tjə]}_{\text{DIM}}$$

For this analysis to go through, final post-stress syllables must be included as weak syllables in the foot, regardless of whether they have schwa (14a) or a vowel other than schwa (14b).[1] If the final syllable is preceded by an unstressed syllable, however, it forms a foot by itself (14c). The word ['meːdiəm] 'medium' is a monomorphemic ternary foot. Such feet in Dutch always have an onsetless syllable in final position, while the preceding syllable has [i] or [y] (Kager 1985).

(14)   a.   b.   c.   d.

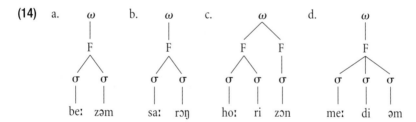

PRE-r LENGTHENING causes tense vowels in Dutch to be long before [r]. The effect of the rule is particularly noticeable in the case of tense [i,y,u], which are short in other contexts. Thus, [bit] 'beetroot', [brysk] 'brusque' and [zʊul] 'sultry' have short vowels, while [biːr] 'beer', [byːrt] 'neighbourhood' and [zʊuːrt] 'rind' have long vowels. The domain of this rule is the foot. Examples are given in (15), in which the primary and secondary stresses have been indicated in accordance with the foot structure outlined above. Interestingly, the rule cannot be directly related to stress: it applies in primary stressed syllables in (15a,b), in secondary stressed syllables in (15d,e) and in an unstressed syllable in (15c) (cf. (14b)).

---

[1] Some speakers will give the form [saːrɔŋətjə] as the diminutive of 'sarong'. There are very few words that have the required context of a post-stress, final syllable with a lax vowel and a sonorant consonant. Trommelen and Zonneveld (1989) assume that, at least at earlier stages of the derivation, Dutch foot structure is somewhat different. In particular, all closed syllables are feet in their analysis (see also Gussenhoven 1993).

(15) a. ʋíːr   'algae'
      b. ʋìːroːk   'incense'
      c. ɑ́rtyːr   'Arthur'
      d. óːliʋìːr   'Oliver'
      e. piːrəmɛ́nt   'barrel organ'

If the rule requires the vowel and [r] to be in the same foot, rather than in the same word, one should expect a word like [piˈraːt] 'pirate', in which the final foot [raːt] contains [r] but not the preceding [i], not to undergo it. This is indeed the case, as shown in (16).

(16) piráːt   *piːráːt   'pirate'
      huráː   *huːráː   'hurray'
      kɔ́rdyrɔj   *kɔ́rdyːrɔj   'corduroys'
      àtmiráːl   *àtmiːráːl   'admiral'

Q136 English [ŋ] obligatorily appears before dorsal consonants in the words in (1), but varies with [n] in the words in (2) (Kiparsky 1979). What is the domain of the obligatory occurrence of [ŋ]? Motivate your answer.

(1) íŋk   *ink*
     íŋkrəmənt   *increment*
(2) ıŋkríːs   *or* ınkríːs   *increase* (verb)
     íŋkriːs   *or* ínkriːs   *increase* (noun)

Q137 Dutch [h] is pronounced in the words in (1), but despite the spelling, no [h] is pronounced in the words in (2) and (3). What determines the occurrence of [h]? What conclusion can be drawn with respect to the prosodic structure of the word in (3)?

(1) [hút]   'hat'
     [áː.bra.hàm]   'Abraham'
     [jo.hɑ́.nəs]   'John'
     [ho.tɛ́l]   'hotel'
(2) *Niehe*   [ní.ə]   (proper name)
     aloha   [a.lóː.a]   'aloha'
     tahu   [táː.u]   'tofu'
(3) *marihuana* [màː.ri.u.áːna]

15.4 STRESS AND MORPHOLOGY

Up until now it has been tacitly assumed that the domain for the foot construction rules is the entire word. That is, feet were constructed only after the complete word had been formed. This is an oversimplification. In many languages, the normal stress pattern is interrupted by the morphological structure of words. In English, for instance, stress in complex words does not follow the same pattern as stress in underived words, as is evident from a comparison of the complex word *Japanése* with the simplex word *Sócrates*. We will now briefly discuss one way in which the morphological structure of words can be taken into account by the stress rules of a language. Consider the following Latin forms in (17).

(17)   a. *i*   *tá*   *que*   'and so'
           l   l

         b. *ple*   *rá*   *que*   'the majority'
           l   l

         c. *vi*   *rúm*   *que*   'and the man'
           l   h

         d. *ré*   *ne*   *gat*   'deny-again-3sg-pres-indic'
           l   l

In (17a,b), stress is on a light penultimate syllable. This is surprising, because in words of more than two syllables stress is always on the antepenult if the penult is light, as in (17d). The forms in (17) are all morphologically complex: the first three consist of a stem to which a clitic *-que* 'and' is attached, while the last form consists of a verb stem to which a prefix *re-* 'again' is attached. Apparently, the stress rules have to take into account the morphological structure of words: a prefix like *re-* has no effect on the stress algorithm, while a clitic like *-que* does. A possible way to account for this in metrical theory is to divide the morphological operations (prefixation, suffixation, compounding, cliticization) into two blocks: a cyclic and a noncyclic block (Halle 1990, Halle and Kenstowicz 1991). The assumption is that after each morphological operation the stress rules are reapplied. The crucial difference between the morphological operations in the cyclic block and those in the noncyclic block is that in the cyclic block all previously assigned metrical structure is erased by the STRESS ERASURE CONVENTION every time the stress algorithm is applied again. In the noncyclic block, the STRESS ERASURE CONVENTION is not active, which means that previously assigned metrical structure is still there after the morphological operation. A reapplication of the stress rules can then only apply to free, i.e. not already metrified, elements. Morphological operations that do not disrupt the stress pattern of simple words are thus located in the cyclic block, while morphological operations that do interrupt the normal stress pattern are located in the noncyclic block. For the forms in (17) this means that prefixation takes place in the cyclic block, whereas encliticization takes place in the noncyclic block. In (18) we have illustrated this by contrasting the prefix *re-* with the enclitic *-que*.

(18)   *Cyclic block*

	ne	*gat*	*i*	*ta*
	l	h	l	l
EXTRAMETRICALITY		<σ>		<σ>
MORAIC TROCHEE	(x)		(x)	
STRESS ERASURE CONVENTION	*ne*	*gat*	*i*	*ta*
	l	h	l	l

PREFIXATION	re	ne	gat		i	ta	
	l	l	h		l	l	
	re	ne	gat		i	ta	
	l	l	h		l	l	
EXTRAMETRICALITY			<σ>			<σ>	
MORAIC TROCHEE	(x	.)			(x)		

Noncyclic block

	re	ne	gat		i	ta	
	l	l	h		l	l	
	(x	.)			(x)		
ENCLITICIZATION	re	ne	gat		i	ta	que
	l	l	h		l	l	h
EXTRAMETRICALITY	(x	.) <σ>			(x)		<σ>
	re	ne	gat		i	ta	que
	l	l	h		l	l	h
MORAIC TROCHEE	(x	.) <σ>			(x)	(x)	<σ>
END RULE FINAL	(x		)		(	x	)

The application of the stress rules in the noncyclic block can, in the case of *itaque*, only apply in the penultimate syllable, given that the previously assigned metrical structure (the foot assigned to the first syllable of *ita* in the cyclic block) must be respected. This leaves the penultimate, light syllable as the only free element. For a more detailed discussion, see Jacobs (1997). In the last section of this chapter, we will briefly discuss how stress patterns are accounted for in the non-derivational framework of Optimality Theory.

15.5   STRESS AND OPTIMALITY THEORY

As mentioned in Chapter 4, in Optimality Theory (OT) phonology is thought of as a universal set of constraints which are hierarchically ranked on a language-specific basis. The relation between input and output is accounted for by respectively generating for each input all possible outputs and evaluating these outputs so as to select the optimal one. Importantly, constraints may be violated, depending on the ranking of other constraints. Let us clarify this with a concrete example. Tagalog has a prefix *um-* signalling 'actor trigger' on the verb to which it is attached (see Prince and Smolensky 1993: 34–7, McCarthy and Prince 1993b: 119–21). If the prefix is attached to a vowel-initial verb, such as [aral] 'to teach', the expected result is [umaral]. Surprisingly, however, if *um-* is attached to a consonant-initial verb, such as [gradwet] 'to graduate' or [sulat] 'to write', it behaves suddenly as an infix, producing [grumadwet] and [sumulat], respectively. OT offers a very elegant solution in terms of constraint domination. Two constraints are invoked by Prince and Smolensky (1993: 36). One is a constraint that states that the prefix should be at the left edge of a word, which we will simply term ALIGN for the moment, and the other one is NOCODA, which states that a syllable must not have a coda. If the constraint ALIGN dominates NOCODA, the prefix will always show up as a prefix, much like, for instance, the English prefix *re-*. In order to obtain the Tagalog facts we need to assume the opposite ranking: NOCODA dominates ALIGN. In (19) this is illustrated for an input /um-gradwet/ in a tableau. Recall from Chapter 4 that ☞ indicates the optimal candidate, that * indicates a constraint violation and that ! indicates that a constraint violation is fatal.

(19)

um-gradwet	NOCODA	ALIGN
a. um.grad.wet	***!	#∅
b. gum.rad.wet	***!	#g
☞ c. gru.mad.wet	**	#gr
d. gra.dum.wet	**	#gra!d
e. grad.wu.met	**	#gra!dw

In (19) candidates a and b violate the higher ranked constraint NOCODA three times, and are therefore less optimal than the remaining three outputs, which violate NOCODA only twice. Output c is optimal because it has the prefix *um-* as close as possible to the left edge. In (20) we have listed some possible outputs for an input /um-aral/.

(20)

um-aral	NOCODA	ALIGN
a. a.um.ral	**!	#a
b. a.ru.mal	*	#ar!
c. a.ra.lum	*	#ar!al
☞ d. u.ma.ral	*	#∅

In the final section of this chapter we will illustrate how stress distribution can be accounted for in OT.

15.6　CONSTRAINING STRESS

To characterize right and left dominance in feet, the constraints RHTYPE(I) and RHTYPE(T) given in (21) and (22) are assumed.

(21)   RhType(I): Feet must be iambic.

(22)   RhType(T): Feet must be trochaic.

In order to derive iambic grouping rather than trochaic grouping, the constraint RhType(I) must outrank the constraint RhType(T). If the language is trochaic, the opposite ranking is required. In order to ensure binary grouping, the constraint in (23) FtBin is assumed, and to achieve the effect of extrametricality, the constraint NonFinality is needed:

(23)   FtBin: Feet must be binary (either two moras or two syllables).

(24)   NonFinality: A foot may not be final.

McCarthy and Prince (1993a, 1993b) capture the left-to-right or right-to-left parsing of feet by appealing to their theory of **generalized alignment**. This theory amounts to a family of alignment constraints, which can be used for a variety of purposes. For instance, as we have seen above and in Chapter 4, the position of an affix is determined by a constraint which aligns one of its edges with the corresponding edge of the word. Most commonly, an alignment constraint stipulates that the right or left edge (R/L) of a grammatical category (GCat, among which are the morphological categories Root, Stem, Morphological Word, Prefix, Suffix, etc.) must coincide with the right or left edge (R/L) of a prosodic category (PCat: μ, σ, foot, phonological word (or ω), phonological phrase, etc.; see Chapter 16) according to the general schema in (25).

(25)   General schema for Align
Align (GCat, R/L-Edge, PCat, R/L-Edge): the R/L-Edge of some GCat must coincide with the R/L-Edge of some PCat.

To ensure that footing begins at the edge of a stress domain, the constraints in (26) and (27) are necessary.

(26)   Align (ω, R, Ft, R): the right edge of the phonological word is aligned with the right edge of a foot.

(27)   Align (ω, L, Ft, L): the left edge of the phonological word is aligned with the left edge of a foot.

In a word of three syllables, $(\sigma\sigma)\sigma$ will be more optimal if the ranking (27) » (26) obtains, while $\sigma(\sigma\sigma)$ will be more optimal if (26) » (27). Next, in order to derive iterative footing, the constraints in (28) and (29) are assumed.

(28)   Align (Ft, R, ω, R): the right edge of every foot is aligned with the right edge of the phonological word.

(29) ALIGN (Ft, L, ω, L): the left edge of every foot is aligned with the left edge of the phonological word.

Recall that in OT constraints may be violated, depending on the ranking of other constraints. The constraints ALIGN(Ft) in (28) and (29) above are in competition with the constraint PARSE-σ in (30).

(30) PARSE-σ: Parse syllables into feet.

If this constraint is higher ranked than (i.e. dominates) the ALIGN(Ft) constraint (29), for instance, iterative footing results. The footing (σσ)(σσ) for a word of four syllables will be more optimal than (σσ)σσ. The latter output violates the higher-ranked PARSE-σ constraint, while the former does not.

We illustrate these constraints by deriving the stress pattern of Garawa (cf. Kenstowicz 1994b: 16). Because no monosyllabic feet occur and because the grouping is trochaic, both the constraints FTBIN and RHTYPE(T) must be highly ranked. For Garawa, the alignment constraints in (31) and (32) are necessary.

(31) ALIGN-ω: Align (ω, L, Ft, L) (= (27))

(32) ALIGN-Ft: Align (Ft, R, ω, R) (= (28))

In (33) we illustrate the interaction between these two constraints in an odd-syllabled word like [kamalarinɟi]. As shown in (33), the actual ranking we need is the one in which (31) dominates (32).

(33) a.

kamalarinɟi	Al (ω, L, Ft, L)	Al (Ft, R, ω, R)
☞ a. (káma)la(rìnɟi)		σσσ#
b. ka(mála)(rìnɟi)	σ!	σσ#

b.

kamalarinɟi	Al (Ft, R, ω, R)	Al (ω, L, Ft, L)
a. (káma)la(rìnɟi)	σσσ#!	
☞ b. ka(mála)(rìnɟi)	σσ#	σ

Notice that the constraint FTBIN must crucially dominate the constraint PARSE-σ. If not, the leftover syllable in (33) would be parsed as a foot. Finally, we illustrate the interaction between the constraint PARSE-σ and ALIGN(Ft) in [jakalakalampa] in (34). PARSE-σ must dominate the ALIGN(Ft) constraint in order to derive iterative footing, as shown in (34a).

(34) a.

jakalakalampa	Al (ω, L, Ft, L)	Parse-σ	Al (Ft, R, ω, R)
☞ a. (jáka)(láka)(lámpa)			$\sigma\sigma\sigma$#, $\sigma\sigma$#
b. (jáka)laka(lámpa)		*!*	$\sigma\sigma\sigma$#

b.

jakalakalampa	Al (ω, L, Ft, L)	Al (Ft, R, ω, R)	Parse-σ
a. (jáka)(láka)(lámpa)		$\sigma\sigma\sigma$#, $\sigma\sigma$#!	
☞ b. (jáka)laka(lámpa)		$\sigma\sigma\sigma$#	**

In (34) we only consider output forms that do not violate the constraint Align(ω), i.e. outputs that have an initial foot. Given the higher ranking of the constraint Parse-σ in (34a), a violation of the constraint Align(Ft) (the second foot of candidate (a) in (34a)) is evaluated as being better than a violation of the constraint Parse-σ (the third and fourth syllable of candidate (b) in (34a)). The constraint ranking in (34a) thus derives 'iterative' footing for Garawa. A reversal of the constraint ranking, as in (34b), causes a violation of the constraint Parse-σ (the third and fourth syllable of candidate (b) in (34b)) to be preferred to a violation of the constraint Align(Ft) (the second foot of candidate (a) in (34b)).

Q138 The ranking we have established thus far for Garawa is the following:

FtBin » RhType (T) » Al (ω, L, Ft, L) » Parse-σ » Al (Ft, R, ω, R).

Draw a constraint tableau for an input /ŋankirikirimpaji/ and show what happens to the following six possible output forms.

[(ŋánki) (ríki) (rímpa)ji]
[(ŋán) (kíri) (kírim) (páji)]
[(ŋánki) rikirim (páji)]
[(ŋánki) ri (kírim) (páji)]
[(ŋánki) (ríki) rim (páji)]
[(ŋanki) ri (kírim) (páji)].

It is easy to observe that the constraints discussed so far treat all feet in the same way, that is, no distinction is made yet between the foot with main stress and secondarily stressed feet. Two more alignment constraints (35) and (36) are necessary.

(35) Align (Head, R, ω, R) (H/R): The foot with main stress is aligned with the right edge of the phonological word.

(36)   ALIGN (HEAD, L, ω, L) (H/L): The foot with main stress is aligned with the left edge of the phonological word.

For the Garawa stress pattern we need to assume that ALIGN (HEAD, L, ω, L) dominates ALIGN (HEAD, R, ω, R).

Finally we will consider Hixkaryana stress in the OT perspective. Given that iambs are required, RHTYPE(I) must be higher ranked than RHTYPE(T). Moreover, given that stress is never final, the constraint NONFINALITY must be highly ranked. Furthermore, iambs are assigned from left to right (to use 'derivational' terminology), so ALIGN(Ft,L) dominates ALIGN(Ft,R). As footing is exhaustive, the constraint PARSE-σ must dominate the Alignment constraint. Also, no degenerate feet are permitted, which points to the ranking of FTBIN above PARSE-σ. This gives us the hierarchy in (37).

(37)   RHTYPE(I) » FTBIN » NONFINALITY » PARSE-σ » ALIGN (Ft, L, ω, L).

In (38) we consider some of the possible candidates for an input [tohkur^{j}ehona].

(38)

tohkur^{j}ehona	RHT(I)	FTBIN	NONFIN	PARSE-σ	ALIGN
a. (tóh)ku(r^{j}ehó)na				**	$\sigma\sigma$#!
b. toh(kúr^{j}e)(hóna)	*!*		*	*	σ#, $\sigma\sigma\sigma$#
c. (tóh)(kur^{j}é)(hó)na		*!		*	σ#, $\sigma\sigma\sigma$#
☞ d. (tóh)(kur^{j}é)hona				**	σ#

In (38), we have not considered a possible candidate in which the first two syllables are grouped into a foot. If a candidate [(tohkú)(r^{j}ehó)na] were added to tableau (38), it would wrongly be characterized as the optimal form. It is obvious that the first foot is not a proper quantity-sensitive iamb. In order to ensure the quantity-sensitivity of stress in languages like Hixkaryana, two constraints have been proposed, the Weight-to-Stress Principle (WSP), demanding that heavy syllables are stressed and Weight-by-Position (WbP), discussed in section 11.5. They are here listed as (39) and (40), respectively. In tableau (41), which illustrates the final ranking for Hixkaryana, they have been collapsed to a single constraint QS.

(39)   Weight-to-Stress Principle (WSP): Heavy syllables are stressed.

(40)   Weight-by-Position (WBP): A coda consonant is moraic.

(41) /tohkurʲehona/	RʜT(I)	FᴛBɪɴ	NᴏɴFɪɴ	QS	Pᴀʀsᴇ-σ	Aʟɪɢɴ(Fᴛ/L)	H/R
(tòh)ku(rʲehó)na					**	#σσ!	σ
toh(kúrʲe)(hòna)	*!*		*	*	*	#σ, #σσ	
(tòh)(kurʲè)(hó)na		*!			*	#σ, #σσσ	σ
☞ (tòh)(kurʲé)hona					**	#σ	σσ
(tohkù)(rʲehó)na				*!	*	#σσ	σ
(tóh)(kurʲè)hona					**	#σ	σσσ! σ
(tòh)(kurʲè)(honá)		*!				#σ, #σσσ	

Q139 Latin main stress is quantity-sensitive, as shown by the forms in (a). In some varieties of Macedonian (cf. Baerman 1999) stress is fixed on the antepenultimate syllable, as shown by the forms in (b).

(a) Latin quantity-sensitive stress		(b) Macedonian quantity-insensitive stress	
cá-me-ram	'(bed)room'	dó-ve-dam	'brIng-1SG-PRES'
so-lí-cu-lum	'little sun'	do-vé-de-te	'bring-2PL-PRES'
pe-dés-ter	'on foot'	do-vé-dox-te	'bring-2PL-AORIST'

Determine what the ranking of the constraints Aʟ(ω, L, Fᴛ, L), Aʟ(ω, R, Fᴛ, R), NᴏɴFɪɴᴀʟɪᴛʏ, QS and Pᴀʀsᴇ-σ for each language must be.

Q140 Yurakaré (van Gijn 2006), has a stress pattern exemplified by the following words:

tá.ta 'father'
ku.dá.wa 'lake'
ti.pó.ho.re 'my canoe'
ma.là.ɲo.lé.ju 'don't fall in love with him'

The following seven constraints are necessary to correctly characterize output forms:

Aʟ (ω, L), Aʟ (ω, R), NᴏɴFɪɴᴀʟɪᴛʏ, (H/L), (H/R), Pᴀʀsᴇ-σ and FᴛBɪɴ.

Assuming output candidates that have iambic feet, propose an analysis and illustrate it with tableaux for [táta], [tipóhore] and [malàɲoléju].

Q141 Cavineña (Key 1968), a Quantity-Insensitive language, displays the stress pattern illustrated in the following data.

é.na	'water'
ki.rí.ka	'paper, book'
à.si.ká.da	'dirty'
ma.tò.ha.i.wa	'cactus-like plant'
a.tà.ta.wá.ha	'kind of bee'

The following constraints will enable you to characterize the correct output forms:

a. FTBIN
b. ALIGN(Ft, L, ω, L)
c. ALIGN(Ft, R, ω, R)
d. RHTYPE(T)
e. RHTYPE(I)
f. PARSE-σ

1. Identify the pairs of constraints that are crucially ranked.
2. Demonstrate the interaction of each pair by giving two tableaux for some input form, one with the correct ranking and one with the incorrect ranking.

Q142 In Creek (Haas 1977, Hayes 1995), main stress is realized as an H-tone. The following words are representative.

i.fá	'dog'
i.fó.ci	'puppy'
po.cós.wa	'axe'
a.pa.ta.ká	'pancake'
ak.to.pá	'bridge'
al.pa.tó.ci	'baby alligator'
naf.ki.ti.ka:.ji.tá	'hit-pl-obj'

Provide an OT account that characterizes the foot to which the H-tone will be associated.

15.7 CONCLUSION

We have discussed the refinements that led to the revised metrical theory of Hayes (1995). The syllabic trochee, the iamb and the moraic trochee have been used to describe the stress patterns of Garawa, Weri, Hixkaryana, Classical Latin and Cairene Arabic. The notion of catalexis was introduced and it has been shown that destressing rules are no longer needed. After that, we discussed the foot as a domain for segmental processes that have the effect of increasing the durational unevenness in languages with iambic rhythm, and as a domain for segmental rules that are not – or no longer – obviously related to optimizing rhythm. In addition, we considered the way in which the morphological structure of words can be taken into account by the stress rules of a language. Finally, it was demonstrated how stress distribution can be accounted for in Optimality Theory. Our final chapter considers phonological adjustments whose structural description somehow makes reference to more than one word, and deals with the theory of **Prosodic Phonology**.

Phonology above the word

16.1   INTRODUCTION

The phonological structure of languages extends beyond the syllable and the foot. There is a hierarchy of phonological constituents, so that lower, and thus typically smaller constituents, are contained within higher, and thus typically larger ones. For instance, the foot is contained within, or dominated by, the phonological word, and phonological words are grouped into phonological phrases, etc. Instead of 'phonological constituent' the term 'prosodic constituent' is often used, particularly for the higher constituents, like the phonological phrase, the intonational phrase and the phonological utterance. The entire structure above the syllable is often referred to as the 'Prosodic Hierarchy'. This line of research began with Selkirk (1972) and was consolidated by Nespor and Vogel (1986), Hayes (1989) and, for the phonological word, Booij (1985), among others.

In this chapter, we discuss and illustrate the phonological utterance (U), the intonational phrase (IP), the phonological phrase (φ) and the phonological word (ω). In (1), an example of a sentence is given that has been parsed into these constituents. The next two lower constituents are the foot, which was discussed in Chapters 14 and 15, and the syllable, which was discussed in section 11.6. Notice, for instance, that weak forms, the function words *were* and *to*, are not separate phonological words, but are included with the following form in the same ω. In fact they aren't even feet, since they have no stress. Before discussing the prosodic constituents in more detail, we first deal with three general questions. First, how do prosodic constituents manifest themselves? Second, what is the general structure of the prosodic hierarchy? And third, what determines the prosodic structure of specific sentences?

(1)

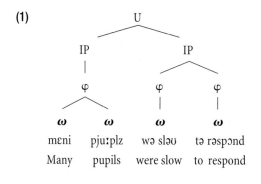

U		phonological utterance
IP IP		intonational phrase
φ φ φ		phonological phrase
ω ω ω ω		phonological word

mɛni   pjuːplz   wə sləʊ   tə rəspɔnd
Many   pupils   were slow   to respond

16.2   GENERALIZATIONS INVOLVING PROSODIC CONSTITUENTS

Prosodic constituents manifest themselves in four ways:

1. Boundary strength. There is a greater degree of articulatory integration in lower constituents than in higher ones. For instance, within an English syllable like [læmp] as in *Lampton*, the articulatory gestures occur relatively quickly after each other, but within higher-ranking constituents, the sequence of movements in [læmp] will be less tightly coordinated, as in *A fu[ll amp]utation* or *A [lamb p]assed by*. That is, prosodic breaks between higher constituents are stronger than those between lower constituents. Boundary strength will reveal itself in a number of phonetic measures. The extent to which the articulation of a vowel is influenced by that of a vowel or consonant in a preceding syllable will depend on the strength of the boundary between the trigger and the vowel concerned. Such **coarticulation** will cause a schwa to be closer in [əpiː] than in [əpɑː], in anticipation of the tongue position of the following vowel. However, this effect will be stronger if the two vowels occur within an ω, as in [ə]*ppeal*, than when they occur in different ωs, as in *Emm*[ə] *Peel* (cf. Cho 2004). Also, the duration of the last syllable of a prosodic constituent is typically longer as the lengthening is stronger (or 'higher', thinking hierarchically), which is known as **final lengthening**. Equally, the initial segments of a constituent are more clearly pronounced as the boundary is stronger, which is known as **initial strengthening** (Keating, Cho and Hsu 2004).

2. Boundary tones. Higher constituents are often characterized by intonational boundary tones. When that happens, the boundary is particularly easy to hear. Examples of this will be given when we discuss the phonological phrase and the intonational phrase.

3. Postlexical phonological processes. Prosodic constituents frequently determine the distribution of segments and the application of phonological processes. We have already seen in section 11.6 how the syllable functions in phonological generalizations, and in section 15.3.2, we saw the foot in the same role. The ways in which reference is made to phonological constituents have been classed into three types. They were given as 'rules' by Selkirk (1980), who had phonological processes in mind, but they might usefully be extended to any distributional facts.

    a. Domain limit constraints. Reference is made to the left or right edge of a constituent. In many languages, phonological words must end in a consonant, as in Tagalog for instance, although syllables occur freely without a coda word-internally.

    b. Domain span constraints. The context and the focus of some generalization must occur with a single constituent of some rank. For instance, as we will see below, Italian has a rule of s-VOICING, which causes [z], never [s], to appear between vowels contained within a phonological word.

c.   Domain juncture constraints. The context of the generalization may include the left and right edges of adjacent constituents of some rank, provided this boundary occurs within some higher constituent. For instance, as we will see, [s] is optionally voiced to [z] in Dutch if it occurs finally in the phonological word and the next phonological word begins with a vowel, provided this boundary falls within an Intonational Phrase.

4.   Phonology-sensitive syntax. Lastly, it has been observed that syntactic and morphological rules may be sensitive to the size of constituents (Zec and Inkelas 1990). English has HEAVY NP SHIFT, which allows the movement of the object in (2) to clause-final position. However, a condition on the rule is that the object NP must consist of more than one phonological phrase. For this reason, (3a) cannot move its NP. By contrast, (3b) shows that either order is fine if the object NP contains more than one phonological phrase.

(2)   V NP to NP

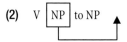

(3)   a.   He gave the book to her aunt (* … to her aunt the book)
       b.   He gave to her aunt the book about Mozart (*or*: the book about Mozart to her aunt)

16.3   THE STRICT LAYER HYPOTHESIS

What does the prosodic hierarchy look like? A common view is that the constituents obey the STRICT LAYER HYPOTHESIS, which is perfectly obeyed by representation (4).

(4)   (   )U
       (   )(   )IP
       (   )(   )(   )(   )φ
       (   )(   )(   )(   )(   )(   )(   )ω

There have been a number of formulations of this principle (Selkirk 1984, Ladd 1996). We give it as (5).

(5)   STRICT LAYER HYPOTHESIS (SLH): A prosodic constituent of rank n is immediately dominated by a single constituent of rank $n + 1$.

An ω, for example, will be dominated by φ. If it isn't, as in (6a), the structure is non-exhaustively parsed, in this case into constituents of rank 2. (In Chapter 15, we saw that nonexhaustive parsing of syllables into feet in fact does sometimes occur; we come back to this point in section 16.9.) As a result, segment A in (6a) may begin a syllable without at the same time beginning a foot. If an ω were to be dominated by two φs, we would create the incoherent occurrence of a φ-boundary within an ω.

This type of violation of the SLH, shown for the boundary between A and B in (6b) and known as 'improper bracketing', is ruled out completely. Third, if a constituent were to dominate a constituent of the same rank, we would have recursiveness. A structure is recursive if some constituent appears within a constituent of the same rank or a lower rank. In (6c), for instance, two constituents of rank 1 are contained within a constituent of the same rank. There have been various claims that same-rank recursiveness in prosodic phrasing must in fact sometimes be recognized.

(6)   a. (   )3   b. (   )3   c.
               (   )2   (   )(   )2   (   )1
           (A   )(   )1   ( )(A B)( )1   (   )(A   )1

As observed in Chapter 3, recursiveness in the morphosyntactic structure is one of the hallmarks of human language. It explains why sentence length is infinite, as in *This is the cat that caught the rat that stole the cheese that lay on the table that …*, where every NP except *This* has the structure $[…[…]_S]_{NP}$, as in [*the cat* [*the cat stole the cheese*]$_S$]$_{NP}$, in which the S has an NP which takes the form $[…[…]_S]_{NP}$, and so on, *ad infinitum*. Similarly, sentences may appear as premodifiers within NPs, as in *an I-couldn't-care-less attitude*.

16.4   FACTORS DETERMINING PROSODIC PHRASING

What determines where these prosodic constituents begin and end? Not surprisingly, an important factor is the morphosyntactic structure. It would, to give an extreme example, be unexpected for the main break in (7a) to occur between *to* and *arrive*, with smaller breaks as indicated. Rather, we would expect something more like (7b). In fact, in (7b), the smaller domains are phonological phrases and the larger ones intonational phrases. As will be clear, they correspond with syntactic phrases, unlike the bracketed parts of (7a). By somehow marking off the meaningful constituents in the pronunciation, parsing of the expression will be easier for the listener.

(7)   a.   {(The first) (train to)} {(arrive is the) (one from Paris)}
        b.   {(The first train) (to arrive)} {(is the one) (from Paris)}

However, a secondary role is played by constituent length. Since morphosyntactic constituents of a given rank may vary hugely in length, a one-to-one correspondence between phonological and morphosyntactic constituents would put unreasonable demands on speakers. For instance, the large NP after *see* in (8a) is syntactically equivalent to the word *her* in (8b). It would be quite a strain on the speaker to produce a phonological phrase that runs all the way from *the old* to *road*, while it would equally be awkward to produce two in quick succession for *I can see* and *her*. In (8a) there is too much phonological structure and in (8b) too little for a comfortably rhythmic occurrence of prosodic breaks. There would appear to be a tendency for constituents to consist of two lower constituents (Selkirk 2000).

(8)   a.   I can see the old customs office at the end of the bend in the road
       b.   I can see her

Not surprisingly, a phonological phrase tends to be produced for each of the NP-internal phrases in (8a): *(the old customs office), (at the end), (of the bend)* and *(in the road)*. And in (8b), the NP *her* will be incorporated with the preceding *see* into a single phonological word, pronounced [siːə], to rhyme with *Maria*. This incorporation of phonologically weak words into adjacent words is called **cliticization**, and *her* here is a clitic that attaches to the host *see*. Cliticization of phonologically weak words in phonological word formation is a specific case of what is called **restructuring**, the incorporation of phonologically light structures with adjacent words into a phonological constituent which it would otherwise have had to itself. We will see an example in section 16.5.4. Languages must be expected to have ways of preventing short phonological constituents.

In (8a), the correspondence between the syntactic and the phonological structure is still in a sense one to one, since inside the large NP, the 'maximal projection', there are smaller phrases, PPs and an NP, or XPs for short, which correspond to phonological phrases. However, also when the syntax is identical, different prosodic structures may be imposed on the grounds of length. For instance, an intonational phrase boundary is more likely after the subject NP in *Hippopotamuses like to swim in the river* than in *John likes to swim in the river*. Languages will vary in their preference for reflecting the morphosyntactic structure in the phonology at the expense of an even distribution of phonological constituents.

A third factor is the **information structure** of the sentence. If someone answers the question *When was Mozart born?* by saying *In January 1756*, all of the information expressed is new to the hearer who posed the question. However, if the same expression was said in response to *Was Mozart born in January 1756 or in February 1756?* only *January* would be the new information. These different focus constituents are indicated in (9a) and (9b), respectively. Languages have different ways of encoding such differences in information structure, or focus structure, and one of them is the prosodic phrasing. We will see an example of this in the discussion of the phonological phrase in Bengali. Other languages, like English, use pitch accents for this purpose (see Chapter 10).

(8)   a.   In [January seventeen fifty-six]$_{FOC}$
       b.   In [January]$_{FOC}$ seventeen fifty-six

Alignment constraints will be able to take care of the coincidence of morpho-syntactic constituents and prosodic constituents. Selkirk's (2000) ALIGNXP, for instance, given in (10), can be used to describe the phonological phrasing of the Basque sentence in (11a). It explains why (11b) is ungrammatical, because the right edge of the XP meaning 'to Amaia's grandmother' does not end a φ. The coincidence of prosodic constituents and focus constituents can likewise be accounted for by means of alignment constraints.

(10)   ALIGNXP: Align the right edge of an XP with the right edge of a φ.

(11) a. $_\varphi$(Amaien amumari)$_\varphi$ $_\varphi$(liburua)$_\varphi$ $_\varphi$(emon dotzo)$_\varphi$
Amaia-GEN grandmother-DAT book give AUX
She gave the book to Amaia's grandmother
b. *$_\varphi$(Amaien amumari liburua)$_\varphi$ $_\varphi$(emon dotzo)$_\varphi$

An example of a constraint that considers phonological length is BINARY (Elordieta 1997), a specific form of the general phenomenon that constituents mustn't be too short or too long. In fact, syntactically well-behaved (13b) is ungrammatical, because (12) outranks (10).

(12) BINARY: The first φ of the sentence must contain minimally two ωs.

(13) a. $_\varphi$(Amaiari amumen liburua)$_\varphi$ $_\varphi$(emon dotzo)$_\varphi$
Amaia-DAT grandmother-GEN book give AUX
She gave grandmother's book to Amaia
b. *$_\varphi$(Amaiari)$_\varphi$ $_\varphi$(amumen liburua)$_\varphi$ $_\varphi$(emon dotzo)$_\varphi$

Q143 If the syntactic structure of (13a) were to be used as a response to *Did she give Joseba's book to Amaia?*, the focus constituent would be *amumen*, the 'new' information. The left edge of this kind of focus constituent must be aligned with a φ-boundary, as expressed in (1).

(1) ALIGNFOC: Align the left edge of a FOC-constituent with the left edge of a φ.

The prosodic structure of the reply, in translation 'She gave GRANDMOTHER'S book to Amaia', is the one given as ungrammatical in (13b) of the text.

1. How would you account for the fact that the first φ consists of a single ω?
2. What would the prosodic structure be of the equivalent of 'She gave grandmother's BOOK to Amaia'?

We now turn briefly to the four prosodic constituents. These are not the only prosodic constituents that are discussed in the literature. For instance, an 'accentual phrase' and an 'intermediate phrase' are often referred to.

16.5 THE PROSODIC CONSTITUENTS

16.5.1 The utterance

Nespor and Vogel (1986) illustrate the domain span effect of the phonological utterance, or U, on r-LINKING in the standard variety of English spoken in England, RP. Like many other varieties, RP disallows the [−cons] consonants [h,j,w,r] in the coda. Morphemes that end in nonhigh vowels ([ə,ɪə,ɛə,ɔː,ɑː,ɜː], as in *villa, idea, fair, paw, car, stir*) are followed by [r], if the next morpheme begins with an onsetless syllable, as illustrated in (14). (The [r] is traditionally known as 'linking r' when there is an [r] in the spelling, and as 'intrusive linking r' if there is not.) In (14a,b), r-LINKING is seen to apply within the word and across words. However, the upper limit is the U: while it can apply across two sentences addressed to the same listener and not separated by a pause, it cannot apply across two sentences addressed to different listeners, even if they are spoken without an intervening pause. The examples (14c,d) illustrate that the U is not necessarily isomorphic with a single syntactic sentence, but that there is nevertheless an upper limit to what can be accommodated within the same U.

(14) a. stɜː   *stir* $_U$(… sti[r]ing …)$_U$
     b. fɛə   *fair* $_U$(A fai[r]idea)$_U$
     c. ˈʃiːlə   *Sheila* $_U$(Hi Sheila! [r]Everything all right?)$_U$
     d. ˈpiːtə   *Peter* $_U$(Hi Peter!)$_U$ *[r] $_U$(Open the window, Sheila)$_U$

16.5.2 The intonational phrase

The intonational phrase, or IP (often also I) tends to correspond to the **root sentence**, i.e. a single [NP VP]-structure without extrapositions or interruptions. Selkirk (1978) gives (15b), in which the extraposition *in Pakistan* and the restrictive relative clause *which is a weekday* have been assigned to separate IPs, leaving the root sentence, which would otherwise be a single IP (15b), to be divided over two IPs. However, as was the case with U, the division of speech into IPs is not purely syntactically driven. In particular, when the subject is longer than a single lexical word there will tend to be an IP boundary between the subject NP and the VP, as shown in (15c).

(15) a. $_I$(In Pakistan)$_I$ $_I$(Tuesday)$_I$ $_I$(which is a weekday)$_I$ $_I$(is a holiday)$_I$
     b. $_I$(Tuesday is a holiday)$_I$
     c. $_I$(The second Tuesday of every month)$_I$ $_I$(is a holiday)$_I$

The domain span effect of the IP can be illustrated with a rhythmic stress retraction rule affecting certain adverbials in Dutch, like [ɑltɛit] *altijd* 'always', which can appear in a variety of sentential positions in the same IP. They have the word stress on the second syllable when no other pitch accented word follows in the same IP, as illustrated in (16a,b). The retraction of the stress to the first syllable occurs when the word is followed by a word with a pitch accent within the IP, as illustrated in (16c,d). (The pitch accent is indicated by [ˊ].)[1]

(16) a. $_I$(Naar de wáterstanden luistert ze altíjd)$_I$
       to the water level reports listens she always
       'The water level reports she will always listen to'
     b. $_I$(Waar ze altíjd naar luistert)$_I$ $_I$(zijn de wáterstanden)$_I$
     c. $_I$(áltijd luistert ze naar de wáterstanden)$_I$
     d. $_I$(Ze luistert áltijd naar de wáterstanden)$_I$

In many languages the IP is bounded by intonational boundary tones, a domain limit phenomenon from which the constituent derives its name. In English, nonfinal IPs are frequently closed by H% after a H*L pitch accent, which causes the final syllable of *incident* in (17a) to have high pitch. The same H*L H% pattern may be

---

[1] This rhythmic phenomenon is distinct from the Dutch Rhythm Rule that applies to adjectives in NPs, the English equivalent of which is dealt with in 16.2.3 (Gussenhoven 1983).

used for questions, as shown in (17b). IPs usually begin with an intitial %L$_I$. The second IP in (17a) has 'declarative' intonation, and ends in %L$_I$.

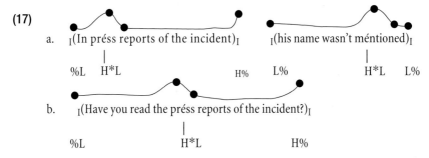

(17)
    a. $_I$(In préss reports of the incident)$_I$ $_I$(his name wasn't méntioned)$_I$

          %L   H*L   H%   L%   H*L   L%

    b. $_I$(Have you read the préss reports of the incident?)$_I$

          %L   H*L   H%

16.5.3 The phonological phrase

Although languages vary in the details of the correspondence, the phonological phrase, or φ, tends to correspond to the syntactic phrase. Hayes (1989) shows that the φ defines the domain of the English RHYTHM RULE. In (18a), *Chinese* is an adjective inside the NP *the Chinese dishes*, while in (18b) *the Chinese* is an NP, the indirect object of *gives*. An adjustment of the stress pattern from *Chinése* to *Chinese* under the influence of the following main stress on *dishes* takes place in (18a) but not in (18b). Similarly, the German Rhythm Rule is sensitive to the German φ in (19a), the headless object NP *das hell-blaue* forms a φ by itself, while in (19b), it forms part of the NP, and hence the φ, *das hell-blaue Bild*.

(18)   a. On Tuesdays, he gives $_φ$(the Chínese díshes)$_φ$
          b. On Tuesdays, he gives $_φ$(the Chinése)$_φ$ $_φ$(díshes)$_φ$

(19)   a. Ich fand $_φ$(das hèll-bláue)$_φ$ $_φ$(schön)$_φ$
          'I found the light-blue one beautiful'
          b. Ich fand $_φ$(das héll-blaue Bíld)$_φ$
          'I found the light-blue picture'

In Bengali, the φ is phonologically marked by a final boundary tone H$_φ$ if it contains an intonational pitch accent L*, as shown in (20a). Because the right-hand boundary of the φ is sensitive to the focus of the sentence in Bengali, (20a) contrasts with (20b), whose focus is confined to the first constituent of the compound word for 'fishhead'. (The focus is indicated by capital letters in the glosses. The examples also include an IP-final L$_I$.) The Bengali φ equally defines the domain of the rule of r-DELETION (Q43) and a regressive voicing process (Hayes and Lahiri 1991).

(20)
    a. tumi $_φ$(kon matʃʰer-matʰa)$_φ$ $_φ$(ranna-korle)$_φ$)$_I$

               L*   H$_φ$ L$_I$
         you   which fishhead   cooked
         'Which FISHHEAD did you cook?'

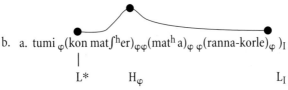

b.　a. tumi $_\varphi$(kon matʃʰer)$_{\varphi\varphi}$(matʰ a)$_\varphi$ $_\varphi$(ranna-korle)$_\varphi$)ᵢ

L*　　　　Hᵩ　　　　　　　　　　　　　Lᵢ

'The head of which FISH did you cook?'

Again, syntactic constituency does not provide the only relevant information for deriving φ-structure. Constituents to the right of the NP head in English, such as the PP *of ancient China* in the NP *the Chinése of áncient Chìna,* form their own φ, as shown by the absence of rhythmic stress shift on the word *Chinése*. However, when the postposed PP does not contain a lexical head, like the PP *on him* in the NP *that report on him*, a single φ is formed containing the whole NP. The relevance of this distinction was shown by Zec and Inkelas (1988), who pointed out that the syntactic rule of HEAVY NP SHIFT, which places an object NP in sentence-final position, only applies if the NP is composed of at least two φs. This is shown in (21), taken from Inkelas (1989). In the ungrammatical b-example, the object is only a single φ.

(21)　a. Mary gave to Susan $_\varphi$(that report)$_{\varphi\ \varphi}$(on Dukakis)$_\varphi$
　　　　b. *Mary gave to Susan $_\varphi$(that report on him)$_\varphi$

The examples in (22a,b) (Nespor and Vogel 1986) illustrate another way in which nonsyntactic information is relevant to φ-formation in (American) English, as revealed by the behaviour of the RHYTHM RULE. In (22a), [ˌriːprə'duːs] *rèprodúce* has the main stress on the last syllable, which pronunciation is as expected when it is the last word in the φ. However, in (22b) it has undergone stress shift, a pronunciation that requires that it should be followed by another accented word in the same φ. This is explained by the assumption that if the Adverbial Phrase consists of a single phonological word, it can optionally be included in the φ on its left, instead of forming its own φ.

(22)　a. Rabbits $_\varphi$(rèprodúce)$_\varphi$ $_{\varphi}$(quíckly and dìligently)$_\varphi$
　　　　b. Rabbits $_\varphi$(réprodùce quìckly)$_\varphi$

Q144　What is the φ structure of sentences (1) and (2)? Why is (2) ungrammatical?

(1)　I was explaining to the students the problem of the double negation in Middle English
(2)　*I was explaining to the students the problem

Q145　The English rhythm rule can apply in (1), but not in (2). How would you account for this difference?

(1)　This is répresènted in síx. (i.e. in (6))
(2)　This is rèpresénted in síx á. (i.e. in (6a))

16.5.4 The phonological word

Frequently, when a phenomenon is said to be word-based it is in fact confined to the domain of the **phonological word**, or ω (also known as the **prosodic word**). Crucially, the ω does not correspond in a one-to-one fashion to the morphological word. For instance, while compounds represent 'words' in the sense of morphological categories like Noun, Verb or Adjective, in many languages each of the constituent parts forms a phonological domain for (consonant or vowel) harmony, word stress and syllabification. Thus, VOWEL HARMONY in Turkish is confined to the constituents of the compound, as shown in (23), from Nespor (1998), where the vowels in one constituent are all [+back] and the vowels in the other are other all [−back]. In German, the MOP (MAXIMUM ONSET PRINCIPLE, cf. Chapter 11) does not apply across the internal boundary in a compound, as shown in (24), while in Greek, each of the constituents has its own word stress, exactly as if they formed an NP, as shown in (25).

(23) a. jemek odasɯ   'dining room'
        b. el jazɯsɯ   'handwriting'

(24) a. mʊnt.aːrt (*mʊn.taːrt)   'dialect (*lit.* mouth type)'
        b. aɪs.lœfl (*aɪ.slœfl)   'ice spoon'

(25) a. omáða erɣasías   'work team' (*omaða erɣasías)
           (cf. meɣália erɣasía   'big works')
        b. zóni asfalías   'safety zone' (*zoni asfalías)

Italian s-VOICING, shown in (26), provides an example of an ω domain span rule. It voices nongeminate [s] between vowels, as illustrated in (27) (Nespor and Vogel 1986, 1997). The rule applies in a simplex word in (27a), in a suffixed word in (27b), but does not apply across a prefix and its base (27c) or a combination of a stem and a word (27d), even though all four items in (27) are single morphological words. The generalization that brings this disparate group of morphosyntactic constituents under one heading is the ω.

$$\text{(26)} \quad \text{ITALIAN s-VOICING} \quad s \rightarrow z /\ _\omega(. . . \mid \underset{\underline{\quad}}{\overset{\text{V C V}}{. . .)}}_\omega$$

(27) a. 'kaza   'house'
        b. ka'zina   'house + DIM'
        c. aso'tʃale   *azo'tʃale   'a-social'
        d. 'filoso'vjetiko *'filozo'vjetiko 'pro-soviet'

A constituency effect of the Dutch ω was noted by Booij (1985). Dutch coordinated NPs allow deletion of identical parts in the coordinated constituents. Schematically, the situation can be represented as A*B̸* and *CB*, where the slash marks the deleted item. Crucially, the deleted portion in the left-hand coordinate is not a morphological (or syntactic) constituent. This is illustrated in (28). The deleted B corresponds to the head noun of an NP in (28a), to a noun within a compound noun in (28b), to a verbal stem in (28c) and to an adjectival suffix in (28d). While the deleted portions are quite heterogeneous when viewed from a morphosyntactic perspective, their common phonological characteristic is that they form separate syllabification domains, i.e. *ω*s. Dutch does not generally syllabify across words, while all prefixes and certain suffixes like *-schap* and *-achtig* do not syllabify together with the base they are attached to, forming separate *ω*s.

(28) a. $[[grote]_{Adj} [maten]_N]_{NP}$ en $[[kleine]_{Adj} [maten]_N]_{NP}$
$_\omega$(grote)$_\omega$ $_\omega$(en)$_\omega$ $_\omega$(kleine)$_\omega$ $_\omega$(maten)$_\omega$
'small (sizes) and large sizes'

b. $[[minimum]_N [maten]_N]_N$ en $[[maximum]_N [maten]_N]_N$
$_\omega$(minimum)$_\omega$ $_\omega$(en)$_\omega$ $_\omega$(maximum)$_\omega$ $_\omega$(maten)$_\omega$
'minimum (sizes) and maximum sizes'

c. $[in [voer]_N]_N$ en $[uit [voer]_N]_N$
$_\omega$(in)$_\omega$ $_\omega$(en)$_\omega$ $_\omega$(uit)$_\omega$(voer)$_\omega$
'im(port) and export'

d. $[[zwanger]_{Adj} schap]_N$ en $[[moeder]_N schap]_N$
$_\omega$(zwanger)$_\omega$ $_\omega$(en)$_\omega$ $_\omega$(moeder)$_\omega$ $_\omega$(schap)$_\omega$
'pregnant(hood) and motherhood'

The assumption that the deleted portion should minimally be a *ω* is supported by the impossibility of deleting suffixes that **do** syllabify with the base. Dutch has two adjective-forming suffixes meaning 'like'. The suffix *-achtig* [ɑχtəχ] is like *-schap* in (28d), and forms its own *ω*, but the suffix *-ig* [əχ] is incorporated into the *ω* of its base. Accordingly, deletion of *-achtig* is possible in (29a), while in (29b) no deletion is possible.

(29) a. $[[paars]_{Adj} achtig]_{Adj}$ en $[[groen]_{Adj} achtig]_{Adj}$
$_\omega$(paars)$_\omega$ $_\omega$(en)$_\omega$ $_\omega$(groen)$_\omega$ $_\omega$(achtig)$_\omega$
'purple(-like) and green-like'

b. $[[paars]_{Adj} ig]_{Adj}$ en $[[groen]_{Adj} ig]_{Adj}$
$_\omega$(paarsig)$_\omega$ $_\omega$(en)$_\omega$ $_\omega$(groenig)$_\omega$
'purple-like and green-like'

Q146 In Dutch, prevocalic [s] is often voiced to [z] after voiced segments, as shown in (1). However, no voicing is possible in the examples in (2). What determines when [s] may be voiced?

(1) $[['hœys]_N [ɑrts]_N]_N$	[z]	'family doctor'
$[[ʋɑs]_{Aux} ['aːrdəχ]_{Adj}]_{VP}$	[z]	'was friendly'
$[['mɛns]_N [aːp]_N]_N$	[z]	'orang-utan'
$['mɪs [oːχst]_N]_N$	[z]	'failed harvest (mis-harvest)'
$[['ɛis]_N ɑχtəχ]_{Adj}$	[z]	'ice-like'
(2) $[hɛis]_V ən]_V$	*[z]	'hoist+INF.'
$[kɑns]_N ən]_N$	*[z]	'chance+PLUR.'
$['mɑsaː]_N$	*[z]	'mass'

16.6 DERIVING PROSODIC CONSTITUENTS

With the ω we have come to the lowest prosodic constituent which can somehow be related to morphosyntactic constituency. What the ω and higher constituents have in common is that at least part of their formation is dependent on the morphosyntactic structure of the language. The question of how the relation between the two kinds of constituency is to be expressed has received different answers in the literature. In Nespor and Vogel (1986), the relation is based on a variety of morphosyntactic properties. A typical statement of such a relation might be 'Include the head of the syntactic constituent S, together with all the prosodic constituents of rank C on its non-recursive side, in Prosodic Constituent of rank C+1.' (The non-recursive side is the left side in right-branching structures, and vice versa.) Selkirk (1986), with reference to a proposal in an earlier version of Chen (1987), suggests that the unifying element in the relation between prosodic and morphosyntactic constituency is reference to edges. Her theory is known as EDGE-BASED PROSODIFICATION, and is given in (30).

(30) EDGE-BASED PROSODIFICATION: The right (left) boundary of a prosodic constituent C corresponds to the right (left) boundary of a morphosyntactic category X.

The claim in (30) is that, to derive a prosodic constituent, all we need to know is which syntactic constituent it 'co-begins' or 'co-ends' with, so to speak. As has become clear from the discussion in the preceding sections, the role of nonsyntactic factors like length tends to be stronger as the rank of the prosodic constituent is higher, and we therefore illustrate the theory with a low-ranking prosodic constituent, the Dutch ω. This constituent can be derived with the help of morphological information only (cf. Booij 1977: 103, van der Hulst 1984: 85). As is the case in Italian, suffixes are syllabified with their base, but prefixes never are. This suggests that the ω co-begins with the beginning of the morphological category 'word', i.e. any stem or derived word. This excludes prefixes and, as we will see in the next section, certain function words, like pronouns and prepositions. This is informally expressed in (31). This description predicts that constituents of the compound form individual ωs, which is correct. It will be clear that EDGE-BASED PROSODIFICATION is the precursor of Alignment Constraints in Optimality Theory.

(31) ω: Lexical Category, Left

In (32a) we see that separate syllabification domains are created for prefixes and stems. This is because the prefix begins a lexical category (the complex word) and so does the base. (The end of a nonfinal ω is of course defined by the beginning of the next.) Similarly, (32b) illustrates how separate domains are created for the constituents of compounds: each of them begins a lexical category, while the first, additionally but redundantly, begins the compound, another lexical category. In (32c) we see that suffixes are included in the ω on the left, because suffixes do not begin lexical stems.

(32)	Morphology	ω-structure	Syllabification	
a.	[ɔnt [εiχən]$_V$]$_V$	$_ω$(ɔnt)$_ω$ $_ω$(εiχən)$_ω$	ɔnt.εi.χən	'dispossess'
	[ɔn [eːvən]$_{Adj}$]$_{Adj}$	$_ω$(ɔn)$_ω$ $_ω$(eːvən)$_ω$	ɔn.eː.vən	'uneven'
b.	[[rεin]$_N$ [aːk]$_N$]$_N$	$_ω$(rεin)$_ω$ $_ω$(aːk)$_ω$	rεin.aːk	'Rhine barge'
	[[kεrk]$_N$ [œyl]$_N$]$_N$	$_ω$(kεrk)$_ω$ $_ω$(œyl)$_ω$	kεrk.œyl	'barn owl'
c.	[[teːkən]$_V$ ɪŋ]$_N$	$_ω$(teːkənɪŋ)$_ω$	teː.kə.nɪŋ	'drawing'
	[[ʋandəl]$_V$ aːr]$_N$	$_ω$(ʋandəlaːr)$_ω$	ʋan.də.laːr	'walker'

As pointed out by Inkelas (1989) and Booij (1996), prosodic structure, like any other aspect of the phonological representation of words or morphemes, can be included in underlying representations. As we saw in (28d) above, many Dutch full-vowelled suffixes are not included in the ω on their left, like the nominalizing suffix -*schap* and the adjectival suffix -*achtig*, which do not syllabify with their base. In the lexicon, these suffixes will therefore be listed as ωs. (It would, incidentally, not be difficult to give a phonological characterization of the suffixes that display this behaviour.)

16.6.1 Clitics

Pronouns, auxiliary verbs, conjunctions and the like cannot be given ω status by (31) in Dutch, since they do not belong to a major word class. But since they are words, not affixes, they cannot attach to some other item in the lexicon that *is* a major-class item. Many function words are in fact included in ω postlexically. If (31) is also valid postlexically, the prediction is that function words in Dutch should behave like suffixes, i.e. be included in the phonological word to their left. This is indeed what we find. In (33a) the article [ən] encliticizes onto the preceding verb form [rip] 'called'. This explains why the article cannot, in natural speech, be pronounced [ʔən] in this context. The same goes for the preposition [ɪn] and the definite article [ət] in (33b) (Booij 1996).

(33)	a.	[rip]$_V$ [ən]$_{Art}$	Hij $_ω$(ri.pən)$_ω$ kat
			'he called a cat'
	b.	[χaːt]$_V$ [ɪn]$_{Prep}$ [ət]$_{Art}$	Het $_ω$(χaː.tɪ.nət)$_ω$ putje
			'it goes into the drain'

Other function words, also those that lack an onset, have a full vowel, like the conjunctions [ɔf] 'or' and [εn] 'and'. These words are at best only variably syllabified with the preceding word, and they will therefore have to be given ω status in the lexicon, along with the suffixes that form their own ω, like -*schap*. It has also been noted that certain function words and affixes behave neither as elements that are included in the same ω as their host word nor as elements that form an ω by themselves. Nespor and Vogel (1986) postulate the Clitic Group as a constituent between the ω and the φ in order to account for phonological processes that occur between words and such recalcitrant morphemes, but which fail to occur in other morpheme combinations. An example is the prestressing of Latin -*que* 'and', discussed in Chapter 15.

16.6.2   The syntactic residue

The U, IP, φ, ω and, perhaps, the Clitic Group are the prosodic constituents which define the relevant domains of processes that apply above the word level. Prosodic theory thus distinguishes itself from theories that claim that such rules can refer directly to syntactic structure, such as Kaisse (1985). Nevertheless, instances have been found of rules that apply across words, which do apparently refer to syntactic categories, as would appear to be the case for French LIAISON (Hayes 1990, Post 1997). Hayes (1990) proposes that such 'residual' syntax-sensitivity should be accounted for in the lexicon. That is, the phonological rules that produce the required forms are in fact lexical rules, and the forms they produce are thus available in the lexicon, ready for insertion into syntactic phrases. To give an example, the phonological rule that shortens final long vowels in Hausa verbs is syntactically conditioned: it only applies if a direct object that contains a major class noun immediately follows. This is illustrated in (34a), which contrasts with (34b), where the morphosyntactic condition is not met.

(34)   a. náː káːmà kiːfiː   'I have caught a fish'
       b. náː káːmàː ʃí   'I have caught it'
          náː káːmàː wà múːsáː kiːfiː   'I have caught Musa a fish'

The lexical rule is given in (35); its morphosyntactic conditioning is expressed by the 'Frame' given below it. (Because the only category that can occur initially in a VP before an NP is a V, it is not necessary to label the word as a Verb in the rule.) Thus, when a verb is to be inserted in a sentence, the more specific form produced by FINAL VOWEL SHORTENING is chosen if the morphosyntactic condition applies.

(35)   FINAL VOWEL SHORTENING V → ∅ / [...V —] $_{\text{Frame 1}}$
       Frame 1: [— NP...]$_{\text{VP}}$

The assumption that syntax-dependent rules are in fact lexical rules puts such alternations in a comparable position with phrasal allomorphy of the sort that is seen in the English indefinite article, which is [ən] before vowels but [ə] elsewhere. As the name suggests, phrasal allomorphs are rival phonological forms whose distribution is governed by properties of the surrounding words. There are, however, two differences between these two cases worth mentioning. First, the forms in (35) are generated by a rule, because they involve a whole class of words rather than a single morpheme, and second, in (35) the conditioning is morphosyntactic rather than purely phonological. Hayes refers to forms like English [ən] and Hausa [káːmà] as **precompiled**, the idea being that they come ready-made from the lexicon. A prediction of this treatment is that rules like (35) might have exceptions.

16.7   PROSODIC CONSTITUENCY BELOW THE PHONOLOGICAL WORD

Below the ω, the prosodic hierarchy could be argued to continue with the foot (F) and the syllable. However, these constituents cannot, as a rule, be derived from morphosyntactic constituency, and are thus only subject to phonological well-formedness conditions. Another difference with the prosodic constituents discussed so far is that the SLH (7) does not apply with the same force to constituents below the word. In particular, stray monosyllabic syllables need not be included in foot structure, as we saw in Chapter 15. In English an initial, open prestress syllable like [tə] in *Tamara* neither belongs to the foot *mara* nor, in view of its obviously unstressed character, forms a foot by itself. As as result, the syllable is directly attached to the ω node, as shown in (36), a clear case of nonexhaustiveness (Pierrehumbert and Beckman 1988: 148). In Dutch, such initial prestress syllables remain unfooted regardless of whether they are closed or not, so that both [mi'nyt] 'minute' and [kɑn'toːr] 'office' have an unfooted initial syllable (Gussenhoven 1993).

(36)

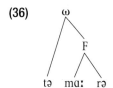

Likewise, ambisyllabic representations can be interpreted as involving improper bracketing: the ambisyllabic consonant is in the coda of one and in the onset of another (Kiparsky 1979, Jensen 1993). Even if the violation occurs below the level of the syllable, one might argue that the syllable is at least 'guilty by association'. By the same token, the relation between segments and syllable affiliations might be viewed as being in the ambiguous transition zone between 'association lines' (which routinely enter into many-to-one linkings) and the branches of tree structures that indicate constituent membership. There thus seems no good reason for rejecting ambisyllabic representations, certainly when considering the advantages of this representation in Chapter 11. Indeed, in addition to the postlexical ambisyllabicity in English dealt with in that chapter, there are further considerations for assuming that ambisyllabicity may even exist in lexical representations. Dutch and German foot structure, for instance, leaves no doubt that intervocalic single (superficially non-geminate) consonants, like [t] in Dutch [kɔn'fɛti] 'confetti', close the syllable on their left (as well as open the syllable on their right). One reason for assuming they are in the coda is that the main stress never falls to the left of a closed penultimate syllable, and that the penultimate syllable of a word like [kɔn'fɛti] behaves just like a closed penultimate syllable in a word like [a.'lɑs.kaː] 'Alaska' in this respect (*['aː.lɑs.kaː], *['kɔnfɛti]). In these cases, the consonant is ambisyllabic in representations that exist 'before' foot structure is erected and crucially contributes to the weight of the syllable (van der Hulst 1985).

16.8   CONCLUSION

Phonological rules that apply above the level of the word appear to be constrained by prosodic constituents that form a hierarchical structure which is not directly mappable onto the morphosyntactic structure. We have seen that these prosodic constituents not only define the domains at or within whose edges phonological adjustments occur, but are also constituents that are referred to by rules of syntax. Just as syllabic and foot structure is available in the lexicon (cf. Chapter 9), so the prosodic structure appears to be visible to the syntax. That is, morphosyntactic structure exists simultaneously with the phonological structure. The distinction between lexical and postlexical rules, which separates phonological rules that can refer to morphological information and which potentially have exceptions from those that can only refer to phonological representations and which cannot have exceptions, could be maintained above the level of the word by assuming that phonological rules for which syntactic information is relevant are in fact lexical rules. Such syntax-sensitive rules only apparently apply above the level of the word, and actually produce the appropriate alternants in the lexicon. During the construction of the sentence, these precompiled forms are inserted in the specific contexts instead of the rival, more general alternant.

Prosodic structure is considerably more orderly than syntactic structure. The STRICT LAYER HYPOTHESIS, which forbids improper bracketing, recursivity and non-exhaustiveness, constrains the prosodic structure from the ω onwards. The phonological constituents below the ω are not usually derivable from morphosyntactic structure, and may deviate from these well-formedness requirements in limited ways. In particular, not all syllables need to be included in foot structure, while consonants may be simultaneously part of two syllables, a representation known as ambisyllabicity.

Epilogue

Writing a textbook can be a dangerous enterprise. Especially in a fast-developing discipline such as phonology, there is always the risk that the book is outdated at the moment of publication. We have tried to give our textbook a longer life not only by providing an overview of the state of the art but also by presenting the arguments that have led to changes in theoretical frameworks, while constantly trying to keep in mind the kinds of question that a beginning student of phonology might ask. By trying to make this book meet the beginning student's needs, we have also felt free to deviate from a strict chronological treatment of theories. For instance, at an early point, when we were dealing with the nativization of loanwords, we introduced the latest version of phonological theory: Optimality Theory. This same didactic goal characterizes most of the exercises. Rather than rehearsing the material of each chapter, they are designed to make students sensitive to linguistic arguments, and more often than not present new data and new questions.

The history of generative phonology can be divided into three main periods. Starting with the idea that sound can be linearly sliced up into discrete matrices of segments, the main emphasis of linear phonology from the early 1960s has been on the exact formulation of rules that manipulate strings of segments. Chapters 7 and 8 present an overview of this linear framework of phonology. As so often in the development of science, the joint effort of many researchers quickly led to new insights. Starting in the late 1970s, phonologists have convincingly shown that phonological theory is in need of an enriched representation of phonological structure. The replacement of linear phonology by nonlinear models greatly increased our understanding of phonological structure and at the same time reduced the number of possible phonological rules. As such, it offers a more adequate theory of possible phonological processes. The developments and arguments that led to nonlinear phonology form the topics of Chapters 10–16. In the early 1990s, when nonlinear models were being consolidated, nonlinear theory appeared well equipped to return to the issue of how to deal with phonological adjustments.

During the first two periods of its history, phonology remained derivational: rules changed underlying structures into surface structures. With the advent of Optimality Theory that picture, too, changed. The phonological rule itself has been abandoned and replaced by a universal set of constraints that may be ranked on a language-specific basis. The ranking of constraints decides what will be the surface structure for any given input form in a given language.

Our hope is that students who have studied this book will feel we have succeeded in giving them a sound understanding of phonology, and will have come to share with us the excitement of realizing that nontrivial questions about sound structure can be formulated and answered. We also hope that it will have provided them with the right kind of background wherever scientific questions have a bearing on the sounds of language, as will often be the case in psycholinguistics, speech technology, neurolinguistics and sociolinguistics. And, fortunately, for those who want more there are excellent further textbooks available: *Phonology in generative grammar* by Michael Kenstowicz, *The handbook of phonological theory*, edited by John Goldsmith, *The Cambridge Handbook of Phonology*, edited by Paul de Lacy, John McCarthy's *A Thematic Guide to Optimality Theory*, *Optimality Theory* by René Kager and *The Blackwell Companion to Phonology,* edited by Marc van Oostendorp, Colin Ewen, Elizabeth Hume and Keren Rice.

Key to questions

Chapter 1

Q1 In Japanese songs, the notes are sung on moras: all the Japanese lines have seven moras. Line 2 has a moraic [n] in the second syllable of *re.mon*, line 3 has one in the first syllable of *min.na*, which is also the first half of a long consonant, lines 4 and 5 have diphthongs in *fai.to* and *a.oi*, each counting for two moras, and line 6 has a mora in first half of the long consonant in *rap.pa*.

Q2

- A. A 'silent letter' in the spelling of a word fails to correspond to a segment in the pronunciation with which that letter typically corresponds in other words. For instance, in the majority of cases, *h* corresponds to [h] in English words, as in *honey* ['hʌni], but it fails to do so in *honest* ['ɒnəst] or *Thomas* ['tɒməs].

- B. It is often difficult to equate letters with segments, because the segment that a letter corresponds with often depends on other letters in the same word. Letters can hardly be said to be 'silent' if their absence changes the correspondent segment of another letter. The *gh* in *light* have the effect of suggesting [aɪ] as the correspondent of *i*, because the spelling *lit* would suggest a pronunciation [lɪt], not [laɪt]. In fact, it doesn't make a great deal of sense to talk about 'the pronunciation of a letter'. Letters have names, like English [eɪ] for *A,* and that's how you pronounce them.

Q3

- A. The syllable [hi] could be accented or unaccented, and the answer is therefore 'two'. In fact, both *hí* and *hi* exist, 'fire' and ' day', respectively. Three words could be made with [kentoo], *kéntoo, kentóo* and *kentoo*. Here, the last two are actual words, the nouns 'guess' and 'investigation'. The fact that this disyllabic structure has four moras is not relevant, since the accentable element is the syllable.

- B. Words that have the same pronunciation, like English [lɛd] (*lead,* 'type of metal') and [lɛd] (*led,* past tense of *lead* 'guide') are known as homophones. And yes, English *lead* 'to guide' and *lead* 'type of metal' are homographs.

Q4 The briefest answer is that no English word will ever have the sound sequence [lð] or [ðəp]. Word-initially, [ð] can only appear in the closed class of grammatical words (function words), as in *the, these, that, their, there, thence, thus,* etc., and there is no function word that begins with [ðəp]. Inside words, [ð] only appears after a vowel, as in *mother* and *to breathe*. By contrast, the sound sequence [dɪstɛnd] occurring in the underlined part of *wildest endings* is perfectly well-formed as a word, in fact represents the word *distend*.

Q5   The suffix *-able* attaches to verbs that can take a direct object. *To die* is an intransitive verb and thus cannot take a direct object, while *seem* is a copular verb and thus is followed by an adjectival or nominal predicate, like *nice* or *a nice person*. By contrast, *imagine* takes a direct object, like *a better world, this* or *that the world is flat*.

Q6   In *unscratchable* there is a verb *scratch*, the base of *scratchable*. In *road tax increase* there are the nouns *road, tax, increase, road tax* and *road tax increase*. That is, its structure is:

$$_N[_N[_N[\text{ road }]_N {}_N[\text{ tax }]_N]_N {}_N[\text{ increase }]_N]_N$$

Q7   There are six NPs: *He, the letter, a pen he bought in Italy, a pen, he* and *Italy*. In addition there is the deleted NP *that* (*A pen* that *he bought in Italy*), a relative pronoun that takes the place of the Direct Object of *bought*, viz., *a pen*.

Q8   If the vocalizations that represent morphemes did not have structure, there would be no segmental structure, and consequently there would be no segments that could be switched round. For the relevance of speech errors for phonological structure, see Levelt (1989: ch. 9) and Shattuck-Hufnagel (1992).

Q9   Yes, sign languages for the deaf have morphosyntactic structure as well as phonological structure, just like spoken languages. The difference is that the medium in which the phonological units are expressed is not human vocal sound, but gestures. There are many sign languages in the world, and there is no genetic relationship between the dominant sign language and the dominant spoken language in any community. They are entirely comparable functionally and in terms of processing speed. A person who is deaf at birth and does not learn a sign language will be linguistically and cognitively deprived in the same way as any hearing person would who is artificially prevented from learning a spoken language. The haunting story of the slow pace with which this insight spread to the community of therapists is told in Sacks (1989). It is only recently that research into the morphosyntactic and phonological structure of sign languages has got off the ground.

Q10

1. The word for 'field' begins with [ð] because according to FRICATION a word-initial plosive like [d] is not tolerated when the word occurs in non-initial position in the sentence.

2. 'Cows are grazing in the field' in language II is [ni xaputi fula].

3. Since fricatives would uniquely occur at the beginning of non-initial words, any occurrence of a fricative would signal the beginning of a word. Detecting the word boundaries in speech is a nontrivial task for the hearer. It must be realized that there are no pauses between words, as should be readily evident to anyone listening to unfamiliar languages. For more information on the

relevance of phonological structure for parsing strategies, see Cutler (1995) or McQueen and Cutler (1997).

Q11   *Syllables*   *Morphemes*
[ɛ], [lə], [fənts]   [ɛləfənt], [s]
[pɑːm], [ɔɪl]   [pɑːm], [ɔɪl]
[ʌn], [sɛt], [lɪŋ]   [ʌn], [sɛtl], [ɪŋ]

Q12

1. No, [ɪkt] is a well-formed syllable, and occurs as a rhyme in *licked, nicked, strict*, etc. There just so happens not to be a morpheme with that shape.

2. The sequence [mrʌt] does not represent a well-formed English syllable.

Chapter 2

Q13   Since the glottis is closed, the air in the lungs is trapped. This prevents the higher air pressure in the lungs from creating a pressure difference across the larynx. The sounds you were making were therefore non-pulmonic. In section 2.8 we will see how air pressure differences can be created in the mouth without the aid of the vocal folds or the lungs.

Q14   Starting on the left, the speech wave form for *ceased* will show a strongly turbulent phase caused by the friction of [s], followed by a periodic signal of the vowel [iː], which is similar to that of [aː] in Fig 2.2, but with the periods showing a resonance profile more like that in Fig 2.3; the periodic vibration fades away and there follows strong turbulence for [s], ending in a straight line representing the silence during the closure of [t], after which the explosion of the [t] will just be visible.

Q15   The period is 4.94 ms. Therefore, the fundamental frequency is 1,000 (ms) divided by 4.94 (ms), or 203 Hz.

Q16   The answers really depend on the kind of English, but we have tried our best to pick out sounds that are stable across the different varieties. There are close front vowels in *here* and a mid-close/mid-open front vowel in *friends*. A velar plosive, [k], occurs in *make*. For [f] in *friends,* friction is produced at the point where the upper incisors make contact with the lower lip, and for [z] in the same word, alveolar friction as preduced. There may be some oral cavity friction for an emphatic pronunciation of [h] in *here,* but typically what friction there is will be produced in the larynx.

Chapter 3

Q17   The vowel system contains two articulatory routines that are each used once only, nasalization only for [o] to give [õ] and breathy voice for[a] to give [a̤]. More probably, there would just be nasalization for all the vowels, perhaps without nasalized high vowels, to give 10 or 8 vowels in all, or just breathy voice for all the vowels, again giving 10 vowels. Of course, both features may be present, to give 16 or 20 vowels in all.

Q18 The explanation would be that three vowels can be distinguished so clearly with so little effort that languages will develop them with a degree of probability that approaches certainty, but that we must not revise our view of the world if a language were to be found that had fewer vowels.

Q19
1. (C(C))V(V).
2. Yes, as in the second syllable of 'lizard type', for example.

Q20
1. To answer the question for our own native language, English has [θ], which is absent from Dutch, while Dutch has [y], unlike English.
2. The final consonant of German *Kiev* will be [f] because of FINAL DEVOICING.

Q21
1. The total number of segments in !Xũ is very large indeed.
2. The number of vowels in Pawaia is large compared with the small number of consonants.
3. The number of vowels in Haida is small compared with the large number of consonants.
4. While the number of consonants of Norwegian is close to the world average, the number of vowels is rather large.

Q22 The smaller the number of segments, the smaller will be the number of contrasts, and the sooner the need arises to add further segments. For the same reason, binary numbers (numbers that consist of 1 and 0 only) will be longer than decimal numbers as soon as their value exceeds 2.

Q23 The voiced uvular stop will be most likely to be absent, because the space between the uvular closure and the glottis is even smaller than that between the velar closure and the glottis.

Q24
1. Your graphs should look like two parallel inverted Vs, with the lower one representing the voiced plosives.
2. The [p] and the [g] have lower positions than in the theoretical graphs. The reasons for this must be the same as those that were given for the relative frequency of the system gaps for [p] and [g] in section 3.3.5: the first is relatively hard to hear because of the absence of a resonance chamber in front of the place of articulation, while the second is relatively hard to produce because of the rapid increase in air pressure in the small chamber between the velar closure and the glottis, which will impede the air flow through the glottis needed to allow the vocal folds to vibrate.

Chapter 4

Q25 *[tuʔa] contains the illegal segment [t], *[plai] has an illegal CC onset, while *[kehunanal] has an illegal coda in the last syllable.

Q26   *[meŋ] does not have the required two syllables, while *[leʔem] ends in [m], which is not allowed in Konjo codas.

Q27   The narrow transcriptions are [tsɯ̥kemono], [ʃi̥tá] and [ótʃiba]. In effect, the devoiced vowel is phonetically deleted, and the first two words could also be given as [ts̩kemono], [ʃtá], where ˌ indicates a syllabic consonant.

Q28   Before [ɯ], [t] affricates to [ts]. If [ɯ] were used, therefore, the word for 'toast' would be [toːsɯtsɯ], which output is less similar to the English word than [toːsɯto]. (There are exceptions to this strategy, since 'donut' is [doːnatsɯ].)

Q29

1. The only consonant that can appear word-finally in Japanese is [n].

2. The consonants that can appear in the coda of non-final syllables are [m,n,ŋ]. (Japanese also has intervocalic geminate consonants, which simultaneously function as coda of one syllable and onset of the next.)

3. A vowel is added after the word for 'rubber', but not after the word for 'manganese' because word-finally only [n], not [m], is allowed as a coda consonant.

4. On the basis of these data, [s] and [h] can be said to be the voiceless fricatives of Japanese.

5. The fact that the onset clusters [bl-] and [dr-] in the words for 'tin' and 'hypochondria' are broken up into separate syllables suggests that Japanese has no complex onsets other than C[j].

Q30

1. The onset clusters [br-] and [fl-] and the coda cluster [-lt] are broken up into different syllables.

2. Clusters that are not broken up, that is, are not fully interpreted, are the onset clusters [st-] and [sk-] and the coda clusters [-nd] and [-nt].

3. Hawaiian [p] is used for English [b,f,p]. These consonants are all articulated with the lips.

4. Hawaiian [k] is used for English [t,d,s,ʃ,z,θ,k]. These consonants are all articulated with the tongue.

5. We feel uncertain of what the vowels would be, but the consonants would be [p,l,k]. [palaki] and [poloka] are among the possible forms.

6. The sound [s] is not part of the segment inventory of the language, which is why it is replaced by a native segment. It is improbable that the fully native speaker of Hawaiian cannot hear the difference between [s] and [k]. Speakers may feel that the difference is somehow not important, much in the same way as speakers of Dutch or German can hear the difference between English *bet* [bɛt] and *bat* [bæt], but nevertheless pronounce both as [bɛt].

Q31

1. The constraint in (11), Max-IO (deletion of segments is prohibited) is responsible for ruling out [kɪs].

2. Max-IO has to be ranked above Dep-IO because otherwise [kɪs] would become the optimal output form.

kɪsz	Max-IO	Dep-IO
[kɪs]	*!	
☞ [kɪsɪz]		*

Q32

ʃəvø	*ʃ/ʒ	Ident (F)
ʃeve	*!	
☞ seve		*

Q33

1. In *[gazi] there are two voiced obstruents, in violation of Lyman's Law, but in [gami] there is only one, since [m] is a sonorant.

2. The reason why Rendaku fails in (2) is that in all three cases Lyman's Law would be violated in the second word in the compound, since Rendaku would lead to two voiced obstruents in the word (e.g. *[gaze]).

3. Lyman's Law must outrank Rendaku, as in this tableau.

/kita-kaze	Lyman's Law	Rendaku
☞ [kita-kaze]		*
[kita-gaze]	*!	

Q34

lem	Align-stem-right	Dep-IO	CodaCond	Ident(F)
leme	*!	*		
leʔem		**	*!	
☞ leʔeŋ		**		*

1. Dep-IO is not crucially ranked above CodaDond, as the same form, [leʔeŋ] would still be the optimal output form.

lem	ALIGN-STEM-RIGHT	DEP-IO	IDENT(F)	CODACOND
leme	*!	*		
☞ leʔem		**		*
leʔeŋ		**	*!	

2. Yes, CODACOND is crucially ranked above IDENT(F), because the reverse ranking would produce [leʔem] as the optimal output form.

Chapter 5

Q35

1. In Southern Swedish, [ʀ] and [r] are allophones of the same phoneme, because their distribution is determined by the phonological context.

2. In Dutch, they are stylistic variants, because their distribution is determined by the formality of the situation.

3. In Provençal, they are different phonemes, because they can be used to form a minimal pair.

Q36 In Tolitoli, the retroflex lateral flap [ʟ] occurs after back vowels ([o,u,a]), whereas [l] occurs after front vowels ([i,e]) and word-initially.

Q37 [x] and [ç] are different phonemes in Plautdiitsch, because they contrast, as shown by the minimal pairs given in the question.

Q38 Old English [ç] occurs after front vowels (in the examples, [i,iː,eː,æː]), whereas [x] occurs after the back vowels (in the examples, [uː,oː,ɔ,ɑː], and [ə] as the second element of a diphthong).

Q39 [r] and [l] are allophones of the same phoneme in Korean. Regardless of whether [r] or [l] is in the English input forms, Korean has [r] in the onset, as shown by *melon,* for instance. In the coda, [l] occurs consistently. (In British English, there is no coda [r]; any coda [r] in any American English input words is left untranslated.)

Q40 *Sew* and *sewage* are unrelated, both semantically and phonologically. *Blow* and *blew* are arguably derivable from the same UR, but since the number of forms that would go by the rules that would be required to transform [bləʊ] into [bluː] is very small (cf. *grow, know, throw*), it would seem more reasonable to list the past form. For a derivational description, see Halle and Mohanan (1985). The same consideration applies to the different verbal and nominal stems *-ceive* and *-ception.* There is not even a remotely reasonable case to be made for *brother – fraternal* (cf. the different phonological relations between *mother – maternal* and *father – paternal*). *Cork – corkage* are regularly related phonologically via attachment of the nominal suffix [ɪdʒ], though the form needs to be listed in the lexicon because of its specialized meaning 'fee to be paid for opening the guest's own wine in restaurants without a licence to sell wine'. The forms *talk* and *talked* indubitably contain the same UR: the phonology is regular and the semantics of the inflected form is predictable from its morphological structure.

Q41

1. If *list* were [lɪs] underlyingly, its present participle would be *['lɪsɪŋ] instead of the correct ['lɪstɪŋ].

2. Its past participle form would be [lɪst], produced by DEVOICING of [d] after the voiceless obstruent [s]. If [lɪst] is assumed as the UR, ə-INSERTION would insert a schwa between the suffix [d] and the stem, preventing DEVOICING from applying.

Q42

A. The words are [ʃuːrəz] and [pɛrsəd]. Because the plural and past+participle suffixes have syllabic forms after non-sibilant sounds, these must have been non-alternating [əz] and [əd], respectively. (In present-day English, these words are [ʃau.ərz] and [prɛst]. Presumably, Middle English [pɛrs] and [prɛs] were alternative forms, of which the second survived.)

B. Historically, there was a process of vowel deletion after non-sibilants, causing [z] and [s] to develop in those contexts, and a similar process of vowel deletion after all sounds except coronal plosives. However, a present-day grammar of English will contain vowel insertion rules, not deletion rules, after sibilants before [z] and after [t, d] before [d]. This shows that the rules of a grammar need not correspond to historical sound changes, as indeed is to be expected, given that grammars are created by making simple generalizations over contemporary input data.

Q43 Given that the first name comes before the surname, [tɔn] is the better choice. In combination with the surname, [tɔm] would be ambiguous between [tɔm] and [tɔn], since the latter is likely to assimilate to [tɔm] before the [b] of *Bleekveld*. With [tɔn], it is possible to suppress the assimilation, as in ['tɔn 'bleːkfɛlt], avoiding the ambiguity. In effect, the parents should be advised not to choose a neutralized output.

Q44

1. The alternants of each prefix in Balantak are [sa-], [sam-], [san-], [saŋ-] and [to-], [tom-], [ton-], [toŋ-].

2. After [sa-], the initial segment of the base is [w,l,n,ŋ,m,r], and after [to-] it is [j,w,l,ŋ,r].

   After [sam-], the initial segment of the base is [b], and after [tom-] it is [b,p].
   After [san-], the initial segment of the base is [t,s], and after [ton-] it is [t,d,s].
   After [saŋ-], the initial segment of the base is [k,g], or a vowel, just as it is after [toŋ].

3. The underlying forms must be /saŋ, toŋ/.

4. A deletion rule is required to delete [ŋ] of the prefix before a base starting with a sonorant consonant ([n,ŋ,m,l,r,j,w]) and a place assimilation rule is required to assimilate the place of articulation of the prefix-final [ŋ] to that of the base-initial consonant. Before vowels nothing needs to be done, which would not be the case if different URs were chosen. With /tom, sam/ or /ton, san/, the assimilation to [ŋ] would have to be effected in the unnatural context 'before dorsal consonants or a vowel'. If /to, sa/ were chosen, an insertion rule would be required to insert [ŋ] before the unnatural context of 'obstruents and vowels'.

Chapter 6

Q45

1. [p,t,k]

2. [p,t,k]

3. [p,t,k]

4. Evidently, [p,t,k] form a natural segment class.

Q46

1. With two binary features F and G, eight natural segment classes can be referred to. Four classes are defined by using one binary feature with each possible value: +F, −F, +G, −G. An additional four are defined by using two features with every possible value combination: +F+G, +F−G, −F+G, −F−G.

2. The combination of [+cons,−son] defines the class of obstruents ([p,f,t], etc.), [+cons,+son] defines the class of sonorants ([n,r,l], etc.), [−cons, −son] defines the class of laryngeal segments ([h,ɦ,ʔ] and [−cons,+son] defines the class of glides ([j,w,ʋ], etc.).

Q47   In Dutch, [ə] is inserted between the noun stem and the diminutive suffix, when the noun stem ends in a [+cons,+son] segment, that is, after the class of sonorants excluding glides and vowels. If we referred to only [+son], the glide [j] would wrongly be included.

Q48   In Cordoba Spanish, the assimilation process creating geminates applies to [+cons] segments. Glides and laryngeal segments, [−cons] segments, do not trigger it.

Q49   The class of sounds subject to degemination in Dutch can be characterized by the feature [+cons].

Q50   All obstruents are voiceless at the end of a syllable in Dutch. This class can be characterized by the features [+cons,−son]. Since [h] cannot occur word-finally in Dutch, the specification [−son] would suffice.

Q51

p	t	k	ʔ
b	d	g	
f	s	x	h
v	z	ɣ	

[−son]

[+son]

m	n	ŋ

[−approx]

[+approx]

	lr	[+cons]

[−cons]

w	j

i	a	u

Q52 Segments that may appear after [sp,st,sk] in English, [l,r,j,w] and the vowels, can be characterized by the feature [+approx].

Q53 The plosives acquire the feature [+constr].

Q54 In Southern Oromo, the combination of the features [+constr, −voice, +cons] is necessary to distinguish [t'] from the three consonants that do not trigger i-EPENTHESIS. The feature [+constr] is necessary to distinguish ejective [t'] from [t], [−voice] is necessary to distinguish it from [ɗ] (which is [+constr] as well), and, finally, the feature [+cons] is necessary to distinguish [t'] from the glottal stop [ʔ].

Q55 The class of segments before which the long vowels appear in Scottish English can be characterized as [+cont, +voice].

Q56
1. The devoicing applies to [b,d,g,dʒ], but not to [z].

2. The group of plosives and affricates is [−cont]. Fricatives are [+cont].

Q57 The class of vowels undergoing the nasalization process in Corsican can be referred to by the feature [−high] as the class of non-high vowels.

Q58 The class of consonants triggering r-DELETION in Bengali can be characterized by the feature [CORONAL].

Q59   The feature [back] is involved in the UMLAUT process in the Dutch dialect of Wehl: it is [−back] in the plurals.

Q60

1. The complementary distribution of [r] and [l] is determined by the preceding vowel. The [l] occurs after a back vowel and [r] occurs after a front vowel. [l] also occurs word-initially.

2. The context of [r] can be stated as 'after a vowel with the feature [−back]', whereas the context for [l] cannot be expressed in terms of distinctive features. Although the word-internal occurrence of [l] can be expressed as 'preceded by a vowel with the feature [+back]', there is no feature to refer to word-initial position.

3. If /l/ is chosen as the underlying representation a single rule can account for the surface complementary distribution pattern: /l/ becomes [r] after a front vowel.

Q61

1. [+spread]
2. [CORONAL, −cont, −son]
3. [LABIAL, +voice, −cont] *or* [LABIAL, +voice, +cons]
4. [−cons] ([+son] is superfluous, as there are no laryngeal segments in the language.)
5. [+back, −high]

Q62

1. [+cont, −son] (Recall that [h,hʷ] are not specified for [±cont], p. 82.)
2. [+constr]
3. [CORONAL, −anterior, −son]
4. [CORONAL, +nas]
5. [+back, +round] (We must not include the rounded consonants, and assume the class of V or [+syll].)

Chapter 7

Q63   Rule (6) applies to both [d]s. At the first application, the first [d] corresponds to the focus [−son] and the second to C_0, and at the second application the second [d] matches the focus [−son], while the term C_0 corresponds to no consonant.

Q64   Rule (1) says 'Insert a schwa before a word-final postvocalic [r]' and rule (2) says 'Delete [r] before consonants or at the word end'.

Q65   Your answer should consist of four copies of rule (10). In one of them, α and β are replaced with + and +, respectively, in a second with + and −, in a third with − and +, and in the fourth with − and −.

Q66

1. The rule says that word-final mid vowels are raised, that is, word-final [e] and [o] become [i] and [u].

2. This rule states that a front vowel is deleted before another vowel, if the two vowels have the same height. That is, [e] is deleted before [e] and [o], [i] is deleted before [i] and [u] and [æ] is deleted before [æ], [a] and [ɔ].

3. The rule says that a coronal voiceless stop is inserted between [n,ɲ] (a coronal nasal) and [s, ʃ] (a coronal voiceless fricative) in word-final position. That is, word-finally, [t] is inserted between [n] and [s] and [c] between [ɲ] and [ʃ].

Q67

1. $[-\text{son}] \rightarrow [-\text{voice}] / [-\text{son}] \, (\# \#) —$

2. $\emptyset \rightarrow \partial / \begin{bmatrix} +\text{cons} \\ +\text{approx} \end{bmatrix} - \begin{bmatrix} \text{LABIAL} \\ -\text{son} \end{bmatrix}$

3. $V \rightarrow [\alpha\text{back}] / \begin{bmatrix} +\text{high} \\ \alpha\text{back} \end{bmatrix} C_0 + —$

Instead of just C_0, also $C_0)_\sigma$ is correct, but the reference to the syllable is implicit in C_0, since it stipulates that no further vowels may appear after the focus V of the rule.

Q68

	vaːrn			vaːrn
n-DELETION	–	ə-INSERTION		ə
ə-insertion	ə	n-DELETION		Ø
Output	[vaːrən			vaːrə]

Q69

1.
underlying forms	morphemes
we	3rd-PL-OBJ ('them')
n	PROGRESSIVE
oʔ	3rd-SG-SUBJ ('he')
Ø	3rd-SG-OBJ ('it' has no phonological form)
netale	'lick'
picena	'cut'

2.
	/netale+oʔ/	/we+picena+n+oʔ/	/we+picena+oʔ/
CONTRACTION	netleoʔ	wepcenanoʔ	wepcenaoʔ
TRUNCATION	netleʔ	n.a.	wepcenaʔ
	[netleʔ]	[wepcenanoʔ]	[wepcenaʔ]
	'he licks it'	'he is cutting them'	'he cuts them'

Q70

1. The diminutive form of [flɑm] is [flɑməcə]. If PLACE ASSIMILATION applied before ə-INSERTION, [flɑm+tjə] would incorrectly end up as [flɑmpjə], as shown.

	/flam+tjə/		/flam+tjə/
ə-INSERTION	flam+ətjə	PLACE ASSIMILATION	flam+pjə
DEGEMINATION	–	ə-INSERTION	–
t-DELETION	–	DEGEMINATION	–
PLACE ASSIMILATION	–	t-DELETION	–
PALATALIZATION	flam+əcə	PALATALIZATION	–
Output	[flaməcə]		*[flampjə]

2. The diminutive form of [feːst] is [feːʃə]. If t-DELETION applied before DEGEMINATION, /feːst+tjə/ would incorrectly end up as [feːʃcə], as shown.

	/feːst+tjə/		/feːst+tjə/
ə-INSERTION	–	ə-INSERTION	–
DEGEMINATION	feːs+tjə	t-DELETION	feːst+jə
t-DELETION	feːs+jə	DEGEMINATION	–
PLACE ASSIMILATION	–	PLACE ASSIMILATION	–
PALATALIZATION	feːʃə	PALATALIZATION	feːʃcə
Output	[feːʃə]		*[feːʃcə]

3.	/hɛmt+tjə/		/hɛmt+tjə/
ə-INSERTION	–	ə-INSERTION	–
DEGEMINATION	hɛmØ+tjə	PLACE ASSIMILATION	vac.
t-DELETION	–	DEGEMINATION	hɛm+tjə
PLACE ASSIMILATION	hɛm+pjə	t-DELETION	–
PALATALIZATION	–	PALATALIZATION	hɛmcə
Output	[hɛmpjə]		*[hɛmcə]

Q71   Given that the laterals [l] and [ʎ] in Sittard Dutch do not trigger k-FRONTING, they should be considered [+cont] segments. If they were [−cont], they would trigger k-FRONTING.

Q72   The difference between Wehl Dutch and the standard language is that in Wehl Dutch ə-INSERTION apparently only applies if the sonorant in the structural description of the rule (cf. rule (22)) is [CORONAL].

Q73

1. In the dialect of Utrecht, the alternants of the diminutive suffix are [-χi], [-əχi], [-i], [-si], [-tsi], [-pi] and [-ki].

2. All the rules in (29) (ə-INSERTION, DEGEMINATION, t-DELETION and PLACE ASSIMILATION) except PALATALIZATION exist in Utrecht Dutch.

3. The required rules are AFFRICATION, by which [t] becomes an affricate [ts], and a rule by which [t] becomes [χ], which we will term FRICATION. If FRICATION is ordered between ə-INSERTION and DEGEMINATION and if AFFRICATION is ordered last, the rules can be formulated as follows:

FRICATION $[t] \rightarrow [\chi] / V \underline{\quad} V$
AFFRICATION $[t] \rightarrow [ts] / \underline{\quad} i]_{DIM}$

4.	ɛi-ti	rɔk-ti	bɔm-ti	raːm-ti	bɔχt-ti	fut-ti	bɔrt-ti
ə-INSERTION	–	–	bɔm-əti	–	–	–	–
FRICATION	ɛi-χi	–	bɔm-əχi	–	–	–	–
DEGEMINATION	–	–	–	–	bɔχ-ti	fu-ti	bɔr-ti
t-DELETION	–	rɔk-i	–	–	bɔχ-i	–	–
PLACE ASSIMILATION	–	–	–	raːm-pi	–	–	–
AFFRICATION	–	–	–	–	–	futsi	bɔrtsi
Output	[ɛiχi	rɔki	bɔməχi	raːmpi	bɔχi	futsi	bɔrtsi]

Q74 Sittard Dutch [bɛɲcə] could be derived from /bɛɲc-kə/, /bɛnt-kə/, /bɛɲ-kə/, /baɲc-kə/, /bant-kə/ or /baɲ-kə/. The last three possibilities will be identical to the first three after UMLAUT (rule (31)), while the further derivation will proceed as illustrated in (35) for /mɛɲ-kə/ and in (36) for /lɛɲc-kə/ and /tɛnt-kə/. It could not be derived from /bɛn-kə/ (or /ban-kə/), because n-ASSIMILATION bleeds k-FRONTING, as illustrated in (35) for /pan-kə/.

Q75 1. s-INSERTION needs to apply before ə-INSERTION, because otherwise /slaŋ-kə/ would incorrectly end up as *[slaŋəkə] instead of [slaŋəskə]. VOWEL LAXING needs to be applied after ə-INSERTION, because otherwise /oːr-kə/ would first become /ɔr-kə/ and then be subject to ə-INSERTION, ending up incorrectly as *[ɔrəkə] instead of [ɔrkə].

2.	/slaŋ-kə/	/snɔr-kə/	/oːr-kə/
S-INSERTION	slaŋ-skə	–	–
ə-INSERTION	slaŋ-əskə	snɔr-əkə	–
VOWEL LAXING	–	–	ɔr-kə
Output	[slaŋəskə]	[snɔrəkə]	[ɔrkə]

Chapter 8

Q76

1. Rule 1 could be termed VOICED PLOSIVE DELETION, rule 2 POST-NASAL VOICING and rule 3 PLACE ASSIMILATION, but more or less explicit names would also be correct.

2.	/n+gomo/	/n+kuja/
(1) VOICED PLOSIVE DELETION	nomo	*n.a.*
(2) POST-NASAL VOICING	*n.a.*	nguja
(3) PLACE ASSIMILATION	*n.a.*	ŋguja
	*[nomo]	[ŋguja]
	/n+gomo/	/n+kuja/
(1) VOICED PLOSIVE DELETION	nomo	*n.a.*
(3) PLACE ASSIMILATION	*n.a.*	ŋguja
(2) POST-NASAL VOICING	*n.a.*	ŋguja
	*[nomo]	[ŋguja]
	/n+gomo/	/n+kuja/

(2) POST-NASAL VOICING	*n.a.*	ŋguja
(1) VOICED PLOSIVE DELETION	nomo	nuja
(3) PLACE-ASSIMILATION	*n.a.*	*n.a.*
	*[nomo]	*[nuja]

	/n+gomo/	/n+kuja/
(2) POST-NASAL VOICING	*n.a.*	nguja
(3) PLACE ASSIMILATION	ŋgomo	nguja
(1) VOICED PLOSIVE DELETION	ŋomo	ɳuja
	[ŋomo]	*[ɳuja]

	/n+gomo/	/n+kuja/
(3) PLACE ASSIMILATION	ŋgomo	ŋkuja
(2) POST-NASAL VOICING	*n.a.*	ŋguja
(1) VOICED PLOSIVE DELETION	ŋomo	ɳuja
	[ŋomo]	*[ɳuja]

	/n+gomo/	/n+kuja/
(3) PLACE ASSIMILATION	ŋgowo	ŋkuja
(1) VOICED PLOSIVE DELETION	ŋomo	ŋkuja
(2) POST-NASAL VOICING	*n.a.*	ŋguja
	[ŋomo]	[ŋguja]

Only the last order derives the correct surface forms [ŋomo] and [ŋguja].

Q77

1. PROGRESSIVE DEVOICING should devoice fricatives after a voiceless obstruent and REGRESSIVE VOICING should voice obstruents preceding a voiced plosive. The order depends in part on how explicit the formulation of the rules is. With the least explicit formulations, the order is FINAL DEVOICING, PROGRESSIVE DEVOICING, REGRESSIVE VOICING and DEGEMINATION.

2. PROGRESSIVE DEVOICING $\begin{bmatrix} +\text{cont} \\ -\text{son} \end{bmatrix} \rightarrow [-\text{voice}] / [-\text{voice}](\#)$ —

   REGRESSIVE VOICING: $[-\text{son}] \rightarrow [+\text{voice}] / —(\#)\begin{bmatrix} -\text{cont} \\ +\text{voice} \end{bmatrix}$

It is unnecessary to specify the focus of PROGRESSIVE DEVOICING as [+voice], since any [−voice] fricatives would retain their specification as [−voice]. That is, the rule would apply without effect, i.e. vacuously. Second, in the right-hand context of REGRESSIVE VOICING, instead of [−cont] also [−son] could be specified, if we assume that PROGRESSIVE DEVOICING applies first, which rule leaves only voiced plosives behind in the context concerned.

3.	/ʋɑnd#teːχəl/	/lup#zœyvər/	/kaːz#zaːk/
FINAL DEVOICING	ʋɑnt#teːχəl	*n.a.*	kaːs#zaːk
PROGRESSIVE DEVOICING	*n.a.*	lup#sœyvər	kaːs#saːk
REGRESSIVE VOICING	*n.a.*	*n.a.*	*n.a.*
DEGEMINATION	ʋɑn#teːχəl	*n.a.*	kaː#saːk
	[ʋɑnteːχəl]	[lupsœyvər]	[kaːsaːk]

	/kɔp#bɑl/	/leːz#brɪl/
FINAL DEVOICING	*n.a.*	leːs#brɪl
PROGRESSIVE DEVOICING	*n.a.*	*n.a.*
REGRESSIVE VOICING	kɔb#bɑl	leːz#brɪl
DEGEMINATION	kɔ#bɑl	*n.a.*
	[kɔbɑl]	[leːzbrɪl]

Q78 In Kaatsheuvel Dutch, the diminutive form of the river *Linge* will be [lɪŋəkə], given that the final schwa, contrary to the epenthetic schwa, is already present when s-INSERTION (21) applies.

Q79 The rules FLAPPING and PRE-FORTIS-CLIPPING stand in a counterbleeding order. The reverse order would decrease the number of forms to which PRE-FORTIS-CLIPPING (8) could apply.

Q80 The tableau you have drawn up should look as follows. Voiced plosives in intervocalic position are now wrongly predicted to be realized as voiceless, and, voiceless plosives remain unaltered.

/la gana/	SPIRANTIZATION	IDENT(CONT)	VOICING	IDENT(VOICE)
[la gana]	*!			
☞ [la kana]			*	*
[la ɣana]		*!		
/la kama/	SPIRANTIZATION	IDENT(CONT)	VOICING	IDENT(VOICE)
[la gama]	*!			*
☞ [la kama]			*	
[la ɣama]		*!		*

Q81 Your tableau should look like this, with still the same result: incorrect optimal [pana].

/pan+æ/	PALATALIZATION	IDENT(ANTERIOR)	æ-BACKING	IDENT(BACK)
panæ	*!		*	
paɲæ		*!	*	
☞ pana				*
paɲa		*!		*

Q82 With IDENT(ANTERIOR) as the selector, two outputs are potentially sympathetic: the first and the third. The third output candidate is better than the first in not having a violation of æ-BACKING and will therefore become the sympathetic candidate. As shown, this leads to the sympathetic candidate becoming the optimal candidate.

/pan+ae/	æ-Backing	Id (back)	Palatalization	⊛ Cumul	Id (anterior) selector - ✶
panæ	*!		*	*	
paɲæ	*!			*	*
☞ pana⊛		*			
paɲa		*			*!

Q83   First level

/la gana/	Ident(voice)	Voicing	Spirantization	Ident(cont)
[la gana]			*!	
[la kana]	*!	*		
☞ [la ɣana]				*
/la kama/	Ident(voice)	Voicing	Spirantization	Ident(cont)
[la gama]	*!		*	
☞ [la kama]		*		
[la ɣama]	*!			*

Second level, with inputs /la ɣana/ and //la kama/

/la ɣana/	Voicing	Ident(voice)	Ident(cont)	Spirantization
[la ɣana]			*!	*
[la kana]	*!	*	*	
☞ [la ɣana]				
/la kama/	Voicing	Ident(voice)	Ident(cont)	Spirantization
☞ [la gama]		*		*
[la kama]	*!			
[la ɣama]		*	*!	

Chapter 9

Q84

1. The lexical representation of 'breakout' is [œytbraːk], the form prior to the application of postlexical REGRESSIVE VOICING.

2. Because it is a postlexical rule, REGRESSIVE VOICING would not be expected to have exceptions, which prediction is correct.

3. Native speakers would say the last consonant of the prefix is [t], a judgement which they are expected to base on the lexical representation.

Q85

1. PLAIN PLOSIVE VOICING is not structure preserving, because its products, voiced plosives, do not belong to the lexical segment inventory.

2. AFFRICATION is a structure-preserving rule, because [tʃ,tʃʰ] already occur in the lexical segment inventory.

3. [maɟi] resulted from the application of PLAIN PLOSIVE VOICING, which causes the plosive to be [+voice], and PALATALISATION, which causes it to be [−ant], resulting in [t] coming out as [ɟ]. Similarly AFFRICATION and PLAIN PLOSIVE VOICING changed [t] into [dʒ] in [kudʒi] by causing it to be [+strident, +voice].

4. Properties that are consistent with the status of AFFRICATION as a lexical rule are (a) its inability to apply across word boundaries, given that the right-hand context is a suffix, and (b) the fact that it is structure preserving, while (c) the fact that it refers to morphological information necessarily implies that it is a lexical rule.

Q86

1. (1) VOWEL NASALIZATION $V \rightarrow [+nas] / \_\_\_ n)_\sigma$
   (2) n-DELETION $n \rightarrow \emptyset / [V, +nas] \_\_\_)_\sigma$
   (3) ə-DELETION $ə \rightarrow \emptyset / \_\_\_)_F$

2.

	fin	fin-ə
VOWEL NASALIZATION	ɛ̃	−
n-DELETION	∅	
ə-DELETION	−	∅
Output	[fɛ̃	fin]

3. If [n] resyllabifies as an onset in the syllable [ɔm] after VOWEL NASALIZATION, but before n-DELETION, the vowel will be nasalized, but [n] be preserved. The resyllabification was earlier given as LIAISON.

4. n-DELETION must be postlexical, because it must apply after words, in this case [yn] (or rather its lexical representation [œ̃n]) and [ɔm], combine into phrases.

5. ə-DELETION must be postlexical, because, again, information about the following word is needed to decide whether it is deleted. In this case, [ə] does not delete in the context [d] ___ [d]. This failure of ə-DELETION between identical consonants can be seen as an OCP effect: if [ə] did delete, a sequence of identical consonants would be created.

6. VOWEL NASALIZATION must apply before a word-final [n] is resyllabified into a following onsetless syllable. Therefore, if it is postlexical, it must be ordered before LIAISON. This would be unexpected, as generalizations would normally refer to the prosodic structures that are present at the relevant level of representation. As it happens, the rule has exceptions, such as the loanwords and proper names *abdomen* [abdɔmɛn], *pollen* [pɔlɛn], *Citroën* [sitroɛn] and *Le Pen* [lə pɛn].

7. We could either assume an UR [ɔndə], which will be converted to [ɔ̃d] by a 'free ride' on the grammar that we need anyway, or we could assume [ɔ̃də] as the UR, which is possible because nasalized vowels are produced by a lexical rule and must by implication belong to the lexical segment inventory. If we go by the rule-of-thumb that we do not make URs more abstract than they need to be, the second option would be preferred. Perhaps psycholinguistic research may some day tell us whether this question is meaningful.

Q87   No, the rule applies freely to all forms, also to the underived form /pɑd/ 'toad'.

Q88

1. The rule that produces [ɛː] is lexical, because it must refer to the morphological status of [d] to be able to distinguish *made* and *stayed*, for instance.

2. The rule is not neutralizing, since the product of the rule, [ɛː], does not already appear independently in other words.

3. It is not structure-preserving, for the same reason. However, because the rule is evidently lexical, there is the prediction that [ɛː] could readily be incorporated in URs, in loanwords, for instance.

4. The rule does not show the effect of Non-Derived Environment Blocking, because it readily applies to a morphologically non-complex form like *day*.

Q89

1. BATH-raising is a lexical rule, because it refers to morphological information like 'underived stem'. It is debatable whether it is structure preserving. The output vowel may coalesce with [ɛə] of *bared* or [ɪə] of *beard,* in which case its output already exists (Wells 1982: 511).

2. If a child learning Danish as a second language were to pronounce *Dansk* 'Danish' (Danish [dænsk]) as [dɛənsk] or [dɪənsk], that would show BATH-raising is productive.

Q90   In unguarded speech, RP *cents* and *sense* would be expected to be homophonous, since the phonological representations are the same. Phonetic implementation rules are not expected to take account of the history of the phonological surface representation they are required to translate into phonetics. Nevertheless, speakers would appear to be able to take all sorts of consideration into account when pronouncing linguistic expressions, and may for instance apply fewer optional assimilations in less frequent forms, or make words they use for the first time in their discourse longer than other words. In this connection, Hayes (1994) speaks of 'the beast' in man, suggesting that speakers can influence their speech behaviour from outside the language system, so to speak.

Q91   The lengthening must be created during phonetic implementation. Languages vary in the extent to which they allow lengthening in sonorant segments before voiced obstruents in the coda, Arabic being extremely reluctant and English extremely liberal in this respect (Kluender et al. 1988). If we were to interpret the duration differences as resulting from phonological duration distinctions, English would have to be analysed as having a four-way quantity opposition, for instance.

Q92 When the assimilation produces a segment which is indistinguishable from [ʃ], it is reasonable to assume that the assimilation is phonological, i.e. that the features of the right-hand [ʃ] have spread to the left-hand consonant. However, where the assimilation results in a gradual shift from [s] to [ʃ], it is reasonable to describe it as the effect of phonetic implementation. In a gestural model, for instance, the tongue tip gesture for [s] could be shortened and/or that for [ʃ] be extended forward in time.

Chapter 10

Q93

1. The underlying tone pattern for both words is LH.

2. The association in Tharaka must not start with the second TBU, but with the first.

3. The Tharaka word for 'way of releasing oneself quickly' will be realized as [mòérékáŋgérié]. The underlying representation

mo	e	rɛk	aŋg	eriɛ
L	H	L		H

will be realized as

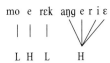

mo e rɛk aŋg e r i ɛ

L H L   H

Q94

1. The word [amakosi] will be realized as [ámàkòsí]. After the initial lexically specified association, the following structure obtains.

ama   kosi

H L   H L

which by the ASSOCIATION CONVENTION (7a and 7b) will be changed into

ama   kosi

H L   H L

2. Part (c) of the ASSOCIATION CONVENTION cannot apply, given that contour tones on short vowels are disallowed in Zulu. Thus, [ámàkòsí] is ruled out, and the final L tone will therefore be deleted.

Q95   After a low-pitched beginning of *Has* due to %L, there is a rise to the beginning of the syllable *John,* where a falling-rising pitch movement occurs. The pitch accent H*L and the boundary H% are pronounced in the same syllable, as shown in

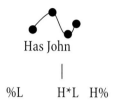

    Has John

         |

   %L   H*L   H%

Q96   The word [ikpa] would have a single L. On the assumption that the OCP remains in force after the morphological operation of REDUPLICATION, the sequence of two L-tones in the reduplicated form would be reduced to a single one, which is associated with as many vowels as remain in the word. There would thus be no need for the TWIN SISTER CONVENTION to operate.

Q97

1. H, L, HL, LH, LHL

2. When LHL occurs with a single syllable, as in the case of the word for 'companion', all three tones are pronounced. Unlike Etung, therefore, the language does not obey the NO CROWDING CONSTRAINT in (9).

3.
   njaha   kpakali

Q98   The fact that H spreads to all syllables, and never to only some, suggests that there is only one L-tone which is responsible for the low-toned syllables. When this L-tone is deleted, all TBUs with which it was associated will associate with H.

Q99

1.
   akivara   ataasiq   akivaa

2. The direction of association is right-to-left, since the rightmost TBU always has tone.

3. Yes, they are. If there is one more TBU, the HLH melody shifts right by one TBU.

   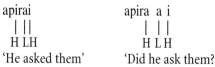
   apirai   apira a i

   'He asked them'   'Did he ask them?

4. Since in the last two syllables there are four TBUs and three tones, the leftmost H must spread to an extra TBU on the left if it occurs in the same syllable.

Chapter 11

Q100   They all break the Sᴏʟʟᴀʙʟᴇ Cᴏɴᴛᴀᴄᴛ Lᴀᴡ.

Q101
1. First, the Amharic words have one, two or three syllables, while the disguised forms all have two. Second, the Amharic words have a variety of vowels, but the disguised forms always have [ai] and [ə], in that order.

2. The consonants are preserved, but the vowels are not.

3. The number of different consonants in the word. If there are at most two different consonants, there are three surface consonants in the disguised form, and if the number of different consonants in the word is three, there are four surface consonants in the disguised form.

4. Use the template CVCVC if there are at most two different consonants, and CVCCVC if there are three. Associate the consonants to the C-slots, left-to-right, one-to-one, spreading the last. Associate [ai] and [ə] to the V-slots.

5. In Arabic, adjacent C-slots and adjacent V-slots associate with the same vowel or consonant, creating long vowels and geminates, but in this secret language adjacent C-slots are filled by different consonants if available.

6.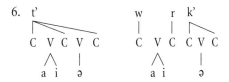

Q102   First, a V-slot associates with at most one vowel segment, which causes all diphthongs, which consist of two vowel segments, to be long. Second, association is left-to-right, one-to-one, only [iaa] can arise from the association of [ia] to VVV, never [iia].

Q103   Together with its syllable node, a word-initial V-slot is deleted if associated with a high vowel after a V-slot. The high vowel re-associates leftward with the remaining V-slot, creating a diphthong, as shown below for the relevant structure in *catalá universal*. The transcriptions with consonantal glides indicate the non-syllabic nature of the remaining vowel.

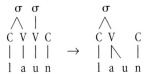

Q104 Since Koya has maximally two moras, and WEIGHT-BY-POSITION, these structures must be as given below.

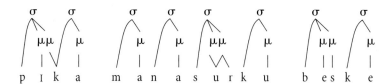

Q105 The number of moras in the prefinal syllable. If there is one, the following schwa is deleted. Tera must have WEIGHT-BY-POSITION, since otherwise this generalization across short vowels-plus-coda consonants and long vowels could not be made.

Q106 Lenakel appears to stress the last syllable if it contains a long vowel, and the penultimate otherwise. The language does not therefore equate coda consonants with the second halves of long vowels and thus has no WEIGHT-BY-POSITION.

Q107

1. In the Bakwiri word game, the segments of the second syllable are placed in the first, and vice versa. The location of tonal and moraic structure is unchanged, however. [ndàkóó] therefore becomes [kòndáá].

2. In [lùùŋgá] a long vowel occurs in the first syllable, but [liòβá] has two different vowels in the same syllable.

3. The word for 'door' has a short (monomoraic) second syllable, and only one of the two vowels can be moraic. The game form must therefore either be [βààlíw] or [βààljó]. The first of these must be excluded because the language has no codas.

4. The glottal stops are there because the syllables concerned begin with a vowel. The glottal stops are more perceptible word-internally than at the beginning of a word.

Q108 In Kinshingelo, the segment strings in the last two *syllables* of the *word* are reversed, while the *tonal* and moraic (*timing*) structure remain intact. Obviously, this operation cannot be carried out without reference to these elements of the phonological representation, which must for that reason exist.

Q109

1. All syllables that are not stem-final are short, regardless of whether they were short in the stem, as in b, d, e, or long, as in a, c, e, f.

2. The vowel in the stem-final syllable is long if its syllable has no coda, but short if it does.

3. In a moraic representation we can say that stem-final syllables have two moras. The adjustment of the vowel duration then follows from the presence of the stem-final consonant. For the word-final syllable, we can either assume these are obligatorily trimoraic, forcing the vowel to be long, or that they

obligatorily have a long vowel, in which case the final consonant is non-moraic. Assuming the first option, here are the structures for 'house':

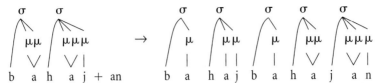

With a CV-tier, the equivalence of the rhymes in the stem-final syllables is less easily expressed, because the first occurrence would be VC and the second VV. This case represents the same type of argument against the CV-tier as the one given in the text on the basis of compensatory lengthening.

Q110

1.

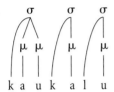

2. Regardless of their ranking, the three constraints will select [kau.ka.lu] as the winner, as shown by the tableau. Because ONSET and DEP(σ) are unranked, as indicated by the dotted column separation lines, we cannot determine for which of these constraints [a.lu.ka.lu] incurs its fatal violation, which is why they are both indicated as fatal. For the same reason, the shading of cells is suspended.

σ σ μμ μ / μ kalu k a l u	ONSET	DEP(σ)	MAX(μ)
☞ kau.ka.lu		*	
au.ka.lu	*!	*	
a.lu.ka.lu	*!	**!	
ka.lu.ka.lu		**!	
ka.ka.lu		*	*!

3. A constraint that discriminates between [a.θoa.θo] and *[θoo.a.θo] is ALIGN-STEM-LEFT, which requires the first segment of the input to correspond with the first segment of the output, parallel to ALIGN-STEM-RIGHT, as discussed in section 4.5 for Konjo. Since the first segment in *[θoo.a.θo] ([θ])

obviously doesn't correspond to the first segment in /aθo+a.θo/ ([a]), it incurs a violation for that constraint. It doesn't matter how ALIGN-STEM-LEFT is ranked relative to the other three. The indications of fatal violations again ignore ranking.

σ ∥ μμ ∥ aθo	σ μ ∣ a	σ μ θ o	ONSET	DEP(σ)	MAX(μ)	ALSTEMLEFT
☞ a.θoa.θo			*	*		
a.θa.θo			*	*	*!	
a.θo.a.θo			**!	**!		
θoo.a.θo			*	*		*!

4. The reduplicated form of [ko.kao] would be [koa.ko.kao], which form satisfies ONSET, MAX(μ) and ALIGN-STEM-LEFT, while not violating DEP(σ) more than is needed to preserve RED. Note that the order of the segments is as in the input /kokao+kokao/. The constraint LINEARITY was proposed by Prince & Smolensky (1993) to make this explicit.

Q111 An *SPE*-style account that does not refer to the syllable would have to say that [COR,+approx] is [−cons] in the context before a word boundary or before a consonant, like (1)

$$\begin{bmatrix} \text{COR} \\ +\text{approx} \end{bmatrix} \rightarrow [-\text{cons}] / \underline{\quad} \begin{Bmatrix} \# \\ \text{C} \end{Bmatrix}$$

The conjunction 'either a consonant or a word boundary' is unnecessary if the syllable coda can be referred to.

Q112 In the words in I and III, the [r] is ambisyllabic. In I this is because it occurs internally within a foot, opening a weak syllable (RIGHT CAPTURE), while in III it is because the next word is vowel-initial (LIAISON). It is ambisyllabicity that thus explains the occurrence of the flap.

Q113
1. If the BP rhyme is maximally bimoraic and [ɲ] is ambisyllabic, this consonant will occupy the second mora of the syllable it closes, meaning that there is no room for the second element of a diphthong.
2. We assume that, as in English, foot-internal syllable-initial consonants (e.g. ['sĩnu]) are made ambisyllabic, and thus contrast structurally with foot-initial consonants (e.g. [bo'nɛka]).
3. We can then say that vowels nasalize before nasal consonants within their rhyme.

4. This solution accounts for the fact that all vowels nasalize before [ɲ], because it is ambisyllabic regardless of whether it is foot-initial or foot-internal.

Chapter 12

Q114

1. It is the [CORONAL] node that spreads to the PLACE node of a preceding [t,d,n,l] in English CORONAL ASSIMILATION.

2. It is the PLACE node that spreads from the consonant to the SUPRALAR node of a preceding nasal in Hindi.

Q115 The picture you end up with should look more or less as shown.

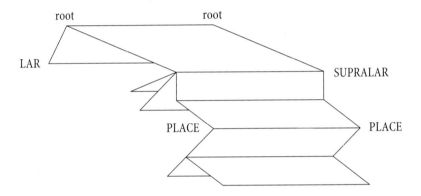

Q116 You cannot, because the PLACE tier and the ROOT tier are not adjacent, and hence do not define a plane.

Q117 Natural feature classes are not phonetically abstract to the extent that the nodes in a feature tree can be defined in phonetic terms. For instance, the laryngeal node could phonetically be defined as 'activity in the larynx', the surpralaryngeal node as 'activity in the vocal tract', etc.

Q118 English PLACE ASSIMILATION can be stated in the display format as follows:

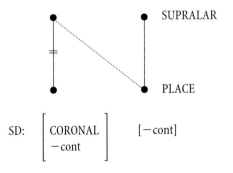

SD: $\begin{bmatrix} \text{CORONAL} \\ -\text{cont} \end{bmatrix}$ $[-\text{cont}]$

Q119

1. In order to account for the Yorkshire English and Durham English assimilation facts, we could assume the *SPE* rules in (1) and (2).
   (1) YORKSHIRE VOICELESSNESS ASSIMILATION [−son] → [−voice]/__ # # [−voice]
   (2) DURHAM VOICING ASSIMILATION   [−son] → [+voice]/__ # # [+voice]

2. Given that the feature [−voice] needs to be referred to in the structural change and the structural description of YORKSHIRE VOICELESSNESS ASSIMILATION, it cannot be left unspecified and be filled in only at the end of the derivation.

Q120   Two ordered rules are necessary to derive the correct Klamath output forms. The first rule should spread the SUPRALARYNGEAL node of a lateral consonant to a preceding [n] or [l]. The second rule should delink the supralaryngeal node of the lateral consonant, which, if it is specified as [−voice] or as [+constricted], will leave behind only its laryngeal specification, causing it to end up as [h] or [ʔ]. The rules can be formalized as (1) and (2) below.

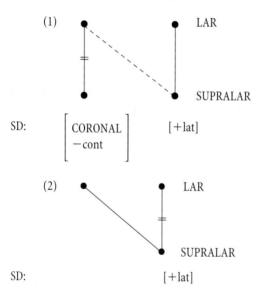

We assume that in the case of [nl] rule (1) creates a geminate structure, as shown.

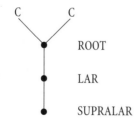

Rule (2) cannot apply to this structure, which will be supplied with the feature [+voice] by default.

Q121

1. The full representation for the four types of initial plosives is the following:

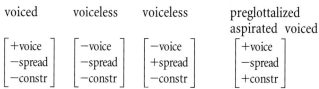

voiced	voiceless	voiceless	preglottalized aspirated voiced
$\begin{bmatrix} +\text{voice} \\ -\text{spread} \\ -\text{constr} \end{bmatrix}$	$\begin{bmatrix} -\text{voice} \\ -\text{spread} \\ -\text{constr} \end{bmatrix}$	$\begin{bmatrix} -\text{voice} \\ +\text{spread} \\ -\text{constr} \end{bmatrix}$	$\begin{bmatrix} +\text{voice} \\ -\text{spread} \\ +\text{constr} \end{bmatrix}$

2. Assuming radical underspecification, the voiced plosives could be characterized by the presence of the feature [+voice] in the underlying representation, the voiceless aspirated plosives by the feature [+spread] and the preglottalized voiced plosives by the feature combination [+voice, +constr]. The features [−voice], [−spread] and [−constr] could then be left unspecified, to be filled in by default rules. This means that the voiceless unaspirated plosives are left unspecified underlyingly.

3. Coda plosives can be left unspecified, as their feature values can be provided by the default rules.

Chapter 13

Q122

1. NASALIZATION in Sundanese should transfer the nasality of a nasal consonant to any following vowel, but is blocked by any consonant, except when this is a laryngeal segment.

2. If the rule is formulated such that it spreads [+nas] from a nasal consonant to the SUPRALARYNGEAL node of a following vowel (V-position), it will be blocked by any segment that has a supralaryngeal specification. Since [h] and [ʔ] do not have a SUPRALARYNGEAL node, these segments are invisible for the spreading [+nas], and their transparancy is straighforwardly accounted for.

Q123

1. One default rule needs to assign [−voice] to a stem-initial obstruent and one needs to assign [+voice] to an intervocalic obstruent.

2. The two [±voice]-melodies are [−voice] and [+voice] [−voice]. Similar to the avoidance of the first TBU at the start of the tonal association in Kikuyu in Chapter 10, the melodies cannot associate to a stem-initial obstruent. The features must not spread, because a [−voice] melody would produce ungrammatical forms like *[itupi] and *[titupi] if it did.

3. Whereas [ʊdɔdɔ] does not have an underlying [±voice] melody, [ədəpigɔ] is specified for a [+voice][−voice] melody.

4.

Underlying form	/iTuPi/	/TəTəKaKe/
Melody association	[−voice]	[+voice][−voice]
	/ituPi/	/TədəkaKe/
Default rules	[itubi]	[tədəkage]

5. The form is not ungrammatical, because the second consonant in [kɔnɔpiɔ] is a sonorant and therefore not a [±voice]-bearing segment. The underlying [−voice] melody, skipping the stem-initial obstruent, will therefore be associated to the third consonant.

Q124   Yes, if there is only one lexical 'floating' [+ATR] feature, it must either be on the left or on the right of any occurrence of [−ATR] linked to a segment.

Q125
1. In the Finnish word game Siansaksa, the initial (C)V-sequences of two words are inverted. BACK HARMONY applies so as to spread the feature [±back] from left to right through the word, whereby the vowels [i] and [e] are transparent, neither undergoing nor imposing BACK HARMONY. For instance, exchanging [sa] and [hæ] in [saksalaisia hætyːtetːiːn] initially gives [hæ]-[ksalaisia] and [sa]-[tyːtetːiːn], which BACK HARMONY turns into [hæksælæisiæ satuːtetːiːn].

2. The analysis accounts for the fact the fact that the first word in the game form in (a) is not *[hæsælæisiæ], because only the initial (C)V sequence is inverted and not the entire first syllable.

3. The analysis accounts for the fact that the second form in (a) is not *[satyːtetːiːn], because [a], being a back vowel in Finnish, will trigger BACK HARMONY, changing [y] into [u].

4. Because [i] is transparent, it neither undergoes nor imposes BACK HARMONY, which is why, in [hitsansa], the original back vowels remain back.

Q126   Complex segments like *[px] or *[dŋ] would require more than one specification for both place and manner. Apparently, a segment cannot be a complex place segment and a manner-contour segment at the same time. Indeed, such representations would raise the question why both manner phases should not occur at both places of articulation, to give *[pfkx].

Q127   The first consonant and the first vowel of a verb stem are reduplicated, as in [fafja], derived from [fja]. Since [fefle] and [kpokplo] are derived from the verbs stems [fle] and [kplo], respectively, it must be the case that while [fl] is a cluster, [kp] is a single consonant, a complex place segment. Similarly, [ts] is a single segment in [tsitsi], from [tsi], because if [ts] were a cluster, the reduplicated form would be [titsi].

Q128
1. If the two suffixes did not have different underlying forms, they would be realized identically in their unassimilated form in the (a) examples.

2. The dental consonants in the third column are [CORONAL,+ant,+distr], the alveolar ones in the fourth column are [CORONAL,+ant,−distr], while the palatoalveolar consonants in the last column are [CORONAL,−ant,+distr].

3. It is impossible to account for CORONAL HARMONY by leftward spreading of the [CORONAL] node to consonants unspecified for [CORONAL], because

the transparent coronal consonants would incorrectly be assimilated, while the consonants that have a [CORONAL] node would incorrectly be left unassimilated, besides incorrectly blocking the spreading of the [CORONAL] node.

4. If it is assumed that laterals and [t,d,t'] are unspecified for [CORONAL] underlyingly, they will get a [CORONAL] node with the features [+ant, −distr] by a default rule. Before that happens, CORONAL HARMONY can spread the [CORONAL] node of the rightmost coronal consonant to preceding consonants that have a [CORONAL] node, delinking these nodes and spreading to the next consonant on the left if there is one.

Chapter 14

Q129   Main stress in Passamaquoddy is on the penultimate syllable if that syllable is heavy (i.e., contains a full vowel), as in item (b), and if it is not, main stress is on the antepenultimate syllable provided it is heavy, as in item (c). If neither of these syllables is heavy, as in items (a), (d) and (e), main stress is on the penultimate or antepenultimate syllable, depending on which of these two is separated by an odd number of syllables from the rightmost preceding full-vowelled syllable. Thus, in [mekənutəsə́pənik], item (a), main stress is on the antepenult, because an odd number of syllables, one, intervenes between this syllable and the rightmost preceding heavy syllable [nu], whereas in [eləkiləkə́pən], item (d), main stress is on the penult, which is separated by an odd number of syllables from the rightmost preceding heavy syllable [ki]. If the word does not contain any heavy syllables at all, main stress is on the penult or the antepenult, whichever is separated by an odd number of syllables from the beginning of the word. Thus, in item (e), main stress must be on the antepenult, in order to be separated by an odd number of syllables from the left word-edge, three in this case.

Q130

1. Input forms which show that the main stress is not invariably located at some fixed distance from a word edge, e.g. always the first, or always the second, or always the last, etc., but varies between first and second, or between last and penultimate, whereby the edgemost syllables with main stress have long vowels and/or are closed. In the next section, it will be seen that the first or last syllable of the word may be extrametrical, so that 'first and second' may in fact be 'second and third', etc.

2. If the language learning child only comes across words in which the main stress is located within a two-syllable window at one word edge, she has no reason to assume unbounded stress, but if additionally she comes across words with the main stress outside that window, i.e. on the third syllable from the same edge or beyond, stress must be unbounded. In the next section, we will see that, due to extrametricality, the two-syllable window may in fact be a three-syllable window.

Q131   The stress pattern of Icelandic can be accounted for by constructing iterative QI-ld feet from left to right, followed by the construction of a left-dominant unbounded word tree, as illustrated for *'höfðingjá* and *'biográfià*.

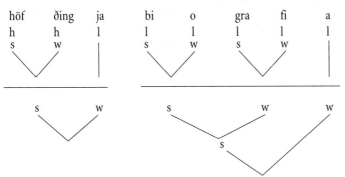

Q132   The examples show that main stress is on the first syllable if it is heavy and on the second if it is not, and a QS foot is thus required. By looking at a word which starts with two light syllables, like [ko.jó.ŋo], we can determine that this foot must be right-dominant, for if it was left-dominant, main stress would wrongly be predicted on the first syllable in that word. A QS-rd foot is therefore required. Since there is no secondary stress, feet must be assigned non-iteratively.

Chapter 15

Q133
1. The Turkish stress system exemplified by these words must be QS, for otherwise stress would be on a fixed syllable.

2. The fact that stress is never on the final syllable can be accounted for by assuming final syllable extrametricality.

3. In order to determine whether a moraic trochee or an iamb is needed to account for the Turkish non-final stress pattern, words with light antepenultimate and penultimate syllables should be considered, like *tornavida* and *çikolata*. Assuming final syllable extrametricality, a moraic trochee would incorrectly locate the stress on the antepenult, **tornávida*, **çikólata*. By contrast, an iamb will correctly stress the penultimate syllable under the same assumption of final extrametricality.

Q134
1. To explain the existence of both *corníce* and *cálice*, final extrametricality could be assumed to be a lexical property in Italian. If the final syllable (or mora) of *calice* is extrametrical, but not the final syllable of *cornice*, the construction of a moraic trochee at the right word edge will correctly produce stress on the penult in *cornice* and on the antepenult in *calice*.

2. Main stress on a final light syllable can be accounted for, if, like final extrametricality, final mora catalexis is a lexical property. Words like

cittá and *colibrí* are specified as having a final catalectic mora, and the construction of a moraic trochee at the right word edge will, again, correctly produce stress on the final syllables of these words.

Q135 Hayes' (1995) analysis of Turkish non-final stress (moraic trochees plus final foot extrametricality under clash) would wrongly predict final stress in *Indiyanapólis* and in *Üsküdar,* given that the final foot will not be made extrametrical, as there is no clash, as shown below.

```
In    di    ya    na    po    lis
mm    m     m     m     m     mm
(x.)  (x    .)    (x    .)    (x.)

Üs    kü    dar
mm    m     mm
(x.)        (x.)
```

Q136 The domain of the obligatory occurrence of [ŋ] is the foot. That is, if the nasal and the dorsal consonant are within the same foot, as in *íncrement,* the nasal is obligatorily realized as [ŋ], whereas if they are not, as in the verb *in(créase)* or the noun *(ín)(crèase),* the nasal may be realized as either [n] or [ŋ].

Q137 Dutch [h] is not realized in foot-internal position. The fact that [h] is not realized in the word *màrihuána* thus suggests that the first three syllables of [maː. ri.u.aː.na] form a single foot.

Q138

/ŋankikirikirimpaji/	FᴛBɪɴ	RʜTʏᴘ (T)	Aʟ (ω, L, Fᴛ, L)	Paʀsᴇ-σ	Aʟ (Fᴛ, R, ω, R)
[(ŋánki) (ríki) (rimpa)ji]				*	σσσσσ σσσ! σ
[(ŋán) (kíri) (kirim)(páji)]	*!				σσσσσσ σσσσ σσ
[(ŋánki)rikirim (páji)]				**!*	σσσσσ
☞[(ŋánki)ri (kírim) (páji)]				*	σσσσσ σσ
[(ŋánki)(ríki)rim (páji)]				*	σσσσσ σσσ!
[(ŋanki)ri (kírim) (páji)]		*!		*	σσσσσ σσ

Q139 The first form of each language shows that NᴏɴFɪɴᴀʟɪᴛʏ must dominate the constraint that requires a word to end in a foot, Aʟ (ω, R, Fᴛ, R). The second form of each language shows that the constraint requiring words to start with a foot is less important than the one requiring words to end in a foot. Therefore, Aʟ (ω, R, Fᴛ, R) must dominate Aʟ (ω, L, Fᴛ, L). Finally, the last form of each language shows that QS must dominate Pᴀʀsᴇ-σ in Latin, but that for Macedonian Pᴀʀsᴇ-σ must dominate QS.

Q140

/tata/	NᴏɴF	FᴛBɪɴ	Pᴀʀsᴇ-σ	Aʟ (ω, L)	Aʟ (ω, R)	H/R	H/L
(táta)	*!						
(tatá)	*!						
☞ (tá)ta		*	*		σ	σ	
ta(tá)	*!	*	*	σ			σ
/malaɲoleju/	NᴏɴF	FᴛBɪɴ	Pᴀʀsᴇ-σ	Aʟ (ω, L)	Aʟ (ω, R)	H/R	H/L
mala(ɲolé)ju			**!*	σσ	σ	σ	σσ
(malà)(ɲolé)(ju)	*!	*				σ	σσ
(mà)(laɲò)(lejú)	*!	*					σσσ
☞(malà) (ɲolé)ju			*		σ	σ	σσ
(malá) (ɲolè)ju			*		σ	σσ!σ	
/tipohore/	NᴏɴF	FᴛBɪɴ	Pᴀʀsᴇ-σ	Aʟ (ω, L)	Aʟ (ω, R)	H/R	H/L
☞ (tipó)hore			**		σσ	σσ	
ti(pohó)re			**	σ!	σ	σ	σ
(tì(pohó)re		*!	*		σ	σ	σ
(tipò)(horé)	*!						σσ
(tipò)(hó)re		*!	*		σ	σ	σσ

Q141

1. First, Rʜᴛʏᴘᴇ (T) » Rʜᴛʏᴘᴇ (I). The four-syllable word [àsikáda] shows that Rʜᴛʏᴘᴇ (T) must dominate Rʜᴛʏᴘᴇ (I) in order to get a trochaic pattern, instead of an iambic [asikidá]. Second, FᴛBɪɴ » Pᴀʀsᴇ-σ. Footing a trisyllabic word like [kiríka] will produce one stress, with one syllable left unfooted, showing that FᴛBɪɴ must crucially rank above Pᴀʀsᴇ-σ, in order to get [kiríka] instead of [kirìka]. Third, Aʟ (Ft, R, ω, R) » Aʟ (Ft, L, ω,L). Assuming a trochee,

the same trisyllabic [kiríka] shows that the foot must be right-aligned with a word, not left-aligned. In the lefthand column the correct rankings are shown, and the incorrect rankings are shown on the right.

/asikada/	RhType(T)	RhType(I)
☞ (àsi)(káda)		**
(asì)(kadá)	*!*	

/asikada/	RhType (I)	RhType (T)
(àsi)(káda)	*!*	
☞ *(asì)(kadá)		**

kirika/	FtBin	Parse-σ
(kì)(ríka)	*!	
☞ ki(ríka)		*

/kirika/	Parse-σ	FtBin
☞ *(kì)(ríka)		*
ki(ríka)	*!	

/kirika/	Al (Ft, R, ω, R)	Al (Ft, L, ω, L)
(kíri)ka	σ!	
☞ ki(ríka)		σ

/kirika/	Al (Ft, L, ω, L)	Al (Ft, R, ω, R)
☞ *(kíri)ka		σ
ki(ríka)	σ!	

Q142 In order to get final stress/H-tone in [apataká], we need to assume iambs rather than trochees, that is, RhType (I) » RhType (T), and also that footing needs to be iterative, that is, Parse-σ » Al (Ft, L, ω, L). Trisyllabic [ifóci] shows that a word must start with a foot rather than end with one, that is, Al (Ft, L, ω, L) » Al (Ft, R, ω, R), and that no monosyllabic light feet are allowed, giving FtBin » Parse-σ. Finally, in order to get final main stress/H-tone, we need to assume that Align (Head, R, ω, R) (H/R) dominates Align (Head, L, ω, L) (H/L). The constraint ranking is illustrated for [ifoci] and [apataka].

/ifoci/	RhT(I)	RhT(T)	FtBin	Parse-σ	Al (Ft, L)	Al (Ft, R)
i(fóci)	*!			*	σ	
i(fòci)		*		*	σ !	
(ifó)(cì)		*	*!			σ
☞ (ifó)ci		*		*		σ

/apataka/	FtBin	Parse-σ	Al (Ft, L)	Al (Ft, R)	H/R	H/L
(apá)(takà)			σσ	σσ	σ!σ	
(apá)taka		*!*		σσ	σσ	
apa(takà)		*!*	σσ			σσ
☞ (apà)(takà)			σσ	σσ		σσ

Chapter 16

Q143

1. Binary must rank below AlignFOC, which makes the violation of Binary unavoidable.

2. When *liburua* is the focus constituent, a φ-boundary must appear before it. Lower-ranking Binary will now make itself felt again by forcing *Amaiari* and *amumen* to occur in the same φ, despite the requirement of lowest-ranking AlignXP that there must be a φ-boundary before the XP *amumen liburua*. With *liburua* as the focus constituent, the prosodic structure will be ₍φ₎(*Amaiari amumen*)_φ ₍φ₎(*liburua*)_φ ₍φ₎(*emon dotzo*)_φ.

Q144 The φ-structures are

(1) ₍φ₎(I was explaining)_φ ₍φ₎(to the students)_φ ₍φ₎(the problem)_φ ₍φ₎(of the double negation)_φ ₍φ₎(in English)_φ

(2) ₍φ₎(I was explaining)_φ ₍φ₎(to the students)_φ ₍φ₎(the problem)_φ

Example (2) is ungrammatical because a condition on Heavy NP Shift is that the NP that is moved must contain minimally two φs, and in (2) it contains only one, *the problem*.

Q145 In *This is represented in (6)*, the adverbial phrase *in six* can be included with its verb *represented* in the same φ, a case of restructuring, because the next constituent is a single phonological word *in six*, where *in* is a function word and as such a weak syllable. As a result, the stress pattern of *règpresénted* changes to *répresènted* before *síx* in the same φ. However, in *This is represented in (6a)*, the adverbial *in six a* consists of two phonological words, *in six* and *a*. As a result, it is not included in the same φ as *represented*, so that the RHYTHM RULE cannot apply.

Q146 In the examples in (1), the vowel is the first segment of a lexical category N or Adj. As a result, it begins an ω, causing the preceding [s] to be in a different ω. Incidentally, this domain juncture rule will require that the two ωs occur in the same IP.

References

Abercrombie, D. (1967). *Elements of general phonetics*. Edinburgh: Edinburgh University Press.

Agostini, P.M. (1995). *L'usu di a nostra lingua*. Privately printed by Sammarcelli, Biguglia (Corsica).

Aitken, A.J. (1981). The Scottish vowel-length rule. In M. Benskin and M.L. Samuels (eds), *So meny people longages and tonges: Philological essays in Scots and Mediaeval English presented to Angus McIntosh*. Edinburgh: M. Benskin and M.L. Samuels, 131–57.

—— (1984). Scottish accents and dialects. In P. Trudgill (ed.), *Language in the British Isles*. Cambridge: Cambridge University Press, 94–114.

Andersen, T. (1987). The phonemic system of Agar Dinka. *Journal of African Languages and Linguistics* 9: 1–27.

Anderson, S.R. (1974). *The organization of phonology*. New York: Academic Press.

Archangeli, D. (1988). *Underspecification in Yawelmani phonology and morphology.* New York: Garland Press.

—— and Pulleyblank, D. (1993). *Grounded phonology*. Cambridge, MA: MIT Press.

Árnason, K. (1985). Icelandic word stress and metrical phonology. *Studia Linguistica* 39: 93–129.

Baerman, M. (1999). *The evolution of fixed stress in Slavic*. Munich: Lincom.

Bailey, C.-J. (1985). *English phonetic transcription*. Dallas: Summer Institute of Linguistics, and Arlington: University of Texas.

Beckman, M.E. (1986). *Stress and non-stress accent*. Dordrecht: Foris.

Bermúdez-Otero, R. (forthcoming). *Stratal optimality theory*. Oxford: Oxford University Press.

Bhat, D.N.S. (1978). A general study of palatalization. In J.H. Greenberg, C.A. Ferguson and E. Moravcsik (eds), *Universals of human language* II: *phonology*. Stanford, CA: Stanford University Press, 47–92.

Bladon, A., Clark, C. and Mickey, K. (1987). Production and perception of sibilant fricatives. *Journal of the International Phonetic Association* 17: 39–65.

Blevins, J. (1995). The syllable in phonological theory. In Goldsmith, 206–44.

Boersma, P. (1998). *Functional phonology*. Utrecht: LOT.

Bolognesi, R. (1998). *The phonology of Campidanian Sardinian*. The Hague: HAG.

Booij, G. (1977). *Generatieve fonologie van het Nederlands*. Utrecht: Spectrum.

—— (1984). Syllabestruktuur en verkleinwoordsvorming in het Nederlands. *Glot* 7: 207–26.

—— (1985). Coordination reduction in complex words: a case for prosodic phonology. In van der Hulst and Smith, 143–60.

—— (1988). On the relation between lexical and prosodic phonology. In P.M. Bertinetto and M. Lopocaro (eds), *Certamen phonologium: papers from the 1987 Cortona phonology meeting*. Turin: Rosenberg & Selier, 389–418.

—— (1995). *The phonology of Dutch*. Oxford: Oxford University Press.

—— (1996). Cliticization as prosodic integration: the case of Dutch. *Linguistic Review* 13: 219–42.

Boxwell, H. and Boxwell, M. (1966). Weri phonemes. *Papers in New Guinea Linguistics* 5: 77–93.

Broe, M. (1992). An introduction to feature geometry. In Docherty and Ladd, 149–65.

Browman, C.P. and Goldstein, L. (1989). Articulatory gestures as phonological units. *Phonology* 6: 201–51.

Busenitz, R.L. and Busenitz, M.J. (1991). Balantak phonology and morphophonemics. In Sneddon, 29–47.

Catford, J.C. (1988). *A practical introduction to phonetics*. Oxford: Clarendon Press.

Ceccaldi, M. (1988). *Dictionnaire Corse–Français*. 2nd edn. Paris: Klincksieck.

Charette, M. (1989). The minimality condition in phonology. *Journal of Linguistics* 25: 159–87.

Chen, M. (1987). The syntax of Xiamen tone sandhi. *Phonology Yearbook* 4: 109–49.

Chen, Y. (2006). Emphasis, syllable duration, and tonal realization in Standard Chinese. *Speech prosody 2006*. Dresden: TUD Verlag der Wissenschaften, 382–85.

Chesswas, J.D. (1963). *The essentials of Luganda*. London: Oxford University Press.

Cho, T. (2004). Prosodically conditioned strengthening and vowel-to-vowel coarticulation in English. *Phonetica* 32, 141–76.

Chomsky, N. and Halle, M. (1968). *The sound pattern of English*. New York: Harper & Row.

Clements, G.N. (1981). Akan vowel harmony: a nonlinear analysis. In G.N. Clements (ed.), *Harvard studies in phonology* 2. Bloomington: Indiana University Linguistics Club.

—— (1985). The geometry of phonological features. *Phonology Yearbook* 2: 223–52.

—— (1986). Compensatory lengthening and consonant gemination in Luganda. In Wetzels and Sezer.

—— (1989). A unified set of features for consonants and vowels. MS, Cornell University.

—— (1990). The role of the sonority cycle in core syllabification. In J. Kingston and M.E. Beckman (eds), *Papers in laboratory phonology I. Between the grammar and physics of speech*. Cambridge: Cambridge University Press, 283–333.

—— (1993). Lieu d'articulation des consonnes et des voyelles: une théorie unifiée. In B. Laks and A. Rialland (eds), *L'architecture et la géométrie des représentations phonologiques*. Paris: CNRS.

—— (1999). Affricates as noncontoured stops. In O. Fujimura, B. Joseph and B. Palek (eds), *Item order in language and speech*. Prague: Charles University Press, 271–99.

—— (2004). Feature economy in sound systems. *Phonology* 20: 287–333.

—— and Ford, K. (1979). Kikuyu tone shift and its synchronic consequences. *Linguistic Inquiry* 10: 179–210.

—— and Hume, E.V. (1995). The internal organisation of speech sounds. In Goldsmith, 245–306.

—— and Keyser, S.J. (1983). *CV-phonology*. Cambridge, MA: MIT Press.

Coates, W. A. and De Silva, M.W.S. (1960). The segmental phonemes of Sinhalese. *University of Ceylon Review* 18: 163–75.

Cohen, A., Ebeling, C.L., Fokkema, K. and van Holk, A.G.F. (1972). *Fonologie van het Nederlands en het Fries*. The Hague: Nijhoff.

Cohn, A. (1990). Phonetic and phonological rules of nasalization. PhD, UCLA.

Connell, B. and Arvaniti, A. (eds) (1995). *Papers in laboratory phonology IV. Phonology and phonetic evidence*. Cambridge: Cambridge University Press.

Coupez, A. (1969). Une leçon de linguistique. *Africa-Tervuren* 5: 1–5.

Cutler, A. (1995). Spoken word recognition and production. In J.L. Miller and P.D. Eimas (eds), *Speech, language and communication*, vol. XI of E.C. Carterette and M.P. Friedman (eds), *Handbook of perception and cognition*. New York: Academic Press, 97–136.

—— (2011). *Native listening: language experience and the recognition of spoken words.* Cambridge, MA: MIT Press.

de Lacy, P. (ed.) (2007). *The Cambridge handbook of phonology.* Cambridge: Cambridge University Press.

Dell, F. and Vergnaud, J.-R. (1984). Les développements récents en phonologie: quelques idées centrales. In F. Dell, D. Hirst and J.-R. Vergnaud (eds), *Forme sonore du langage.* Paris: Hermann, 1–42.

Derbyshire, D. (1979). *Hixkaryana.* Amsterdam: North-Holland.

Docherty, G.J. and Ladd, D.R. (eds) (1992). *Papers in laboratory phonology II. Gesture, segment, prosody.* Cambridge: Cambridge University Press.

Dresher, E. and Lahiri, A. (1991). The Germanic foot: metrical coherence in Old English. *Linguistic Inquiry* 22: 251–86.

Duanmu, S. (2000). *The phonology of Standard Chinese.* Oxford: Oxford University Press.

Elbert, S.H. and Pukui, M.K. (1979). *Hawaiian grammar.* Honolulu: University Press of Hawaii.

Elimelech, B. (1976). *A tonal grammar of Etsako.* UCLA Working Papers in Phonetics 35.

Elordieta, G. (1997). Accent, tone and intonation in Lekeitio Basque. In F. Martínez-Gil and A. Morales-Front (eds), *Issues in the phonologies of the major Iberian languages.* Washington, DC: Georgetown University Press, 3–78.

Evans, N. (1995). Current issues in the phonology of Australian languages. In Goldsmith, 723–61.

Ewen, C.J. (1995). Dependency relations in phonology. In Goldsmith, 570–85.

Firth, J.R. (1957). Phonological features of some Indian languages. In J.R. Firth (ed.), *Papers in linguistics 1934–1951.* Oxford: Oxford University Press.

Flemming, E. (1995). *Auditory representation in phonology.* PhD dissertation, UCLA.

Friberg, T. and Friberg, B. (1991). Notes on Konjo phonology. In Sneddon, 71–115.

Fromkin, V. (ed.) (1978). *Tone: a linguistic survey.* New York: Academic Press.

Fry, D. (1955). Duration and intensity as physical correlates of linguistic stress. *Journal of the Acoustical Society of America* 35: 765–9.

—— (1958). Experiments in the perception of stress. *Language and Speech* 1: 120–52.

Furby, C.E. (1974). Garawa phonology. *Papers in Australian Linguistics* 7: 1–11.

Gafos, D. and Dye, A. (2011). Vowel harmony: opaque and transparent vowels, in Oostendorp *et al.* (2011).

Giegerich, H.J. (1992). Onset maximisation in German: the case against resyllabification rules. In P. Eisenberg (ed.), *Silbenphonologie des Deutschen.* Tübingen: Gunter Narr.

Gimson, A.C. (1989). *An introduction to the pronunciation of English* (2008; 4th edn) revised by A. Cruttenden. London: Arnold.

Goldsmith, J.A. (1976). *Autosegmental phonology.* Bloomington: Indiana University Linguistics Club.

—— (1989). *Autosegmental and metrical phonology* (7th edn). Oxford: Blackwell.

—— (ed.) (1995). *The handbook of phonological theory.* Cambridge, MA: Blackwell.

Graaf, T. de (1990). Grasu glas. Fonetische contrasten Japans–Nederlands. *Tabu* 20: 47–57.

Grimes, B. (1988). *Ethnologue,* pts 1 and 2. Fort Worth, TX: Summer Institute of Linguistics.

Gurevich, N. (2004). *Lenition and contrast. The functional consequences of certain phonetically motivated sound changes.* New York/London: Routledge.

Gussenhoven, C. (1978). Het Nederlandse diminutief-suffix: schwa-insertie nader bekeken. *Nieuwe Taalgids* 71: 206–11.

—— (1983). Stress shift and the nucleus. *Linguistics* 21: 303–39.

—— (1986). English plosive allophones and ambisyllabicity. *Gramma* 10: 119–41.

—— (1990). Tonal association domains and the prosodic hierarchy in English. In S. Ramsaran (ed.), *Studies in the pronunciation of English.* London: Routledge.

—— (1991). The English rhythm rule as an accent deletion rule. *Phonology* 8: 1–35.

—— (1993). The Dutch foot and the chanted call. *Journal of Linguistics* 29: 37–63.

—— (2004). *The phonology of tone and intonation.* Cambridge: Cambridge University Press.

—— and Rietveld, A. (1992). Intonation contours, prosodic structure and preboundary lengthening. *Journal of Phonetics* 20: 283–303.

Haan, J. (1996). Umlaut en diminutiefvorming in een Oostgelders dialect. *Taal en Tongval* 48: 18–37.

—— (2002). *Speaking of questions: an exploration of Dutch question intonation.* Utrecht: LOT Press.

Haas, M. (1977). Tonal accent in Creek. In L. Hyman (ed.), *Studies in stress and accent.* Los Angeles: USC, 195–208.

Hale, M. and Reiss, C. (2008). *The phonological enterprise.* Oxford: Oxford University Press.

Halle, M. (1959). *The sound pattern of Russian.* The Hague: Mouton.

—— (1985). Speculations about the representations of words in memory. In V. Fromkin (ed.), *Phonetic linguistics: essays in honor of Peter Ladefoged.* Orlando, FL: Academic Press.

—— (1990). Respecting metrical structure. *Natural Language and Linguistic Theory* 8: 149–76.

—— and Clements, G.N. (1983). *Problem book in phonology.* Cambridge, MA: MIT Press.

—— and Idsardi, W. (1995). General properties of stress and metrical structure. In Goldsmith, 403–43.

—— and Kenstowicz, M. (1991). The free element condition and cyclic vs. noncyclic stress. *Linguistic Inquiry* 22: 457–501.

—— and Mohanan, K.P. (1985). Segmental phonology of Modern English. *Linguistic Inquiry* 16: 57–116.

—— and Vergnaud, J.R. (1978). Metrical structures in phonology. MS, MIT.

—— —— (1987). *An essay on stress.* Cambridge, MA: MIT Press.

Hamans, C. (1985). Umlaut in a Dutch dialect. In van der Hulst and Smith, 381–96.

Hardcastle, W.J. and Laver, J. (1997). *The handbook of phonetic sciences.* Oxford: Blackwell.

Harris, J. (1994). *English sound structure.* Oxford: Blackwell.

Harris, J.W. (1983). *Syllable structure and stress in Spanish.* Cambridge, MA: MIT Press.

Hayes, B. (1981). A metrical theory of stress rules. PhD, MIT. Distributed by Indiana University Linguistics Club.

—— (1985). Iambic and trochaic rhythm in stress rules. *Berkeley Linguistics Society* 13: 429–46.

—— (1987). A revised parametric metrical theory. *Northeastern Linguistics Society* 17: 274–89.

—— (1989). The prosodic hierarchy in meter. In P. Kiparsky and G. Youmans (eds), *Rhythm and meter.* Orlando, FL: Academic Press, 201–60.

—— (1990). Precompiled phonology. In Inkelas and Zec, 85–108.

—— (1992). Commentary on F. Nolan, 'The descriptive role of segments: evidence from assimilation'. In Docherty and Ladd, 280–86.

—— (1994). 'Gesture' in prosody: comments on the paper by Ladd. In P. Keating (ed.), *Papers in Laboratory Phonology III. Phonological structure and phonetic form.* Cambridge: Cambridge University Press, 64–75.

—— (1995). *Metrical stress theory: principles and case studies.* Chicago: Chicago University Press.

—— and Lahiri, A. (1991). Bengali intonational phonology. *Natural Language and Linguistic Theory* 9: 46–99.

Hayward, K. and Hayward, R.J. (1992). Amharic (illustrations of the IPA). *Journal of the International Phonetic Association* 22: 48–52.

Himmelmann, N.P. (1991). Tomini-Tolitoli sound structures. In Sneddon, 49–70.

Holst, T. and Nolan, F. (1995). The influence of syntactic structure on [s] to [ʃ] assimilation. In Connell and Arvaniti, 315–33.

Holt, E. (ed.) (2003). *Optimality Theory and language change.* Dordrecht: Kluwer.

Hombert, J.M. (1973). Speaking backwards in Bakwiri. *Studies in African Linguistics* 4: 227–35.

—— (1986). Word games: some implications for analysis of tone and other phonological constructs. In Ohala and Jaeger, 175–86.

Hooper, J. (1976). *An introduction to natural generative phonology.* New York: Academic Press.

Hualde, J.I. (1992). *Catalan.* London: Routledge.

Huisman, R., Huisman, R. and Lloyd, J. (1981). Angaatiha syllable patterns. In P.M. Healey (ed.), *Angan languages are different: four phonologies.* Huntington Beach, CA: Summer Institute of Linguistics, 51–62.

Hyman, L.M. (1970). How concrete is phonology? *Language* 46: 58–76.

—— (1975). *Phonology: theory and analysis.* New York: Holt, Rinehart & Winston.

—— (1985). *A theory of phonological weight.* Dordrecht: Foris.

—— (1992). Moraic mismatches in Bantu. *Phonology* 9: 255–65.

—— and Ngunga, A. (1994). On the non-universality of tonal association 'conventions': evidence from Ciyao. *Phonology* 11: 25–68.

Inkelas, S. (1989). *Prosodic constituency in the lexicon.* New York: Garland Press.

—— and Zec, D. (eds) (1990). *The phonology-syntax connection.* Chicago: University of Chicago Press.

Iverson, G.K. (1993). (Post)lexical rule application. In S. Hargus and E.M. Kaisse (eds), *Studies in lexical phonology.* San Diego, CA: Academic Press.

Jacobs, H. (1989). Nonlinear studies in the historical phonology of French. PhD, Nijmegen.

—— (1990). On markedness and bounded stress systems. *Linguistic Review* 7: 81–119.

—— (1994). Catalexis and stress in Romance. In Mazzola, 49–65.

—— (1997). Latin enclitic stress revisited. *Linguistic Inquiry* 28: 48–61.

—— and Gussenhoven, C. (2000). Loan phonology: perception, salience, the lexicon and OT. In J. Dekkers, F. van der Leeuw and J. van de Weijer (eds), *Optimality Theory. Phonology, syntax and acquisition.* Oxford: Oxford University Press, 193–210.

—— and van de Weijer, J. (1992). On the formal description of palatalisation. In R. Bok-Bennema and R. van Hout (eds), *Linguistics in the Netherlands 1992.* Amsterdam: Benjamins, 123–35.

Jakobson, R. (1968). *Child language, aphasia, and phonological universals.* The Hague: Mouton.

—— (1990). *On language.* Edited by L.R. Waugh and M. Monville-Burston. Cambridge, MA: Harvard University Press.

—— Fant, G. and Halle, M. (1952). *Preliminaries to speech analysis.* Cambridge, MA: MIT Press.

Jeanne, L.M. (1978). Aspects of Hopi grammar. PhD, MIT.

—— (1982). Some phonological rules of Hopi. *International Journal of American Linguistics* 48: 245–70.

Jensen, J.T. (1993). *English phonology.* Amsterdam: Benjamins.

Jones, D. (1967). *The phoneme: its nature and use.* London: Cambridge University Press.

Jones, R.B. (1961). *Karen linguistic studies.* Berkeley and Los Angeles: University of California Press.

Joos, M. (1942). A phonological dilemma in Canadian English. *Language* 18: 141–4.

Jun, S.-A. (1993). The phonetics and phonology of Korean. PhD, Ohio State University.

Kager, R. (1985). Cycliciteit, klemtoon en HGI. *Spektator* 14: 326–31.

—— (1993). Alternatives to the iambic-trochaic law. *Natural Language and Linguistic Theory* 11: 381–432.

—— (1995). Consequences of catalexis. In H. van der Hulst and J. van de Weijer (eds), *Leiden in last*. The Hague: Holland Academic Graphics, 269–98.

—— (1999). *Optimality Theory*. Cambridge: Cambridge University Press.

Kahn, D. (1976). Syllable-based generalizations in English. PhD, MIT. Distributed by Indiana University Linguistics Club.

Kaisse, E.M. (1985). *Connected speech*. London: Academic Press.

Katamba, F. (1989). *An introduction to phonology*. London: Longman.

Kaye, J. (1975). A functional explanation of rule ordering in phonology. *Parasession on Functionalism*. CLS, 244–252.

—— (1989). *Phonology: a cognitive view*. Hillsdale, NJ: Laurence Erlbaum.

Keating, P.A. (1987). Palatals as complex segments: x-ray evidence. Paper presented at the 1987 Annual Meeting of LSA, San Francisco.

—— (1991). Coronal places of articulation. In Paradis and Prunet, 29–48.

—— (1990). Phonetic representations in a generative grammar. *Journal of Phonetics* 18: 321–34.

——, Cho, T., Fougeron, C. and Hsu, C. (2004). Domain-initial articulatory strengthening in four languages. *Papers in Laboratory Phonology VI*. Cambridge: Cambridge University Press.

—— and Lahiri, A. (1993). Fronted velars, palatalized velars, and palatals. *Phonetica* 50: 73–101.

Keller, C. (1993). The phonology of Brao. MS, Summer Institute of Linguistics, Dallas, TX.

Kennedy, R. (2008). Bugotu and Cheke Holo reduplication: in defence of the emergence of the unmarked. *Phonology* 25, 61–82.

Kenstowicz, M. (1994a). *Phonology in generative grammar*. Oxford: Blackwell.

—— (1994b). Cyclic vs. noncyclic constraint evaluation. *MIT Working Papers in Linguistics* 21: 11–42.

—— (1979). *Generative phonology*. New York: Academic Press.

—— and Kisseberth, C. (1977). *Topics in phonological theory*. New York: Academic Press.

Kerswill, P.E. (1987). Linguistic variation in Durham. *Journal of Linguistics* 23: 25–49.

Key, M. (1968). *Comparative Tacanan phonology*. The Hague: Mouton.

Kim, H. (1997). *The Phonological representation of affricates: evidence from Korean and other languages*. PhD dissertation, Cornell.

—— (2001). A phonetically based account of phonological stop assibilation. *Phonology* 8, 81–108.

Kim, J.-M. (1986). *Phonology and syntax of Korean morphology*. Hanshin.

King, R.D. (1969). *Historical linguistics and generative grammar*. Englewood Cliffs, NJ: Prentice-Hall.

Kiparsky, P. (1968). Linguistic universals and linguistic change. In E. Bach and R. Harms (eds), *Universals in linguistic theory*. New York: Holt, 170–202.

—— (1973a). 'Elsewhere' in phonology. In S. Anderson and P. Kiparsky (eds), *A Festschrift for Morris Halle*. New York: Holt, 93–106.

—— (1973b). Phonological representations. In O. Fujimura (ed.), *Three dimensions of linguistic theory*. Tokyo: TEC.

—— (1977). The rhythmic structure of English verse. *Linguistic Inquiry* 8: 189–247.

—— (1979). Metrical structure assignment is cyclic. *Linguistic Inquiry* 10: 421–42.

—— (1982). *Explanation in phonology*. Dordrecht: Foris.

—— (1982). From cyclic phonology to lexical phonology. In Hulst and Smith, 131–75.

—— (1985). Some consequences of lexical phonology. *Phonology Yearbook* 2: 82–138.

—— (1991). Catalexis. MS, Stanford University and Wissenschaftkolleg zu Berlin.

—— (1993). Blocking in nonderived environments. In S. Hargus and E. Kaisse (eds), *Studies in lexical phonology*. San Diego, CA: Academic Press, 277–313.

Kluender, K.R., Diehl, R.L. and Wright, B.A. (1988). Vowel-length differences before voiced and voiceless consonants: an auditory explanation. *Journal of Phonetics* 16: 153–70.

Koefoed, G.A.T. (1979). Paradigmatische invloeden op fonetische processen. *Glot Special*. Vakgroep Nederlands, University of Leiden, 51–72.

Kooij, J. (1982). Epenthetische schwa: processen, regels, domeinen. *Spektator* 11: 315–25.

Koopmans-van Bcinum, F. (1980). *Contrast reduction: an acoustic and perceptual study of Dutch vowels in various speech conditions*. Amsterdam: Akademische Pers.

Koster, J. (1975). Dutch as an SOV language. *Linguistic Analysis* 1: 111–136.

Kubonzono (1999). 'Mova and syllable,' In N. Tsujimura (ed), *The handbook of Japanese linguistics*. Oxford: Blackwell, 31–61.

Kuroda, S.-Y. (1967). *Yawelmani phonology*. Cambridge, MA: MIT Press.

Ladd, D. R. (2008). *Intonational Phonology*. 2nd edition. Cambridge: Cambridge University Press.

Ladefoged, P. (1971). *Preliminaries to linguistic phonetics*. Chicago: University of Chicago Press.

—— (1991). What do we symbolize? Thoughts prompted by bilabial and labiodental fricatives. *Journal of the International Phonetic Association* 20: 33–6.

—— (2006). *A course in phonetics*. 5th edn. Boston, MA: Thomson/Wadsworth.

—— and Maddieson, I. (1996). *The sounds of the world's languages*. Oxford: Blackwell.

Lahiri, A. and Blumstein, S.E. (1984). A re-evaluation of the feature coronal. *Journal of Phonetics* 12: 133–45.

—— and Evers, V. (1991). Palatalization and coronality. In Paradis and Prunet, 79–100.

—— and Koreman, J. (1988). Syllable weight and quantity in Dutch. *West Coast Conference on Formal Linguistics* 7: 217–28.

—— and Marslen-Wilson, W. (1991). The mental representation of lexical form: a phonological approach to the recognition lexicon. *Cognition* 38: 245–94.

Lass, R. (1976). *English phonology and phonological theory*. Cambridge: Cambridge University Press.

—— (1984) *Phonology*. Cambridge: Cambridge University Press.

Laughren, M. (1984). Tone in Zulu nouns. In G.N. Clements and J. Goldsmith (eds), *Autosegmental studies in Bantu tone*. Dordrecht: Foris, 183–234.

Laver, J. (1994). *Principles of phonetics*. Cambridge: Cambridge University Press.

Leben, W.R. (1973). Suprasegmental phonology. PhD, MIT.

—— (1978). The representation of tone. In Fromkin, 177–219.

Levelt, W.J.M. (1989). *Speaking from intention to articulation*. Cambridge, MA: MIT Press.

Li, B. (1996). *Tungusic vowel harmony: description and analysis*. The Hague: Holland Academic Graphics.

Liberman, M. and Prince, A. (1977). On stress and linguistic rhythm. *Linguistic Inquiry* 8: 249–336.

Lieber, R. (1987). *An integrated theory of autosegmental processes*. New York: State University of New York Press.

Lindau, M. (1978). Vowel features. *Language* 54: 541–63.

Lloret, M. (1995). The representation of glottals in Oromo. *Phonology* 12: 257–80.

Lombardi, L. (1990). The nonlinear representation of the affricate. *Natural Language and Linguistic Theory* 8: 375–425.

McCarthy, J.J. (1985a). *Formal problems in semitic phonology and morphology*. New York: Garland.

—— (1985b). Speech disguise and phonological representation in Amharic. In van der Hulst and Smith, 305–12.

—— (1988). Feature geometry and dependency: a review. *Phonetica* 45: 84–108.

—— (1999). Sympathy and phonological opacity. *Phonology* 16: 331–99.

—— (2002). Sympathy, cumulativity, and the Duke-Of-York gambit. In C. Féry and R. van de Vijver (eds.), *The syllable in Optimality Theory.* Cambridge: Cambridge University Press.

—— (2002). *A thematic guide to Optimality Theory.* Cambridge: Cambridge University Press.

—— (2003). Comparative markedness. *Theoretical Linguistics*, 29: 1–51.

—— (2007). *Hidden generalizations. Phonological opacity in Optimality Theory.* Equinox.

—— and Prince, A. (1993a). Generalized alignment. *Yearbook of Morphology*, 79–154.

—— —— (1993b). Prosodic morphology I. MS.

—— —— (1994). The emergence of the unmarked: optimality in prosodic morphology. *Northeastern Linguistics Society* 24: 333–79.

—— —— (1995). Faithfulness and reduplicative identity. *University of Massachusetts Occasional Papers* 18: 249–384.

McCawley, J.D. (1986). Today the world, tomorrow phonology. *Phonology Yearbook* 3: 27–43.

McQueen, J.M. and Cutler, A. (1997). Cognitive processes in spoken-word recognition. In Hardcastle and Laver, 566–85.

Maddieson, I. (1984). *Patterns of sounds.* Cambridge: Cambridge University Press.

—— and Precoda, K. (1990). *UPSID-PC. The UCLA Phonological Segment Inventory Database.*

Marantz, A. (1982). Re-reduplication. *Linguistic Inquiry* 13: 435–82.

Mascaró, J. (1976). Catalan phonology. PhD, MIT.

Mazzola, M.L. (1976). *Proto-Romance and Sicilian.* Lisse: Peter de Ridder.

—— (1994). *Issues and theory in Romance linguistics.* Washington, DC: Georgetown University Press.

Meyer, A.S. and Belke, E. (2007). Word form retrieval in language production. In M.G. Gaskell (ed.), *The Oxford handbook of psycholinguistics.* Oxford: Oxford University Press.

Mohanan, K.P. (1986). *The theory of lexical phonology.* Dordrecht: Reidel. Distributed by Indiana University Linguistics Club 1982.

—— (1992). Describing the phonology of non-native varieties of language. MS. National University of Singapore.

Morais, J., Cary, L., Alegria, J. and Bertelson, P. (1979). Does awareness of speech as a sequence of phones arise spontaneously? *Cognition 7*, 323–331.

Moulton, W.G. (1962). The vowels of Dutch: phonetic and distributional classes. *Lingua* 6: 294–312.

Nagano-Madsen, Y. (1993). Phrase-final intonation in West Greenlandic Eskimo. *Working Papers in General Linguistics and Phonetics* 40. Lund University, 145–55.

Nespor, M. and Vogel, I. (1986). *Prosodic phonology.* Dordrecht: Foris.

—— —— (1998). Stress domains. In H. van der Hulst (ed.), *Word prosodic systems in the languages of Europe.* Berlin: Mouton De Gruyter.

Nettle, D. (1995). Segmental inventory size, word length, and communicative efficiency. *Linguistics* 33: 359–67.

Newman, P. (1970). *A grammar of Tera.* Berkeley and Los Angeles: University of California Press.

Nieuweboer, C. (1998). *The Altai dialect of Plautdiitsch (West-Siberian Mennonite Low German).* PhD dissertation, University of Groningen.

Nijen Twilhaar, J. (1990). *Generatieve fonologie en de studie van Oostnederlandse dialecten.* Amsterdam: P.J. Meertens-Instituut.

Odden, D. (1986). On the Obligatory Contour Principle. *Language* 62: 353–83.

—— (1995). Tone: African languages. In Goldsmith, 444–75.

Oftedal, M. (1985). *Lenition in Celtic and in Insular Spanish: the secondary voicing of stops in Gran Canaria.* Oslo, Universitetsforlaget.

Ohala, J.J. (1979). The contribution of acoustic phonetics to phonology. In B. Lindblom and S. Öhman (eds), *Frontiers of speech communication research*. London: Academic Press, 355–63.

—— (1986). A consumer's guide to phonological evidence. *Phonological Yearbook* 3: 3–26.

—— (1989). Sound change is drawn from a pool of synchronic variation. In L.E. Breivik and E.H. Jahr (eds), *Language change: contributions to the study of its causes*. Berlin: Mouton de Gruyter.

—— (1997). The relationship between phonetics and phonology. In Hardcastle and Laver, 674–94.

—— and Jaeger, J.J. (eds) (1986). *Experimental phonology*. Orlando, FL: Academic Press.

Ohala, M. (1983). *Aspects of Hindi phonology*. Delhi: Motilal Banarsidass.

Palmer, F.R. (1970). *Prosodic analysis*. London: Oxford University Press.

Paradis, C. and Prunet, J.F. (eds) (1991). *The special status of coronals: internal and external evidence*. San Diego, CA: Academic Press.

Pet, W.J.A. (1979). Another look at Arawak phonology. *International Journal of American Linguistics* 45: 323–31.

Phelps, E.F. (1975). Iteration and disjunctive domains in phonology. *Linguistic Analysis* 1: 137–72.

Pierrehumbert, J.B. (1980). *The phonetics and phonology of English intonation*. PhD dissertation MIT. Published 1990, New York: Garland.

—— (1990). Phonological and phonetic representation. *Journal of Phonetics* 18: 375–94.

—— (2002). Word-specific phonetics. In C. Gussenhoven and N. Warner (eds), *Laboratory phonology* 7. Berlin: Mouton de Gruyter, 101–139.

—— and Beckman, M.E. (1988). *Japanese tone structure*. Cambridge, MA: MIT Press.

Poser, W.J. (1990). Evidence for foot structure in Japanese. *Language* 66: 78–105.

Post, B. (2000). Pitch accents, Liaison and the phonological phrase in French. *Probus* 12: 127–64.

Postal, P. (1968). *Aspects of phonological theory*. New York: Harper & Row.

Prince, A. (1985). Improving tree theory. *Berkeley Linguistics Society* 11: 471–90.

—— and Smolensky, P. (1993). *Optimality Theory: constraint interaction in generative grammar*. New Brunswick, NJ: Rutgers University.

Pulleyblank, G.D. (1986). *Tone in lexical phonology*. Dordrecht: Reidel.

—— (1988). Vocalic underspecification in Yoruba. *Linguistic Inquiry* 19: 233–70.

Recasens, D., Fontdevila, J. and Pallarès, M.D. (1995). A production and perceptual account of palatalization. In Connell and Arvaniti, 265–81.

Reetz, H. and Jongman, A. (2009). *Phonetics: transcription, production, acoustics, and perception*. Chichester: Wiley-Blackwell.

Rietveld, A.C.M. and Loman, H.G. (1985). / h/, Stemloos of stemhebbend. *Glot* 8: 275–85.

Rischel, J. (1974). *Topics in West Greenlandish phonology*. Copenhagen: Akademisk.

Robins, R.H. (1957). Vowel nasality in Sundanese: a phonological and grammatical study. In J.R. Firth (ed.), *Studies in linguistic analysis*. Oxford: Blackwell, 87–103.

Roca, I.M. (1994). *Phonological theory*. London: Routledge.

Rubach, J. (1990). Final devoicing and cyclic syllabification in German. *Linguistic Inquiry* 21: 79–94.

—— (1994). Affricates as strident stops in Polish. *Linguistic Inquiry* 25, 119–143.

—— (1996). Shortening and ambisyllabicity in English. *Phonology* 13: 197–237.

—— (2000). Glide and glottal stop insertion in Slavic languages. A DOT analysis. *Linguistic Inquiry* 31, 271–317.

Ruhlen, M. (1976). *A guide to the languages of the world*. Stanford University Language Universals Project.

Sacks, O. (1989). *Seeing voices*. Berkeley: University of California Press.

Sagey, E.C. (1986). The representation of features and relations in non-linear phonology. PhD, MIT.

Schachter, P. and Otanes, F.T. (1972). *Tagalog reference grammar*. Berkeley: University of California Press.

Schane, S.A. (1971). The phoneme revisited. *Language* 47: 503–21.

—— (1973). *Generative phonology*. Englewood Cliffs, NJ: Prentice-Hall.

Schelberg, P.J.G. (1979). *Woordenboek van het Sittards dialect*. Amsterdam: Rodopi.

Schuh, R.G. (1978). Tone rules. In Fromkin, 221–56.

Seiler, W. (1985). *Imonda, a Papuan language*. Canberra: Australian National University.

Selkirk, E. (1978). On prosodic structure and its relation to syntactic structure. In T. Fretheim (ed.), *Nordic prosody II*. Trondheim: TAPIR, 111–40.

—— (1982). Syllables. In Hulst and Smith, 337–83.

—— (1984). *Phonology and syntax: the relation between sound and structure*. Cambridge, MA: MIT Press.

—— (1986). On derived domains in sentence phonology. *Phonology Yearbook* 3: 371–405.

—— (1995). Sentence prosody: intonation, stress, and phrasing. In Goldsmith, 550–69.

—— (2000). The interaction of constraints on prosodic phrasing. In M. Horne (ed.). *Prosody: theory and experiment. Studies presented to Gösta Bruce*. Amsterdam: Kluwer, 231–261.

Senft, G. (1986). *Kilivila: the language of the Trobriand islanders*. Berlin: Mouton de Gruyter.

Sezer, E. (1983). On non-final stress in Turkish. *Journal of Turkish Studies* 5: 61–9.

Shattuck-Hufnagel, S. (1992). The role of word structure in segmental serial ordering. *Cognition* 42: 213–59.

Shaw, P. (1991). Consonant harmony systems: the special status of coronal harmony. In Paradis and Prunet, 125–57.

Siegel, D. (1974). Topics in English morphology. PhD, MIT. Distributed by Indiana University Linguistics Club.

Silverman, D. (1992). Multiple scansions in loan word phonology. *Phonology* 9: 289–328.

Sipma, P. (1913). *Phonology and grammar of Modern West Frisian*. London: Oxford University Press.

Sluyters, W. (1990). Length and stress revisited: a metrical account of diphthongization, vowel lengthening, consonant gemination and word-final vowel epenthesis in modern Italian. *Probus* 2: 65–102.

Smolensky, P. (1996). On the comprehension/production dilemma in child language. *Linguistic Inquiry*, 27–4: 720–731.

Sneddon, J.N. (ed.) (1991). *Studies in Sulawesi linguistics II*. Jakarta: NUSA (Universitas Katolik Indonesia Atma Jaya).

Spajić, S., Ladefoged, P. and Bhaskarararo, P. (1996). The trills of Toda. *Journal of the International Phonetic Association* 26: 1–21.

Steriade, D. (1987). Redundant values. In *Parasession on autosegmental and metrical phonology*. Chicago: Chicago Linguistic Society, 339–62.

—— (1995). Underspecification and markedness. In Goldsmith, 114–74.

Stevens, K.N. (1997). Articulatory–acoustic–auditory relationships. In Hardcastle and Laver, 462–506.

Stowell, T. (1979). Stress systems of the world, unite! *MIT Working Papers in Linguistics* 1: 51–76.

Ternes, E. (1973). *The phonemic analysis of Scottish Gaelic*. Hamburg: Helmut Buske.

Tiersma, P. (1985). *Frisian reference grammar*. Dordrecht: Foris.

Tranel, B. (1981). *Concreteness in generative phonology.* Berkeley: University of California Press.

Trommelen, M. (1983). *The syllable in Dutch, with special reference to diminutive formation.* Dordrecht: Foris.

—— and Zonneveld, W. (1983). *Generatieve fonologie van het Nederlands.* Muiden: Coutinho.

—— —— (1989). *Klemtoon en metrische fonologie.* Dordrecht: Foris.

Tyler, S.A. (1969). *Koya: an outline grammar.* Berkeley: University of California Press.

Vago, R. (1988). Vowel harmony in Finnish word games. In H. van der Hulst and N. Smith (eds), *Features, segmental structure and harmony processes II.* Dordrecht: Foris, 185–205.

van den Berg, B. (1975). De morfonologische regels voor de vorming van het verkleinwoord in het dialect van de stad Utrecht. *Taal en Tongval* 27: 95–102.

van den Broecke, M.P.R. (1976). *Hierarchies and rank orders in distinctive features.* Assen: Gorcum.

van, Gijn, R. (2006). *A grammar of Yurakaré.* PhD dissertation, Nijmegen.

van der Hulst, H. (1984). *Syllable structure and stress in Dutch.* Dordrecht: Foris.

—— (1985). Ambisyllabicity in Dutch. In H. Bennis and F. Beukema (eds), *Linguistics in the Netherlands.* Dordrecht: Foris, 57–66.

—— and Smith, N. (eds) (1985). *Advances in non-linear phonology.* Dordrecht: Foris.

—— and van de Weijer, J. (1995). Vowel harmony. In Goldsmith, 495–534.

van de Weijer, J.M. (2002). An optimality theoretical analysis of the Dutch diminutive. In H. Broekhuis and P. Fikkert (eds), *Linguistics in the Netherlands 2002.* Amsterdam: Benjamins, 199–209.

van Oostendorp, M. *et al.* (2011). *The Blackwell companion to phonology.* 5 vols. Malden MA; Oxford: Wiley-Blackwell.

Venneman, T. (1972). On the theory of syllabic phonology. *Linguistische Berichte* 18: 1–18.

—— (1988). *Preference laws for syllable structure and the explanation of sound change.* Berlin: Mouton de Gruyter.

Vos, F. (1963) Dutch influences on the Japanese language. *Lingua* 12: 341–88.

Wang, H.S. and Derwing, B.C. (1986). More on English vowel shift: the back vowel question. *Phonology Yearbook* 3: 99–116.

Wells, J.C. (1982). *Accents of English.* London: Arnold.

—— (2008). *Longman pronunciation dictionary,* 3rd edn. Harlow: Pearson-Longman.

Wetzels, W.L. (1990). Umlaut en verkleinwoordvorming in het Schinnens. *Gramma* 14: 139–68.

—— (1997a). Bakairi and the feature 'voice'. *Número Especial do Boletim da Associação Brasileira de Lingüística (ABRALIN)* am Homenagem a Aryon Rodrigues. Universidade Federal de Alagoas (UFAL), Maceió, Brazil.

—— (1997b). The lexical representation of nasality in Brazilian Portuguese. *Probus* 9: 203–32.

—— and Sezer, E. (eds) (1986). *Studies in compensatory lengthening.* Dordrecht: Foris.

Whitley, M.S. (1978). *Generative phonology workbook.* Madison: University of Wisconsin Press.

Wiese, R. (1986). Nichtlineare Phonologie: Eine Fallstudie des Chinesischen. *Linguistische Berichte* 102: 93–135.

Xu, Y. (2006). Tonal alignment, syllable structure and coarticulation: toward an integrated model. *Journal of Italian Linguistics* 18, 125–157.

Yip, M. (1988). The Obligatory Contour Principle and phonological rules: a loss of identity. *Linguistic Inquiry* 19: 65–100.

—— (1993). Cantonese loanword phonology and Optimality Theory. *Journal of East Asian Linguistics* 2: 261–91.

Zec, D. and Inkelas, S. (1990). Prosodically constrained syntax. In Inkelas and Zec, 365–78.

Zsiga, E. (1997). Features, gestures, and Igbo vowel assimilation: an approach to the phonology/phonetics mapping. *Language* 73: 227–74.

Language index

The language index below was modelled on the one in Laver (1994) and composed with the help of Grimes (1988).

Language	Family	Geographical area	Page numbers
!Xū	Khoisan	Namibia, Angola	32, 35, 43, 39
Akan	Niger-Kordofanian, Kwa	Ghana (South)	84, 202, 203
Amharic	Semitic	Ethiopia, Egypt	90, 168
Angaatiha	Trans-New Guinea, Angan	Papua New Guinea (Moroba Province, Menyamya District)	37
Arabela	Zaparoan	Peru (Arabela River)	36
Arabic	Semitic	Saudi Arabia, Algeria, Bahrain, Chad, Egypt, Ethiopia, Iraq, Jordan, Kuwait, Lebanon, Libya, Morocco, Oman, People's Democratic Republic of Yemen, Qatar, Somalia, Sudan, Syria, Tunisia, United Arab Emirates, Yemen, Arabic Republic	31, 43, 166–168
Cairene Arabic		Egypt (Cairo)	218, 219, 230, 231, 244
Gulf Arabic		United Arab Emirates, Saudi Arabia	27
Tetouan Arabic		Morocco (Tetouan)	220
Arawak	Arawakan	Surinam, French Guiana, Guyana, Venezuela	29
Bakairí	Carib	Brazil (Mato Grosso)	42, 201
Bakwiri	Niger-Kordofanian, Bantu	Cameroon (South)	175, 207, 208
Balantak	Austronesian	Indonesia (East central Sulawesi)	71
Basque	Isolate	Spain, France	250, 251
Bengali	Indo-European, Indo-Aryan	Bangladesh, India, Singapore, United Arab Emirates	89, 250, 253, 254
Brao	Austro-Asiatic, Brao-Kravet	Laos, Cambodia	197
Bugotu	Austronesian	Solomon Islands	178
Bura	Afro-Asiatic	Nigeria	204
Burmese	Sino-Tibetan	Burma, Bangladesh	43
Cantonese	Sino-Tibetan, Chinese	Guangdong	49
Catalan	Indo-European, Romance	Spain (Northeast)	29, 37, 172
Cavineña	Tacanan	Bolivia (Beni River)	244
Chipewyan	Athabaskan	Canada (North-west Territories, Saskatchewan)	30
Chuave	Trans-New Guinea, Chimbu	Papua New Guinea (Chimbu Province)	38, 43

Subject index

This subject index lists only the sections and chapters in which the subject concerned is dealt with fully, and does not list all pages on which the topics is mentioned.